YOU'LL BE HEARING FROM US!

Operation Anthropoid – the assassination of SS-Obergruppenführer Reinhard Heydrich and its consequences

Niall Cherry
with
Tony Moseley, Jonathan Saunders & John Howes

Helion & Company Limited

Helion & Company Limited
Unit 8 Amherst Business Centre
Budbrooke Road
Warwick
CV34 5WE
England
Tel. 01926 499 619
Email: info@helion.co.uk
Website: www.helion.co.uk
Twitter: @helionbooks
Visit our blog http://blog.helion.co.uk/

Published by Helion & Company 2019
Designed and typeset by Mach 3 Solutions Ltd (www.mach3solutions.co.uk)
Cover designed by Paul Hewitt, Battlefield Design (www.battlefield-design.co.uk)

ISBN 978-1-912866-22-9

British Library Cataloguing-in-Publication Data.
A catalogue record for this book is available from the British Library.

For details of other military history titles published by Helion & Company Limited contact
the above address, or visit our website: http://www.helion.co.uk.

We always welcome receiving book proposals from prospective authors.

Contents

List of Illustrations

Abbreviations

MHIP Military History Institute Prague
NC Niall Cherry
BG Bob Gerritsen
SP Scriptorium Prague

List of Maps

Introduction

I remember many years ago when I was a teenager finding a book in the Second World War section of my local library called *Seven Men at Daybreak* by Alan Burgess, which dealt with Operation Anthropoid and the assassination of Reinhard Heydrich. Somehow resisting my normal urge to steal it, I borrowed it and seem to recall reading it in just a few hours. I was enthralled by the story and over the years re-read the book occasionally; I always said that I'd like to go and see the locations in Prague for myself. In the years that followed, other priorities took up my time but I always had Operation Anthropoid at the back of my mind. Then, in 2014, I found on the internet a book about Operation Anthropoid called *The Mirror Caught the Sun* by John Martin, and I ordered a copy. This reawakened my interest, and when I later met John and Tony Moseley at a premiere in Liverpool of the excellent film called *'Anthropoid'*, in which John appears fleetingly in the ambush scene, he told me he carried out tours relating to Anthropoid. I easily convinced my long-suffering wife that it would be nice if I went on one of them. I made the booking and duly arrived in Prague in August 2017. Although I had met John before, I hadn't realised he was a man after my own heart and a fellow 'anorak', as were the majority of the people on the trip. Needless to say, this tour really opened my eyes to what happened in 1942 and I was enthused to dig deeper. Operation Anthropoid was perhaps unique in the history of the Second World War, as not many plans to execute a senior Nazi official came to fruition. The retribution exacted afterwards also went down in history as amongst the most savage reprisals carried out by an evil regime.

I was able to enlist three good friends to help with this spadework about the killing of Heydrich, and so a few words about them. Jonathan Saunders is an Anthropoid enthusiast and, in his spare time, a tour guide for Military History Tours. Tony Moseley is a Pardubice historian and Operation Silver A enthusiast.

I have known the third member of the team, John Howes, for many years. He gave great support to the project by being 'our go-to man' for information from the National Archives.

A number of people have helped in this journey: thanks to Kevin Barnes, Zdeněk Špitálnik, George Scott, Anita Moravec, Claire Cherry-Hardy, Gerry Manolas and Marta Majerčik. The research for this book has been challenging, as you really need to be a fluent speaker of three languages – English, German and Czech – none of which I claim as being proficient in! I must also bear responsibility for any mistakes in the translation of documents.

It should be noted that in places we use the term Czechoslovakia and in other the Protectorate of Bohemia and Moravia. In general terms, patriots used the original term for their homeland but the German invaders and local sympathisers used the 'Germanic' name for the occupied territory. Also in places when using words from German reports etc., the Germanic version of a Czech place name is used. For example, Panenské Břežany is also referred to as Jungfern Breschan. Additionally, in German reports they used 'German' versions of first names – for example, Wenzel Novák is their version of Václav Novák. We hope the reader will not find this too confusing, but to maintain accuracy to the original document we felt it a necessary inclusion.

Finally, a big thank-you to Duncan Rogers for agreeing to my choice of subject for yet another book for Helion!

Niall Cherry

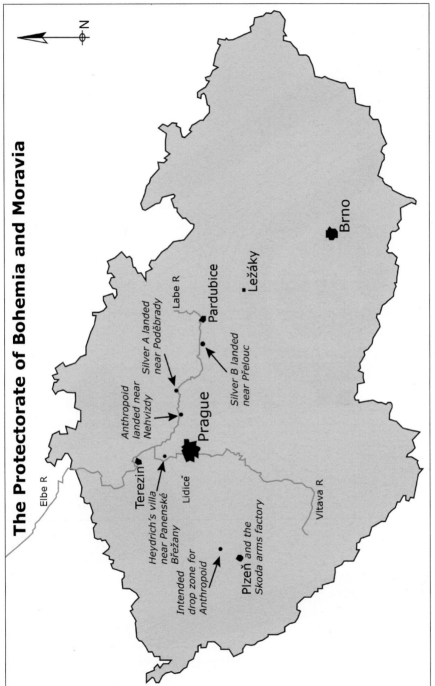

The Protectorate of Bohemia and Moravia

N

Elbe R

Terezín

Heydrich's villa
near Panenské
Břežany

Intended
drop zone for
Anthropoid

Lidice

Plzeň and the
Skoda arms factory

Anthropoid
landed near
Nehvizdy

Silver A landed
near Poděbrady

Labe R

Prague

Silver B landed
near Přelouc

Pardubice

Ležáky

Vltava R

Brno

The Protectorate of Bohemia and Moravia.

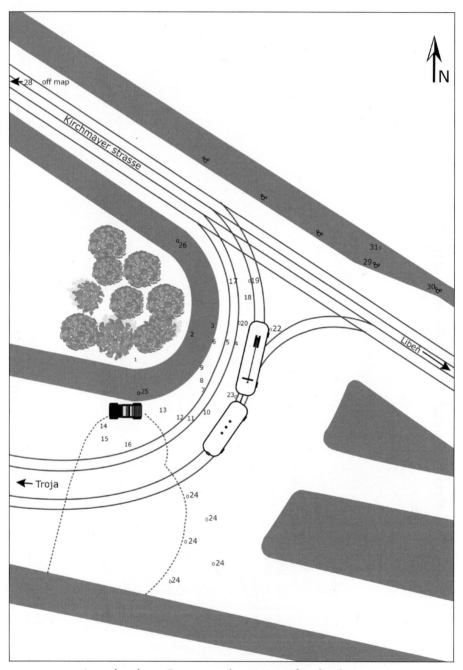

A map based on a Gestapo one showing items found at the scene.

b

1. Cable and photograph.
2. Coat.
3. Machine pistol *(Sten gun)*.
4-5. Parts of mudguard.
6. Wood strip from car.
7-8. Metal parts from mudguard.
9. Metal parts from mudguard.
10. Smalles metal fragments.
11-12. Tape for fixing safety pin *(from No. 73 grenade)*.
13. Wooden parts of car bodywork.
14. Cartridge calibre 7.65mm *(.32)*, not fired.
15. Metal fragment (probably from car).
16. Bomb shrapnel.
17. Bakelite parts from bomb *(parts of No. 247 fuze)*.
18. Rubber fragment, probably from car.
19-22. Smallest bomb fragments.
23. Parts of car upholstery.
24. Upholstery and wooden parts from car.
25. Insulating tape from bomb.
26. Witness Helene Pechar.
27. One cartridge case Kynoch 7.65mm *(.32)*.
28. Three cartridge cases Kynoch 7.65mm *(.32)*.
29. The escape bicycle, with which one of the assasins *(Jan Kubiš)* escaped to Libeň, stood against this mast.
30. Police recovered a ladies bicycle leaning against this mast, the bag of which contained a stick magazine for a Sten and a bomb.
31. At this point the assassin who had escaped to Libeň discarded a bag containing a bomb and a (flat or golf) cap.

The list of items found at the scene.

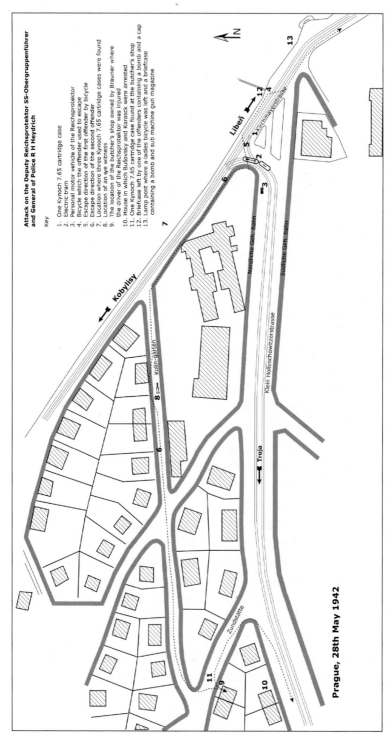

Attack on the Deputy Reichsprotektor SS-Obergruppenführer and General of Police R H Heydrich

Key

1. One Kynoch 7.65 cartridge case
2. Electric tram
3. Personal motor vehicle of the Reichsprotektor
4. Bicycle which the offender used to escape
5. Escape direction of the first offender by bicycle
6. Escape direction of the second offender
7. Location where three Kynoch 7.65 cartridge cases were found
8. Location of an eye witness
9. The location of the butcher's shop owned by Brauner where the driver of the Reichsprotektor was injured
10. House in which Bušovský and Karasck were arrested
11. One Kynoch 7.65 cartridge case found at the butcher's shop
12. Briefcase left by one of the offenders containing a bomb and a cap
13. Lamp post where a ladies bicycle was left and a briefcase containing a bomb and sub machine gun magazine

Prague, 28th May 1942

The escape route of Jozef Gabčík based on a map from the Gestapo report.

1

The Road to Prague

To try and give justice to the story of Operation Anthropoid it is necessary to look back to the time of the Great War of 1914–18. The main protagonists were on one side the 'Allies' – consisting of Britain and its Empire, France, Italy and Russia – and on the other the 'Central Powers', largely Germany and the Austro-Hungarian Empire. No country entered the conflict expecting to end up on the losing side, but this is what happened for Austro-Hungary. Even before the Armistice was arranged by Germany on 11 November 1918, major events were unfolding in the two kingdoms of the Austro-Hungarian Empire. The empire had been ruled by the Austrian Habsburg family for many generations and consisted of a diverse population, including ethnic Germans, Russians, Poles, Hungarians, Czechs and Slovaks. Some of these people had for many years been calling for self-determination, including the Czechs and Slovaks, who primarily populated three 'provinces' of the Habsburg Empire: Bohemia, Moravia and Slovakia.

Prior to the Great War, the Habsburgs had started to loosen the reins of control across their empire, but the outbreak of the global conflict in 1914 brought a sudden end to these reforms. Amongst the Czechs and Slovaks there were cultural differences, as although they spoke very similar languages, they were very different peoples. This is partly explained by the fact that the Austrians looked on Bohemia and Moravia as their territory, whilst the semi-autonomous Kingdom of Hungary was more influential in Slovakia. Bohemia was the most developed industrial region under Austrian control, whereas Slovakia was the most industrialised part of the Hungarian Kingdom. Furthermore, the Hungarians were far more determined to assimilate the Slovaks than the Austrians were to assimilate the Czechs. Yet the similarities between them led, prior to 1914, to the idea of an independent 'Czecho-Slovak' state amongst their two peoples.

With the outbreak of hostilities in 1914, Czechs and Slovaks were conscripted into the Austro-Hungarian Army to fight on the side of the Central Powers. However, a little-known part of the Great War was the role of the Czechoslovakian Legions, who fought for the Allies on both the Eastern and Western Fronts.

When war was declared, Czech and Slovak exiles in Russia asked the Russian Government to support their quest for independence, and as a show of solidarity suggested the raising of a unit from their people to fight alongside the Russian Army. This offer was accepted and a Czecho-Slovak unit went to the Eastern Front in October 1914. However, the number of potential recruits and replacements was limited, so volunteers were sought amongst the Czechs and Slovaks who had been fighting in the Austro-Hungarian Army but were now residing in Russian prisoner of war camps.

The large number of Czechs conscripted into the Austro-Hungarian Army were not particularly keen to fight for the Austrians and would rather have been fighting for their own independence; therefore, as prisoners of war, they were ripe for 'recruiting' onto the Allied side.

However, recruiting from the 'enemy' was frowned upon by the Russian military hierarchy, and the idea was only pursued tentatively. The numbers that volunteered were low. But in 1917 this policy of recruitment was changed by Russia's new Provisional Government, and the Czechs were welcomed with open arms; enough soldiers were recruited to enable the formation of the Czechoslovak Rifle Brigade. This unit distinguished itself during the Kerensky Offensive in July 1917, when they overran Austrian trenches during the Battle of Zborov.

Following their performance at Zborov, the Russian Provisional Government, which had replaced the Tsar, asked the Czechoslovak National Council for permission to further expand their forces in Russia, and soon two divisions had been formed – numbering around 40,000 men. In the latter part of 1917, the Bolsheviks were gaining strength and power in Russia. They desired an end to the fighting, and when they seized total control in November 1917, they started peace talks with the Germans. These culminated in the Treaty of Brest-Litovsk, which ended the fighting on the Eastern Front – at least for Germany – in 1918.

As a result of the Russo-German Armistice on the Eastern Front, Tomáš Masaryk, chairman of the Czechoslovak National Council, who had been in Russia since 1917, began planning for the Czechoslovak Legion's departure from Russia and transfer to France, in order that the Czechoslovaks could continue to fight against the Central Powers and press for their independence. However, for various reasons this failed to materialise and the Legion became embroiled fighting in the Russian Civil War.

The Czechs also fought throughout the war on the Western Front. Since August 1914, Czechs who wanted to fight against the Central Powers were allowed to join the Foreign Legion in France. Enough men volunteered to form a company, but they suffered heavy casualties fighting near Arras in May and June 1915. The company was subsequently disbanded, with the survivors transferred to other units. From the end of 1917, in both France and Italy, 'independent' Czech units were created from former prisoners of war, repeating the process that had taken place in Russia. A further source of manpower were émigré Czech volunteers recently arrived from America.

In return for their service, the right of Czechs and Slovaks to form an independent Czechoslovakian state was recognised by France in June 1918. This followed the Pittsburgh Agreement of 31 May 1918, in America, a memorandum of intent made by the Czech and Slovak émigré communities. This agreement contained the following points:

1. We approve [sanction] the political programme, which endeavours to bring about a Union of the Czechs and Slovaks in an independent state comprising the Czech Lands, (the lands of the Bohemian Crown) and Slovakia.
2. Slovakia will have its own administration, its own diet and its own courts.
3. The Slovak language will be the official language in schools and in public life in general (in Slovakia).
4. The Czechoslovak state will be a republic; its Constitution will be democratic.
5. The organisation of the collaboration of the Czechs and the Slovaks in the United States will be amplified and adjusted according to the needs and according to the changing situation, by mutual agreement.
6. Detailed rules concerning the organisation of the Czechoslovak state are left to the liberated Czechs and Slovaks and their legal representatives (to establish).

This agreement was fulfilled when, on 28 October 1918, Tomáš Masaryk declared the creation of an independent Czechoslovakia, following which he was soon elected the country's first president. In the turmoil that existed in the last few weeks of the Great War and the first few weeks of peace, the establishment of an independent Czechoslovakia was not easy, but institutions and processes were gradually put in place to run a democracy.

Against this backdrop, the newly formed Czechoslovak Republic was allowed to attend the Paris Peace Conference, which began in January 1919. The conference approved the establishment of Czechoslovakia and set out its territorial boundaries, which included the lands of Bohemia, Moravia, Silesia, Slovakia and Carpathian Ruthenia. Some of these areas contained what are now known as 'ethnic minorities'. To give the minorities some reassurance, in September 1919 Czechoslovakia signed the Minorities Treaty, which placed these people under the protection of the League of Nations.

It was not without difficulty to keep all these different peoples together under a single nation, but to his credit, Masaryk developed a form of 'coalition politics' that lasted for nearly all his presidency. However, these minorities, primarily Germans, Hungarians and Poles – and indeed the entire Versailles Peace Treaty – would cause future problems. Masaryk eventually resigned on grounds of ill-health on 14 December 1935 and died less than two years later. He was succeeded as president by Edvard Beneš.

Although Masaryk's presidency had been successful, simmering away in the background in 1930s Czechoslovakia were nationalist thoughts and ideas amongst the 'non-Czechs'. One of the more vociferous parties was the Slovak People's Party, led by Andrej Hlinka. In addition, relations between the 'Sudeten Germans' – a mixture of Austrians and Germans – and the Czechs became increasingly uneasy.

Historically, the Germans and Austrians had always looked down upon the Czechs. However, under the republic the new equality was at first convivial, as the rich industrial Sudetenland and its extensive German population enjoyed relative prosperity.

This changed with the Wall Street Crash in 1929, when exports dived, unemployment increased and the ethnic Germans felt their suffering was greater than that of the Czechs. Unemployment amongst the ethnic Germans was double that of the Czechs, most likely because more Czechs were involved in farming and agriculture and were thus not exposed to the industrial downturn in the same way as Sudeten Germans.

Relations between Sudeten Germans and Czechoslovaks continued to deteriorate, coinciding with the rise to power in Germany of Adolf Hitler and the *Nationalsozialistische Deutsche Arbeiterpartei* (NSDAP, hereafter referred to as the Nazi Party). Nationalism and identity was reawakened within the Sudeten German population, which Hitler was able to exploit. With the support of the Nazi Party, the Sudeten German Party was formed and in the 1935 parliamentary elections received over 65 percent of the Sudeten German vote.

Beneš responded to Nazi interference by signing the Czechoslovak-Soviet Treaty of Alliance, believing this would guarantee the republic, but Soviet aid was linked to France coming to Czechoslovakia's assistance first. It is important to remember this Treaty could only be triggered if the French intervened on the side of Czechoslovakia.

Relations between Czechoslovakia and Nazi Germany were never good. Otto Strasser fled into exile in Prague after he was expelled from the Nazi Party in 1930. From his base in Prague, Strasser attempted to split the Nazi Party by forming the Black Party – an anti-Nazi party composed of former and disillusioned members of the Nazi Party, mainly from its left wing. The Black Party was responsible for a supposed assassination attempt on Hitler in 1937 by Helmet Hirsch, a German-Jew living in Prague. The Black Party was also responsible for broadcasting anti-Nazi propaganda into Germany from Czech territory. The broadcaster was Rudolf Formis, another ex-Nazi.

Thus Czechoslovakia and Beneš were regarded with scorn by Hitler, who was determined to smash them. Hitler already had designs on the prosperous Sudetenland. In 1937, Hitler told his Foreign Minister, Konstantin von Neurath, and other senior military officials, that he intended to absorb Bohemia and Austria into the Reich, with a vague mention about the need to expel two million Czechs and the eventual elimination of the Czech nation. This eventually led to Field Marshal Werner von Blomberg, the German Minister of War, drafting a plan for an aggressive war against Czechoslovakia, *Fall Grun*, or Case Green.

In March 1938, the leader of the Sudeten German Party, Konrad Henlein, secretly met with Hitler in Berlin, where Hitler instructed him to start agitating the Sudeten Germans to demand independence from Czechoslovakia.

Previously, Henlein had been a moderate, favouring more autonomy for the Sudeten Germans. However, he was aware he owed his 1935 electoral success to financial support from Nazi Germany. He also realised he needed to re-establish his credentials over his deputy, the ardent Nazi, Karl Hermann Frank.

In April, Henlein issued the Karlsbad Programme, which ostensibly called for autonomy for the Sudetenland but in effect would serve Hitler by either bringing the Sudetenland directly into the Third Reich or creating a political crisis which Hitler could then manipulate to annex the Sudetenland.

The increased pressure on Beneš and his government was further exasperated by terrorist incidents. These were blamed on an ethnic German group called the *Ordnersgruppe*, with the result that on 16 September 1938, the Czech Government banned the *Ordnersgruppe*. Henlein responded the next day by forming a new organisation called the *Sudetendeutsche Freikorps*. Both these groups were trained and equipped by the Nazis. This led to further deterioration in the already very poor relations between Prague and Berlin. The emerging political situation was looked on with horror in both London and Paris. The Prime Minister in London, Neville Chamberlain, wanted very much to follow a policy of appeasement. Beneš later felt that 17 September 1938 was the beginning of the undeclared Czech-German conflict.

The British policy of appeasement had been introduced in the hope of avoiding war by allowing Hitler to expand German territory virtually unchecked. Britain and France had already stood by in 1936 when German troops reoccupied the Rhineland (which was meant to be a demilitarised zone that protected France's eastern border with Germany), and they stood by again in March 1938 when Nazi Germany annexed Austria with the *Anschluß*.

It was against this backdrop that a meeting was arranged in Munich in September 1938, which had far-reaching repercussions. There were thought to be around three million ethnic Germans living in the Sudetenland, and more critically, the region contained a number of important industrial facilities that would be useful to the German military machine. Hitler felt that this area was a prime target for his growing empire, and it was clear in 1938 that he was now determined to seize it. Military assessments by the Western powers concluded that the Czechs by themselves had not the faintest hope of resisting Nazi Germany. Hitler had told his generals in May 1938 that he intended 'to smash Czechoslovakia by military action in the near future'; though some of his confidants had the impression that at this point he did not want a general European war. Chamberlain went to Germany three times in September 1938 to discuss the situation with Hitler, at Berchtesgaden and then at Bad Godesberg, where Hitler demanded not only the prompt German annexation of the Sudetenland but that all predominantly German areas elsewhere in Czechoslovakia should be allowed to join the Third Reich. Back on 20 May, Hitler had told the Hungarian Prime Minister Béla Imrédy that he was sure the British and French would do nothing effective, and he was proved right.

Like almost everyone in Europe, including most Germans, Chamberlain believed anything was preferable to a repeat of the Great War of 1914–18. He misunderstood Hitler, whom he believed could be appeased by concessions. Neither Chamberlain nor the French saw good reason to go to war to preserve Czechoslovakia, which had only been created in 1918. At the same time, if the quest for peace failed, Britain needed to buy time in which to re-arm, though this inevitably also meant giving Germany more time to continue re-arming. From this distance in time it is absurd to think that no Czech representative participated in the Munich Conference, where other countries decided the future of Czechoslovakia almost as an afterthought. Chamberlain had asked for the Czech Ambassador to Germany to come to Munich as an adviser, but subsequently he was not allowed to be present in the same room as

Hitler. On the night of 30 September 1938, a Czech Government statement agreed to cede Czech territory where 50 percent or more of the population was German, but protested against the demand for a plebiscite in areas without a German majority.

At Munich, Hitler obtained what he wanted – the domination of Central Europe – and German troops marched into the Sudetenland on the night of 1 October. The day before, the Czech Government had no choice but to accept the Munich Agreement. General Jan Sirovy, the Czech Premier, told his people by radio that he had experienced the most tragic moment of his life: "I am fulfilling the most painful duty which can ever have fallen upon me, a duty which is worse than dying … the forces arrayed against us oblige us to recognise their superiority and act accordingly." In Germany, Josef Goebbels, the Nazi Minister of Propaganda, said: "We have all walked on a thin tight rope over a dizzy abyss … The world is filled with a frenzy of joy. Germany's prestige has grown enormously. Now we are really a world power again."

As part of the Munich Agreement, all predominantly German territory in Czechoslovakia was to be handed over by 10 October. Poland and Hungary seized the opportunity to occupy other parts of the country, and within a few months the Czechoslovak Republic ceased to exist.

When Chamberlain left Munich, Hitler reportedly said, 'If ever that silly old man comes interfering here again with his umbrella, I'll kick him downstairs.' In contrast to Hitler's view, the French and British premiers had flown home in triumph to tumultuous welcomes from their peoples, who felt huge relief that another European war had been avoided. Chamberlain went straight to Buckingham Palace, where he appeared on the balcony with George VI and Queen Elizabeth to the plaudits of the crowd below, and then on to Downing Street, where he told the admiring throng, 'I believe it is peace for our time.'

As soon as the Munich Agreement had been signed and German troops were entering the Sudetenland, Hitler was plotting the occupation of the rest of Czechoslovakia. On 21 October, he ordered that the *Wehrmacht* 'must be prepared at all times for … the liquidation of the remainder of Czechoslovakia'. Hand-in-hand with these instructions, the Nazis set about doing their best to destabilise the Czech Government. For example, Hermann Goering, head of the *Luftwaffe*, held a meeting with leading Slovaks on 17 October and offered Nazi support if they campaigned for their own independence from the Czecho-Slovak state. He later wrote: 'A Czech state minus Slovakia is even more completely at our mercy. Air base in Slovakia for operation against the east very important.'

Hitler was politically shrewd at this time, using Britain and France's apparent unwillingness to stand up to Nazi Germany to stall for time. The Munich Agreement laid down that Germany, Britain and France would make a separate treaty guaranteeing Czechoslovakia's independence. When the British and French governments eventually approached Germany about the guarantee in February 1939, Hitler replied that he needed to 'await first a clarification of the internal development of Czechoslovakia'. The guarantee was never signed, and by early March there was open rioting in Slovak towns, Slovakian nationalists calling for autonomy from the

Czechoslovak state. At the same time, separatists in Carpathian Ruthenia (a small area at the eastern end of Czechoslovakia) demanded independence.

Hitler seized the moment and entered into negotiations with the Slovak leader, Jozef Tiso. Tiso visited Hitler in Berlin on 13 March, returning to Bratislava the next day to report to his parliament that Nazi Germany offered Slovakia their protection if they immediately declared independence. If they did not, then Nazi Germany would have no further interest in Slovakian affairs and leave their ongoing territorial disputes to be decided by themselves, Hungary and Poland. Slovakia was too weak to resist Hungary and Poland on its own, and its parliament declared independence to ensure the continuation of German protection.

Following closely behind Tiso's visit to Berlin was Emil Hácha, the new Czechoslovakian President. Hácha was not in the best of health and had a heart condition, which made his doctors insist he travel by train to Berlin rather than flying. He left Prague at 1615 on 14 March and did not arrive at Anhalter Station in Berlin until 2240. Met with due consideration appropriate to his position as head of state, his party was then taken to the impressive Adlon Hotel. However, these were false signs of friendship and decorum. Hácha was given only an hour to wash and change his clothes, and then just before midnight he was taken to the Chancellery, where he first met with the German Foreign Minister, Joachim von Ribbentrop. The physically exhausted Hácha was then forced to wait until 0115 on the 15th for his interview with Hitler. Hácha was informed that German troops had already occupied the Czech city of Ostrava, and this would be followed by a full invasion commencing that same morning at 0600. Hácha was told if Czechoslovakia did not resist German protection (and occupation), then the Czech government would retain a level of autonomy. If, however, the Czechs resisted, then Germany would occupy Czechoslovakia by force. Goering, who was also present, curtly told Hácha that his *Luftwaffe* would obliterate the Czech cities. It was with this threat that Hácha collapsed and had to be brought round by an injection from Hitler's personal physician. Once Hácha regained consciousness, the threats continued. Finally, at 0355, to avoid Czech bloodshed and at the same time realising he was sealing his fate in history, Hácha signed a prepared document to 'place the fate of the Czech people and country in the hands of the Führer'.

Within hours on 15 March, the main force of German troops advanced over the border into Czechoslovakia. The anti-Nazi American journalist and historian William Shirer commented: 'A long night of German savagery now settled over Prague and the Czech lands.' Slovakia was given independence under German 'protection', while Ruthenia was given to Hungary.

Back in London, Chamberlain announced the news to the House of Commons later that morning; his statement was very weak and admitted that Hitler had, for the first time, annexed a non-Germanic population, but he did not condemn Hitler's action as a breach of faith, saying only that it was not in 'the spirit of Munich'.

Instead, Chamberlain emphasised that no aggression had taken place, and that the German actions had been 'with the acquiescence of Czechoslovakia'. He ended by reasserting the Government's aim 'to substitute the method of discussion for the method of force in the settlement of differences'. The official protest to Germany was even weaker, beginning: 'His Majesty's Government has no desire to interfere unnecessarily in a matter with which other governments may be more directly concerned ...'

Chamberlain's views were not shared by many people in the country, and the newspapers were particularly condemning of the behaviour of Germany. The outcome of the occupation of Czechoslovakia was that Britain and France made a declaration to Germany that they would come to the aid of Poland – which it was felt was next on Hitler's radar – if it was invaded.

However, this was of no comfort to the men and women of the now occupied Czechoslovakia – many of whom were not prepared to live under German rule, including politicians and members of the Armed Forces.

Beneš had already left Czechoslovakia. He had resigned after the Nazi occupation of the Sudetenland and had been replaced by the aged and infirm Hácha. By the end of October 1938, Beneš was in London with a few of his close confidants. After war was declared in September 1939, Beneš became the driving force behind the Czechoslovak National Liberation Committee. Then in 1940, with Britain needing as many Allies as it could find, Churchill recognised the committee as the Czechoslovakian government-in-exile. Beneš was 'elected' as president, claiming that his 1938 resignation was under duress and therefore null and void.

In the early days of the war it was not easy for the Czechs to become ingrained into the British political and military hierarchy, and they were often ignored. But gradually things changed and they found the best way into the British military community was by sharing the intelligence they received from Prague, supplied by an agent codenamed A-54. A-54 was the double agent Paul Thummel, ostensibly working as a Gestapo agent but actually supplying information to the Czech Intelligence Service. Thummel's contact in Prague was Captain Václav Morávek. After the German occupation, Morávek had formed, at the suggestion of retired General Josef Bílý – a leading member of the Czech anti-Nazi movement – a resistance unit in conjunction with two other former officers, Josef Mašín and Josef Balabán. Calling themselves *Obrana národa*, they had the original intention of inciting a rebellion. However, the rapidity and completeness of the German takeover made the likelihood of a successful uprising impossible, and Morávek, Mašín and Balabán concentrated on providing the government-in-exile in London with information obtained through Thummel. The information he supplied would later include details of the German plan to invade the Soviet Union. The quality of the intelligence provided by the Czechs impressed the British and did give Beneš' government a form of legitimacy.

One of Beneš' trusted associates in London was Colonel František Moravec, who in 1937 became head of the Czech Military Intelligence Services. He had been born in 1895 and during the Great War was a member of both the Serbian and Czechoslovak Legions, fighting against the Central Powers. After the Munich Agreement he remained in Czechoslovakia and continued to head the intelligence services. However, just before the German occupation in March 1939, Moravec, together with 10 of his intelligence officers, escaped from Prague on a chartered KLM flight to London via Rotterdam. He later commented on his escape:

While sitting in the Dutch plane flying towards England, I found myself suddenly swept by black thoughts. The bitter struggle of the past years, the blood and sweat of so many, what had it amounted to? The republic of Masaryk was dead. For the second time in my life I was an exile. My wife and children were lost to me, abandoned in the stricken country below, somewhere under the swirling flakes, left to the mercies of our invaders. Bitterness welled within me. As our plane passed over the frontier mountains of Czechoslovakia, I put my head in my hands and cried.

A number of Czech secret files had already been brought out in the 'Diplomatic Bag' and handed over to British Intelligence. Although relations between the British and the Czechs had at first been frosty and difficult, as the summer of 1940 drew to a close and it was clear that Germany had not achieved air supremacy over Britain, relations improved. Winston Churchill, who had become Prime Minister in May, replacing Chamberlain, came up with a cunning plan to strike back at the Germans. As well as calling for 'special service' troops, later to become the commandos, he requested that a corps of 5,000 paratroopers be formed and a secret underground army recruited and trained to "set Europe ablaze!". From these words the Special Operations Executive (SOE) was formed, an organisation that would have a major role in the Operation Anthropoid story.

Although the Czechoslovak Army was formally disbanded after the March 1939 occupation, except for a small ceremonial unit, large numbers of military personnel from all services wanted to fight the Germans if a European war came, which seemed likely. For many, the only option was to leave and volunteer to serve in another nation's army. Romania and Poland were the two common escape routes before their borders were also closed. For most, their final intended destination was France and service in the Foreign Legion, but around 900 Czechs, sensing that Poland might be Nazi Germany's next objective, volunteered to serve with the Polish Army in a 'Czech and Slovak Legion'. Those who had remained in Poland were interred by the Russians after the Soviet invasion of Poland on 17 September 1939. They themselves would be conscripted into the Soviet armed forces after the commencement of Operation Barbarossa by the Germans on 21 June 1941. From amongst their number were chosen the Czech parachutists and agents dropped into Czechoslovakia by the Soviets.

For this story, however, we concentrate on those who went to France. Many arrived by sea at Boulogne via Poland in early 1939, and from here they were taken to the Foreign Legion recruiting centre at Lille to complete their attestation, and thence to the Legion depot at Sidi-bel-Abbès in Algeria. It is believed that of the Legion volunteers, around 40 were parachuted back into their homeland over the coming years.

As the men adjusted to life in the Legion, storm clouds gathered over Europe, culminating in war breaking out on 3 September. The French Government released the Czechs from the Foreign Legion in accordance with a pre-agreement to form the 1st Czechoslovak Infantry Division in the event of a European war. The men were transported by ship from Oran to Marseille, and then to their new depot at Agde.

When they took their place in the French Army's order of battle on 1 January 1940, some were wearing French kit from the Great War and the division lacked adequate resources in artillery, anti-tank and anti-aircraft weapons.

It is reported that by March 1940, a total of 13,614 men of Czech nationality had joined the French forces, including those who had travelled from Britain, America and beyond; 11,814 were serving in the Army and 1,800 in the Air Force. The Army contingent paraded at Agde on 7 March to commemorate the 90th anniversary of the birth of Tomáš Masaryk. They had been able to form two regiments of infantry – which in British terms was just about a division. The 1st Infantry Regiment was assigned to the French 23rd Infantry Division and the 2nd Infantry Regiment to the 239th Infantry Division. They were a tiny remnant of a Czech Army that, before the Munich Agreement, had consisted of 40 infantry divisions.

The 'Phoney War' in Western Europe lasted until the early summer of 1940. The German invasion of France and the Low Countries then commenced on 10 May. The French had pinned much faith on the Maginot Line to stop any German invasion, but crucially this defensive line did not extend along the Belgian/French border, Belgium being regarded by the French as a neutral neighbour.

However, the main German thrust was made through neutral Belgium, thus bypassing the Maginot Line. The Germans expected to tempt the British Expeditionary Force (BEF) into Belgium to meet their advance. This is exactly what happened, allowing the rapidly moving German forces – adopting the new *Blitzkrieg* tactics – to outmanoeuvre the slow-to-react BEF and French Army and force the Allies to retreat. Armoured German thrusts reached the Channel coast, cutting off the BEF and a large contingent of French forces in north-east France and Belgium.

This culminated in the evacuation of 338,000 troops from Dunkirk at the end of May and early June, including as many as 90,000 French troops. But for the bulk of the French Army, the Battle of France would continue further to the south.

The Czech soldiers had left their homeland due to a German invasion, but now a few months later their adopted country was on the verge of defeat and occupation by the same German forces. With the evacuation of the BEF, the Germans began *Fall Rot* (Case Red) on 5 June – the conquest of the rest of France.

The 60 French divisions that remained put up a determined resistance but were unable to resist the German air superiority and armoured mobility. German forces advanced deep into France without being checked, occupying Paris on 14 June virtually without a shot being fired. The Battle of France ended in the humiliating surrender of French forces just three days after Paris fell.

The Czech soldiers did try to put up some resistance, the 1st Regiment (at Coulommiers) and the 2nd (on the Marne) attempting to halt the 16th German Infantry Division. However, due to a lack of support they had their flanks turned and had to fight a rearguard action back across France: they eventually regrouped at Narbonne under General Sergej Ingr, commander of Czech forces in France, before being told to head to the port of Sète on the French Mediterranean coast. The Czechs had fought well but now the choice was simple – they must try to get to Britain to continue the fight.

The British Admiralty agreed to assist with the evacuation of the surviving Czech forces. They made available a mixed group of ships, including three destroyers, one of which was HMS *Keppel*. The log book for HMS *Keppel* records the following:

June   Nominated for evacuation of British civilian personnel From southern France after French capitulation.

20th   Passage from Gibraltar to Gulf of Lyon.

22nd   Embarked British civilians, Czech and Polish troops at Port Vendres and Sète.

23rd   Took passage to Gibraltar with embarked personnel.

To supplement the Admiralty force, merchant ships were commandeered from Egypt and used to transport this mixed bag of troops and civilians. Two of these merchant ships were the *Rod el Farag* and the *Mohamed Ali el Kebir*, which carried a significant number of the Czech contingent. They first sailed to Gibraltar, where the *el Kebir* joined convoy HG 36, which left on 28 June and reached Liverpool on 8 July 1940. The *Rod el Farag* joined a slightly later convoy and also arrived at Liverpool just four days after the *el Kebir*. Only around 4,000 Czechs managed to escape from France. Whilst it could be argued this was not a great numerical success, it was from amongst these 4,000 servicemen that some of the finest sons of Czechoslovakia would emerge.

2

How to Strike Back?

Once the basic building blocks were in place for a Czech government-in-exile being fully recognised by the British, and with SOE gaining in strength and experience, both the British and Beneš governments felt the time was right in 1941 to plan operations to strike at the Germans in their province of Bohemia and Moravia. As well as identifying suitable targets, potential agents had to be identified. In theory there was a potential source of candidates in the 3,000-or-so-strong Czech Brigade – now part of the British Army.

The Czech Brigade had been formed after the arrival of the remnants of the Czech Legion in Britain in July 1940, when the Czech formation was poorly equipped, being at the bottom of the supply chain for equipment. Whilst the Czechs had fought tenaciously, they had never been in a condition to even delay the German advance, never mind stop it. When France signed the Armistice, it is said that many 'French Slovak' soldiers who had been 'conscripted' into the formation deserted and went back to their homes in France.

In keeping with the situation at Dunkirk, much of the heavy equipment had to be left behind in France by the Czech forces. The overriding memory of many Czech soldiers was contempt for France, whom they felt had not only abandoned them over the Munich Agreement but also whilst they had been fighting for France.

After the remnants of the Czech forces arrived in England in mid-July they were reformed into what became known as the 1st Czechoslovak Mixed Brigade Group. This formation originally numbered around 4.000 men, enough for two infantry battalions and some supporting arms and services. However, this number decreased when many men transferred as aircrew to the Czech squadrons forming in the RAF.

At the same time, the HQ of Czech Intelligence was set up in a large building in Porchester Gate, London. The 22nd Liaison (Czech) Unit was formed, with British officers appointed to ease relations and provide additional help with the variety of problems that would no doubt arise; for example, communication equipment was only provided after the intervention of the Liaison Unit.

The opening entry in the War Diary of No. 22 Military Mission, dated 22 August 1940, reports:

No. 22 Military Mission was formed to train and work with Czechoslovak Forces in this country, and act as liaison between Czechoslovak personnel, Commands and Departments. Previous to formation of this Mission a British Camp Commandant Major E.H. Tamplin MC RA, with a staff of British Officers and NCOs, was administering the camp issuing stores and rations. For purposes of training, the Brigade was attached to III Corps, Commander Sir James Marshall-Cornwall for assistance. Colonel Pollock, General Staff from Mission to Norway, appointed Commandant.

The Czech Section of SOE had been established under Captain Peter Wilkinson. When the Nazis' Protectorate of Bohemia and Moravia had been formed, Wilkinson had been in Prague on a special nine-month study leave. Colonel Colin Gubbins, who was the senior officer in SOE, felt that Wilkinson was an ideal candidate to head the Czech Section. He was given the remit to arrange training of selected candidates and assist with the planning of operations and transportation of agents to their deployment in the field. In addition, Wilkinson was to make the Czech government-in-exile aware of the overall strategy of SOE and report back to his own chiefs what it was the Czechs wanted to achieve.

A major step forward in Czech relations came in April 1941, with the arrival of intelligence concerning the German plans to invade the Soviet Union. Beneš, at a meeting with Churchill, was able to impress him with this information, which had been obtained from agent A-54, who even gave the invasion date. At the same time, Beneš presented Churchill with a request for equal recognition of his presidency and government as existed between Britain and its other allies. This shrewd move worked, and a British official from the Foreign Office who was friendly with Beneš reported to him that he had seen written by Churchill on the minutes, "I do not see why the Czechs should not be placed on the same footing as the other Allied Governments." Underneath, the Foreign Secretary, Anthony Eden, had written, "I agree."

Back in July 1940, the Czech forces evacuated from France had been sent to Cholmondeley Park in Cheshire to reorganise. Here they suffered a minor mutiny by around 550 of the 4,000-strong unit. These men refused to obey orders and requested they be discharged from the Army. At this time, with invasion fever at a high level, it was inconceivable that the authorities would allow 550 'aliens' to be discharged. These soldiers were first sent to a camp at Sutton Coldfield, then transferred to the Pioneer Corps. At the time it was felt it had weeded out from the ranks of the Czechs some of the weaker soldiers. However, it was a source of embarrassment for both the British and the Czech government-in-exile and was quietly forgotten.

During August 1940, the Czechs had been redesignated as the Czech Mixed Brigade Group and modelled on the standard British Army brigade structure, although it only had two infantry battalions as opposed to the normal three.

The War Diary of No. 22 Military Mission concludes the entry for the month of August with observations as to the condition of the Czech Brigade:

Organisation.

A War Establishment for a Czechoslovak Independent Infantry Brigade Group has been approved by the War Office. It would be the task of the Mission to assist in the training, administration and equipment of the Czechoslovak Independent Infantry Brigade Group in accordance with this War Establishment.

Training.

No training had been attempted prior to the arrival of the Mission. A number of Officers had been sent on attachment to units of the 2nd London Division. In the majority of cases attachments had little more than social value.

Morale.

Morale was greatly affected by experiences in France. There was apprehension lest the British should direct them as the French had done, giving them equipment at the last minute and fling them into the 'line'.

There was some internal dissension which had resulted in some 550 men being separated from the main body and interned at Sutton Coldfield.

A document (WO178/21) in the National Archives at Kew giving a list of equipment issued to the Czech Army in August 1940 contains the following:

Rifles and Pull throughs	1,541
Bayonets and Scabbards	1,541
Vickers Machine Gun	12
Lewis Machine Gun	1
Pistols .45	45
Pistols, Signalling	14
Guns, Field 75mm	4
Guns, Anti-Tank 2 Pounder	2

Then the next month more items arrived:

Transmitting Wireless Sets	4
Bren LMG	42
Lorries and Trucks	15
Ambulances	8
Badges 'Czechoslovakia'	2,000
Lorries 3 Ton Breakdown	1
Motor Cycles and sidecars	10
Lorries 30cwt 4 wheeled GS	14
Lorries 3 Ton 4 wheeled	27
Anti-Tank rifles .55	24
Greatcoats	1,456

Then, and no doubt much to the Czechs' relief, it seems in October 1940 they were finally issued with some ammunition, as the No. 22 Military Mission War Diary records:

Ammunition .22	80,000 rounds
Ammunition .55	400 rounds
Ammunition .303 belt packed	15,000 rounds
Ammunition .303	124,840 rounds

The War Diary does not contain any returns on the number of men in the Czech Brigade, but a clue to that figure can be gauged from the issue of gas masks, battle-dress trousers and boots from November 1941. Whilst you could argue that trousers and boots could be issued at more than one pair per man, it is difficult to see why they would be issued with more than one gas mask:

Battle dress, trousers	3,050
Pairs Boots	3,050
Respirators, Anti-Gas	3,000

Therefore, the early strength of the brigade had been over 3,500 men, and possibly nearer 4,000 when considering those who had volunteered as aircrew and transferred to the RAF. However, the 'mutiny' in August lowered the strength by 550, so the brigade must have numbered around 3,000 men at the end of 1940.

By the end of October 1940, the Czech Brigade had moved from Cheshire to the Midlands town of Leamington Spa, where they would stay for around two years. Their headquarters were in Harrington House, a large Victorian villa in Newbold Terrace, which has since been demolished. Whilst the troops were in the Leamington Spa area, friendly relations were established between locals and the young men far from their homeland.

For the rest of 1940 and into 1941, training continued and morale improved. Some of their countrymen had already seen direct action in the Battle of Britain as fighter pilots or aircrew. One Czech observer at the time said:

> The Czech soldiers can never hold their heads up in Prague unless they have been in actual combat with the Germans. It is true that a large proportion were involved in the retreat across France but that is not considered sufficient and the men themselves realise full well that they will receive no welcome in their own country unless they have actually fought the Germans in the later stages of the war; and of course it is the urgent wish of every man in that Brigade to want to have a go.

Then in April 1941 there was a visitor from London – Major Josef Strankmüller, deputy of Colonel Moravec, head of Czech Military Intelligence. His visit was meant to be secret, but did not stay so very long, as it soon became clear that

Strankmüller's task was to 'talent spot' men for a return to their homeland as secret agents. At this stage, the aim was to assist the Czech Home Army with 'proper' soldiers who had knowledge of weapons, explosives, demolition, sabotage and subversion. Another important aspect was the insertion of communication teams so that there was a more regular flow of intelligence and better communications between London and Czechoslovakia. The men they were looking for would need to be self-reliant, highly professional in their job and, more importantly, be able to survive behind enemy lines for long periods, avoid detection and handle the stress and pressure of operating in German-held territory. Each potential agent had to consider that if they were caught by the Germans, they may face death or, worse still, torture to reveal the identities of other agents or resistance helpers.

It is said that after looking at a number of candidates, around 40 names were put forward to be subject to further investigation for their suitability. They were then interviewed and asked if they would consider volunteering to return to their homeland as secret agents.

Operation Barbarossa, the German invasion of the Soviet Union in June 1941, greatly complicated matters for the Czech government-in-exile. In very quick time, the Soviet Union were sending their own agents in to Czechoslovakia to make contact with former members of the Czech Communist Party. The Czech government-in-exile was now in a race to gain control of resistance from within Czechoslovakia. Beneš knew that if the Soviets positioned themselves to assume political control upon the successful conclusion of the war, then the London Czechs would be marginalised. On the other hand, the British wanted to do all they could to help their new ally.

Beneš now had little option but to infiltrate his own agents into Czechoslovakia. In August 1941, General Ingr, by now the Minister of National Defence, informed the Home Army that when the nights were longer, teams of agents would be dropped into Czechoslovakia for the purposes of intelligence gathering, communications and sabotage.

Amongst the early volunteers from the Czech Infantry Brigade were the following individuals who would play a major part in the Anthropoid story.

Jozef Gabčik was born on 8 April 1912 in Poluvsie, near Žilina, in Slovakia. After leaving school he trained to be a locksmith. In 1932, he joined the Czech Army and served with the 14th Infantry Regiment, and upon discharge in 1937 he worked in a military poison gas factory. In 1939 he crossed the border and entered Poland, making his way to France, where he joined the French Foreign Legion. During the fighting in France in 1940 he was awarded the Czech War Cross. He escaped to Britain in July 1940 and became the second-in-command of No. 2 Platoon, No. 3 Company, of the 1st Czech Battalion.

Jan Kubiš was born on 24 June 1913 in Dolni Vilémovice, near Třebič, and before joining the Czech Army in 1935 had trained as a furnaceman in a brickworks. He served with a number of units, including the 31st Infantry Regiment and the 13th Guard Battalion. In June 1939 he escaped to Poland and then to France, joining the

French Foreign Legion and subsequently the Czech Division when war broke out in September 1939.

He wrote in his diary an account of how he crossed illegally into Poland on 14 June 1939:

> I will never forget the day I walked through the woods from 4 a.m. to 3 p.m. It was a fairly dangerous journey, as the border between Poland and us was heavily guarded by German customs officials and others employed by the Germans. While walking through the woods I met a forester, he was called Ručka. Fortunately he has a good patriot and I gave him my grenade which I had been carrying for my own protection. He directed me to a Mr Slaviček, a blacksmith in the village of Morávka. When I met him I felt able to share my plan with him and he offered to help. He sold me two shovels and advised me on what to say if I should get stopped by the authorities. More importantly, he showed me exactly where the border was. The crossing went without a hitch and I was able to move quietly and unmolested through the woods. When I was approaching the village of Rieka, which was in Poland, I realised I was soaked to the skin and my shoes were full of water. I knocked on one door and they directed me to another house and I was able to explain that I had escaped from Czechoslovakia and wanted to join the Czech Army-in-Exile. He then became very friendly and helpful. He fed me and dried out my clothes.

During the fighting in France, Kubiš was awarded the French *Croix de Guerre* and the Czechoslovak War Cross. Another entry in his diary records a typical day during the German invasion in the summer of 1940:

> No breakfast. No lunch and the enemy, having located our positions, treated us to several hour-long artillery bombardments. Numerous shells exploded above our heads. Our machine gunners did their best to retaliate. The order to withdraw came at 2100 hours. I had quite a job keeping the squad calm. Eventually we started our long march back during which I saw unforgettable scenes of many mutilated corpses. I was also very tired but after 50 kilometres I forced myself to sing and even crack jokes which helped me to forget the tiredness. Eventually we reached Sète and were ordered to hand over our weapons. I had two hand guns and together with Lance Corporal Gabčik we decided to keep them. We were worried that we might be searched and so we decided to hide them. We borrowed a tin opener from somewhere and in a quiet corner near the sea, cut open the bottoms of our water bottles and hid our pistols inside.

After arrival in England in 1940, Kubiš became second-in-command of No. 1 Platoon, No. 3 Company, of the 1st Czech Battalion.

Gabčik and Kubiš became close friends, and when based in the Cholmondeley Castle area developed a friendship with the Ellison family – especially their two daughters, Lorna and Edna – who lived in the small village of Ightfield, about 4 miles south-east of Whitchurch in Shropshire. Lorna recounted to author John Martin in the 1990s how they met:

> My elder sister Edna and I had been to the cinema in Whitchurch. In those days, especially with the war going on, there wasn't much else to do. As we walked to get our bus home, we passed a soldier in uniform, sitting on a wall near the car park. He was also waiting for a bus, to take him back to Cholmondeley Castle. He smiled as we went past and when we got on the bus, he came up, wrote something on a piece of paper and passed it to us through the bus window. My sister, Edna opened the note and said: "Ooh look, he wants to meet us here tomorrow afternoon. What do you think Mum will say?" When we got home and showed Mum the note, Mum said "I don't mind, behave yourselves and go on the condition that you are both back here by 5 p.m."

This was the first meeting of the Ellisons and Jan Kubiš. He began to visit the family regularly, and they asked him if he had a friend he would like to bring with him. John Martin's interview with Lorna continued:

> Jan always had his camera and photograph album with him, so one day he put the album on the table and said to Edna and I "You choose one." We all had a look through it having a good old giggle and eventually we stopped on one picture and said; "That one." The man in the photograph had a right old mischievous grin. Jan couldn't believe it and said; "How strange, that's my best friend Jozef." It was a photograph of the two men taken together whilst they were in Africa. I remember the photograph well, as they were both sat on a wall. So the next visit he bought Jozef with him and that was the beginning of our very special friendship.

Karel Svoboda, born on 18 October 1912, served in the Czech Army from 1932–34 with the 2nd Frontier Battalion at Trutnov. After his service he worked as a draftsman with Popper and Hruška in Prague. He was amongst the many soldiers and ex-servicemen who crossed over to Poland in June 1939, and then on to France to serve in the Foreign Legion and later the Signals Company of the 2nd Infantry Regiment. After being evacuated from France, he served with the HQ Company of the 2nd Czech Battalion.

František Pavelka was a little younger than some of his contemporaries, being born on 29 November 1920. He was a philosophy student at Masaryk University in Brno at the beginning of the Nazi occupation. He avoided arrest when the Germans raided the university and, for a short time, found employment in the Telegraphic Office at Brno. He did not leave Czechoslovakia until March 1940, crossing first into Hungary and then Yugoslavia. Like so many others, he ended up in France, where he volunteered for the Czech Army and took part in the campaign in May and June – though it must be said with very little training beforehand! Once in England, he was assigned to the Signals Platoon of the 2nd Czech Battalion.

Adolf Opálka was born on 4 January 1915. In 1935 he started officer training at the Military Academy in Hranice, graduating with the rank of lieutenant in 1937. In July 1939, he escaped to Poland and from there travelled to France and joined the French Foreign Legion, serving in Sidi-bel-Abbès and later in Oran. Following his transfer to the Czech Army in France in 1939, he saw combat against the Germans in 1940. He was also evacuated to England and served as commander of a machine-gun platoon.

Jozef Valčik was born on 2 November 1914. Upon finishing school he became an apprentice tanner and worked in a shoemaking factory until 1936. He was then called for his national service and served with the 22nd Infantry Regiment. His escape route from Czechoslovakia after the German takeover was different to the others, his travels taking him through Yugoslavia, Turkey, Syria and then to France. In March 1940 he was posted to the 2nd Infantry Regiment. In England he served as Company Sergeant Major of No. 1 Company of the 2nd Czech Battalion.

Karel Čurda was born on 10 October 1911 in Stará Hlína, near Treboň. He started his National Service in 1933 and decided to sign-on as a regular soldier. After having served throughout the country, he left for Poland in June 1939, following the well-trodden path to France, joining the French Foreign Legion and thence the Czech Division. Although he did not see combat in France, he did escape to England, where he served in the Transport Company of the Czech Brigade.

Jiří Potůćek was born on 12 July 1919 and seems not to have served prior to the Second World War. At some point after war broke out it is believed he was sent on a business trip to Yugoslavia, from where he travelled on to France and either volunteered or was volunteered for the Czech Army. Given his lack of experience, it is likely he did not see any action in France, but nevertheless he crossed to England and was a part of the signals team at Czech Brigade HQ.

Vladimir Škacha was born on 17 May 1920 and originally trained as a bricklayer. He reached France via Poland in July 1939. He then served with the French Foreign Legion in Algeria and was selected for a course at the NCO's School at Agde. During the fighting in France in June 1940, he saw combat and was later recommended and awarded the Czechoslovak Medal for Gallantry in the Face of the Enemy. He sailed for England on the *Rod el Farag*, alongside Gabčik and Kubiš, and served with No. 3 Company of the 1st Czech Battalion.

Jan Hrubý, born on 4 March 1915, trained as a waiter, becoming head waiter at a hotel in Zlin. He completed his national service and afterwards worked for a period in Germany. He returned home in 1939 before leaving for France via Hungary and the Balkans. During the fighting in May and June 1940, he served with the 1st Infantry Regiment and was awarded the Czechoslovak War Cross. Escaping to England, he served with No. 1 Company of the 1st Czech Battalion. Hrubý is believed to have spoken four languages, which would, no doubt, have improved his application when being considered for special duties.

Jaroslav Švarc was born on 11 May 1914, and after completing his education he joined the family sweet and confectionary business. He enlisted in the Czech Army in 1936 and reached NCO rank. In November 1938 he was on border security duties and was involved in several incidents with Hungarian forces. In March he was demobilised and, in January 1940, escaped to France via Hungary, Yugoslavia and Syria. He served in France in May and June 1940 with the 2nd Infantry Regiment and travelled to England on the *Rod el Farag*.

Jozef Bublik, born on 12 February 1920, was the son of a Czech Legionnaire, his father having been wounded fighting against the Allies in Italy, taken prisoner and subsequently fighting in the Czech Legion in 1918. Bublik had been a student in 1939, and when his university was closed down he left Czechoslovakia via the Balkan route to France. If he fought in France during 1940, then it was with minimal training. Nevertheless, he was evacuated to England and served with No. 2 Company of the 2nd Czech Battalion.

Vilem Gerik was born on 28 December 1920 and was apprenticed as a radio mechanic. In November 1939, he left Czechoslovakia via Hungary, Yugoslavia and Beirut for France, where, in April 1940, he was placed with the 8th Company of the 1st Czechoslovak Infantry Regiment, taking part in the fighting against the Germans. In Britain, he served with the signals platoon of the 2nd Battalion.

Ivan Kolařík was born on 22 March 1920 and after leaving school he studied medicine to follow his dream to become a doctor. After the closure of the universities in 1939 he left for France via Slovakia and the Balkans. Once in France, he joined the Czech Army as a private and served with No. 8 Company of the 1st Infantry Regiment, seeing action against the Germans. He was evacuated to Britain on the *Rod el Farag*, and in England was a member of No. 2 Company of the 1st Czech Battalion.

Oldřich Pechal, born on 12 May 1913, became a cadet at the Military Academy in Hranice in 1935. He graduated as a lieutenant in 1937 and elected to serve in the infantry. After the German occupation he left for France via Poland, and on 8 September 1939, joined the Czech Army at Agde. He served first with the 3rd Infantry Regiment and then as Support Company commander with the 2nd Infantry Regiment. After successfully being evacuated to England, he was made commander of the Czech Machine-Gun Company.

Arnošt Mikš was born on 27 June 1913. When he left school he was apprenticed to a stone mason. He underwent his national service between 1936 and 1938 and was discharged as a sergeant. Following the occupation, he took the Balkan pipeline to France and joined the Czech Army there on 13 January 1940. He was appointed as second-in-command of a machine-gun platoon and saw action against the Germans in May and June 1940. After arriving in England he was appointed as second-in-command of a platoon in a rifle company in the 1st Czech Battalion.

These were just some of the brave men identified as suitable for special operations back in their homeland.

3

Enter Reinhard Heydrich – Operation Anthropoid Takes Shape

After the German occupation of Czechoslovakia in 1939, the country was divided into two parts – one became known as the Protectorate of Bohemia and Moravia and the other Slovakia. Germany was happy to treat Slovakia as a satellite country with its own autonomous government, provided it fell in line with Nazi thinking.

In Bohemia and Moravia, the Germans appointed a *Reichsprotektor* to protect German interests in the new territory. The first person to hold this position was the former German Foreign Minister, Konstantin von Neurath. Emil Hácha remained as the 'theoretical' head of state with the title of State President, but in reality he had no powers and was used by the Germans as a tool to provide legality to their occupation.

German officials took over in the government departments and the SS assumed control of the police, as well as setting up offices of the *Gestapo* across the Protectorate. Heinrich Himmler, the leader of the SS, appointed the Sudeten German politician, Karl Hermann Frank, as head of the SS and police in Bohemia and Moravia. The new regime also had consequences for the Jews, who, as in Germany and Austria, were banned from working in the civil service and denied many of their normal rights. Political parties, other than the Czech National Socialist Party, and trade unions were banned, and press and radio censored.

In keeping with the future methods employed in other conquered countries, the Germans took a keen interest in those industries which would benefit them, as well as looking upon Czech agriculture and food production as necessary exports for Germany, whilst rationing was introduced for the Czechs. There were important industries in Bohemia and Moravia, and the Germans did their best to improve production in the coal mines, the iron and steel works and, most importantly for them, the arms industry. The Skoda works at Plzeň was said to be the second-largest single armaments factory in Europe behind the Krupps factory in Essen. The importance of this additional factory to the German war machine can be gauged by a comment Hitler made in a speech in which he claimed that by occupying Czechoslovakia, Germany gained 2,175 artillery pieces, 469 tanks, 500 anti-aircraft guns, 43,000 machine guns, 1,090,000 military rifles, 114,000 pistols and about a billion rounds of ammunition. This amount of weaponry was sufficient to arm about half of the *Wehrmacht* at this time.

Despite these early repressive measures, the first few months under German rule were moderate compared to what was to come. As the year of 1939 moved forward, culminating in the German invasion of Poland on 1 September and the outbreak of the Second World War, daily life for the Czechs became much tougher, resulting in Czech demonstration against the occupation on 28 October 1939, the 21st anniversary of Czechoslovak independence. German security forces responded to these demonstrations by shooting into the crowds. One man was killed instantly and another, Jan Opletal, a medical student, gravely wounded by a gunshot to the stomach. Opletal died on 11 November, and his funeral march four days later caused further widespread demonstrations, especially amongst students.

The Germans had given permission for Opletal's coffin to be taken by procession through Prague on 15 November, en-route to the station for transport to his home for burial. More than 3,000 students were present at a memorial service at the Institute of Pathology and the adjacent chapel. Hundreds of students followed his coffin afterwards, and more locals joined the procession. The Czech hymn, '*Kde domov můj*', was sung over and over again. When they reached Charles Square, anti-German sentiment was overflowing and a confrontation developed between members of the procession and the German security services. The students withdrew into the building of the Technical University. The Germans allowed them to leave in small groups, but the cunning students regrouped and, continuing their anti-Nazi protest, tried to reach the city centre. Two days later, *Reichsprotektor* von Neurath, likely under pressure from Berlin to act with a heavy hand, ordered what became known as the *Sonderaktion Prague*, or Special Operation Prague. All Czech universities and colleges were closed and approximately 1,850 students arrested, of whom nine were later tried and executed, with around 1,200 sent to Mauthausen concentration camp.

Now they were at war, the German intention was to put an end to all resistance and leave the Czech peoples in no doubt as to who were their masters. Back in London, Beneš and Moravec were encouraged by these signs of Czech resistance. London was already in contact with, and influencing, the Central Committee for Resistance in Czechoslovakia, which had been formed shortly after the occupation but consisted of disparate resistance groups. At the start of 1940, the main resistance groups consolidated to form the Central Leadership of Home Resistance, otherwise known as the *Ústřední Vedení Odboje Domácího*, hereafter referred to as ÚVOD.

ÚVOD was made up of three groups – the *Obrana Národa* (the Defence of the Nation), the *Politické Ústředí* (the Political Centre) and *Petiční výbor Věrni zůstaneme* (the Committee of the Petition that We Remain Faithful), which consisted of trade unionists and left-wing intellectuals. Following the launch of Operation Barbarossa, the German invasion of the Soviet Union, there was a fourth main resistance group, the *Komunistická Strana Československa* (the Communist Party of Czechoslovakia), which worked on the periphery of ÚVOD whilst maintaining the right of independence of action.

As would take place with the other occupied countries that had governments-in-exile, the BBC granted the Beneš government facilities to broadcast news and programmes back to their homeland. Many Czechs risked arrest by listening to these broadcasts, which was the only viable option for the government-in-exile to send messages to the people back home. In September 1941, a significant broadcast was made that was designed to demonstrate how much power Beneš could wield. On 14 September, the BBC Czech Service called for a boycott of the Protectorate press, which was no more than a propaganda tool for the Nazis. It was effective: in the days that followed, sales dropped by up to half, much to the Nazis' chagrin. Beneš explained at the time that this had two main purposes for his government. The first was a test mobilisation of public support and the potential for an armed uprising that could be co-ordinated from London, Secondly, it was evidence that the Czechs at home would obey and take more notice of broadcasts from London than those broadcast by Moscow Radio. On 21st September 1941, the government-in-exile broadcast that the boycott should be ended and sent a message of congratulations to ÚVOD; Beneš informed the Home Army that the demonstration had served its purpose but to continue would undoubtedly provoke German reprisals. It had shown the resolve of the Czech people to listen to London and that there was a will to resist. The boycott brought favourable comments in the British press and radio, creating popular good will for Beneš' government. It was also around this time that ÚVOD was advised that the first parachute agent from Britain would soon arrive.

Increased Czech resistance, albeit of a passive nature, had not gone unnoticed by the German security forces. The exasperated Prague security services sent a report directly to Hitler to complain that von Neurath was too weak with the Czechs, that there was a go-slow action in the factories and other forms of passive resistance. This was the catalyst for the appointment of Reinhard Heydrich as *Reichsprotektor*.

On 27 September, it was announced in the press and on the radio that "the *Reichsprotektor* of Bohemia and Moravia, Herr Konstantin von Neurath had made a request to the *Führer* that he be given leave on medical grounds. The *Führer*, under such circumstances had agreed to the *Reichsprotektor's* request and *SS-Obergruppenführer* and *General der Polizei*, Reinhard Heydrich, was appointed as Acting *Reichsprotektor* of Bohemia and Moravia." While Heydrich was initially only appointed for von Neurath's leave of absence, in truth von Neurath had been sacked and Heydrich was now in charge.

Reinhard Heydrich was born in Halle an der Saale, near Leipzig, in Saxony, on 7 March 1904. His father and mother were musicians of some repute in Saxony. Heydrich had been a child during the Great War, but during the aftermath of the Versailles Treaty he witnessed the turmoil in Germany and became involved with the *Freikorps*, jobless former soldiers from the Great War who banded together to act as paramilitary armed 'muscle' for right-wing political groups. Aged only 15, it is probable he acted as no more than a runner, but this was the first inkling that Heydrich wanted a military career. His parents had expected him to become a violinist, although as a child he wanted to be a chemist.

Shortly after his 18th birthday, Heydrich entered the *Reichsmarine* as an officer cadet. He specialised in naval signalling, and by 1928 had risen to the rank of *Oberleutnant zur See*. His widowed grandmother had married Gustov Suss, Suss being a Jewish name. As a result, both Heydrich and his father had endured a lifetime of prejudice as it was believed they were Jewish. This prejudice continued into Heydrich's naval career, so he remained aloof and a loner. Despite this reserve when in male company, Heydrich found that women were attracted to him, but this would lead to his downfall in the Navy.

On 6 December 1930, Heydrich met Lina von Osten; 12 days later they become unofficially engaged. This became official after Heydrich had spoken with Lina's father on Boxing Day 1930. However, a press announcement of their engagement led to another woman accusing Heydrich of already having been engaged to her. This woman's father was a close friend of Admiral Raeder, Commander-in-Chief of the *Reichsmarine*. Heydrich was charged by a naval court with 'conduct unbecoming to an officer and gentleman': namely his two proposals of marriage. Raeder's connection ensured the verdict went against Heydrich, and he was dismissed from the Navy.

Heydrich was now unemployed and his prospects uncertain. However, through the influence of Baron von Eberstein, a senior member of the SA – the *Sturmabteilung*, the paramilitary wing of the Nazi Party – and whose wife was Heydrich's godmother, Heydrich was granted an interview with Reichsführer SS Heinrich Himmler in Munich in June 1931. The position available to Heydrich was to form an intelligence agency for the Nazi Party. Himmler was so impressed by Heydrich's proposals during the interview that he was offered the post immediately. Within a year, Heydrich's new agency was renamed the *Sicherheitsdienst* (Security Service), shortened to SD.

The SA were commonly known as Storm Troopers or the Brown Shirts, receiving the latter nickname from the colour of the shirts they wore. From 1921–33, the SA disrupted the meetings of the political opponents of the Nazis, as well as defending the halls where Hitler made his public speeches. Their members played a very important role in the formative years of the Nazi Party. By 1933, however, the SA had become a potential threat to Hitler. Himmler also saw an opportunity to usurp the SA with his SS. Heydrich's SD fabricated evidence against the head of the SA, Ernst Röhm, which when presented to Hitler led to the culling of the SA leadership in what became known as the 'Night of the Long Knives'.

The SS was the common name of the *Schutzstaffel*, which translates literally to 'Protection Squadron'. It had been formed purposely to be independent of the SA and in effect consisted of the bully boys of the NSDAP (*Nationalsozialistische Deutsche Arbeiterpartei*, or Nazi Party). The origins of the SS can be found in a small unit known as the *Saal-Schutz* (Hall Security), made up of NSDAP volunteers to provide close personal security at speeches and party meetings in Munich in the early 1920s, whilst the SA provided general security. In 1925, Heinrich Himmler joined this unit, which had by then been reformed under the name *Schutzstaffel*. An ambitious Himmler held several senior positions, until finally in January 1929 he became *Reichsführer-SS*. Under his direction, the SS grew from a small paramilitary formation to one of the most powerful organisations in Nazi Germany. From 1929 until the regime's collapse in 1945, the SS was the foremost agency of security, surveillance and terror within Germany and German-occupied Europe.

The SD, a branch of the SS, was the intelligence-gathering body of the Nazis. The SD was formed in March 1931, but was not formally known as the SD until June 1932. Its purpose was to act as an exclusive SS intelligence agency, reporting direct to Himmler. In 1933, Hermann Goering established the *Gestapo* (the secret police service), which acted as a rival to the SD until it came under the control of Himmler and Heydrich the following year.

Himmler had very clear ideas as to the purpose of the SD: "The SD will discover the enemies of the National Socialist concept and it will initiate counter-measures through the official police authorities."

In theory, the SD was under the control of the Minister of the Interior, Wilhelm Frick, as was the *Gestapo*, but few doubted that the SD's real masters were Himmler and Heydrich. The SD consolidated the numerous police forces, including the *Kripo* (the criminal police force), *Schupos* (the urban constabulary) and the Reich Central Security Office. Members of the SD were thought of as the elite of the elite – professionals who were responsible for the security of the Third Reich.

Under Heydrich, the SD was the primary agency responsible for intelligence analysis and held executive measures in suppressing numerous internal and external enemies of the Nazi state. The SD established intelligence offices in all the occupied territories. It investigated any individual or group that did not accept the authority of the Nazi state. The *Gestapo* then arrested these political opponents and, where deemed appropriate, incarcerated them in special camps using the police authority granted by an order of 'Protective Custody'.

When Heydrich became Acting *Reichsprotektor* of Bohemia and Moravia, he retained his position as *SS-Obergruppenführer und General der Polizei* and Head of the Reich Main Security Office, which since September 1939 had been the name of the now combined SD, *Gestapo* and *Kripo*.

Heydrich arrived in Prague on the evening of 27 September 1941 with three objectives:

i)   crush Czech resistance;
ii) increase armaments production;
iii) prepare the way for ultimate Germanisation of all Czech lands.

Even before Heydrich had arrived in Prague, the Czech Prime Minister, General Alois Eliáš, had already been arrested on his orders. Eliáš was tried just four days later, found guilty of communicating with the Beneš government-in-exile and sentenced to death. President Hácha asked Hitler via Heydrich that Eliáš be spared, and although Hitler gave no ruling, it suited Heydrich to keep Eliáš alive in prison but under the threat of the death penalty.

The arrival of Heydrich would also result in Hácha's already difficult and compromised position as president becoming far worse. He was invited to a meeting with Heydrich, but this was a one-way discussion that left Hácha heart-broken and speechless. Heydrich is said to have given Hácha three choices as he outlined the new regime's plans for Bohemia and Moravia – suicide, resignation or carrying on but being fully responsible for the consequences of full collaboration. Hácha chose the last option, but truly believed that by further sacrificing himself, his reputation and his place in history, he could alleviate some of the hardship that would otherwise have fallen on his countrymen.

Other notable victims in the early days of Heydrich's arrival in Prague were the acting leaders of the military resistance – Generals Josef Bilý and Hugo Vojta. Bilý had retired from the Army in 1935, but after the occupation had helped in the establishment of the Defence of the Nation, an anti-Nazi military resistance organisation. As this was an illegal organisation, Bilý had lived in hiding but was arrested in November 1940 and had been in protective custody since then. It is not clear if he had a trial, but he was executed on the evening of 28 September 1941. His reported last words to the firing squad were, "Long live the Czechoslovak Republic! Fire you dogs!" General Vojta, who had been the military leader of the Sokol organisation that promoted Czech nationalism, was executed alongside him. A number of other senior Army officers were also executed in the weeks that followed, many as early as 1 October, just four days after Heydrich's arrival as Acting *Reichsprotektor*. It was clear that iron discipline would now be applied to Nazi rules and regulations in Bohemia and Moravia under Heydrich, whom Hitler called "the man with the iron heart".

London was kept well informed of what was going on via its home intelligence network. The Czech government-in-exile was alarmed by reports that between 28 September and 28 November 1941, the German military courts in Prague had sentenced to death 233 Czech citizens. Of these, 135 were shot by firing squad at Ruzyně Barracks and 88 were hung.

The War Office file on Heydrich (now held at the National Archives at Kew) contains a synopsis of a report which is itself based on a report from the news agency Reuters, dated 27 September 1941, regarding Heydrich's appointment in Prague, 'Reported Appointment of Reinhard Heydrich to the position of Reichs Protector Bohemia and Moravia'. The synopsis provides an idea of the feeling that existed in London at the time:

1.   Czechoslovakia has seethed with discontent ever since Hitler took the country under his 'protection'. On various occasions since the outbreak of the war there have been purges, perhaps the most notorious being the brutal liquidation of hundreds of Czech students in the autumn of 1939.
2.   Industrial sabotage and 'go-slow' tactics have been frequently reported. The most recent case was the large explosion in the Skoda works [in] Plzeň, caused, according to Moscow, by a time bomb. There have been other cases previously of 'dud' production in the Skoda plant.
3.   Baron Konstantin von Neurath, an ex-Foreign Minister and ex-Ambassador was appointed first Protector of the Czechs. He is not a Party man, but a professional diplomat who has – like other non-Party men such as Meisener and von Papen – been able through much adroitness and lip-service, to

maintain [his] position in the Nazi organisation. In von Neurath's case his star began to wane when von Ribbentrop, convinced of the subtlety of his own approach to the English problem, ousted him from the post of Ambassador to the Court of St. James in 1937. When in turn Ribbentrop was recalled, he again scored off von Neurath by succeeding him as Reichs Minister of Foreign Affairs in February 1938. Von Neurath after a temporary eclipse emerged again to become Reichs Protector in Prague immediately after the occupation of Bohemia and Moravia in March 1939.

4. His rule has not been an unmixed blessing either to the Czechs or to himself. An aristocrat and a courtier by birth and by tradition, there must inevitably be features of the Nazi regime which have made it very difficult for him to accept wholeheartedly the fullest implications of 'Hitlerite' rule. There are grounds for supposing that the policy vis a vis the Czechs did not exclude a certain, and possibly expanding degree of collaboration. This policy has proved a personal failure and it is consequently logical that a completely fanatical Nazi boss should have been appointed to take over the position of Reichs Protector.

5. An obvious choice for this role was Reinhard Heydrich, SS Gruppenführer, Chief of the Reichs Security Police and the Security Service of the SS, and ipso facto of the Gestapo. As Himmler's right-hand man, and therefore probably the second most dangerous man in German occupied Europe, there can be no doubt of the immediate consequences of this drastic appointment.

6. It is interesting to note that only at the beginning of September; Heydrich paid a lightning visit to Norway where resistance to the Gestapo also demanded ruthless intervention. That Heydrich has his ear to the ground and senses the rising tide of revolt not only in occupied [Europe] but also in the home territory is shown by his recent demand – reported on 4th September – for an extra body of informers to be recruited from the general public.

The Deputy *Reichsprotektor*, Karl Hermann Frank, had harboured his own ambitions to replace von Neurath, but if he felt any disappointment he did not show it and became a loyal servant to Heydrich. Frank was born in Karlovy Vary (then part of the Austro-Hungarian Empire) on 24 January 1898. This was part of the Sudeten lands that in 1918 became part of the Czechoslovak Republic. Even before the formation of the republic, Frank had felt himself completely 'German', developing a hatred towards the Czechs and the Slovaks that consumed him. He tried to enlist in the Austro-Hungarian Army during the Great War but was rejected as he was blind in one eye. He married Anna Muller in January 1925 and had two sons. They would later divorce, and in April 1940 Frank married Karola Blaschek, with whom he had three more children. As early as 1923, he joined the NSDAP and was involved in setting up several branches of the Nazi party in northern Bohemia and Silesia. He opened a bookshop that became a hotbed of Nazi propaganda. In 1933, Frank joined and helped organise the Sudeten-German Homeland Front, which evolved into the Sudeten German Party; he worked for a while in their public relations and propaganda department and later was elected as a Sudeten German Party member of the Czechoslovakian parliament. His radical views came to the notice of Himmler, who made him an *SS-Brigadeführer* in November 1938. This was one month after the German occupation of the Sudetenland, and he was made Deputy *Gauleiter* for the region. Further promotion and responsibility came in 1939, when he was made Higher SS and Police Leader and Secretary of State of the *Reich Protektorate* of Bohemia and Moravia, along with his promotion to *SS-Gruppenführer*. Frank's true role was to act as a counterbalance to von Neurath, whose appointment had been primarily to appease Britain and France. Although he was von Neurath's deputy, Frank was answerable directly to Hitler, Himmler and Heydrich. In the coming months he reported on von Neurath's soft approach to the Czechs, which would eventually culminate in von Neurath's removal from office. When Heydrich arrived in Prague, Frank approved of the strong actions that were taken by the new *Reichsprotektor*. Together, they formed a strong working relationship to protect German interests in Bohemia and Moravia.

A week after Heydrich's arrival in Prague, the first British-based agent was ready to be inserted into Czechoslovakia. This mission was codenamed Operation Percentage, and its purpose was to help increase the amount of radio communication between the Home Army in Czechoslovakia and London. It was in the early hours of 4 October 1941 that František Pavelka, a signals specialist, was dropped by parachute near Koudelov, in the Čáslav area. Pavelka was tasked with establishing contact with ÚVOD, delivering a message from General Ingr that he had memorised and handing over crystals for radio transmitters/receivers and a new cypher key. Pavelka was also carrying the SOE Mk III radio. Shortly before he left London, it is reported that Colonel Moravec, of Czech Military Intelligence, tried to encourage him with the words, "With a bit of luck all will be well. Of course, there is a certain danger involved, not that I am saying you will put your neck into a hangman's noose, but nothing is 100 percent certain even though from our side all has been prepared meticulously and with caution."

As would become a feature of many of the parachute insertions, Pavelka was dropped in the wrong location. Despite landing about 20 miles away from where his reception committee awaited his arrival, near Nasavkry, he was after a few days, with the help of local patriots, able to contact the ÚVOD organisation. He travelled to Prague at a time when the German security forces were pursuing Czech resistance workers, and ultimately they picked up a trail that led to Pavelka. He was arrested by the *Gestapo* on 25 October 1941, still in possession of his radio set. He was later pictured in his jump suit and interrogated over several months. It appears Pavelka only gave up information that he believed the Germans already knew. The names he surrendered were fabricated. Eventually the Germans sent him to Berlin, and he was executed at Plötzensee prison in January 1943.

The German invasion of the Soviet Union in June 1941 brought several complications for Beneš. He feared the dormant Communist Party in Czechoslovakia would mobilise in support of the Soviet Union and, by so doing, reinvigorate internal support and win over a large number of Czech citizens – before the Nazi occupation, the Communist Party had been well established in Czechoslovakia. As it turned out, the Communists were not organised for resistance in 1941. But much later on, Beneš was proved right to be fearful. The invasion of Russia had mobilised the resistance in France, which had become much more aggressive. Operation Barbarossa meant the French Communists, free from the ties of the non-Aggression Pact between Germany and the Soviet Union, now focused themselves on active resistance. Up to this time, Beneš had been content with the passive resistance in his homeland, which, subsequent to the Germans' violent reaction to the student demonstrations in 1939, had not elicited too much in the way of retribution. Now Beneš found himself under pressure to match the activities of the French resistance. It was around this time that the idea of an assassination attempt first materialised.

Whilst the exact evolution of the assassination plan is not known for certain, it is likely that both Beneš and Colonel Moravec were the driving forces. Originally there were two candidates: Emanuel Moravec, a former Czech Army officer now turned Quisling, and later a detested Minister of Education in Hácha's government, or Deputy *Reichsprotektor* Karl Hermann Frank. However, the wave of executions and arrests that marked the arrival of the Acting *Reichsprotektor* determined Heydrich as the target.

It is likely that the plan of assassination was motivated from a political rather than a military base point. In addition, there was increased pressure on Beneš from the British for the Home Army to act, not helped by the fact Beneš had also lost his trump card; contact had been lost between London and Václav Morávek and, therefore, access to the intelligence provided by the German double agent, A-54, had ceased.

As well as running agent A-54, Morávek had, in conjunction with two other officers – Josef Balabán and Josef Mašin – been instrumental in coordinating the different resistance movements in Czechoslovakia once they had been consolidated to form ÚVOD. These three officers became known by the *Gestapo* as 'The Three Kings of the Czech Resistance'. By the latter part of 1941 only Morávek remained free at large. Balabán was amongst those officers executed at Ruzynè Barracks in October 1941, whilst Mašin had been in the hands of the *Gestapo* since May 1941. A-54, Paul Thummel, had also been arrested and was under suspicion of supplying information to the Czech resistance movement; he would be released but rearrested within a few months.

London now had a period of operating blind. Beneš and Colonel Moravec decided to send in a parachutist group, Operation Silver A, with the task of renewing contact with Morávek. In the meantime, a high profile assassination would re-establish the political legitimacy and credibility of Beneš' government-in-exile with the British.

Under von Neurath, output in the all-important industries of arms, coal, iron and steel had been below the expected targets of production. These were all crucial industries for the Nazi war machine. It was also an area where the Czechs could assert their passive resistance, by working slowly or producing inferior products. Heydrich had decided on a 'carrot and stick' approach (which he called 'a whips and sugar' policy). He would reward those who worked well for the Reich but act with brutality towards those who shirked or acted against Nazi Germany.

One of his carrots, or pieces of sugar, was to crack down on the black market and those who operated it – Heydrich claimed that black marketeers were responsible for the food shortages across the Protectorate. In the early wave of arrests after Heydrich's arrival, around 190 of them were for 'economic crimes'. The sugar was when Heydrich ordered the confiscated black market foodstuffs be sent to the canteens of the armaments factories. He followed this with opportunities for the shop floor workers to voice their grievances and suggest ways of improving production. On 24 October, Heydrich received a delegation from the Czech workers and promised to raise living standards. In the following weeks the tobacco and fat rations were raised for certain categories of workers, health schemes were provided and increased wages introduced for the munitions workers based on increased output. Heydrich also apparently arranged that 200,000 new pairs of boots be given to industrial workers. It turned out that these moves did increase production; he was clever enough to realise that if the Czech worker was to produce more, he had to eat. Heydrich calculated the Czechs would work all the harder to keep these concessions, more so when this was coupled with the potential stick (or whip) of being arrested for sabotage, with all the implications that meant.

Heydrich's final carrot and attempt to increase productivity was to lift martial law in Prague and Brno and release some of the students who had been under protective custody since 1939, as a gesture of goodwill. Heydrich wanted to feed the Czechs the message that collaboration worked, although from December 1941 this message was tainted when it was announced that Czechs could be conscripted and sent on 'war work' anywhere in Germany. From April–November 1942, it is recorded 80,000 Czechs were sent to Germany.

Heydrich would further manipulate the government of Bohemia and Moravia by the creation of a Ministry of Labour under the leadership of a German bureaucrat, Walter Bertsch. Bertsch would be responsible for the day-to-day economic running of the Protectorate and became very effective in uncovering any dissension against the Nazi rulers. He ruled that all civil service discussions would be conducted in German, and similarly all documentation and records had to be kept in the German language.

In the months that followed, Bertsch presided over a massive reorganisation in the Czech industries and amongst the workforce. Companies whose output was deemed not necessary for the war effort were either closed down or made to manufacture alternative war-related products. An estimated 100,000 workers were moved from what was thought of as unsuitable employment into what the Nazis did deem as suitable. In February 1942, the standard 8-hour day in the armaments industry was changed to a 12-hour one, and shift patterns were reviewed in other industries. If further evidence is required as to how highly prized Czech-made weapons were, in March 1942, Himmler attempted to divert the entire output of the Skoda arms factories to the Waffen-SS.

To counter adverse changes, Heydrich offered further carrots to the workforce; in April 1942, social security payments were increased by 30cent, May Day was proclaimed as a public holiday and 3,000 armaments workers and their families were offered free holidays in luxury hotels that would normally have been unaffordable to them. Other workers were offered free tickets for football matches, the cinema or the theatre via the workers' organisations. The Germans used their propaganda machine to portray Heydrich as the friend of the workers, and in the press it was claimed he "was carrying out an unparalleled social reform which recognised for the first time in Czech history the value of the Czech worker". With the benefit of hindsight, it can be said that Heydrich's measures were little more than a smokescreen, to increase arms production and at no cost to the Nazis. The hotels, for example, were commandeered and other costs met by Czech employers and insurance companies.

Another key role was played by the Ministry of Education and Propaganda, led by the Czech Quisling, Emanuel Moravec, once a fierce nationalist and opponent of the Munich Agreement but now a fanatical supporter of the Nazis. Heydrich welcomed his support and regarded him as a useful tool to get into the Czech psyche. Moravec's role from late 1941 was to reform the Czech education system, break what the Nazis saw as the hold of nationalistic school teachers over young people and to eventually produce more compliant workers for German industry. To achieve this, Moravec planned an overhaul of the education system. Secondary school education would be reduced by two years. Learning the German language became a mandatory school subject, and to enforce this it was intended schooling should take place in Germany when possible. Moravec also headed the Board of Trustees for the Education of Youth, which created youth groups based on the Hitler Youth idea for children between 10 and 18 years of age. Through linking Czech national culture to the Reich, it was intended that Czech children would develop an unwavering link to the ideals of Nazi Germany.

Whilst Heydrich set out on his mission to break down the Czech population, so the planning of another mission was underway in Britain. Post-war, both Beneš and Colonel Moravec distanced themselves from responsibility for Operation Anthropoid, but in the absence of distinct documentary evidence, it must be assumed that authority for the mission came from the top, if not the very top.

The first batch of soldiers selected by Major Strankmüller, Moravec's deputy, were, by the middle part of 1941, undergoing training at the hands of SOE instructors at various secret locations the length and breadth of Britain. The initial training course for those selected, numbering 40 or so men across several batches, was a remote location in the Scottish Highlands near Arisaig. The facility was known as STS 25, which was centred on three locations at Traigh, Garramor and Camusdarrach. STS stood for Special Training School. The course itself lasted four weeks and was normally conducted for groups of 20 men. It was modelled on the Army commando course and included activities such as rock climbing, field firing exercises, silent killing and unarmed combat. Two of the trainers were Captain William Fairbairn and Captain Eric Sykes. The pair had both served between the wars in the Shanghai Municipal Police and were known for their unconventional fighting methods. They were specialists in silent killing methods and together designed the Fairbairn-Sykes fighting knife, which was issued to Special Forces during the war. Jozef Gabčík was in the first batch at Arisaig. The second batch of trainees went through STS 25 from 16 August to 12 September 1941; Jan Kubiš was amongst their number.

Arisaig was followed by parachute training at RAF Ringway near Manchester before the men moved to Station XVII at Brickendonbury, Hertfordshire, for training in explosives and demolition.

Very few records relating to SOE training have survived. Within the records of No. 1 Parachute Training School RAF Ringway, no details exist for any of the Czech soldiers who returned to their homeland in 1941 and 1942. (However, a succinct report dated 17 August 1941, does exist for one of the Czech trainees and has been included in the photographs section).

It was decided that a two-man team would carry out Operation Anthropoid. Warrant Officer Jozef Gabčík and Sergeant Karel Svoboda were selected from amongst those men who by the beginning of October 1941 had completed their SOE training programmes. According to a meeting note in the Colonel Moravec archive, Gabčík and Svoboda were summoned to a meeting held on 3 October 1941:

3rd of October 1941: Present: Colonel Moravec, Lieutenant Colonel Bartík, Major Palečēk, Major Krček, Warrant Officer Gabčík and Sergeant Svoboda.

Colonel Moravec told Warrant Officer Gabčík and Sergeant Svoboda the following:

"We are being informed from radio and newspapers about senseless killings back at home. Germans are murdering the best of the best of our people. This situation means war, so we shall not cry; we shall not weep, but act. Our people back at home worked, but now they are in a position in which the possibilities are restricted. It's our turn now; we who are abroad must help. One of the tasks will be entrusted to you. October is the month of our national holiday, our Liberation Day. It is desirable in this situation, when our people will 'celebrate' our saddest holiday of our liberation, to underline this holiday. It has been decided to emphasise it by a deed, which would be recorded in history the same way as these killings. There are two main figures in Prague representing these killings. K. H. Frank and new arrival, Heydrich. In our opinion and as well as in the opinion of our leading representatives, one of them has to pay a heavy price; we should show them that we can hit back. This will be the task assigned to you. Tomorrow you are leaving to retrain for a night parachute jump. You are both going home so you must help each other. It will also be necessary for the reasons, which will become known to you that you will have to execute the task without co-operation with our people back home. When I say without co-operation I mean just until the accomplishment. After the task is over, you will get all the help and protection you need from our people. The method and date of the execution has to be devised by you. You will be dropped at a location, which can guarantee the best possible landing. You will be equipped with everything we can get for you. According to our best information you will get help from all the good people you will turn to. But you will have to act with the highest caution and composure. I can't stress enough how historically important the task is and how high the risk is. It depends on conditions you'll create for yourself, your cleverness etc. We will talk about it some more after your return from additional training. Now I have already said that the task is of great importance, so if you have any doubts, then please speak out."

Additional note: Gabčík and Svoboda both agree to assume the responsibility for the task. They will both leave 10th of October, the same year.

It was significant that in order to represent the Czechoslovak Republic, one man came from Slovakia (Gabčík) whilst the other was Czech (Svoboda).

As instructed, the two men returned to No. 1 Parachute Training School at RAF Ringway, for training in night jumps. It was whilst undertaking one of these jumps that Sergeant Svoboda suffered a training accident on 5 October, ruling him out of the operation. Svoboda had fractured his skull, noted as a swelling on the head in this hand-written chronology (translated) from the Colonel Moravec files:

Operation Anthropoid

2nd October 1941	Accommodation secured for 2 persons in area.
3rd October 1941	10:45 arrival of Gabčik and Svoboda
	15:10 meeting with the Chief: Bartík, Paleĉek, Strankmüller, Krček and both men.
	A night time departure with Major Keary – Strankmüller will provide notes.
5th October 1941	16:00 arrival in London – Svoboda injured his head when jumping from a static balloon (an English Army colonel who also jumped was injured even more seriously).
6th October 1941	Svoboda was sent, accompanied by Musil, to a Red Cross doctor.
	Afternoon meeting with Major Wicki, Captain X, Strankmüller and Šustr.
	Both men (Gabčík and Svoboda) briefed and equipment and arms issued.
	Afternoon issue of civilian clothes.
	17:00 men dismissed.
	Telephone inquiry to Headquarters regarding instructions for tomorrow's departure – 7th October at 09:30 remains in effect – it will be a test with the explosive devices and followed by weapon training.

7th October 1941   09:00 Svoboda reports sick. He is suffering from a swelling on the head and says it must be as a result of the bad
landing he had earlier. He states his entire body is aching,
especially his back.
Šustr informed. Only Kubiš fit for operation. This message
acknowledged, and a decision delayed until noon.
Meanwhile Gabčik (on standby) to leave alone at the
appointed time.

The two-man team had been reduced to one as it was clear Svoboda would be out
of action for a few weeks at least. To his credit, Gabčík was prepared to continue
the operation alone if necessary. It can be assumed that Strankmüller looked for a
replacement amongst the men who had undergone SOE training, but most accounts
state Gabčík suggested Jan Kubiš as Svoboda's replacement.

However it came about, Kubiš was approached and agreed to take part in Operation
Anthropoid. Clearly, Kubiš would need to be trained in night jumps and so some
reality came to the timeline. An early jump into the Protectorate was cancelled, and
Gabčík and Kubiš were given the chance of enhanced training.

Meanwhile, the RAF were looking at possible drop zones for the agents, as outlined
in the following two documents:

Document No. 1
6th October 1941
To S/Leader Barham   From Captain Dodds-Parker
(copy to S/Leader Farley)
I attach maps of the dropping point for Operation Anthropoid. The first priority
is for the point as marked on the Protectorate maps – this is enclosed in a circle
marked 3 on the 250,000 Air Map [the maps were not retained when the file
was thinned-out before release to the National Archives].

The second priority is the point in a circle marked 2 WSW of the first point
near Lake Cekonsky Ryb.

This operation has now been postponed 24 hours and arrangements made for
7th October now hold good for 8th October.
Signed A.D. Dodds-Parker

Document No. 2
From Captain Hon P.R. Rea   6th October 1941
Operation Anthropoid
This confirms agreed dropping points in the Plzeň area in order of priority.
Map: Europe: 1/250,000 (Air) Sheet M.33/7 (Plzeň)
1st Choice North of main road crossing main railway. 2km W of Cerhovice,
33km ENE of Plzeň 15°46'E 49°51'N
2nd Choice West side of lake at Cekov, 2km West of Karéz, 3km S of Zbirch,
27km ENE of Plzeň 13°45'E 49°40'N

3rd Choice 2½km NNE of Jarov, 7km E of Kaznéjov, 18km NNE of Plzeň 13°29'E 49°53'N

4th Choice NW corner of isthmus formed by river, 4km N of Chrast, 3km S of Planá, 13km NE of Plzeň 13°31'E 49°49'N

5th Choice W of Hor-Stupno railway station, 4km SSW of Radnice (next station), 7km NE of Chrast, 16km NE of Plzeň 13°34'E 49°49'N

Signed P.R. Rea Captain

Once the Czechs had accepted the assassination would not be carried out on 28 October, the urgency of the mission seems to have diminished. The flight to Czechoslovakia did not occur in October, or even November. Various reasons have been put forward for the length of this delay: new forged identity papers for Kubiš were not ready in time; the realisation that more training was required in assassination techniques; and synchronising a drop opportunity with the hard-pressed RAF, who had to assign a long-range aircraft and a crew experienced enough to undertake a somewhat challenging flight.

There was also concern regarding Operation Percentage (with František Pavelka), which had left Britain on the night of 3/4 October. There had been no messages from Pavelka, and the normal flow of messages from the Home Army had also ceased. It is likely the Czechs adjusted their focus to re-establishing this essential radio contact. Two communications teams were being prepared for a return to the homeland; these were known as Silver A and Silver B and consisted of teams of three and two agents respectively.

During the rest of October, Gabčík and Kubiš revisited the STS locations after briefly practising parachute training and night drops at RAF Ringway. Between 14 and 18 October, both men returned to Arisaig and received further training under the auspices of Captain Eric Sykes in explosives and small-arms skills. When they left Arisaig a favourable report followed them:

They have completed the training in the given time as prescribed by London. During the hand grenade throwing tests both their strength and accuracy were excellent. They undertook two night exercises. Mistakes made during the first exercise were not repeated during the second task. Apart from a few hesitant moves, their work in difficult conditions was very consistent. Regardless of what type of training they had to undergo, they showed great resolution and enthusiasm. It was a pleasure to work with them. An excellent pair.

On 20 October, they travelled south to Station XVII at Brickendonbury Manor, near Hertford, for further instruction in industrial sabotage and the use of explosives and fuses. One of the instructors at Station XVII was Major C.V. 'Nobby' Clarke, who had worked mainly in the motor industry. He was a veteran of the Great War and came to the attention of the authorities after submitting a scheme entitled 'A Consideration of New Offensive Means', which he sent to the Admiralty in early 1940. As a result, he quickly found himself commissioned as a lieutenant in the Intelligence Corps. In

April 1941, he was selected for promotion to major with a further comment added that he had "a special knowledge of explosives". His promotion was approved and for reasons which are not clear he was at No. 1 Parachute Training School at RAF Ringway in July 1941, where, on 8 July, he had a bad landing, sustaining a "sprain fracture left ankle. Moderate severity." It was fortunate that the injury was not considered likely to interfere with Clarke's future efficiency as an officer. Part of the training under Major Clarke was how to handle grenades or bombs with sensitive fuses, which would lead to him playing a significant role in Operation Anthropoid.

The training continued into November. By 8 November, Gabčík and Kubiš had moved to STS 2, located at the Villa Bellasis near Dorking in Surrey, south of London. Their training at Villa Bellasis was termed 'continuation and skill enhancement training'. This again covered small-arms training and grenade throwing, but also included skills that would be of use in Czechoslovakia, such as counter-surveillance techniques.

On 1 December, Gabčík and Kubiš were at the Czech Intelligence HQ in London, where both men signed a pledge stating:

> The substance of my mission basically is that I will be sent back to my homeland, with another member of the Czechoslovak Army, in order to commit an act of sabotage or terrorism at a place and in a situation depending on our findings at the given site and under the given circumstances, and I will do so effectively so as to generate the sought-after response not only in the home country but also abroad. I will do it to the extent of my best knowledge and conscience so that I can successfully fulfil this mission for which I have volunteered.

It is believed, although unsurprisingly no evidence exists to confirm it, that a meeting was held on 6 December, at which Gabčík and Kubiš met with President Beneš, Colonel Moravec and Major Strankmüller. It is alleged that Gabčík told Beneš: "Do not worry, Mr President, we will do it for you."

An indication of the type and level of training undertaken by Gabčík and Kubiš, plus the operational orders given them, is summarised in the following two file notes found at the National Archives in London. The first file note is dated 30 May 1942, but refers to training conducted immediately after Kubiš had been assigned to replace Svoboda:

> Target: Liquidation of Heydrich.
> Personnel: 2 W/O's recruited from the Czech Army.
> Planned: 10/10/41.
> Date of recruitment: 20/10/41.
> Training.

Prior to their recruitment these men attended para-military course in Scotland and were subsequently specially trained jointly by the Czech Section and the

Training Section. The latter training included instruction by the following specialists:-

Captain Fairbairn at Station XVII for one day.

Major Clarke at Station XVII for one day.

Captain Sykes and Captain Bush at Arisaig for six days.

In addition a number of discussions on tactical planning were held between the two W/O's, Officers of the Czech Section and Major Clarke at which specialist explosive charges were designed by the latter and finalised by Major Wood at Station XII.

The party was subsequently held at STS2 for six weeks and continued training throughout this period.

Orders and Instructions given to the party:

As it was known that Heydrich lived at the Castle [Hradcany] in Prague it was agreed that the attack should take place when he was travelling in his car from the Castle to his office or to any known appointment.

Practical experiments proved that such an anti-personnel attack on a car must be carried out at a corner where it is forced to slow down. The two men were therefore told to obtain as much information as possible about Heydrich's movements in the first place and then to get a job as road sweepers. On the day chosen for the operation they were to begin sweeping the road at a selected corner. Their explosives and arms were to be concealed in their dustman's cart and were to consist of three one-pound contact fused bombs, one four-second Mills bomb, one Colt 38 Super automatic pistol to be carried by No 1, and one one-pound contact fused bomb, one Colt 38 Super automatic pistol and one Sten gun (optional) to be carried by No 2. The first bomb was to be thrown by No 1 at the front of the car when it came within 15 yards in order to kill the driver and so force the car to stop. The second bomb was then to be thrown broadside to hit the rear window, the panel just behind it or the rear door. Simultaneously No 2 would open up with the Sten gun (or with his pistol if he had not been able to conceal the Sten under his coat). The Mills bomb was to be thrown by No 1 if Heydrich was not already dead, as contact bombs cannot be relied upon to explode if they hit soft surfaces. The last contact bomb was to be retained by No 2 as a reserve in case of failure of the primary attack. If a hit were not scored the party was to kill Heydrich at close quarters with their Colt 38 Super automatic pistols, which they would carry in shoulder holsters.

In the event of the operation being successful the Colt pistols and spare bombs were to be used during the withdrawal, which was to be made separately.

A suitcase containing 30 pounds of Plastic Explosive was also to be concealed in the dustman's barrow. This suitcase was to be fitted with a five-second delay fuse and could be thrown bodily at the car or, as a last resort; No 1 was to rush the car with the suitcase in his hand while No 2 threw his last bomb at the front axle.

At the request of the party themselves this operation was planned so that no attempt at withdrawal should be made or considered until Heydrich had been successfully liquidated, and they made it quite clear that, unless the initial action were entirely successful, both members of the party would share Heydrich's death.

The second report was written by Captain Alfgar Hesketh-Prichard, a highly regarded officer in SOE who worked for the Czech Section. He had been asked to oversee the training of Gabčík and Kubiš:

Report by Captain Hesketh-Prichard dated 22nd January 1942.

The operation Anthropoid, consisting of 2 agents was despatched by parachute on the night of 28/29th December 1941. They carried with them a package containing two metal boxes, the contents of which are shown in the attached schedule.

The object of the operation is the assassination of Herr Heydrich, the German Protector in Czechoslovakia and the small box contains equipment for an attack on him in car on his way from the Castle in Prague to his office. The larger box contains assorted equipment for alternative attacks by:-

(a) Getting into the castle.

(b) Getting into his office.

(c) Placing a bomb in his car or in his armoured train.

(d) Blowing up his railway train.

(e) Mining a road along which he is going to travel.

(f) Shooting him when he is appearing at some ceremony.

The time and place of this operation will be decided on the spot but the agents concerned have been trained in all methods of assassination known to us. They intend to carry out this operation whether or not there is any opportunity of subsequent escape.

This project is not known to the Czech organisation within the Protectorate.

The training reports from Arisaig survive for Gabčík and Kubiš and contain interesting summary information on the two would-be assassins, which, if not outstanding, were solid reports:

Training History Sheet
Serial No 2
Name in Full   Gabčik, Jozef
Age 28   Nationality Czechoslovakian
Description   Short, thick set, 141lbs weight. Hair fair, Eyes brown
Knowledge of Languages
Civil Employment   Locksmith
Military Employment and Qualifications:
Warrant Officer Czechoslovakian Army; was employed for 3 years in a Military
    Poison Gas Factory 1935–38. Army 1932–35. Polish Legion 1939. French

Foreign Legion 6 weeks. Served in France gained his country's Military Cross.

Training Report

STS No 25

Health   V Fit

Character   V Good

Particular Standard or Ability in Regard To: -

I Physical Training   V Good

II Fieldcraft   Good

III Close Combat   V Good

IV Weapons Training   Good

V Explosive and Demolition   Good   Test 86%

VI Communications   V Good   Morse Code 12 words per minute

VII Reports

VIII Map Reading and Sketching Fair Map Reading Test 68% Sketching Fair

IX Intelligence

X SS Work

XI Irregular Warfare

XII Sabotage

XIII Combined Operations

XIV Political and General

XV Advanced Technical Training

XVI Driving or Riding:-

(i) Bicycle   Yes

(ii) Motor Bicycle   No

(iii) Motor Car   Yes

XVII Any other particulars   swimmer   good skier

Commandant's Remarks.

A smart and well-disciplined soldier. He has not the brains of some of the others and is slow to acquire knowledge. He is thoroughly reliable and very keen and has plenty of common sense. He has self confidence in practical work, but lacks it as far as brain work is concerned. He is a good leader when sure of his ground and he obeys orders to the last detail. He is surprisingly good at signalling. Also appears to have technical knowledge, perhaps of use. (Worked in Poison Gas Factory.)

Grade F

8th August 1941

Training History Sheet

Serial No 2

Name in Full   Jan Kubiš

Age 28   Nationality Czechoslovakian

Description   Medium Height and build. Hair brown, eyes blue, complexion fresh.

Knowledge of Languages

Civil Employment   Furnanceman in Brick Works

Military Employment and Qualifications:

Enlisted 1935 and served thereafter. French Foreign Legion Algiers 2 months. Served in France. Now Warrant Officer. French Croix de Guerre and Czechoslovakian C de G.

Training Report

STS No 25

Health   V Good

Character   Slow but reliable, solid, popular.

Particular Standard or Ability in Regard To:-

I Physical Training   Very Good

II Fieldcraft   Good

III Close Combat   V Good

IV Weapons Training   Good

V Explosive and Demolition Good Test 90%. Slow in practice and instruction

VI Communications Good   Test Morse 7 words pm

VII Reports

VIII Map Reading and Sketching   V Good 98%

IX Intelligence

X SS Work

XI Irregular Warfare

XII Sabotage

XIII Combined Operations

XIV Political and General

XV Advanced Technical Training

XVI Driving or Riding:-

(i) Bicycle   Yes

(ii) Motor Bicycle   Yes

(iii) Motor Car   No

XVII Any other particulars   Good swimmer

Commandant's Remarks.

A good reliable soldier, quiet and comes in for a certain amount of good natured teasing. Classification 'D' might work up to 'B'.

11th September 1941

Meanwhile, planning for Operations Silver A and Silver B was progressing. Lieutenant Alfréd Bartoš, Warrant Officer Jozef Valčik and Lance Corporal Jiří Potůček had been chosen as the three-man team for Silver A. Their mission was to search out members of the home resistance movement, specifically Captain Václav Morávek, and to renew radio communication with London. Silver B was a two-man team consisting of Staff Sergeant Jan Zemek and Sergeant Vladimír Škacha. Their task was to deliver a radio to the home resistance and to set up a further communication link with London.

The agents signed a similar undertaking to the Anthropoid group. The following is a translation of that signed by Jiří Potůček, dated 29 October 1941:

> The main task is that, together with two other Czechoslovak Army officers, I will be sent to my homeland to establish radio communications with the Headquarters of the Czechoslovak Army in Great Britain. I will also if specific information is forthcoming make contact with our Home Army.
>
> I will make my upmost efforts to accomplish this task, which I volunteer for in my own free will.

It was agreed with the RAF that all three groups would be dropped on the same night, from the same aircraft. In preparation for his departure, Kubiš made a diary note: "I am not sure of the future as a special task is asked of me, a very dangerous one, but I am not afraid, I will embrace it with gusto and nothing is going to stop me."

The RAF had allocated a long-range aircraft from their special duties squadron No. 138 to fly the mission. The pilot selected was Flight Lieutenant Ron Hockey. While 138 Squadron normally flew on operations out of RAF Tempsford, near Sandy in Bedfordshire, for this mission Hockey flew to RAF Tangmere on the south coast of England, where his passengers would embark on 28 December. Travelling with the parachutists but on a return journey was an observer from the Czech Government, Major Jaroslav Šustr.

Šustr provided Gabčík and Kubiš with their last Operational Orders just prior to leaving for their homeland:

> The aircraft will reach the drop zone between 2300 and 2400 German Summer Time on the day of its departure from England, or just after midnight, i.e., in the first hours of the next day. After landing, immediately and with care, bury the parachutes and parachutist clothing, as well as all other items that were necessary only for the flight over.
>
> If need be, hide the equipment and wait in the forest near the landing place until morning. The longer nights with the moon setting in the early hours of the morning will allow you to stay close to the drop zone. As soon as the situation allows, go to the main road and travel to either Plzeň or Rokycany. From the moment that you leave the aircraft, rely on your own initiative and adapt to whatever situation you may find on the ground.
>
> In Plzeň or Rokycany, seek out people according to the addresses you were given in a separate annex and after establishing your credentials using the passwords provided, ask them for any necessary assistance in terms of obtaining lodging, food, or other essentials. Do not mention your specific task for your own safety as well as theirs.
>
> Once you have secured your first contact, you have to discover ways of travelling to Prague, the current circumstances in the Protectorate, the validity of money, or if need be, the issue of new identity cards (you have been provided with two photographs each). You will then carry out your mission at a place and

time and under such circumstances as would be the most advantageous for you as well as for the task itself.

Before you attempt the task, secure new accommodation in a place other than the one you used when you first arrived. Also take into account the place where the operation will be carried out, escape routes and anything you can do to confuse the investigating authorities.

Depending on the situation, after completing the operation you may need to hide for some time and then make yourself known to some of the people whose addresses you have been provided with. Do not go to these people yourselves, send a third party, or arrange a password.

When contacting people, as well as when making them aware of your next location, keep to the order of addresses that you have been given.

Use the money provided to buy everything you need, but do not attract attention by spending unnecessarily or extravagantly. Do not carry large amounts of money.

Once the operation has been completed and when you are later contacted by our people, for which they will be instructed as appropriate, you will hand over the rest of the money to our home organisation and will assist them to the full extent as best you can in carrying out their challenging work, which is most important for our country and nation.

J. Šustr

A surviving document at the National Archives details the items issued separately to Gabčík and Kubiš for their mission:

Most Secret
Operation Anthropoid
No of Agents   2
Appendix A
1 .32 Automatic (Mauser or Colt).
1 Spare Magazine.
16 rounds .32 ammunition.
1 Knife, locking.
1 Compass, pocket. Enamel marching type, unless otherwise specified.
1 First aid dressing.
1 Pocket torch with spare battery and bulb.
1 Tin Horlicks tablets.
1 Tin meat lozenges.
1 Emergency ration (concentrated chocolate).
1 pair Anklets.
1 Tablet 'L' (Lethal).
1 pair gloves, gauntlets.
1 flying suit (overall cover with pockets).
1 Tablet 'B' (Benzedrine).
1 Tablet 'K' (Sleeping)

Appendix B
1 Spade in web carrier.
1 Helmet, padded
1 Parachute (W/T set attached, if required).
1 Spirit flask, full.
For use in aircraft:
1 Sleeping bag, heated.
1 Thermos flask
Sandwiches
Then dropped in a supply canister were the following items:
Small Box
2 38 Supers and shoulder holsters.
4 Spare magazines.
100 Rounds ammunition.
6 Percussion bombs with plastic [explosive].
2 Detonator magazines.
2 4-second Mills bombs.
Large Box
1 Tree spigot.
1 Coil trip wire.
2 Igniters.
1 Spigot bomb.
4-hour time delay for use with 2-lb P.E. charge.
4 Medium magnets.
4 Electric detonators and 30in wire and battery.
1 Sten gun.
100 Rounds ammunition for Sten gun.
32-lbs P.E.
10-lbs Gelignite.
2 yards Cordtex (new).
4 Fog signals.
3 Time pencils.
1 Lethal hypodermic syringe.

Under their all-in-one jump suits, commonly known as a 'striptease suit', Gabčík and Kubiš would be wearing civilian clothes. They had also been issued with money; receipts exist where Gabčík and Kubiš together signed out 5,000 Reichsmarks and 500 Koruna (Czech currency) on 4 December 1941. The Reichsmarks receipts actually totalled 5,020 RM in the following denominations:

RM 5 notes	50
RM 10 notes	470
RM 20 notes	2,000
RM 50 notes	2,500

The Czech currency was made up of 10 Koruna notes. In 1941 the combined value would have been equivalent to approximately £435, which in 2019 terms equates to over £23,000. These were significant funds.

For Hockey and his crew it was an unusual sortie. Operations to Eastern Europe were still rare, even in the darker winter months, and 138 Squadron had only recently received delivery of the longer-range Halifax. Up until then they had been equipped with the Whitley. The Whitley's range was constrained by its low cruising speed (and therefore by the hours of darkness over enemy territory) and its small payload when flown with a full complement of additional fuel-tanks. It's a debateable point whether the RAF would have permitted the flight to have gone ahead in October 1941, when 138 Squadron was in the process of converting to the Halifax.

By December 1941, 138 Squadron had completed its conversion to Halifax bombers. It had been the Polish Forces in Exile, led by General Sikorski, that had lobbied for a Polish squadron to be equipped with a faster, long-range aircraft to at least make contact with and supply for the Polish homeland feasible. A Halifax from 138 Squadron flew a first mission to Poland in early November 1941, but the aircraft had to crash land in Sweden on the return journey, which made the RAF hesitant about supplying another Halifax for the long-range flight to Czechoslovakia. The intention had been for a Czech crew to pilot the aircraft, but most likely with the Polish mission in mind, the RAF allocated the experienced Flight Lieutenant Hockey and his crew.

Hockey took off from the extra-long runway at Tangmere at 2200. The Halifax had a crew of seven, plus Major Šustr as despatcher, and then the seven parachutists; a total of 15 people. The take-off weight of the aircraft was recorded as 59,800lb. Landfall over the French coast was made near Le Crotoy, at the mouth of the Somme estuary. Hockey then set course for the German town of Darmstadt, possibly because the Rhine has a distinctive configuration south-west of the town.

The flight was an eventful one. Enemy aircraft were seen near Darmstadt, but fortunately combat was avoided. Navigation at this time was difficult; the RAF did not have many navigation aids to guide aircrews over enemy territory, except what was known as dead reckoning, using the stars and landmarks on the ground to identify their position.

Dead reckoning was not very accurate, and an investigation in 1941 led to findings that did not make for good reading. It reported that only a small percentage of those crews on operations claiming to drop their bombs accurately on a pinpoint target were actually within 10 miles of the intended target.

The Halifax steadily made its way across France, then Germany via Darmstadt, where the navigator was able to make a definite spot-check on his position, and finally into the airspace above Czechoslovakia. The Anthropoid drop zone, scheduled to be east of Plzeň, was reached first. In the early hours of 29 December, the aircraft came under German anti-aircraft fire which the aircrew mistakenly reported as protecting Plzeň. A heavy fog made dead reckoning on the drop zone almost impossible, but believing the aircraft was five miles south of Plzeň, Gabčík and Kubiš were summoned to the exit by Šustr. The men shook hands, one of them said, "You will soon be hearing from us, we will do everything we can", and then they were gone into the darkness below. The time was 0224.

The aircraft then carried on to the next two drop zones further to the east, dispatching the men of Silver A and Silver B. In his post-operation report, Hockey stated the last two drops had been carried out by 0246. The aircraft then set course for home, landing at Tangmere at 0819 on 29 December. It had been a flight of just over 10 hours.

The following report is from the Operational Record Book of 138 Squadron, dated 28 December 1941:

> Aircraft NF-V L9618 Halifax took off from Tangmere, with F/Lt Hockey Capt. Course set for French coast which was crossed at Le Crotoy. Course then set for Darmstadt and shortly after an enemy fighter sighted astern on port quarter. Two flares dropped by this aircraft, but no attack made on the Halifax, and owing to heavy loading the Halifax took no punitive action and after twenty minutes contact was lost.
>
> Visibility good and several pinpoints obtained despite snow on ground. Darmstadt reached at 00.42 hrs and although another aircraft was seen it was lost shortly after. Course set for target and eventually pinpointing became impossible owing to heavy snow, which blotted out all roads, railways, rivers and small towns. Owing to cloud height was lost and at 02.12 hrs flak was seen ahead and identified to be from Pilsen. Course altered to south of town and then for target area. First part of operation completed by 02.24 hrs (Anthropoid). Course then set for second target and the next operation was carried out within ten miles of the target at 800 ft.
>
> Course then set for third target, but bad visibility prevented identification of the landscape. Operation completed at 02.46 hrs within twelve miles. Course then set for Darmstadt and flak again met at Pilsen, and no other pinpoint recognised until flak met at Brussels. Course changed to westward at 05.40 hrs. French coast crossed at 07.20 hrs and shortly after the cockpit hood blew up and jammed. Second pilot held the hood to prevent it being jettisoned and fouling the controls, speed reduced to 140MPH. English coast crossed at 08.07 hrs near Selsey Bill and a landing effected at Tangmere at 08.19hrs.

In 1941 there were major problems for bomber crews to find and pinpoint targets in German-occupied territory. Their ability to find such a location depended on pinpoint navigation at relatively low level. At 10,000ft the ground beneath, if visible at all, appears very different from the detailed view available at 2,000–4,000ft, but Hockey also had to contend with deep snow when even a city can be rendered almost invisible in poor visibility at that height. By the time Hockey reached Czechoslovakia there was heavy cloud cover; had he not encountered flak, he and his crew might have had little idea of where they were, even though they mistook the flak from Prague as being from Plzeň.

The flight of the Halifax over the Protectorate did not go unnoticed by the Germans, and a report was prepared on the morning of 29 December 1941:

The Wehrmacht representative with the Reichsprotektor in Bohemia and Moravia.
Prague 29.12.1941
Secret
Group I c Az. 40 No. 2856/41 go.
Re: Enemy flights in the night of 28./29. 12. 41.

To the Reichsprotektor in Bohemia and Moravia z. Hd. By SS-Hauptsturmführer Werth Prague

The entry took place at 02.47 from Eger, then crossed south of Prague and arrived at 03.24 at Pardubice. The return flight went over Brandeis and Melnik to Schlan (04.15) and from there to the west to Karlsbad. For the flight path see attached sketch. Information about any enemy activity on the ground is not available. Anti-aircraft fire was directed at the aircraft from Prague and 98 rounds of ammunition were fired. In the areas flown over, the Wehrmacht has carried out searches after it was reported parachutists and leaflets had been dropped.
For the Wehrmacht representative
The Chief of the General Staff
Major I. Genst.

*Note: the tracked flight plan is included in the photograph section. The aircraft track splits into two at around 0315 and so suggests the Germans thought there were two aircraft flying over Bohemia and Moravia that night; however, their report never explicitly mentions two aircraft.

4

You'll Be Hearing From Us

Gabčík and Kubiš descended to the snow-covered ground below, but unfortunately Gabčík suffered a bad landing on the frozen terrain, injuring his left foot and ankle. The two men were, however, able to make contact with each other and collect their equipment, which they hid together with their parachutes in a hut belonging to a man called Antonin Sedláček. Leaving Gabčík in the hut, Kubiš set out for a nearby village to try to find out their exact location. Given the poor weather conditions, they knew it was likely they had been dropped adrift of Plzeň, but how far they did not know. Kubiš negotiated the fields and tracks into the village of Nehvizdy. Taking a chance, he knocked at the village Rectory. The door was opened by the priest, František Samek, who decided against asking this stranger any questions but was prepared to tell him he was in Nehvizdy, about 12 miles east of Prague. Kubiš calculated this was approximately 70 miles east of their intended drop zone. Thinking quickly, he told Father Samek that he had recently returned from forced labour in Germany and needed to reach Plzeň. Samek, who was himself taking a risk, gave Kubiš directions to the house of František Kroutil, who had been a local leader of Sokol. Whether Father Samek knew or just suspected, Kroutil was also a member of the local resistance and he assisted Gabčík and Kubiš with their travel by train to Rokycany, to the east of Plzeň. This was a vital first link in the chain of help given by many brave Czechs.

The Sokol movement had been formed in Prague in 1862 as a gymnastics organisation for all ages. It was based on the principle of a strong mind in a sound body. Originally just for men, by the 1930s everyone was allowed to join. After the occupation in 1939, the organisation was banned by the Nazis, wary of any large-scale popular movements. One of the reasons the Nazis banned Sokol was because one of the organisation's central articles of faith was upholding pride in their country. However, this did not stop branch meetings being held in secret as Sokol became part of the underground movement. A number of people who were prominent in ÚVOD had been members of Sokol. It appears Gabčík and Kubiš were given conflicting instructions in London before they left. On the one hand they were told to keep their mission secret and not to approach the Home Army, yet they were given contact addresses in the Protectorate to go to for help, and thus would inevitably meet members of the Home Army.

In Rokycany they found the house of Václav Stehlik, where, using a phrase given to them in London, "We are bringing regards from Hradecky", they were able to make contact with the resistance. Stehlik arranged medical treatment for Gabčík with a local doctor, Zdenko Čáp. They remained in Rokycany for a very short time before moving on to Plzeň, where they searched out the home of Václav Král.

Král's address had been given to them by Major Šustr, of the Czech Government, although the suggestion to contact Král had originally come from Adolf Horák, the future commander of the Operation Sulphur group. Král was a police officer and also a member of ÚVOD. He put them in contact with another resistance helper and fellow police officer, Jan Bejbi, who had contacts in Prague. It is believed Gabčík and Kubiš stayed with Král whilst he arranged false employment books for them. Gabčík was suffering from his ankle injury and so remained with Král whilst Kubiš went to Prague. It appears Bejbi passed Kubiš on to Jaroslav Starý from Šestajovice, who would introduce Kubiš to his Prague contacts in the resistance, namely Jan Zelenka and František Pecháček. It was Pecháček who reported Kubiš' arrival to Jindra, what was effectively the Prague resistance group. To all intense purposes, Jindra was led by Ladislav Vaněk, who was apprehensive when told that parachutists had arrived from London. He wanted to meet them and verify their credentials to ensure they were not German stool pigeons trying to infiltrate the resistance movement.

By this time Gabčík was also in Prague, but still struggling to walk on his injured foot, so when the meeting was arranged at Pecháček's apartment in Smichov, only Kubiš went, accompanied by Zelenka, another key member of Jindra. Zelenka was born in 1895 and had worked his entire career as a teacher and then a headmaster. He was a leading figure in the underground Sokol organisation, often going under the pseudonym of 'Hajský', which he chose because prior to the Munich Agreement he had lived and worked in the village of Haj near Duchcov, which was in the Sudetenland. When the Sudetenland was taken into the Reich, Zelenka returned to Prague, where he had lived and worked previously. He soon became a senior member of the Prague Sokol and was lucky to avoid arrest when the organisation was banned.

Vaněk was born in 1906 and had been a chemistry teacher and member of Sokol, rising through the hierarchy to become part of the Executive Committee. He also escaped arrest when Sokol was banned in 1941, after which he went on to be one of the founders of the Jindra group. Vaněk actually took the name 'Jindra' as his own pseudonym. Vaněk survived the war and later gave an account of this meeting:

> I was waiting for them, together with Pecháček, in the flat he had in the Smichov district of Prague. We were sitting there not saying a word, the sound of the bell made us jump. Pecháček went to open the door and he came back with Zelenka-Hajský and a young man we did not know. Only one of the parachutists had come. I must say a few words about Zelenka-Hajský. He was a former headmaster who had escaped from the frontier zone in September 1938, after Munich, when the region where he lived was attached to the Reich. He worked faithfully for our movement and had been assigned to help people who were living outside the law. The stranger was rather short and thicker. He had slightly

protruding cheekbones and thin lips. As he came in he glanced around the room and seemed relieved to find me alone. "I am Ota," he said. "And I am Jindra," I replied. We shook hands, each watching the other. Pecháček brought in tea. I made up my mind to start. "I'd just like to point out this house is guarded and that each of us has something in his pocket." He smiled and without a word took a pistol from his pocket. Then he added, "I'm fond of these gadgets too."

Questions went to and fro for a while, with Kubiš keeping his cards close to his chest but nevertheless confirming he had parachuted in from England. He was asked to name various Czech officers in England, which he did to the satisfaction of the others. This included identifying a picture of Pecháček's son-in-law, who was serving in England. Eventually Kubiš was asked by one of those present, Josef Ogoun, "Do you come from Bohemia?" Kubiš replied in the negative, saying he came from Moravia. Ogoun also came from Moravia and so asked Kubiš what part, to which Kubiš replied that he was from the area of Trebic. As Ogoun later recounted, he said, "I know those parts. Can you tell me what there is extra-ordinary about the railway station at Vladislav?"

Without hesitating, Kubiš answered, "There's a magnificent great bed of roses. I dare say one of the railwaymen is very keen on growing flowers." By this answer, together with the weight of his previous replies and that he spoke of his family still living in the province, Kubiš convinced the Jindra delegation that he was a genuine parachute agent. Jindra agreed they would provide Kubiš with help, although at this stage the mission tasked to Gabčík and Kubiš had not been revealed to the Jindra group.

Now with logistical help from Jindra, the first objective was to move to Prague the equipment they had brought from England, which was still hidden near Nehvizdy. After landing they had hidden their equipment in Antonín Sedláček's shed. Sedláček subsequently made many claims of how he helped the parachutists, but his role was actually very minor. Sedláček discovered the equipment hidden in his shed, some of which had labels written in English. He shared this information with the local policeman, and between them it was agreed this would be logged in the report book as a break-in by poachers. It is probable that Sedláček had picked up their footprints in the snow, but with the exception of Sedláček's own exaggerated testimony there is no evidence that he met either of the parachutists until Kubiš returned in mid-January.

According to a statement from Ludmilla Kroupová, she met Jan Kubiš in the late afternoon of 13 January 1942. She said Kubiš had travelled by train to the station in Mstětice, where he got out around 1630 and started walking towards Nehvizdy. She claimed she had been ahead of Kubiš but he had caught up with her and asked whether she knew who owned the shed behind the village "and whether he is also a good Bohemian?". Kroupová continued:

> I told him that I did not know much about him, but that he was a gardener and I think he is also a good Czech. Then this man told me that he was a parachute agent from England and had landed near Nehvizdy and some things were stored

there in the shed and that he was going to speak to the owner of this hut. He asked me to show him where he lived.

Sedláček later recalled:

> A man came to my apartment and asked to speak to me and asked if I was a good Bohemian, I told him I was. He then told me he was a parachute agent and that they had landed near my shed some days ago. He asked me to go with him to the shed as his equipment was hidden there. I suggested we go there and bring some things back to my apartment which we did and he took them back to Prague leaving at about 2300.

Whilst it would have been against his training, and likely his sanity, to divulge he was a parachute agent, Kubiš may have felt he had no option but to take Sedláček into his confidence, given the nature of the equipment that was stored in the shed. It is less likely Kubiš said such a thing to Ludmilla Kroupová. Her statement was given post-war and there is no way of verifying her comments.

It is believed that four visits were made to Nehvizdy to remove the equipment to Prague. František Kroutil enlisted help from the miller, Břetislav Bauman, who had a van, and Starý completed the removal team. Some equipment was distributed and hidden in safe houses, but other items were buried in the Ďáblice cemetery. This was arranged by Vojtěch Paur, an undertaker in the Libeň district of Prague and brother-in-law of Václav Khodl, an important member of the Jindra network. Paur was able to obtain a false death certificate and paid for the funeral costs. A service was held, attended by several mourners, and then the coffin containing the equipment brought from England was buried. It was not used and so remained hidden until after the war, when the 'corpse' was exhumed.

The two-man Anthropoid team, together with most of their equipment, had now arrived in Prague. In theory the planning for the operation could now start in earnest. A small street in the Žižkov district became the nerve centre for the planning of the operation, as well as providing accommodation for Gabčík and Kubiš and later other parachute agents from England. The Sokol leader, Jan Zelenka, lived in an apartment in Biskupcova, while 100 metres away at 1795/7 Biskupcova lived the Moravec family.

Alois and Marie Moravec had two sons. The eldest son, Miroslav, was at the time in England and serving with the Czech Air Force. Their younger son was christened Vlastimil, but was normally called Ata. Marie had worked on the periphery of the resistance for the Volunteer Sisters of the Czech Red Cross. She was asked to provide accommodation for two visitors, which she readily agreed to. Her home subsequently became the hub for parachutists in Prague, who called her 'Auntie'. Over the coming months, as her task expanded, Marie received help in providing for the parachutists from her former colleagues in the Czech Red Cross.

At some point both Zelenka and the Moravecs learnt that the target for Gabčík and Kubiš was Heydrich, but other members of the resistance organisation were not informed, although many had their suspicions. Through necessity, others were likely told as much as Zelenka, Gabčík or Kubiš dared to tell them; for example, František Šafařík. He had been a former pupil of Zelenka's who since 1933 worked as a carpenter in Prague Castle. After the occupation, Prague Castle had effectively become the Nazi seat of power, and von Neurath and later Heydrich had an office there and often spent their working day there. Šafařík was in a position to obtain useful information about Heydrich and his movements. Post-war, he said that Zelenka visited him several times during the closing months of 1941 and they discussed the situation of Czechoslovakia. He stated Zelenka had told him "Heydrich must be eliminated and that he considered it his patriotic duty." Sometime in January or February 1942, Šafařík was introduced to Gabčík and Kubiš at Čelakovského Park next to the National Museum near Wenceslas Square. At this meeting, Zelenka asked Šafařík to provide information about Heydrich's arrival and departure from the castle. Šafařík agreed, and at a subsequent meeting a few days later he described to them Heydrich's daily itinerary, the layout of the castle, the cars Heydrich travelled in, at what time he arrived and his departure time for home.

To try to complete their cover stories, the Jindra group was also able to arrange suitable papers showing that whilst they were of 'working age', they were both unable to do so because of medical problems. So with the help of a friendly doctor, Stanislav Hrubý, 'sick notes' were written for a Josef Strnad, who was suffering from a duodenal ulcer, and another in the name of František Procházka, who had an inflammation of the gall bladder. Then another member of the organisation, Doctor Lyčka, carried out a review of their fitness each week as required, and signed them off as unfit for work.

Whilst the Anthropoid mission progressed, the other two parachutist groups were also at large. Similar to Anthropoid, these had been dropped in the wrong location. Hockey's navigator recorded that Silver A was dispatched at 0237 east of Čáslav, but in reality they were dropped between Poděbrady and Městec Králové. Silver B was the last to exit the aircraft at 0246, but instead of landing north-west of Ždírec, they landed close to Kasaličky, north-west of Lázně Bohdaneč, near Pardubice. From Hockey's report it is clear that he had been unaware of his location. In his post-operational report, Hockey hints that his orders, at least regarding Silver A and B, were to drop these teams regardless of whether he could find the precise target: "Both the two latter operations were completed under difficult weather conditions owing to their urgent nature and according to instructions received before take-off." The mission of the Silver A group was to re-establish contact between the Military Radio Centre in England and the local home resistance in the Pardubice area in eastern Bohemia. The radio which they had brought with them from Britain was codenamed 'Libuše'. Much of the story of Silver A takes place around Pardubice and the surrounding villages.

Pardubice is a large industrial town on the River Labe (Elbe) 60 miles east of the capital city of Prague. The town's manufacturing factories were taken over by the German occupiers as a centre for production of armaments and oil products, both urgently needed for the Reich war effort. Pardubice was also favourably situated on a vital railway junction from where materials could be easily moved to any part of occupied Europe. Soon after German units moved into Pardubice in March 1939, the *Gestapo* took over the Pardubice *Ředitelství pošt a telegrafů* (post and telegraph offices), a huge labyrinth of a building, with long corridors which ran adjacent behind buildings on the town square. The *Gestapo* officers based here ruled the population of Pardubice and the surrounding area with an iron grip.

Jozef Valčik had been the last man of Silver A out of the Halifax, and he became separated from his colleagues and landed some distance from them. Bartoš and Potůček were able to link up and they made for the nearby village of Podmoky in the hope that Valčik would soon join them. Valčík had the contact details of Adolf Švadlenka at Mikulovice and Miloslav Kostecký in Hošťalovice to the south of Pardubice. He set out for Mikulovice, arriving there on 29 December, and was reunited with Bartoš and Potůček two days later.

Pardubice was the home town of Bartoš. Sending him to a town where he was well known broke one of SOE's fundamental rules – to avoid going to a place where there was a possibility of you being recognised. Bartoš could not resist visiting his mother, who lived very close to several of the safe houses, thus magnifying the danger. Over time it was inevitable that not only rumours started to circulate about the arrival of parachutists from England, but townspeople recognised Bartoš when he was out going about his work. It was only with the very best of good fortune that these rumours did not reach the local *Gestapo*.

Silver A was given help by many local people in the town of Pardubice. At the hub of the resistance group was a former Czechoslovak cavalry officer, Vaclav Krupka, and his wife, the young and glamorous but later controversial Hana Krupková. It cannot be stressed highly enough how important the Krupkas were to operations in Pardubice and the whole of the Protectorate in general. The Silver A resistance group relied greatly on Vaclav Krupka and made extensive use of the family flat at Pernerova ulice 1607, which became a central base for their activities. Bartoš even moved in and lived with the Krupkas for an extended period from February 1942. It was Vaclav Krupka who held the different personalities within the group together and smoothed out the complicated tensions that arose. The Krupka husband and wife team coordinated a courier service for the resistance between Pardubice and Prague, with Hana regularly taking messages to and from the Moravec and Zelenka safe houses in Biskupcova in Prague.

In Pardubice it was arranged for Bartoš to nominally take a job as a salesman with the Sekuritas Insurance Company. Valčik found work as a waiter, using the name Šolc, at the famous Grande Hotel Veselka in central Pardubice, while radio operator Jiří Potůček arranged a cover story to enable him to appear as a worker in the village of Ležáky, where Libuše was hidden.

Potůček first made radio contact with London on 15 January 1942. Other than report their safe arrival, this first broadcast to London warned that their false papers contained errors which even the most one-eyed Czech policeman could not fail to spot.

Whilst London was relieved to be in contact with Silver A, there had been no contact from Anthropoid or Silver B. After messages had passed back and forth between Silver A and London, Bartoš was instructed on 11 February 1942 to find out what had happened to Anthropoid and Silver B.

Talking specifically about Anthropoid, Colonel Moravec later commented: "By my calculations at least ten days must elapse before the men could make proper preparations. Two, then three weeks went by. When four weeks had elapsed and nothing had happened, I began to worry. Had something gone wrong?"

For the Czechs in London, the Anthropoid mission was of extreme political importance, so information on the current position was desperately needed. Moravec wanted to know if the Anthropoid duo were safe or whether they had been captured. If they knew that something had gone wrong, then they could at least consider sending out a replacement team.

Faced with both the delicacy and importance of this situation, Colonel Moravec took the decision to divert Bartoš' team away from their primary mission and ask them to investigate what had happened to Anthropoid. Moravec provided Bartoš with the contact addresses in Plzeň, together with the phrase "Miluska from station seventeen sends greetings to Vysocil". It was hoped the coded reference to the SOE station and the name 'Vysocil', Gabčik's alias, would lead to the underground and the fate of Gabčík and Kubiš.

It is likely that Valčik was sent to Plzeň and followed the Anthropoid trail to Prague ,as it is he who met up with Gabčík and Kubiš in Prague at the end of February 1942. It must have been a pleasing meeting for all three, and for Gabčík and Kubiš a tangible reminder, not that it was needed, of their mission. On 1 March a message was transmitted to London by Silver A that their Anthropoids were alive and well. London was no doubt gratified to learn that the Anthropoid mission was still active, although it is unlikely much more information was transmitted.

The last group to exit the Halifax was the two parachutists of Silver B, Staff Sergeant Jan Zemek and Sergeant Vladimir Škacha. Their drop zone should have been at Ždírce nad Doubravou, near Chotěboř. But like the other groups, they landed far from their intended destination due to navigation problems. As we have said, they were dropped at 0246 near to the village of Kasaličky. The task of Silver B was to deliver the radio code-named Božena to the ÚVOD home resistance group known as Introduction, which was based in the northern Krušné hory mountains.

One of the problems that Gabčík and Kubiš faced was that during his time as Reich Protector, Heydrich's other security responsibilities often took him away from Prague. Heydrich was often required in Berlin, and one example of his absence took place in mid-January 1942 when Heydrich chaired a conference of 15 top-ranking Nazi officials in Berlin. This was the infamous Wannsee Conference to discuss and implement the so-called 'Final Solution to the Jewish Question'. The conference only lasted one day, so it is likely that Heydrich was back in Prague soon afterwards.

As a result of the time Heydrich spent outside of Prague, detailed knowledge of his movements and routine were crucial for any assassination attempt. František Šafařík had been tasked with keeping a record of when Heydrich arrived at Prague Castle, when he departed and whether he had a protection squad with him. Each evening Šafařík dropped a note through the window of the apartment shared by the Kovárniková sisters (Marie Kovárniková and Ludmila Soukupová). There was also a second source of information in the castle, Josef Novotny, who looked after the maintenance of all its clocks. This role gave him access to nearly every room of the castle. He also repaired watches for members of the garrison, which allowed him to snoop or eavesdrop and gather small pieces of additional intelligence that, when added together, helped produce a clearer picture of Heydrich's intended routines. For a few weeks intelligence-gathering continued but no real opportunities appeared for a successful attack on Heydrich. However, it did become clear to Gabčík and Kubiš during this phase that an attempt to kill Heydrich at Prague Castle would not be possible as he was well guarded there. At the beginning of April 1942, Heydrich moved to his 'summer residence', the villa at Panenské Břežany, about nine miles north of Prague. During the German occupation, this village was called Jungfern Breschan.

It was a small, sleepy village of around 500 people. In the early part of the 18th century, a Baroque palace was built in the village and was known as the Lower Castle, although it was never a fortified building. After a redesign along the lines of a French chateau and a series of owners, it was bought in 1909 as a holiday residence by Ferdinand Bloch-Bauer, a Jewish businessman involved in the sugar industry. Hereafter, the residence became more commonly known as the Lower Villa.

Today, Bloch-Bauer is most well known for the two paintings he commissioned of his wife, Adele, by the portrait artist Gustav Klimt. One of these paintings was entitled 'The Woman in Gold', which was the subject of a restitution order returning it to his heirs. In 1939, the widowed Bloch-Bauer fled to Switzerland and the Lower Villa was confiscated by the state and became the summer residence of the Reich Protector of Bohemia and Moravia. A more modest second castle, or more appropriately chateau, was built on the high ground surrounding the village. This became known as the Upper Villa and was home to Karl Hermann Frank and his family.

Heydrich now travelled twice a day to and from his residence, and the nine-mile trip brought new opportunities for Gabčík and Kubiš. The area between Prague and Panenské Břežany was rural, whilst the outskirts of the city from Kobylisy into Hradčany were residential. Gabčík and Kubiš investigated the route and the possibility of attacking his car on the open road between Panenské Břežany and Prague with an item they had brought to the Protectorate with them: the tree spigot. This weapon was developed by Major 'Nobby' Clarke, who had trained Gabčík and Kubiš at Station XVII and adapted the bombs for Anthropoid. The tree spigot was a form of mortar that could be secured to a tree by its screw. It propelled a projectile, which was about 5in in diameter and contained 3lb of high explosive, to a range of about 200 yards. It had a thin metal covering over the explosive which crumpled on impact with the target, thus pushing the explosive charge in close at the point of contact immediately prior to detonation. It could penetrate armoured plate about 2in thick. It was a simple, quiet and easily portable weapon that Major Clarke most likely designed specifically for use by SOE agents. This was an option that Gabčík and Kubiš considered for the assassination attempt.

At one stage Gabčík and Kubiš asked the Jindra organisation for a length of steel cable, which was obtained from a factory worker. They thought they could secure the cable across the road to stop the car. Once the car had been stopped, it would be possible to finish off Heydrich at close quarters. There was a small wood south of the village of Panenské Břežany that was identified as suitable for the plan. However, there were several problems with this scheme. The sound of any explosions or firing would be heard in the village and members of Heydrich's protection team and staff at the villa would be sent to investigate. The road at this point was relatively straight, and if Heydrich was travelling at speed it was possible the car would break the cable. Most of all, Gabčík and Kubiš wanted to give themselves a chance of survival, however small, and this wasn't likely if troops could quickly be alerted and flood the surrounding countryside. As Ladislav Vaněk of the Jindra resistance group later commented: "The countryside around Panenské Břežany offered not the least possibility of hiding or getting away. For those who carried it out [Operation Anthropoid], an attempt in this place would certainly have meant suicide."

Gabčík and Kubiš therefore discounted the cable idea, then in April 1942 they received new instructions that sent them into despair with London and put a temporary halt to their planning of Operation Anthropoid.

5

Operation Canonbury

No doubt it was a cause of great embarrassment to the Czech government-in-exile that the Skoda arms factories in the Plzeň area continued to fuel the German armaments requirements. President Beneš was also mindful of reprisals should the factories be destroyed by a bomb planted by the Home Defence Army. A better option of trying to stop the manufacture of arms would be to ask the RAF to bomb the area. However, this was a long-range target, and in 1941 and 1942 the RAF simply did not have the precision bombing aids to pinpoint a target from a height of around 10,000ft. Furthermore, Plzeň was on the outer fuel extremities and capabilities of a fully loaded bomber force, being located approximately 700 miles from London.

One of the first references to Plzeň as a potential bombing target can be found in a memo dated 15 October 1941, from MX, an SOE officer, to D/AIR at the Air Ministry, which stated:

> Further to our conversation about the bombardment of Plzeň, I now attach at 1A a plan of the town of Plzeň indicating possible bombing targets. 1B a sketch map showing AA defences. 1C a draft brief for the pilots concerned.
>
> I would be grateful if you would press most urgently that this operation should be carried out on the 28th of this month which is, as you know the Czech National Day.
>
> I am also suggesting that the Czechs should take this matter up direct with the Air Ministry, through President Beneš office.
>
> If there are any further points you would like to raise, I will pass them on to the Czechs but, for the moment, our wireless communication is interrupted.

It seems that not much happened as a result of this request and the Skoda factories remained unmolested. Then in April 1942 the matter of arms production raised its head again, with momentum coming from the Czechs in London, as borne out by the following document dated 9 April, outlining the 'Case for Bombing a Target within the Protectorate':

> The underground organisation in Czechoslovakia has made the very strongest representations for the bombing of Skoda Works before the end of this month. The reasons given are as follows:

(1) That a highly organised sabotage group is standing by within the works themselves, and that this group is fully prepared and equipped to destroy the key objectives under cover of a bombing attack.

(2) That the bombing of the Skoda Works has been agreed as the signal for the commencement of the systematic attack on German lines of communication to the Russian Front, which they have been requested to carry out by the Chiefs of Staff. They state that, although the organisation remains intact, the whole network of internal communications has not been fully re-established, and that by no other means could simultaneously offensive action be ensured. For this offensive action it is necessary to convince the people that they are receiving sufficient support from this country to justify the universal reprisals which would result in the fulfilment of their instructions.

(3) That it is imperative to make at least one attack on a military objective within the frontiers of the Protectorate in order to maintain morale in face of constant German propaganda to the effect that the RAF is physically unable to bomb the Protectorate. Up to the present the leaders of the Secret Army have been unable to cite one concrete instance to disapprove this claim.

(4) That the effect of such an attack would be to ensure the immediate consolidation of the Secret Army and to double its strength, as nearly 50% of the ex-service men of which the Army is composed are unwilling to commit themselves to the sacrifice involved without any evidence whatsoever of concrete action by the Allies in response to their most regular and most urgent requests.

The Czech secret organisation is prepared to undertake any necessary action involving the lighting of fires, flares etc. in order to indicate the target to Allied aircraft.

This was acknowledged by an internal SOE memo dated 13 April 1942 in the National Archives file on Operation Canonbury (HS4/35), two RAF raids on the Skoda Works at Plzeň in late April and early May 1942, again from MX to D/AIR, which contained the following: "I understand from M that SO is very taken with this idea and is pressing the Secretary of State for Air. In the meantime MYO is getting full details from the Czechs about the lights, etc. they are prepared to provide."

Shortly before this note, another memo from the same file entered the system, dated 10 April 1942. It read as follows:

From M
To AD/P

The Czechs are raising the subject of bombing the Skoda Works as a question of confidence. They are most anxious that some attempt should be made before the nights get too short and would be content with a sortie of three to four planes merely for the moral effect.

MX spoke to D/AIR who feels the Target Committee might view this question more sympathetically if it had your approval.

I attach a case which is convincing in itself though I am well aware of the difficulties of these long distance flights.

A list of the items believed to be manufactured by Skoda for the Nazi war machine was as follows:

Number of employees: 35,000 at Plzeň only

Manufacturing at present for the German Army:

1. AA shells.
2. Twin automatic guns, 32mm, rpgpm [rounds per gun per minute] 75.
3. Cantilever springs, castings and forgings for guns and tracked vehicles.
4. Howitzers 24cm.
5. 120 heavy locomotives being manufactured.
6. Anti-tank guns 4.7cm.
7. Anti-aircraft guns 8.8cm and the German type 3.7 Flak 36.
8. Special undercarriages for bomber aircraft.
9. Component parts for submarines and destroyers.
10. Artillery ammunition of various calibres.
11. 800 3-ton tractors,
12. Accumulator batteries.
13. Moulding machines for the manufacture of war materials of all kinds.
14. Infantry guns 7.5cm (100 delivered by March 1st 1941).
15. Metal cases of heavy aircraft bombs.

Plzeň, a town of 130,000 inhabitants of which no less than 35,000 are employed in the Skoda Armaments Works, was during the late war, the arsenal of the Austro-Hungarian Empire and remains the principal supplier of general arms to the Germans today.

Among other German weapons, the following come almost exclusively from the Skoda Works at Plzeň:-

10 inch Howitzers

47mm Anti-Tank guns

88 and 37mm Anti-Aircraft guns

75mm Infantry guns

Heavy tanks of the special Czech design

During the last six months, the workers of the Skoda factory have, by means of passive resistance, succeeded in reducing their output so that it is less than 30% of German expectations. Nevertheless times are very hard in Czechoslovakia. The Gestapo have received special orders to suppress the Czech organisations responsible for this passive resistance, and, in the face of so much opposition, the Czechs feel for the moment that they are fighting their underground war alone against almost insuperable odds. The successful bombing of Skoda will serve as a serious setback to German armament production; secondly it will provide an excuse for various minor acts of sabotage which can be safely carried out under its cover and, finally, it will be an encouragement to the Czechs to know that, in this underground fight, they are not alone and that the ever-increasing strength of the RAF means that those at home will have air support for their secret armies just as their army in Britain will be able to count on RAF co-operation when the time comes for the Allies to take the offensive on land.

There is a further memo dated 13 April 1942:

From MX
To D/AIR

We spoke about the possibilities of bombing Skoda Works.

I understand from M that SO is very taken with this idea and is pressing the Secretary of State for Air. I attach a 'case' so that you are briefed for the Targets Committee.

In the meantime MYO is getting full details from the Czechs about the lights etc. they are prepared to provide.

The next document is dated 15 April 1942, entitled 'Bombing of Skoda Works':

The Czech Underground organisation reports that every effort is being made to provide sabotage co-operation for this raid on an unprecedented scale. The following information must be provided 5–7 days before the raid takes place:-
  (1) Pin-point at what time fire should be lighted. This fire should be north or west of Plzeň. If a series of fires laid out according to a pre-arranged plan are required, details must be supplied by the Air Ministry.
      Distribution: Silver A and Anthropoid.
  (2)ETA of aircraft over target.
      Distribution: Silver A and Head of Factory Organisation.
  (3) First scheduled date 22nd April 1942.
      Distribution: Silver A, Anthropoid and Head of Factory Organisation.

Confirmation that the operation will take place must be received by 12.00 hours on the first available day. This will be communicated to Anthropoid by Iodoform. Czech HQ particularly requests that every effort should be made to carry out the operation as near to the first scheduled date as possible.

The Chief of the Czech organisation suggests that consideration should be given to the possibility of the operation being carried out by a squadron led by the SOE Halifax fitted with Rebecca RDF apparatus. The ground beacon can be erected to enable this aircraft to home on a pre-arranged point within 5–10 miles of the target.

This was an interesting development, with the suggestion that a Rebecca homing beacon be used as a location aid, together with the help from the 'Factory Organisation'. It also suggests that the bombers would have to fly in formation to Plzeň, with all the added dangers that entailed from *Luftwaffe* interception. To give the homing beacon its correct name, it was the Rebecca-Eureka System, which was a VHF (Secondary) Radar Interrogator-Beacon. The Rebecca was carried in the aircraft and would pair with the Eureka on the ground. It had been devised in 1941 to assist with drop of supplies to the Allied armies and resistance groups in occupied Europe. Much of the credit for the development of the system went to Doctor R. Hanbury-Brown and J. Pringle of the Telecommunications Research Establishment. After it had been demonstrated to the Army, SOE also became interested in its potential uses for aiding the accurate dropping of supplies and agents.

With the exception of the small-scale sabotage efforts by factory workers, interference with the production at the Skoda Works had been fairly ineffective up to this point.

The document 'Bombing of Skoda Works', dated 15 April, that tacitly gave authorisation to the RAF mission had been preceded earlier that morning with the arrival of a paper from Colonel Moravec that had finished up on the desk of M at the SOE HQ, with a covering note from MX: "Herewith a paper on bombing military objectives in the Protectorate which Colonel Moravec has today prepared for you." A handwritten comment added to the original states: "We will add them to the list."

The report by Colonel Moravec summarised radio transmissions from the Home Army requesting a heavy bombing raid, and outlined targets and what effect aerial bombing might have internally in Czechoslovakia:

> The Problem of Air Bombing of Various Objectives throughout the Protectorate, as described in reports arriving from Czechoslovakia.
>
> 1st October 1941:
> General Opinion: We can be helped in our situation here only by heavy air bombing of local military objectives. Otherwise the sabotage and undermining activity will be extremely difficult.
>
> 4th October 1941:
> Do not enumerate objectives bombed by our airmen but bomb military and production objectives in our Country and most importantly in the Sudeten Territory. People are already waiting impatiently.
>
> 5th February 1942:
> The air bombing of Semtin would be most advantageous in nights from Sunday to Monday when the number of the personnel is the least one. There is a possibility of staking out the aims.
>
> [Semtin is a suburb of Pardubice. It later gave its name to the plastic explosive Semtex).

28th February 1942:

Any display of your strength and power is most impatiently waited for and, in my opinion, already in the utmost necessary.

11th March 1942:

All appeals to sabotage superfluous cannot be undertaken en masse. Especially not on the part of the workmen. What is uniquely necessary: to bomb from the air. Everyone resents very much that this is not being done. The Skoda Works are only weakly protected. Best time for any undertakings would be from Saturday to Sunday.

20th March 1942:

The best would be to subject to strong air bombing the factory plants where ammunition is filled as e.g. at Polička, Nýřany, where there are immense stocks in existence. Furthermore, at Adamov, production of ammunition and no filling, and in the Sudeten. It is being recommended to subject to slighter bombing actions, in order to provoke a nervosity, the Skoda Works and the armament works at Brno. The last shift is the weakest one. The anti-aircraft defence has been everywhere weakened due to its being everywhere not in use. At a distance of 2 km to the south east of the Skoda Works are camouflaged 'imitation' buildings of the factory.

26th March 1942:

You stress in your wireless transmissions the necessity of accelerating the fall of Germany by sabotage activity. The Germans, of course, are fully aware of this danger and have taken all possible measures accordingly. Everybody awaits help from the air only, i.e. from air bombardment which will mean a general signal and a unique opportunity to show sentiments and to destroy spontaneously everything the annihilation of which, under normal conditions, would be possible only under death penalty. All procrastination expresses itself in outbursts of wrath, criticism and hopelessness. Don't delay. We wait for you.

28th March 1942:

The Germans are greatly worried by the possibility of air bombings of the Protectorate, crammed with various and most important branches of war industries. There is nearly no Flak anywhere. The annihilation of Ervěnice would mean so much and the population so nearly furious why you hesitate so much.

1st April 1942:

Any subversive activity, after the events of last autumn and under steadily more rigorous police system, is becoming more and more difficult. Workers who do not surrender their allotted portion in due time are removed and sent to Germany. Consequently, the sabotage activity by slowing down is becoming more and more ineffective. You can help any sabotage only by means of efficient bombing from the air.

15th April 1942:
The uninterrupted working of all the armaments works throughout the Protectorate which had not been, so far, stopped in the least by a single air raid provokes amongst the population vexation.

The final authorisation for a bombing raid on the Skoda Works came in a memo dated 18 April 1942: "The Minister for Air has agreed that aircraft should stand by for this operation from 23rd April 1942. I attach copy of the Iodoform as required by Czech Headquarters."

Major Strankmüller, Moravec's deputy, kept departmental notes relating to the exchange of communications with the Home Army, which confirmed that the parachutists and resistance were kept up to date with the latest position on the proposed bomber raid:

Night 20th–21st April 1942
Czech HQ W/T to Home Organisation; HQ will obtain home proposals as to lighting of fires, with exact positions. HQ will send the operational programme, stating that Rebecca is only from 26th April 1942. Also HQ will give SOE's exact directives as to fires in answer to the home proposals. HQ will also state how they will inform home that the operation will or will not be carried out on the agreed day.

Night 21st–22nd April 1942
Czech HQ W/T to home. HQ obtains final and definite reply of Home Organisation. HQ will also state the method of indicating that operation will take place the same evening. This communication will take place at 01.00 hours. At the same time, HQ will inform home of probability of operation.

Night 22nd–23rd April 1942
Further reply from home to Czech HQ; full agreement executed. Final confirmation of indicated first date of operation.

London had decided that a bombing operation undertaken by the RAF on the Skoda Works would necessitate the use of the parachutist-agents on the ground to set fires and mark the target, leading the raid on the final run-in to the site. This had already been alluded to in the various memorandums that had been issued during April. The parachutists were assigned from Operations Anthropoid, Silver A and Out Distance. The thinking behind this must have been that by using trained and trusted soldiers, it increased the likelihood of a successful bombing raid. This alone is evidence that the Skoda Works was now an important target. Why London detailed Gabčík and Kubiš to this operation, which brought significant dangers and thereby threatened their own mission, is much more difficult to understand.

Operation Out Distance had parachuted into Czechoslovakia on the night of 27/28 March 1942, from a Halifax aircraft flown by a Polish crew under the command of Flight Lieutenant Mariusz Wódzicki. Out Distance was made up of Lieutenant Adolf Opálka, Sergeant Karel Čurda and Corporal Ivan Kolařík. As this parachutist group took a Rebecca location beacon with them, it can be assumed that future bombing raids on Czechoslovakia had already been discussed in London. This most likely was a contributing factor when the Home Army requested bombing of strategic targets in the Protectorate. However, the Rebecca dropped with Out Distance had been hidden upon landing but subsequently discovered by the Germans. This was why the lighting of the guiding beacons became so important.

Bartoš of Silver A, having been informed in advance that more parachutists were being sent to the Protectorate, made arrangements for them to contact him by using coded newspaper advertisements. On the same Halifax as Out Distance were the three members of Operation Zinc: Lieutenant Oldřich Pechal, Sergeant Arnošt Mikš and Corporal Vilém Gerik. This group had been tasked with setting up a resistance network in Moravia and sending intelligence back to London.

Both Out Distance and Zinc suffered misfortunes. Zinc had, unbeknown to them, been dropped across the border in Slovakia near the town of Gbely. They landed safely in a wooded area and were able to collect their equipment together. What they didn't immediately need they hid in a barn and covered with straw. In one account, they are reported as having written on the side of one of the packing cases: "I beg the good person who finds this not to report it to the authorities but to keep it to himself or better to destroy it." They set out by foot to find their way to their correct location. Pechal was carrying a briefcase containing many thousands of Reichsmarks and Kroner, while Gerik carried his portable radio transmitter and Mikš had a briefcase crammed with food and other essential supplies. After about two miles they could see a village ahead. They walked on until they came to a signpost which read Gbely. From this distance in time it is hard to imagine the full extent of their horror as they realised they had not only been dropped many miles away from the intended drop zone (DZ), but would have to make a border crossing. Worse still, since the formation of the puppet state of Slovakia, strict border security existed between Slovakia and the Protectorate of Bohemia and Moravia. This was an unwanted risk, but Zinc had little choice but to break through the frontier.

They agreed amongst themselves that their best option was to cross over as soon as possible under cover of darkness. After walking through Gbely, disaster struck when they ran into a patrol of Slovakian border police. Pechal ordered his men to make a break for it, and they fled into a field next to the road. It appears they were only half-heartedly pursued by this patrol, and with the noise of the chase slowly dying away they were soon alone in a forest. They examined their maps and discussed their options. Gerik said he had an aunt who lived in a nearby town close to the border, and she might be able to offer them temporary shelter. His suggestion was agreed upon, and next morning they moved closer to the border. Gerik went on alone, but soon returned with the unwanted news that his aunt had moved to Bratislava. Once again they considered their ever-reducing options on how to attempt the border crossing. They felt their next best hope was a contact address they had been given in the Moravian border town of Buchlovice. Pechal decided that it would be safest if they travelled independently as the Slovakians would probably be looking for a group of three men. They would meet up again at the address given in Buchlovice.

Pechal waited a few hours to give the others a head start. Mikš and Gerik were able to cross the border without any difficulties, eventually found a railway station and caught a train to Buchlovice. Here they found the correct address, but the door was answered by a lady who she said she did not know when the man of the house would return as he had been arrested some time previously and sent to a camp. Either emboldened by this information of the man's incarceration or in desperation, Mikš and Gerik revealed they had parachuted in from England and needed help. The conversation did not go well; the woman was frightened at the thought of the danger they were bringing to her, and asked them to leave immediately. It was now that her daughter interceded and told her mother they must offer help and allow the men to stay. They were taken to an attic room which had an electric light, so Gerik decided to try to contact London but only succeeded in blowing the fuses in the house. This was the final straw for the mother, who insisted that they leave at once. The daughter gave them the name of a patriot who lived a few streets away, whom she believed would give them help. Mikš and Gerik had no option but to contact this man. Their first meeting started with Mikš and Gerik asking some guarded questions to ascertain if he was a 'good patriot'. He satisfied them enough to again reveal they were parachute agents from England. The man's demeanour changed suddenly; whilst he agreed to temporarily look after their radio set, he was not prepared to let them stay in his house. Mikš and Gerik, expecting Pechal would follow the same sequence to this address, explained that another parachutist may turn up. Saying they would check in daily, they reluctantly headed to some local woods, where they spent the next three nights in utter frustration. On the morning of the fourth day, Mikš and Gerik decided that sitting around in the woods was achieving nothing. Pechal should have turned up by now. They knew his parents lived in Vřesovice, some 30 miles to the south. This had been close to their intended DZ, and they reasoned that Pechal might turn up there. They also had their original contact addresses, so it seemed a natural progression for them to head to Vřesovice. They made the journey without incident and were able to make contact with Pechal's brother. He advised them that Oldřich had been to Vřesovice, but that he was wanted by the police for murder and his face was on 'wanted' posters all over town. However, Pechal's brother knew where he was hiding and would take them to him.

When they had split up, Pechal had waited as agreed before setting off to cross the border. He walked with caution, keeping to the forest tracks through the dark night. Suddenly he was caught in a torch beam, which was accompanied by the command, "'Halt!" This was followed by the noise of a rifle bolt being worked, and Pechal faced a pair of armed guards – Reinhard Schewe and Hanse Walter – on a border patrol. He was asked to produce his identity card, which he duly did, explaining that he had just left the village of Petrova Ves and was taking a short-cut home. But this excuse did not satisfy the guards, one of whom took Pechal's identity card and placed it in his pocket. They told Pechal to accompany them to the local police station, where his story could be verified. As they walked along, Pechal knew that once properly searched, his pistol would be found, and his briefcase carried more money than most Slovaks earned in a year. It is reported he first offered the guards some money to turn a blind eye and let him go, but this seems unlikely as he would have known they were probably sympathetic to the puppet regime and it would have warned them that he was hiding something. It is more likely he resolved to deal with them both and make a break for it.

He swung his briefcase against the rifle barrel of the guard to his left, which caused the guard to drop his weapon. Pechal dropped the briefcase, quickly drew his pistol and shot both guards. The first guard fell to the ground, whilst the other was hit but still able to return fire. His shot missed Pechal, who shot him again, this time fatally. Pechal looked for his briefcase but was unable to find it. He realised he would have to leave it as the noise of gunfire would soon bring men flooding into the area. He decided that the path he had been travelling on was probably only guarded by the one patrol, so it was his best option to continue along it and put distance between himself and the dead guards. This was a good assumption, and he ran for about 30 minutes without being challenged. It was only when he paused for deep breaths that he realised his identity card was still in the pocket of one of the guards.

Meanwhile, the bodies had been found, as had the briefcase. The large amount of currency aroused suspicion that this was not a normal border run, so the police informed the *Gestapo*. An identity card in the name of Oldřich Pešar from Otrokovice had been found on one of the dead guards, which included a photograph of this person. Oldřich Pešar was now a suspect. It was Pechal's bad luck that one of the policemen who saw the identity card in the name of Pešar recognised him as Oldřich Pechal, with whom he had served in the army a few years previously. The *Gestapo now investigated* Oldřich Pechal – his false identity papers had kept his real date of birth, while the similarity in the cover and real name convinced them that they had identified the murderer.

Pechal was able to cross the border the following evening and made for his family home at Vřesovice, where he was reunited with Mikš and Gerik. Pechal knew he was now a danger to the others. He felt safest hiding out in the woods alone, and realised he had little option but to disband Zinc. Mikš and Gerik, however, could continue and make contact with the underground movement via the safe house addresses they had been given in London. They both travelled onto Brno by train and then parted. Mikš wanted to travel north to find his fiancée, whom he knew he could trust, whilst Gerik continued alone to Prague, where he had an address in Wenceslas Square which would put him in contact with the underground movement. It was agreed that Gerik would leave word where he could be contacted with his brother, Antonin, in Prague. It was on these terms that the men parted.

In the same transport aircraft as Zinc had been the Out Distance group, consisting of Lieutenant Adolf Opálka, Sergeant Karel Čurda and Corporal Ivan Kolařík. They had been dropped near Ořechov, to the west of Telč. Their first task was to join up with the Silver A group. The noise of the low-flying aircraft was heard by the village fire patrol, and it is possible this same patrol also saw the three parachutes descend. Either way, the fire patrol alerted the police, who quickly deployed to the area. The parachutists buried their parachutes and what equipment they could find as quickly as they could. However, they left much of their kit unfound, so they must have been aware that their descent had been detected. Opálka decided they should split up, lie low for a few days and then make their way to the safe house they had been given. Opálka probably knew that all three of them had their homes within a radius of about 30 miles, so shelter was relatively close at hand. Opálka made his way to his aunt's home at Rešice, Čurda to his mother's at Trebon. They would both later make their way to Prague via contacts at Pardubice connected to Silver A.

For Kolařík, the landing had not gone well. Somehow he had lost his false identity card in the name of Jan Krátký with his photo. The police who had arrived from Urbanov, about a mile from the DZ at Ořechov, recovered five parachutes, two radio sets and a wallet containing 150 Reichsmarks, the fake identity card plus a photograph signed and dated by Milada Hrušáková, who had been Kolařík's girlfriend.

Kolařík first went to his parents in Valašské Meziříčí. He also visited the home of the Hrušákovás but was told Milada was now engaged to someone else. He decided to move on and seek shelter with his brother in Zlin.

The photo of Milada had also been annotated with the initials 'VM' alongside the date. This led the police to first visit Velké Meziříčí, but no Milada Hrušáková lived there and they moved on to Valašské Meziříčí, where they did find the Hrušá family home. Milada had little option but to identify the photo as a previous boyfriend, Ivan Kolařík, who had disappeared in 1939.

It was not long before the police arrived at his brother's home in Zlin. Whilst they did not find Kolařík, he was aware the net was fast closing around him, so at around noon on 1 April, he swallowed the L pill that he had been issued with in London. He hoped that by committing suicide he might spare the rest of his family, but this proved a false hope as over the coming days, 17 people associated with him were arrested and executed. These included his mother, father and brother, as well as several members of the Hrušáková family.

The position at the beginning of April was that 10 parachute agents from Britain were operating in Czechoslovakia. As regards subterfuge, it had totally failed and the Germans were fully aware of unknown aircraft entering Czech airspace. Furthermore, they had captured parachutists and equipment that could only have come from Britain.

Misfortune also occurred with one of the members of Silver A, Josef Valčik, who had been working as a waiter at the Grande Hotel Veselka in Pardubice. The Veselka bar was regularly used by German officers, and in his daily work Valčik made sure he overheard the many interesting conversations that took place, so he was able to provide additional intelligence to the resistance. His employer and the owner of the hotel was a man called Arnošt Košťál, who was also a member of the Pardubice resistance. Košťál was a very astute operator and had even arranged to divorce his wife, so that in the event of his arrest for resistance activities, she would not be incriminated. The plan worked and although Arnošt was amongst those later arrested, his wife was not and she survived. Košťál would be one of the last executed as darkness fell at the Zámeček in Pardubice on 2 July 1942. The Hotel Veselka stood until 1972, when it was demolished to widen a road junction, an unpopular decision carried out against the wishes of many Pardubice people.

Events in Prague on 21 March were to cause complications for Josef Valčik in Pardubice. Captain Václav Morávek, the last member of the Three Kings (*Tři Kralové*) resistance group in Prague who was still at liberty, fell in a gun fight at the Powder Bridge near Prague Castle. Captain Morávek could best be described as a tough, no-nonsense pistol shooting champion of the Czechoslovak Army, his motto being "I believe in God and in my pistols". He died while attempting to rescue his colleague, Václav Řehák, who had been arrested by the *Gestapo* at a rendezvous in a nearby park. At the time of his arrest, Řehák carried a large amount of money intended for the German double agent A-54 (Paul Thummel), which had originated from England courtesy of Silver A funds.

During an extended gun battle, Morávek fired off 50 rounds using a 9mm pistol in each hand, before being wounded and ending his own life. Unfortunately for Josef Valčik, Morávek also carried new photographs of Valčik which were to have been used for new false identification documents. Despite Morávek trying to destroy the photographic evidence, the shredded images were found by the *Gestapo*. The name of the well-known photographic studio *Vomáčka* of Pardubice on the photos gave away a huge clue. The *Gestapo* now knew the face of one of their major adversaries and where to look for him. The Germans went looking for him in Pardubice, and the Hotel Veselka was soon connected to Valčik; but when the *Gestapo* arrived Valčik had already gone. Arnošt Košťál provided an unlikely cover story that the waiter, whom he called Šolc, had broken one plate too many and been dismissed. Valčik had left Pardubice with the help of his girlfriend, Ludmila Malá. She was later betrayed, likely by Karel Čurda of Out Distance, and when the *Gestapo* came to arrest her on 20 June, she took a poison capsule rather than take the risk of being totured to give the Germans information.

Valčik's face appeared on 'wanted' posters, which were circulated around the Protectorate by the *Gestapo*. He was forced to go on the run, following a route that took him to Dašice, Mnětice, Trnová and then to his parents' home at Valašské Klobouky and his sister's house in Střelna. He was in Brno for a short time, visiting his brother Emil. All this time a safe refuge was being sought for Valčik in Prague, and when the time was considered right, about the middle of April, he was moved to a safe house in the Hanspaulka district of Prague. Eventually he would stay with the Moravecs in Žižkov. He was also selected to be a part of Operation Canonbury in late April 1942.

The majority of the 10 parachute agents were now concentrated in Prague, and London was keen to utilise them operationally. Bartoš received a message via the Libuše receiver/transmitter that the RAF intended to bomb the Skoda Works at Plzeň, which would require support from the ground to ensure the target was clearly marked for the bomber aircraft. It is possible the bombing of targets such as the Skoda munitions factory had previously been considered at the highest level, as the

Out Distance group had bought a Rebecca short-range navigational system whose transmission could be locked into by a Eureka receiver onboard the aircraft.

The RAF had already decided not to just rely on the Rebecca transmitter. They wanted agents in the Protectorate to start fires to help lead the aircraft to the target. The overall commander of the operation on the ground was Lieutenant Alfréd Bartoš from the Silver A group, who first had to send a team on a reconnaissance to the Plzeň area to locate suitable barns and hayricks to the north and west of the target as requested by London. Bartoš chose to send Gabčík and Kubiš, together with Josef Valčik of Silver A and Karel Čurda of Out Distance. Gabčík and Kubiš thought their inclusion absurd, an unnecessary risk that could compromise their main objective. Gabčík, particularly, made his objections known.

The following operational orders were sent out for the bombing raid:

Operation Canonbury 21st April 1942

(1) Action to be taken on the ground.
    (a) A fire will be lighted west of the target and will be burning properly at 01.15 hours so as to be visible to the first fire-raising aircraft whose ETA is 01.30 hours or alternatively:
    If instructions are received to this effect on the day previous to the operation, Rebecca will be placed at a pin-point west of the target and will be switched on at 00.45 hours, so that the first aircraft can home on it to arrive at 01.30 hours.
    (b) As soon as the fire-raising aircraft drops its incendiaries the dummy factory to the west of the target will be set on fire.
    Decisions required.
    (a) Pin-point for fire.
    (b) Pin-point for Rebecca set if used.
    (c) Estimated range at which fire will be visible.

(2) Action to be taken by Bomber Command.
    (a) 6–8 aircraft will take part in the operation and will each carry 4,000 lbs bombs.
    (b) The target date for the operation is 23rd April 1942.
    Bomber Command will confirm operation:
    (i) Possible – by 00.05 hours on day of operation. This information will be passed to Porchester Gate by 00.50 hours, using words: 'Canonbury Possibly On' or 'Canonbury Off.'
    (ii) Scheduled and almost certain – by 12.30 hours. This decision will be broadcast under arrangements made by SOE at 14.30 hours.
    (iii) On – by 16.30. This decision will be passed to Porchester Gate by 17.15 hours and will be broadcast at 18.45 hours, under arrangements made by Czech Headquarters.

Urgent Telegram 24th April 1942
To Controller Bomber Command
From AI 10

In addition to fire to be lighted at Skvrnany a second fire will be lighted 1 kilometre south of target at point 200 metres north of the Goldschneidrovka.
　Visibility of both fires good as barns will be set on fire.
　The dummy factory 4.6 kms east of factory will repeat not be set on fire.
　Meteorological report at 1700 hrs received 1000 hrs following day. Will be telephoned to you if required.

So whilst the operational instructions were being passed from London, it must be assumed that a discussion was going on in the Protectorate about exactly who should light the fires on the ground. As stated, Gabčík and Kubiš were not exactly happy with being told they had to take part in Operation Canonbury and they made their feelings known. It is likely that Bartoš was aware of their original mission, and following Gabčík's protestations he made a decision that it was too risky to involve both of them at Plzeň, so Gabčík could be withdrawn. On 24 April, Ata Moravec escorted, on behalf of Bartoš, Čurda from Pardubice to Plzeň, where Valčík, Kubiš and Opálka were already present. Then Ata returned to Prague, taking Gabčík with him. During the preparations for Canonbury, the men stayed at a number of locations in Plzeň; including with the Králs family in Pod Záhorsem, the Bejbis family in Čechova, the Kučera family in Resslova and the Hrdličková family in Klatovská.

As darkness fell on the evening of 25 April, the agents made their way towards their targets, hiding up until the scheduled time. After midnight, both teams set fire to their barns and made good their escape. Valčík and Kubiš stopped on a small hill and looked back to see flames shooting through the roof of their barn. Opálka and Čurda also successfully set their barn on fire. The agents on the ground had done their job, and it was now up to the RAF to do theirs. The agents made it back to Prague safely, and the following day the local radio broadcast a report saying that a small number of enemy aircraft had penetrated Protectorate airspace and attempted to bomb Plzeň, but all the bombs had fallen in open country and no damage had been caused. At first the parachutists expected this was German propaganda, but it soon became clear that the report was accurate. It was a bitter blow to accept, and back in London it was decided to repeat the exercise within a few days. But Operation Canonbury II would not involve agents on the ground,

From this distance in time, given the supposed importance of targeting the Skoda Works and the amount of correspondence that had been generated in London about attacking it, it is mystifying to find that in the first raid the RAF only allocated six bombers for themission.

Soon after the first raid, Colonel Moravec sent a report on its results to the SOE's Brigadier Gubbins. Dated 30 April, this reads:

The results of the air-raid operation negative. The Skoda Works did not suffer the least damage.

The indicative signs agreed upon, farms set on fire in the vicinity of the Skoda Works were put into effect in due time and exactly according to instructions. The German Police arrested a couple of people suspected to have set these objectives on fire.

There prevails a great disillusionment among the workers of the Skoda Works as there were held many actions of sabotage in preparation in case that the factory or some of its plants would have been hit.

Our Home Organisation requests that the operation be repeated. They point out to be in a position to co-operate even if other objectives would form the target to the operations, so e.g. Semtin near Pardubice, Fantovy závody [The Fanta Works] and chiefly in the case of bombing of important railway junctions.

The public opinion at home has been unfavourably impressed by the fact that [in] broadcasts from London, the Czechoslovakian amongst others gave an account of the action not corresponding to the truth.

In spite of these seemingly adverse results, a report was sent to the Czech government-in-exile by Brigadier Gubbins, dated 7 May 1942. According to an accompanying note, the reports were based on information received from the Protectorate:

Experience gained during the Bombardment Operation on the Skoda Works undertaken on 25th April 1942.

1. The announcing of the action. Next time it will be best to announce it during the 13.30 hrs broadcast and to confirm the start at 22.45 hrs. Afternoon broadcasting from London is often very bad and there might easily arise a misunderstanding.
2. The setting of fires. The fires of orientation were set exactly at spots formerly indicated and the same were visible at a distance of some 30 km from the air. Setting of fires of orientation may be repeated and within various zones due to German reprisals.
3. Action. Three or five planes came over the target and dropped some eight bombs of heavy calibre. Five bombs fell on the close by marshalling yards, the remaining ones we can only hazard at. There was caused a certain amount of damage. One of the planes, flying low, fired his guns at German crews manning the anti-aircraft defences. There is circulating an unconfirmed rumour that legal proceedings have been taken against the Military Commander of the City of Plzeň for neglecting the defence of the plant.
4. Conclusion. According to our opinion the action could have succeeded despite the unfavourable weather conditions. It is of course necessary that the leading aircraft be manned by a crew experienced in long distance navigation. The planes are reported to have actually flown over the target. The bombs, however, were dropped without hitting the target. Groups of

workers at the Skoda Factory are prepared to act against the most important machinery as soon as a favourable moment presents itself. Their despair, may be, therefore, easily understood when they saw they had been deprived of an opportunity to put into action the carefully prepared acts of sabotage due to the failure of this operation.

Additional comments from Gubbins made the following points:

There was some difficulty over the reception of Iodoform as atmospheric conditions were very bad. However the confirmatory broadcast was well received and acted upon. In future we shall use another time for the first broadcast.

We understand that, if the occasion should arise, our agents are prepared to repeat these fires.

The Czechs are quite pleased with even the limited success of this operation and we hope that the second attempt which took place on 4th May 1942 will have been more successful as two of the aircraft taking part reported direct hits. We have as yet no news of this from the Protectorate.

AA Defence of Plzeň.
This has been reinforced by a certain number of AA batteries and by three armoured trains mounting AA guns which have arrived from Essen.

A new commander also is reported to have arrived to take charge of AA defences.

An unconfirmed report maintains that, during Canonbury II, the Germans themselves set on fire the camouflaged dummy 5 miles to the west of the real Skoda Works in order to divert the attention of the pilots.

Persons arrested during Canonbury I, on suspicion of co-operation with the British, have now been released as the Germans consider the fires they lit might have been caused by incendiaries dropped from British aircraft.

Following receipt of the Moravec letter, dated 30 April 1942, a reply was eventually sent, dated 8 May 1942, written from Room 98, Horse Guards, which was Gubbins' office. The date is significant because it followed the second bomber raid against the Skoda Works, on 4/5 May, codenamed Canonbury II. Gubbins' reply reads:

Thank you very much for your note on the first attempt at Canonbury. I am sorry this was not more successful, but the results seem to have been better than we hoped at first, especially considering that there was 10/10ths cloud over the target area.

I look forward to hearing the results of the second attempt at Canonbury as the pilots who took part are more confident that this was successful.

I am forwarding extracts of your report to Bomber Command as they were most helpful in co-operating with us in this matter.

There is one other thing. As you will no doubt have noticed the reports of the second attempt at Canonbury which appeared in the newspapers and over the BBC were much more restrained. I hope that this matter is now under control and that there will be no further difficulties.

It originally appeared that the confidence of the pilots participating in the second raid as reported by Gubbins was not entirely misplaced in the official report, although they could not distinguish between the damage caused by the RAF and that caused by internal sabotage.

The archives also contain a further SOE report on Canonbury II, which is undated:

SOE Report on Canonbury II
This operation took place on 4th May 1942.
According to reports which we have now received the results were as follows:-

(a)   Four bombs in the area between the railway lines and the ponds located to the south west of Koterov.
(b)   Five bombs 2 kilometres west of Blovice.
(c)   One bomb on Rokycany.
(d)   Considerable damage at Ziegleruv Dul, which is a subsidiary of Skoda specialising in the filling of artillery shells.
(e)   Considerable damage at Holysov, which is an ammunition factory working for Skoda.

It has not yet been established how much of the damage at (d) and (e) was due to the bombardment and how much to the Czech organisation.

In the days that followed it became evident that the second raid had not been as successful as first reported. A short note from Squadron Leader Elsworthy at HQ Bomber Command, addressed to Colonel Wilkinson at HQ SOE, dated 9 May 1942, confirmed:

With reference to your queries about Canonbury, I am afraid the following is all I can tell you:-

Canonbury I. Six aircraft each carrying six x 1,000 lb GP bombs filled with RDX [a type of explosive] were despatched. One was shot down without reaching the target, of the remaining five, one only succeeded in locating the target. The pilot of this aircraft asserts that his bombs fell just to the north of the target.

Canonbury II. Five aircraft, each carrying six x 1,000 lb GP bombs filled with RDX were despatched, of which three claim to have attacked the target.

Unfortunately PRU [Photographic Reconnaissance Unit] photographs taken since the attack reveal no damage to the target.

This wasn't quite true, as there had been success thanks to the efforts of the Czech underground. An internal SOE memo, dated 14 May 1942, updated the overall damage assessment:

> ... attach[ed] a report received from the Protectorate regarding the results of the second attempt at Canonbury:
>
> As you will see, [the RAF] did not manage to hit the target but, from the information we have, the damage at Ziegleruv Dul was considerable. There is reason to suppose that a good deal of this was caused by members of the Czech organisation who had been warned and prepared by the Silver A and Anthropoid parties.

It is worth repeating why the RAF attacks were so unsuccessful. At this stage of the bombing campaign, the navigation and bombing aids available to the RAF were still rudimentary and simply not sophisticated enough to allow a bombing force to find such a distant target and bomb it accurately. Even 12 months later, when much-improved navigation aids were available, the bombers still had difficulties: on the night of 16 April 1943, a force of 327 aircraft, made up of 197 Lancasters and 130 Halifax bombers, were tasked to attack the same Skoda factory. As reported in *The Bomber Command War Diaries 1939-1945* by M. Middlebrook and C. Everitt:

> The raid took place by the light of a full moon but was not a success. In a complicated plan, the Main Force was ordered to confirm the position of the Skoda factory visually; the Pathfinders markers were only intended as a general guide. In the event, a large asylum building 7 miles away was mistaken for the factory and only six crews brought back bombing photographs which were within 3 miles of the real target. The Skoda factory was not hit. One report said that 200 German soldiers were killed when their barracks near the asylum was bombed.

6

Hurry Up and Wait

When the agents of Out Distance and Zinc had arrived at the end of March, they had told the Home Army that more agents should be expected at the end of April and proper arrangements to mark out DZs should be carried out, together with a reception party on the ground to meet them. If this was not possible, then the underground should send up-to-date contact addresses to London without delay, before the next full moon period began. It was important that these further agent drops should take place before the start of May, when the long summer days would prevent lengthy flights over enemy territory. Two sorties were arranged to bring in five more parachutist groups. The first of these left on the night of 27/28 April 1942. A Halifax, serial number L9613, from 138 Squadron, flown by a Czech crew under the command of Flying Officer Anderle, was – possibly for the first time on a special operation – dropping their own countrymen back to their homeland. The first three groups were as follows:

> Bioscop – a sabotage group consisting of Warrant Officer Bohuslav Kouba, Sergeant Jan Hrubý and Sergeant Josef Bublik.
> Bivouac – another three-man sabotage group, made up of Warrant Officer František Pospíšil, Staff Sergeant Jindřich Čoupek and Corporal Libor Zapletal.
> Steel – a one-man operation conducted by Lance Corporal Oldřich Dvořák, a communications specialist. He carried a new radio transmitter, together with new radio crystals for the Libuše radio, and other items of equipment for Silver A.

All three missions were dropped together in the Křivoklát area to the west of Prague. Upon landing they gathered their equipment and buried it in a small wood close to their DZ before heading off to their allocated roles.

For the men of Bioscop, this meant travelling direct to Prague and making contact with the Jindra organisation – they had been provided with the new contact addresses prior to leaving England. Contact was duly accomplished with no real difficulties and they were given accommodation in safe houses. Kouba, the commander of Bioscop, was impatient to start work immediately and requested help from Jindra to retrieve the equipment as soon as possible. It was therefore agreed that four men would return to the Křivoklát area and collect what they could. The four who went back were Arnošt Mikš from Zinc and a resistance friend of his, Josef Kušý, together with Josef Valčik from Silver A and Ata Moravec, who was more than willing to be involved in anything he could to help the parachute agents. It was 30 April when the four travelled by train to the nearest station to where the equipment had been buried. They split up into two pairs – Mikš with Kušý and Valčik with Moravec. As Valčik and Moravec moved into the area close to where some of the equipment had been buried, they heard the ominous order "Halt!" An armed policeman appeared, covering them with his rifle. Unbeknown to Jindra and the parachutists, the morning after the agents had landed, a farmer noticed disturbed earth and, deciding to investigate, found the radio transmitter and reported it to the authorities. The area was searched in detail and the two dumps of equipment in the small wood were found and removed. Patrols and ambushes were set up to observe the area and wait for whoever might return to recover the items. Fortunately for Valčik and Moravec, the policeman who challenged them was a patriot. He told them to get out of the area as quickly and as quietly as possible.

For Mikš and Kušý, things did not go so well. At the edge of the wood where some of the equipment had been buried they ran into another patrol and were ordered to put their hands up. Mikš, unwilling to give up without a fight, opened fire at the two-man police patrol, hitting both of them, but was also severely wounded by their return fire. One of the policemen was killed and the other wounded. Kušý went to Mikš' aid, but he was so badly wounded that it was impossible for him to flee. Realising that the sound of gunshots would bring more police to the area, Mikš told Kušý to make good his escape. When Kušý had gone, Mikš placed his pistol against his temple and shot himself rather than face arrest, interrogation and the possibility of giving up information to the *Gestapo*.

The dead policeman was František Ometák and his wounded colleague was Václav Kominek. Upon being informed of the shooting, Heydrich ordered that a state funeral be given for Ometák. Kominek was given a financial reward and a ceremonial pistol engraved with the letters 'RH' and the words in German 'My Honour is Loyalty'. Mikš' body was photographed before being removed by the Germans.

Meanwhile, Kušý, Valčik and Ata Moravec had evaded further police patrols and returned to Běleč, which they had been using as a forward base. At Běleč, Bohuslav Kouba, the commander of Bioscop, was informed of Mikš' death. He decided to leave for Kutná Hora next morning, where he wanted to meet a contact of Mikš' brother. The details remain unclear, but shortly after arriving in Kutná Hora, Kouba found himself surrounded by gendarmes and with no chance of escape, swallowed his L pill and committed suicide.

After parting from Mikš in Brno, Vilém Gerik of Operation Zinc had travelled on alone to Prague. The address he had been given in Wenceslas Square proved useless, and he spent some days walking the streets of Prague searching for the underground movement. He had already made contact with his brother but decided against returning to him, possibly as he did not want to endanger any of his family. Instead, Gerik took the momentous decision on the afternoon of 4 April to give himself up to the Protectorate police. If Gerik, a Slovak, believed he would be safe with the Protectorate police and returned to Slovakia, then he was naive. Once the police realised who Gerik really was, he was handed over to the *Gestapo*.

To what extent Gerik resisted *Gestapo* interrogation is unknown, but he did eventually make a bargain with them. In return for immunity for himself and his family, he agreed to help the *Gestapo*. There is no doubt that Gerik gave the Germans useful background information on the training he had received in England, the Czech intelligence organisation in London and the Zinc group. On 6 April the *Gestapo* took him back to Gbely in Slovakia to recover what remained of the buried equipment. Gerik was also taken to the Křivoklát area to identify the body of Arnošt Mikš. It is understood he was allowed to talk to local villagers, which was how the news reached Prague and the Jindra organisation that a parachute agent had become a *Gestapo* informer.

During the night of 29/30 April, Halifax L9618 from 138 Squadron, again piloted by Anderle, returned to Czechoslovakia and dropped two groups near Věšín, in the area of Rožmitál to the south-west of Prague. These groups were called Intransitive and Tin.

The objective of Tin, made up of Sergeant Ludvík Cupal and Sergeant Jaroslav Švarc, was to assassinate the Minister of Education, Emanuel Moravec.

Intransitive was a three-man team with a remit for sabotage, their first objective being an oil refinery in Kolin. The group consisted of Lieutenant Václav Kindl, Sergeant Bohuslav Grabovský and Corporal Vojtěch Lukaštík.

This drop was fraught with difficulties. Both members of Tin had bad landings, with Cupal actually landing in a tree. He was able to extract himself from his harness, but when dropping to the ground suffered a leg injury.

Whilst Cupal and Švarc met up on the ground, they could not find their equipment and so headed for their contact point in Rokycany. Here they stayed for a few days before Švarc travelled to Prague, where he eventually made contact with Kubiš and Valčik. In June that year, Cupal attempted to assassinate Emanuel Moravec with Lukaštik from the Intransitive group, but they were unable to get close enough to carry out the attempt. Cupal remained at large until 15 January 1943, when he was surrounded by the Germans in Velehrad and committed suicide.

The Intransitive group fared little better. At the beginning of May, the *Gestapo* had found their equipment. The team themselves avoided detection by the Germans for some months, but eventually their luck ran out. Vojtěch Lukaštík was the first to be cornered, being shot in Janovice on 8 January 1943 in an ambush by the *Gestapo*. In the middle of March 1943, Kindl and Grabovský were arrested by the *Gestapo* and both agreed to collaborate with the Germans. Whilst still being held in Pankrác Prison, a note from Grabovský intended for the resistance was intercepted by the *Gestapo*, in which he asked them to tell London he was 'working' for the *Gestapo*. He was held in solitary confinement in Terezin until October 1944, when he was executed. Václav Kindl became one of the leading turned agents for the *Gestapo*, responsible for the Germans penetrating numerous underground groups. His death came in ironic circumstances in May 1944: he accompanied a police operation and was accidentally shot by a member of the *Gestapo* when he was mistaken as a member of the resistance.

London had embarked on a process of the saturation of agents inserted into Czechoslovakia, but for the resistance the influx of agents was a cause of great stress and danger to both the security of the underground movement and the existing agents already working in the Protectorate. An additional problem was that the Germans were collecting much of the equipment dropped. At the point of jumping, aircraft were typically flying at less than 1,000ft. The sound of a low-flying aircraft being easily audible to those who lived below the flight path, the locals often searched for containers, and many, out of fear or for financial reward, decided to report any findings to the Germans. *Gestapo* records include a list of items found up to the end of April 1942:

Arms and ammunition
A large quantity of explosives
5 radio sets
1 homing beacon [also known as the Rebecca set]
72 sabotage charges
6 anti-personnel charges
40 incendiary charges
1,000 detonators and fuses of various designs

This was now becoming an unsatisfactory situation, and a clearly annoyed Bartoš sent London a message on 21 May: "Please cancel any further drops. In practice, you are sending us people for whom we have no use. On the contrary, they are a burden on the organisational network which is undesirable in today's critical times. The Czech and German security authorities have so much information and knowledge about us that to repeat these operations would be a waste of people and equipment." The receipt of this message to the Czech Intelligence service in London must have been a shock, highlighting their lack of understanding of what was happening in their homeland.

It was against this background of German successes regarding the parachute agents that Gabčík and Kubiš were still trying to finalise their knowledge of Heydrich and his daily routine. After Canonbury, they had both obtained bicycles, which meant they could easily ride to the outskirts of Panenské Břežany looking for a suitable location and method to carry out an assassination. Undoubtedly, many members of the Jindra organisation were now aware of the intention of their mission, either through necessity or guess-work, but when asked the purpose of their mission, Gabčík and Kubiš always gave the stock reply, "We are counting the ducks on the Vltava."

Gabčík and Kubiš considered many options to assassinate Heydrich. Some were discounted quite quickly, such as an attack on Heydrich on his train, or the tree spigot or steel cable against his car. Whilst both men were prepared to die if necessary to complete their mission, they both intended to live if possible. Attacking the car in open country would quickly diminish their chances to escape before the area was flooded with German troops and police, so they continued their search in a residential part of Prague, where they hoped a combination of side roads, buildings and the presence of other people would conceal their escape. Once Heydrich had moved to his summer residence and they followed his new routine, they soon started to focus on one particular location on the outskirts of Prague, which would give them almost ideal circumstances to kill Heydrich and flee from the area.

In the northern suburb of Libeň there was a sharp bend where it was necessary for the car in which Heydrich travelled to slow down. This was the junction of Kirchmayer and V Holešovičkách. This location also had the advantage of being a tram terminus, which would provide them with cover as they innocently waited amongst the crowd for their tram. There was another advantage; Heydrich often travelled ahead of, or without an escort, meaning they would just need to deal with Heydrich and his driver. This increased their hopes of escaping the area without entering into a firefight with Heydrich's escort.

Just at the time when Gabčík and Kubiš were considering their final options for the assassination, they were confronted by senior members within the Jindra organisation to explain their actual mission. Whilst accounts differ, it is clear that Jindra knew that an attempt on the life of Heydrich was imminent and real, and there was suddenly concern of the potentially horrendous repercussions that would befall the Czech people. Matters came to a head at a meeting between Vaněk and some of the parachute agents held in late April or early May. Of those present at this meeting, which included Vaněk, Zelenka, Bartoš, Opálka, Gabčik and possibly also Kubiš, only Vaněk survived to give his side of the story. Vaněk told the parachutists he feared the reprisals that would follow an attempt on Heydrich's life would be too great a price for the Czech people to pay. He asked Gabčík to call off the operation. Zelenka, on the other hand, approved of an attempt. Vaněk's plea moved neither Gabčík nor Kubiš. They viewed the operation in very simplistic terms; they had been given orders to carry out a specific mission and had agreed to carry that out whatever the consequences might be for them personally. Orders were orders, and they would obey theirs.

Vaněk later commented:

> The young men asserted that their mission was perfectly clear; they were to organise and carry out the execution. They were soldiers, so they could not find fault with the killing or discuss its point or lack of point, its timeliness or its untimeliness. At the most, they might think it over; but they could do nothing against an order that they had been given.

Vaněk then appealed to Lieutenant Bartoš as the 'commander on the ground', who was prepared to debate the situation, but Gabčík cut Bartoš short and supposedly said, "The killing is necessary and for my part I shall obey the orders I have been given." He then left the apartment, and in the days leading up to the assassination had little time for those who were against his mission.

Having failed to reason with Gabčik or have Bartoš intervene, Vaněk decided to ask London directly. A message was drafted as being from the officials of ÚVOD:

> This assassination would not be of the least value to the Allies and for our nation it would have unforeseen consequences. It would threaten not only hostages and political prisoners, but thousands of other lives. The nation would be the subject of unheard of reprisals. At the same time it would wipe out the last remnants of any organisation. It would then be impossible for the resistance to be useful to the Allies. Therefore we beg you to give the order through Silver A for the assassination not to take place. Danger in delay, give the order at once.

Bartoš also wanted to offer an alternative target so that Gabčik and Kubiš retained a mission. He decided to conclude the message: "If for reasons of foreign policy the assassination is nevertheless essential, pick another person to be killed."

This message was sent during the first days of May, and as ÚVOD did not possess a radio transmitter – the set intended for them had been hidden by Dvořák of Operation Steel after he had landed, but was then discovered and handed to the *Gestapo* the next day – so Bartoš had agreed the message would be sent by the Libuše transmitter.

Meanwhile, Vaněk reported back to his senior colleagues in ÚVOD and argued strongly that they must ensure London cancel any attempt on the life of Heydrich. When no answer was forthcoming from London, ÚVOD, under Vaněk's guidance, prevailed on Bartoš to resend the message. This time the last sentence was altered to read: "If for reasons of foreign policy the assassination is nevertheless essential, another target should be chosen, a quisling, E.M. for example." This second message was sent on 12 May.

'E.M.' referred to Emanuel Moravec, the former Czech Army officer but now an enthusiastic Nazi and the Minister of Education in Hácha's government. Neither Bartoš nor ÚVOD could have been aware at this time that Staff Sergeant Cupal and Sergeant Svarc of Operation Tin had been parachuted into Czechoslovakia on the night of 30 April to undertake the assassination of Emanuel Moravec.

It is likely the receipt of this second message caused increased concern when it landed on the desk of Colonel Moravec. The arrival of the first message would have made it quite clear that the purpose of Operation Anthropoid was known to a number of people in Czechoslovakia. However, there could now be no misunderstanding that the underground was totally against an attempt on Heydrich's life, and that full responsibility for the consequences would be on the conscience of those in London.

There are two accounts of what happened next. The first is that a high-powered meeting was held the following day, at which politicians and intelligence officers were present. In this meeting, the politicians were in favour of respecting the wishes of the underground and cancelling the operation, whilst the intelligence officers argued that the operation needed to proceed as the Allies were expecting a major act of resistance to be delivered by the Czechs. A post-war account from one of Beneš' secretaries, Drtina, said that the president had consulted him about the assassination in the presence of Colonel Moravec:

I, as a former member of the Czech resistance organisation expressed an opinion that the attitude of the home resistance had to be respected and that no action should be taken without the agreement of the home organisations. The President talked in a similar sense to Colonel Moravec who left the meeting with the direct order of the President, the highest commander of the army, to immediately instruct the parachutists to abandon their mission.

Moravec's post-war account was different: "I took the message to President Beneš and the Chief of the British Secret Intelligence Service [Stewart Menzies]. President Beneš ordered me not to answer. The Chief of SIS did not say anything but I have learned since the war that the British insisted on the execution of the order."

After the war, Vaněk, who by this time had switched sides more than once and whose value as an impartial witness was completely compromised, claimed that President Beneš had issued an order confirming the assassination attempt was to go ahead:

> During the last days of our waiting I had a talk with Zelenka who told me an interesting thing. Kubiš and Gabčík had disclosed that about the 20th May they had received a radioed message in a code known only to them. Bartoš, who sent it to them by the Pardubice liaison agent, was unable to decipher it. And it appeared that this message contained a confirmation of the order – which said the attack on Heydrich was to be carried out.

Another source states that although the underground did not receive a direct answer to their early May message, one was received by a clandestine radio station called Vera, which was operating in the home land. This reportedly said the following: "Beech. Do not worry about the terrorist actions. We are convinced that we see the situation clearly and therefore any actions against the official representatives of the German Reich are in the current situation not acceptable to us either. Inform ÚVOD. Pavel."

It was entirely feasible that Gabčík and Kubiš had been given a special code before they left England, so that messages intended for them alone could be decoded by them once received by Libuše. It appears this is what happened. London may well have decided to ignore the message from ÚVOD, but in a continuation of the account given by Vaněk he states a message was sent to Libuše that only Gabčík could decode. Vaněk claimed this confirmed the assassination should be carried out, and afterwards Gabčík commented to the effect that there was nothing they could do because the order had arrived. Vaněk qualified this by saying while he had not seen this message, this was what he had heard was true.

Where Vaněk's evidence cannot be questioned is that London did not cancel the mission, for neither Gabčík nor Kubiš would have ignored such an order, whatever their personal disappointment. The location had been decided. All that was left was to finalise their plan on the day.

A sense of urgency had materialised, as it was around mid-May that the intelligence network was reporting Heydrich would soon be leaving Prague – there was a rumour that Hitler was sending Heydrich to France to perform a similar role as he had in the Protectorate. Heydrich's own diary did not go beyond 27 May, when he would fly to Berlin for a meeting with Hitler.

Therefore, 27 May might have been the last chance for Gabčik and Kubiš to complete their mission. So far, Heydrich's timetable had proved problematical for them. In April, Heydrich had travelled to the Eastern Front, and then in early May he visited Paris and Holland. Gabčik and Kubiš knew Heydrich was due at Hradčany Castle on 27 May, before his flight to Berlin, which had been scheduled for around midday. The date of their attack almost set itself.

7

On a Street Corner
in Prague

The Germans were aware that agents and supplies from England were being dropped in many occupied countries in Europe, with the result that organised resistance to the Nazi occupation had become established. Evidence was clear in the Protectorate of Bohemia and Moravia that agents from England had arrived; several had already been caught or shot in the weeks immediately preceding the attempt on Heydrich's life. The danger of sabotage and assassination could not be ignored. The head of the SS, Heinrich Himmler, visited Prague on 1 May to inspect for himself some of the items recovered from the recent parachute drops. In addition, Heydrich's personal security was reviewed, with suggestions for it to be improved. Himmler told Heydrich he should travel with an escort, and that armour plate should be installed in his cars. Heydrich may have seen the sense in some of these measures, but he did not believe the Czechs were brave enough to attack him, nor did he want to show any form of perceived weakness; so for now he continued to travel with just his driver/bodyguard.

A memo dated 9 May 1942 ordered a temporary police post to be established in Panenské Březany, but this had little impact on how Heydrich travelled. Its purpose was to improve the local security around the village in which Heydrich and his family lived. Even before the Heydrich family moved in to the castle in April 1942, the Czech Gendarmerie had placed officers in the village of Panenské Březany, as revealed by a memo dated 1 April:

Gendarmerie Section Prague.
No. 631 res./1942
Gendarmerie Post Odelenswasser
Subject: Gendarmerie Post reinforcements for the purpose of guarding the Schloss Jungfern Breschan.
To the Commander-in-Chief of the Gendarmerie Prague.

With reference to the telephone instructions issued this morning (by Major Engelmann) it is reported that the Gend.-Posten Odolenswasser, district Prag-Land, has been reinforced by 1 Ensign and 6 Gendarmes.

The reinforcements arrive today in Odolenswasser. The Gend.-Posten Odolenswasser, with a current status of 1 Oberwachtmeister, 1 Ensign and 11 Stabswachtmeisters or Sergeant, takes over this evening the guarding of the Schloss in Jungfern Breschan.

The security of the Schloss is carried out in the day by patrols 2-men strong and at night by patrols 3-men strong.

Concerning the security of the guard duty at the Schloss in Jungfern Breschan (roles and responsibility of the patrols), the provisions of the present order of May 20, 1940, number 1862/4 res./1940, adapted to the reduced number of patrols, in full remain valid. The commanding officer of Odolenswasser was given the necessary instructions verbally today as regards the security service at the Schloss of Jungfern Breschan.

Major Engelmann

It is noted that the Schloss in Jungfern Breschan has already from yesterday, i.e. 1st April 1942, been guarded by Gend.-Posten Odolenswasser.

I. V. of the Czech Gendarmerie commandant:Oberst H Müller.

Otherwise the arrangements for the guarding of the *Reichsprotektor*'s summer residence had not changed since von Neurath had lived there. The security had been set out in a Police Memorandum in 1940:

Liaison Officer for the commander of the Ordnungspolizei to the Ministry of the Interior Prague,

2nd May 1940.

Reference. No. 467.

To the Commander of the Ordnungspolizei with the Reichsprotektor in Prague.

Subject: Residence of the Reichsprotektor in Jungfern Breschan and the security arrangements.

To all Local Divisional Commanders with the exception of the Gendarmerie Commanders in Prague.

The summer residence of Herr Reichsprotektor Freiherr von Neurath in Jungfern Breschan will have a special guard detachment with orders to guard the palace and to act as a bodyguard for the Herr Reichsprotektor.

I order the commanders of the local Gendarmerie Departments, to promptly submit a list of three intelligent, quite reliable, disciplined and possibly single men, of good behaviour, having a military bearing, [and] a well-groomed appearance. Those recommended should either be German speakers or be learning as well as having an impeccable turnout.

The list must contain the following:

1. Number,
2. Surname and first name,
3. Location,
4. Place of birth,

5. Home ownership,
6. School education,
7. Employment before joining in the gendarmerie,
8. Assessment for the last two years,
9. To what extent the German language is mastered,
10. Note. In the 'Note' it must be stated whether the named Gendarmerie is married or single.

On behalf of the Gendarmerie Commander
Oberst Müller

It is known that Heydrich was not too worried about his security arrangements. He certainly felt that he was safe from attack, and so would often travel with just his chauffeur. Any suggestions received from Berlin about changing or increasing his security arrangements were often ignored. He was unaware of the net that was closing in around him.

On the evening of 26 May, Heydrich attended a concert at the Wallenstein Palace, which played many of his father's compositions, the highlight being the Piano Concerto in C-minor. The concert was given by the string quartet of Arthur Bonhardt, accompanied by the pianist Kurt Sanke. The Bonhardt players were from Halle, where Heydrich had been born and where his father's music academy had prospered. Heydrich was accompanied by his heavily pregnant wife. Also in attendance with their wives were most of the high-ranking Nazis in the Protectorate, including Karl Hermann Frank, General Rudolf Toussaint (Commissioner of the Army in the *Protektorate*), Alexander Commichau (*Reichs Arbeits Dienst* commander in the *Protektorate*) and *SS-Brigadeführer* Karl von Treuenfeld (*Waffen-SS* commander in the *Protektorate*).

The concert was a great success and Heydrich, an accomplished musician himself, must have taken enormous pride in hearing his father's music played in the magnificent Wallenstein Palace in the Bohemian capital.

The next morning was a sunny spring day. The date was Wednesday, 27 May, and Heydrich's star was now very much in the ascendancy. In the Protectorate he was effectively a feudal lord, and on this day he had an appointment with Hitler in Berlin that, if rumours could be believed, would extend his own standing in the senior Nazi network. It was possible he would be leaving Prague for good, and if he was, it was because he had been chosen for an even more important task by his *Führer* as reward for his having calmed the Czechs.

In an unusual change to his routine ,Heydrich allowed himself a late breakfast and spent time in the garden with his children. Rather than his usual departure from Panenské Břežany at around 0900, he did not leave until just gone 1000 that morning. In contrast, Gabčík and Kubiš had had an early start to their morning. They had spent the previous night at the Ogoun apartment in Prague-Dejvice and had left just before 0600, departing with the words, "Do not worry if we are not back as usual." Perhaps without thinking too much of the potential consequences, Gabčík took a raincoat and cap from the apartment on his way out.

They most likely used trams to cross the city to Žižkov, where another man, Josef Janacek, kept their bicycles in his garage. A widely accepted account has them cycling to the outskirts of the city to give some flowers to Ema Khodlova, whom they called Mama, and who had been amongst the first to offer them help when they arrived in Prague. However, it is more likely they last visited the Khodls and left the flowers on Mother's Day, which had taken place earlier in May.

If Heydrich had followed his routine, then Gabčik and Kubiš knew he would arrive shortly after 0900, so they would have wanted to have been in their places by no later than 0845. The plan was relatively simple. Josef Valčik, from the Silver A group, would be positioned up the hill, ready to signal with a mirror when Heydrich's car was sighted. Adolf Opálka from the Out Distance team would cross the road in front of Heydrich's car, slowing it down further as it entered the bend. The weapon of choice for Gabčik to carry out the assassination was a Sten gun, potentially the ideal weapon for use on the streets of Prague. In length it was a relatively small weapon and could be broken down into four major pieces – the barrel, body, stock and magazine – each no more than about 12in long – making it ideal to be hidden in a briefcase and then assembled underneath a raincoat.

The Sten was a 9mm sub-machine gun, its name derived from the chief designers' initials, 'S' for Shepherd and 'T' for Turpin, with 'EN' for Enfield where the Royal Small Arms Factory was located. The Sten was described in one early account as "resembling a roughly machined collection of scrap metal that was quite exciting to be around as it tended to go off when knocked". As well as hinting at unreliability, this description also suggests the simplicity of the Sten, which was born from an economic necessity – after the BEF had been evacuated from Dunkirk in 1940, weapons were scarce and Britain was buying Thompson sub-machine guns from America, which were costing around $200 each. It was decided that the Thompsons were too expensive, plus the Americans couldn't supply them quickly enough. Shepherd and Turpin were tasked with designing a cheap weapon which could be mass-produced by relatively unskilled labour. They came up with a weapon that fired 9mm ammunition, the same calibre as used by the Germans, and it only had 47 parts, with just two parts machined; the rest were made of stamped steel and then welded together, so production could be done in small shops rather than in large factories – one of the largest manufacturers was Lines Brothers, a firm whose pre-war business had been toy makers. The magazine held a maximum of 32 rounds, and the detachable stock was basically a length of pipe. The whole weapon could be made in about five hours, and in comparison to the Thompson the cost was just $10 apiece. Being relatively small, easy to break down and conceal, and having a commonality of ammunition with German weapons, made the Sten ideal to send to resistance groups in occupied Europe, and the cost was far easier to write off than a $200 Thompson when the weapon didn't come back!

If, for any reason, Gabčik was unable to carry out the assassination, then Kubiš would place himself just beyond Gabčik. Kubiš carried one of the modified No. 73 anti-tank grenades in his briefcase. The 73 anti-tank grenade was designed in the dark days of summer 1940 when the British Army was facing the very real threat of a German invasion. It is calculated that in 1940, Britain only had around 170 anti-tank guns in the country, whilst over 800 had been left behind in France. In addition, ammunition was in such short supply that it was forbidden to use any live ammunition for training purposes. The No. 73 grenade had a roughly cylindrical shape and plastic screw-on cap, similar to that of a Thermos flask, from which the 'Thermos bomb' nickname was derived. The original version was about 3½-in in diameter and 12-in long, and weighed over 4lb. The explosive content was 3½lb of polar ammonal gelatine dynamite or nitro gelatine – both of which were easily flammable and could be detonated by the impact of small-arms fire. When thrown at a tank or any other vehicle, a weighted tape, which in theory the thrower held in his hand, unravelled and pulled free a safety pin, which was attached to a Type 247 'All-Ways' fuse which then armed and detonated the grenade. An 'All-Ways' fuse meant that it went off whichever way it landed or hit its target. The somewhat heavy weight of this grenade meant most soldiers could only throw it short distances, limiting its range to about 10–15 yards, with the added danger that the thrower would likely need to find cover very quickly or potentially be wounded himself by the blast. It was able to penetrate 2-in of armour and was theoretically the perfect weapon to use on Heydrich's car. The No. 73 grenade was first issued in the last months of 1940, but it was rarely used as an anti-tank grenade; instead, the fuse was usually removed and it was used as a demolition charge. It was withdrawn from service within a year and had been declared obsolete. Nevertheless, Major Clarke, who had assisted with the training of Gabčík and Kubiš in England, modified the grenade, making it lighter by cutting its length by about 50 percent and wrapping adhesive tape around the body to give it temporary strength. It was two of these modified No. 73 grenades that Anthropoid took to Czechoslovakia. The parachutists were also armed with their personal weapon, each having a pistol.

When they arrived at the bend at Holešovičkách, Gabčík left his bicycle across the road by some allotments, pointing down the hill towards Libeň. Kubiš placed his bicycle against the railings on the bend. It is likely that Opálka and Valčík were already there, ready to take up their positions. Gabčík would have assembled the Sten soon after arriving, using the raincoat he had taken from the Ogoun apartment to conceal the weapon. He had taken one magazine from his briefcase, leaving the other inside, hanging from the handlebars of his bicycle. Kubiš took his briefcase with him, which held inside one of the modified grenades – for reasons that are not clear, the other grenade remained in Gabčík's briefcase hanging from the handlebars.

They expected Heydrich to leave the villa at Panenské Břežany no later than 0900. A benefit of the Holešovičkách bend was that it was also a mini-tram terminus. The terminus would give Gabčík and Kubiš immediate cover, but they hoped Heydrich would arrive soon as the longer they lingered there without taking a tram, the more likely they would attract attention, possibly even the police. It would take Heydrich between 20 and 25 minutes to reach the bend from Panenské Břežany.

However, as we have seen, on this day Heydrich did not leave his villa until just after 1000. His driver/bodyguard, *SS-Oberscharführer* Johannes Klein, waited patiently for his boss to give the order to drive him to Prague. Heydrich had chosen to travel in his personal Mercedes 320 Cabriolet B, powered by a 3.2-litre engine, with a top speed of around 80mph. The usual registration number placed on this particular Mercedes was SS-4.

Meanwhile, further south at Holešovičkách, the additional wait proved an anxious time for the four parachute agents: 0930 had passed, then 1000. Why had Heydrich not arrived by now – had something gone wrong? The trams came and went, but the agents had to hold their nerve; surely Heydrich would come soon. Still the clock ticked, – 1020, 1025 and 1030 – and then it would have been Valčik who heard the roar of an engine first. Seing Heydrich's Mercedes come over the brow of the hill, Valčik flashed the warning as the sun hit his mirror. Heydrich, the Butcher of Prague, was on his way. The time was almost 1032.

The No. 3 tram was on the apex of the bend as Klein approached, so the driver moved the Mercedes over to the right, taking him closer to the kerb where Gabčík and Kubiš were positioned. Klein used the brakes as he entered the corner, and then Opálka walked in front of the vehicle and he braked again, this time so hard the car almost stopped. The Mercedes was now no more than 6ft away from Gabčík when he dropped his raincoat and pointed the Sten at the slow-moving car. His eyes almost certainly met Heydrich's, then he pulled the trigger,;then he pulled it again and again, yet nothing happened. His Sten had failed to fire.

At this moment, Klein should have put his foot down hard on the accelerator and driven through Gabčik, but Heydrich was shouting *Anhalten!* ("Stop") and Klein obeyed, bringing the car to a halt. Heydrich simultaneously began to stand up and drew a pistol from the door pocket of the car. The car glided past Gabčik, who was momentarily rooted to the spot, watching in stunned disbelief.

It was now that Kubiš emerged from the shadows, pulling his grenade from the briefcase. The accepted version of what happened next is that Kubiš lobbed the grenade underarm, aiming for inside the Cabriolet, but his throw was poor and the grenade hit near the rear wheel arch. However, if Kubiš had thrown underarm, there would be gentleness to the throw to retain accuracy. If the grenade had landed on the leather upholstery, would the impact have been enough to trigger the fuse? Or did Kubiš, who achieved 90 percent in bombing and demolition in the SOE test at Arisaig, purposely, and with force, throw the bomb at the car's bodywork, as he had been instructed in his training, trusting that the consequences of the explosion would cause Heydrich a fatal injury? Kubiš likely threw hard. The fuse engaged, exploding the grenade on impact, causing a loud blast to reverberate and a plume of smoke to rise above the vehicle. The explosion had caused the car to jump, taking it closer to the near kerb, and the blast wave shattered windows in the No. 3 tram. There followed a stunned silence as people collected their senses and began to react, not least the car's occupants.

Heydrich emerged from the stricken car with pistol in hand, but slightly bent-double as his other hand held his back. One of his would-be assassins was still standing motionless and Heydrich fired in his direction. This was Gabčik, who reacted by dropping the Sten and taking cover behind a telegraph pole as he drew his pistol. The pain in Heydrich's back made him stumble. Gabčik, seeing the opportunity, turned and ran. The route to his cycle was barred by passengers from the tram, so he ran up the hill, the road Klein and Heydrich had driven down.

Kubiš had been hit by shrapnel from his grenade. Blood ran down his face and was smeared on his hands. He threw his briefcase beyond the railings, mounted his bicycle and began to pull away, slowly at first as he had to cycle on an upward gradient. There were people in front of him and he fired his pistol into the air. Behind him, Klein took aim and pulled the trigger, but had inadvertently hit the release catch for the magazine and his chance was missed. Kubiš was away over the brow of the hill and cycling furiously towards Libeň.

Heydrich shouted at Klein, "Get that bastard", pointing to Gabčik, and Klein obediently turned and ran after him.

No definitive report can be found on why Gabčik's Sten failed to work. The stoppage could have been caused by one of several factors:

1.   The safety catch had slipped back on.
2.   Grass cuttings in the mechanism. In Prague in those days it was common for many people to keep a rabbit to supplement their meat ration. Most people lived in apartments, so they were allowed to cut grass from public parks as food for their rabbits. A worker carrying grass around in his briefcase was a common occurrence, and had Gabčík been stopped then a covering of grass may have been enough to hide the Sten from a policeman's cursory glance.
3.   A defective or overloaded spring. During one of the author's basic training in the Army, a wise corporal told him, "if we do go to war and you have a Sterling sub-machine gun just put 28 rounds in the magazine". A full magazine of 32 rounds left the gun 'fully compressed' and weakened the spring. The working parts would go forward but no round would be picked up.
4.   The Sten was of simple and rough manufacture and needed 'fettling'.
5.   Magazine lips – if these were damaged then rounds could jam in the breech. It is likely the weapon had not been test-fired since they arrived in Prague many weeks earlier.
6.   If the retaining cap at the rear was faulty or had come loose, this would stop the gun from firing. Gabčik had not assembled the stock, so the retaining cap may not have been held firmly in place.

The Sten used had been made at the Royal Ordnance Factory at Fazakerley in Liverpool, and had the serial number FF209.

As Gabčik was ahead of Klein, he was able to stop every so often behind cover and fire delaying shots. In 1942 there was a printing works on the Kirchmayerova called Prometheus, and the Germans later found three bullet cases near this spot. Gabčik took the first left turn and was now running down hill. In 1942 this road was called Na Kolinské; it is now Gabčikova. The chase continued down this quiet suburban street until Gabčik reached Na Zápalči at the bottom. Diagonally across the road was an open door of a butcher's shop, and Gabčik ran towards it. Still brandishing his pistol, he came across the owner and asked where the back exit was. The owner, František Brauner, was a Nazi sympathiser and ran past Gabčik out of the shop, almost running into Klein. Gabčik now understood the shop had only the front entrance, with no other exit, and he needed to get out of the shop quickly. He could see enough of Klein, who was about 10 yards away, hidden behind a concrete pillar, to fire two rounds at him, although only one cartridge case was later found by the Germans. Gabčik's aim was good and he hit Klein in the lower left leg. Gabčik was again outside, running until he reached Holesokovich, coming out a couple of hundred yards below where Heydrich's car had come to a stop. He jumped on board a passing tram, away from the scene of the assassination attempt, heading back towards the centre of Prague. Klein had ordered Brauner to run after Gabčik, which he did but in a half-hearted manner, soon returning to help Klein. Gabčik's escape along the Na Kolinské was also witnessed by a newspaper vendor called Karel Douša, who lived at what is now 1236/21 Gabčikova and was later interviewed by the *Gestapo*.

Whilst Klein had been chasing after Gabčík, Heydrich had begun to realise the extent of his wounds. Upon impact, the grenade had blown fragments of metal, both from the grenade and from the car's bodywork, through the rear panel into the interior of the car, tearing through the upholstery. The upward motion of the blast meant the debris caused by the bomb splinters had torn into the lumber region of Heydrich, who by this time was standing up in the car. As Gabčík ran from the scene, Heydrich was overcome by agony and slumped down on the pavement.

For some moments, no one dared approach Heydrich until Marie Navarova stepped forward, recognising him and offering assistance. She was soon joined by a policeman, Michal Lofergyuk, who had been a passenger on a trams. Heydrich is recorded as saying he needed to get to hospital. Navarova, who worked as a nurse, took control of the situation, stopping the first passing vehicle and saying, "Quick! There has been an attack. You must take the Herr *Protektor* to the Bulovka hospital." The driver, Karel Duben, remonstrated that his car, a Zetra, was full of sweets out on delivery to Kobylisy. Duben reluctantly began to empty his car of the boxes of sweets, but Navarova flagged down a second vehicle. This was a small Tatra van belonging to the Holan Company, out delivering floor polish and wax. On this day it was being driven by František Šitta, and he had Theodor Šulc to assist him with the delivery. Šitta argued in vain that his van was unsuitable to transport the *Reichsprotektor* with its nauseating smell of polish, but ultimately he could not refuse and Lofergyuk helped Heydrich into the cab. Šitta got into the driver's seat, noticing that Heydrich held his briefcase in one hand and a pistol in the other. Šitta drove off the way the van was facing, which was down Holesokovich towards Prague. He had only driven a short distance when he realised he was travelling in the wrong direction, so he turned in the road and headed back towards the corner. As they re-approached Navarova, Heydrich ordered Šitta to stop; it was just too painful for him sitting upright in the small cab. Heydrich was helped out of the front cab and manoeuvred into the back of the van, lying on top of boxes of floor polish.

After the war, Navarova was arrested and gave the following statement to the authorities:

On 27th May 1942, in the morning, I went to visit my uncle Josef. When I was on a number 3 tram to Bulovka, I was by chance a witness to the assassination of Heydrich. When the bomb exploded and the tram stopped, I got off the tram and went to the car, and I saw that Heydrich was wounded and he called to me vaguely in German. That's why I stopped the nearest car that was passing the scene, as Heydrich struggled and was limping on one leg, I helped him in a car stopped by me and holding his hand I helped him in and told the driver to take him to the Bulovka hospital. I immediately left the scene of the assassination, and I did not say anymore at the time. When I got home to my apartment, I told my husband what had happened.

Kubiš had left the assassination scene on his bicycle, pedalling downhill in the direction of Libeň, where he knew he could find some form of immediate refuge with the Novak family. The journey was little more than a mile, but would not be uneventful. At the scene of the assassination attempt, Kubiš had briefly been pursued by a policeman, Bedřich Zálenský, but as Kubiš was armed, or possibly because his true loyalty lay with the Czechs, Zálenský disappeared from the scene and his identity remained undetected by the Germans during their investigation. A woman who had been cleaning the steps outside her house, aware that an incident had taken place but most likely unaware of any detail, saw the bloodied Kubiš approaching and threw a bucket towards his bicycle. The bucket banged against his front wheel but did not stop him, and he continued his bid to escape. Further down the hill, he almost ran over two women crossing the road on the bend where the old Sokol gymnasium stood. Although the sight of a man on a bicycle was a common one in Prague, Kubiš must have realised that his bloodstreaked face and bloody hands made him conspicuous to many people, who would later report their observations to the authorities. With this is mind and an uphill stretch ahead of him, he jumped off his bicycle at the Bata shoe shop on the corner of Slavatova and Zenklova with as much casualness as he could muster. He left the bicycle against a post and walked briskly towards Strájnského and the Novak 'safe house'.

It was only a short walk and he ran up the external stairs to the Novak apartment, but nobody answered his knock. Although challenged by one of their neighbours, he knew where to find the key and let himself in. In a short time, Marie Novaková returned from her daily shopping. She immediately sent her youngest daughter, Jindřiška, who had just arrived home early from school, to collect the bloodstained bicycle. It was a dangerous thing to do, and Jindřiška was told to ignore any questions or comments she may receive. Whilst she did collect the bicycle and bring it back to their yard, she was seen by at least four women who noticed the blood on the handlebars. At least one of these women tried to question Jindřiška, but she said the bicycle belonged to her father who had been in an accident and calmly wheeled the bicycle away, taking a circuitous route back home.

Marie Novaková cleaned Kubiš' wounds as best she could. Kubiš had been seen heading towards Libeň and the bicycle had attracted attention, and he knew he needed to move out of this part of Prague as soon as he could. Vaclav Novak provided

Kubiš with a set of his old railway overalls, which it was hoped would explain the bruising around Kubiš' face as an industrial accident to any inquisitive observer. It was arranged that Kubiš would go to the Piskáčeks who lived in Rainerova, just beyond Libeň and on the outskirts of Prague.

Kubiš reached the Piskáček house without further incident. It was now clear his eye injury needed medical attention, so he asked Jaroslav Piskáček if he could contact Doctor Lyčka to come and treat his injuries. Piskáček did not know Lyčka personally, so he went to see another underground resister, Augustine Oktábek, with the request. Oktábek then brought Lyčka to the house that afternoon and he treated Kubiš' eye.

Piskáček's son, Miroslav, collected Kubiš' bicycle from its hiding place in the Novák yard and returned it to the original owner, Jaroslav Smrž.

Meanwhile, after leaving the scene of the attempted assassination, Gabčík had gone straight to the Svatoš safe house at Melanantrichova in the Old Town in central Prague. Upon arrival, Gabčík was described as being agitated but he passed this off by saying he had had to complete an unpleasant job that morning. He gave Marie Svatošová his shirt to clean, whilst he washed himself. With his shirt washed but still wet, he left the Svatoš home, pulling out his Colt pistol and saying, "That bloody thing, one has to carry it everywhere and it is of no use." Josef Svatoš, who lent him a hat and coat, watched out of his window when Gabčík left and noticed that he bought some flowers from the florist next door. It is believed that Gabčik went to the apartment of the Fafeks and then went with one of the daughters, Libena, to buy a green Tyrolean-style hat as a form of disguise. Libena and Jozef had become friends in the months he had been staying in Prague, so she was useful as cover on this shopping trip. If this is true, then the disguise worked as at Charles Square a German asked him for a light for his cigarette. Had the German seen the Tyrolean hat and assumed the wearer was a fellow German? Gabčik passed through Prague to Pankrác and the apartment of his girlfriend, Anna Malinová, where he would stay for the next four days.

The other two parachutists at the scene of the assassination attempt were Adolf Opálka and Josef Valčik. Valčik, after signalling the arrival of Heydrich's car with a mirror, walked up Na Kolinské and then took a tram to his 'safe house' with the Sulek family. Another account suggests that on this day Valčik was at the Zelenka flat, where he met Hana Krupková from Pardubice. She had travelled to Prague to obtain a first-hand account of the assassination that Bartoš could transmit back to London. Opálka, meanwhile, returned to the small apartment of Terezie Kasperová at Velvarská, in the Dejvice district of Prague.

8

The German Reaction

Heydrich's arrival at the Bulovka Hospital led to the first official report of what became known as 'the outrage' – the attempt on the life of Heydrich. At Police officer Jan Jiravský was on duty at the hospital, and it was he who contacted the Police Directorate of Prague with the news that an attack had been carried out. However, it does not appear Heydrich was named as the victim, as the report received and forwarded to the State Police Headquarters in Prague only said that a senior-ranking German official had been involved in an incident and had taken to the Bulovka Hospital. The time this message was received was 1050. Immediately, a number of policemen from the local office went to the hospital to investigate.

The arrival of Heydrich caused panic in the hospital. The duty doctor, Vladimir Snadjr, was called to the emergency department, where he found Heydrich sitting on a trolley, bare-chested, silent and aloof but bleeding from a wound in his lower left back. Doctor Snadjr described this encounter in a later interview:

> Heydrich was alone in the room, stripped to the waist, sitting on the table where we carry out the first examination. I greeted him in Czech; he raised his hand but did not answer. I took forceps and a few swabs and tried to see whether the wound was deep. He did not stir; he did not flinch, although it must have hurt him. Meanwhile a nurse telephoned Doctor Dick, a German, asking him to come to the theatre. At first sight the wound did not seem dangerous – unfortunately. Sometimes, you know, doctors find themselves in a complex situation. Take this case for example. Since I was a decent Czech I was delighted that Heydrich should be in a bad way. All it needed was for him to have been wounded a few inches lower down, in the kidneys, or the spinal column to have been affected and everything would have been straight-forward. But since I was a doctor my duty was to cure not kill. But should you cure fascists? He was a murderer and killing a tyrant is an act that benefits mankind as a whole. Before I could make up my mind Doctor Dick rushed in.

Doctor Walter Dick, a thoracic surgeon, was a Sudeten German. He was head of surgery at the Bulovka. Doctor Dick examined the wound himself, which he reported as being filled with blood clots, pieces of metal and car upholstery. His initial conclusion was that the wound was a minor one, with some shrapnel in the area of the chest wall. He believed it could be cleaned up and debrided under a local anaesthetic. This would remove the dead tissue from the wound to prevent an infection and possible gangrene, and ultimately quicken the process of healing. First an X-ray of the chest needed to be taken in case the damage was more widespread. Heydrich was placed in a wheelchair and taken to the X-ray department. Once there, despite being in obvious great pain, Heydrich walked unaided to the machine where the X-ray was taken. Once developed, it showed the following injuries – a left pneumothorax, a fracture of the 11th rib, a tear in his diaphragm and what seemed to be foreign bodies in Heydrich's spleen. A pneumothorax meant there was air in the pleural cavity, normally caused by perforation of the chest wall or of the lung pleura; in simple terms, a collapsed lung. Fortunately for Heydrich, his kidneys had not been damaged and the shrapnel had missed his spine.

The X-ray proved that Heydrich's injuries required an immediate operation, but Heydrich initially refused, ordering that a Berlin surgeon be brought to Prague to perform any operation. Doctor Dick reiterated to Heydrich that the operation had to be carried out urgently, saying it would put him in danger to wait for an SS surgeon to be sent from Berlin. As a compromise, Doctor Dick suggested that Professor Josef Hohlbaum, a Silesian German and deputy chair of surgery at the nearby Charles V University, be asked to conduct the operation. Heydrich reluctantly agreed to the concession and Professor Holbaum was summoned to the Bulovka.

Whilst Professor Holbaum was travelling across Prague, Heydrich was taken to the operating theatre and prepared for the operation. The anaesthetist was a Czech, Doctor Honek, whom Heydrich begrudgingly allowed to examine his mouth, a necessary process before the anaesthetisation. Professor Hohlbaum was ready to commence the surgery at around noon, supported by Doctor Dick. In one account, in his haste to arrive at the hospital, Professor Hohlbaum had left his glasses behind and these had to be fetched from the university. Doctor Dick was advised to start the operation and Hohlbaum would assist when his glasses arrived. In another account, Doctor Dick observed that Professor Holbaum's hands were trembling as he made the first incision. Doctor Dick eased Holbaum away, commenting, "You are not well, let me take over."

A number of procedures were carried out – the chest wound was debrided, the tip of the fractured 11th rib was removed and a drain inserted into the chest to reinflate the lung. Heydrich had been lying on his right side, but was then turned onto his back and his abdomen prepared for a laparotomy – an incision into the abdomen for exploratory purposes. It was found that the abdominal cavity was filling with blood from Heydrich's spleen, but no other internal injuries could be found. The spleen was removed, together with a large fragment from the grenade and an amount of horse hair and other material, which had come from the seat upholstery and was carried into Heydrich's body by the blast. The abdomen was then closed and a further drain left in place. The surgery had lasted about an hour and there was no reason to think it hadn't been a success.

Meanwhile, word had spread. Confirmation that an attack on the life of the *Reichsprotektor* had set the Nazi security apparatus into motion. Sometime after

1200, Heinz Pannwitz, an *SS-Hauptsturmführer* and head of the Special Investigation Commission in Prague, arrived at the Bulovka and began the process of turning the hospital into a fortress. All other patients were moved to other hospitals or discharged. The windows were whitewashed and troops set up a perimeter, with a machine gun placed on the roof. Armed guards not only patrolled the grounds and entrances, but also the corridors of the hospital.

In the early afternoon, Karl Hermann Frank, head of the SS and police in Bohemia and Moravia, and President Hácha arrived at the Bulovka, along with other senior members of the government. Heydrich had been moved to Doctor Dick's office on the second floor of the hospital, which had been converted into a single ward. It was not until mid-afternoon that Heydrich recovered from the anaesthetic.

It fell to Frank to perform the difficult task of informing Hitler of the assassination attempt and the injuries inflicted upon Heydrich. He telephoned the *Führer's* HQ in East Prussia at about 1215. Hitler's response was to become incandescent with rage. Hitler wanted martial law imposed immediately and the arrest and execution of 10,000 Czechs from those who had carried out, or were suspected of, anti-German activities. But Hitler's wrath was not confined to the Czechs; he also criticised Heydrich for his carelessness, angrily commenting, "Irreplaceable people of Heydrich's political profile cannot afford to travel in an open car without any armour plating and move along the streets of Prague without a proper escort. That was unbelievably foolish not to say idiotic."

News of the attack also reached the leader of the SS, Heinrich Himmler, who in turn ordered his personal physician and senior SS doctor, *SS-Gruppenführer* Karl Gebhardt, to travel immediately to Prague to take over the treatment of Heydrich. Gebhardt arrived in Prague that evening, but as an orthopaedic specialist he confined his role to co-ordinating and supervising Heydrich's post-operative care.

At around 1500, with Heydrich safely under guard at the Bulovka Hospital, Frank held a conference with senior members of the *Gestapo* and other security agencies. He briefed them on the *Führer's* intention, and most of those present shared Frank's concerns over the proposed execution of 10,000 Czechs. Pannwitz, who had already made an initial assessment of the crime scene and those items recovered from the perpetrators, believed it was clear the attack had been planned in England, carried out by parachutists trained there and then sent back to their homeland. He felt it highly unlikely that members of the local resistance could conceive and carry out such an attempt.

At 1526 that afternoon, *SS-Standartenführer* Horst Böhme reported the results of Heydrich's first operation to Berlin via a telex:

> ...a lacerated wound to the left of the back vertebrae without damage to the spinal cord. The projectile, a piece of sheet metal, shattered the eleventh rib, punctured the stomach lining, and finally lodged in the spleen. The wound contains a number of horse hair, probably material originating from the upholstery. The dangers: festering of the pleura due to pleurisy. During the operation the spleen was removed.

Frank had hopes of being asked to take on the position of Acting *Reichsprotektor*, at least until Heydrich was well enough to resume his duties. Howsever, given that rumours had been circulating that Heydrich's future was now in France, Frank must have already considered that he might be elevated to *Reichsprotektor*, a position still nominally held by von Neurath. As it turned out, Frank would be disappointed in this, but when he was asked by Hitler to temporarily take control in the Protectorate, he put in place a set of orders that very afternoon:

Decree by the Reichsprotektor to proclaim a civilian state of emergency in the Protectorate of Bohemia and Moravia from 27th May 1942.

Orders from the Reichsprotektor in Bohemia and Moravia.

Due to the attack on the Acting Reichsprotektor SS-Obergruppenführer Heydrich, the following is imposed:

Article I On the basis of § 1 of the decree of the Reichsprotektor in Bohemia and Moravia on the imposition of the civil state of emergency of 27th September 1941, a civilian state of emergency is imposed with immediate effect on the entire Protektorate of Bohemia and Moravia.

Article II Pursuant to § 2 of the above-mentioned regulation, I order that anyone who accommodates or provides assistance to persons involved in the perpetration of the attack, or who does not file a report with regard to their identity or residence, will be shot dead together with their family members.

This decree comes into force when it is first broadcast on the radio.

Prague, 27th May 1942.

The Reichsprotektor in Bohemia and Moravia:

K.H. Frank.

These basic instructions were further expanded upon by posters and broadcasts in Frank's name, which stated:

1. On 27th May 1942 an attempt on the life of the acting Reichsprotektor SS-Obergruppenführer Heydrich, was perpetrated in Prague. A reward of 10,000,000 Koruna will be given for the arrest of the guilty men. Whoever shelters these criminals, provides them with assistance, or who knows them and does not denounce them will be shot with his whole family.

2. In the Prague Oberlandrat region, martial law is proclaimed by the reading of this ordinance on the radio. The following measures are laid down:

   a. The civilian population, without exception, is forbidden to be out on the streets from 2100 on 27th May till 0600 on 28th May.

   b. All inns and restaurants, cinemas, theatres and other public places of entertainment will be shut and all traffic on public highways is forbidden during the same period.

   c. Any person who appears on the streets in defiance of this proclamation will be shot if he does not immediately stop when ordered.

   d. Other measures are foreseen and if necessary they will be announced on the radio.

These instructions were announced on the German radio at 1630 and on Czech radio just after 1700, repeated at regular intervals thereafter. Other measures had also been taken that afternoon, the Germans mobilising around 8,000 troops and policemen from other areas, with the intention of searching at least 35,000 properties in Prague that night. Roadblocks had already been placed on all the main routes out of the city, and all train and bus travel in and out of Prague was suspended. If the perpetrators were still in Prague, then Frank wanted to make sure they could not escape into the country.

That night in Prague, the curfew took effect at 2100 and the Germans commenced the search of approximately 35,000 homes. Whilst no trace of the parachute agents was discovered by the Germans, some of the many agents in Prague that night did have close scrapes. Opálka returned to the apartment of Terezie Kasperová, where he had spent the previous three nights. When the Germans knocked at the door, he hid in a small cupboard whose entrance was concealed by a sofa. Karel Čurda is said to have hung from a bathroom windowsill over a light well whilst the flat of the Bautz family, where he was hiding, was searched. Both agents escaped detection.

The report produced by the *Gestapo* on the search conducted during the night of 27th/28th May attempted to paint a more positive picture than had really existed:

> On the orders of the Secret State Police HQ in Prague, a large scale search was organised in the city during the night of 27th/28th May 1942. 4,500 men from the security police, SS and NSKK units, ordinary police and Protektorate police, together with 3 Wehrmacht battalions were required to seal off the town and to place sentries in the streets for the searching of houses.
>
> In the course of the search, 541 persons were arrested because they had been unable to reach their homes in time or because they were not carrying identity cards. The stations in which members of the SD had been posted were able to release 430 people after their identities had been checked.
>
> 111 people were transferred to the HQ of the State Police in Prague but 88 were released after a thorough check. In addition to this, 3 or 4 tramps, 1 prostitute and 1 juvenile delinquent were taken to the Prague Police HQ.
>
> Among those detained in custody are: 1 leader of the resistance movement on our wanted list, who has been living clandestinely since October 1941; 4 Jews and 3 Czech women suspected of having slandered the Aryan race; 4 people in possession of excessive quantities of food; 1 woman in possession of ammunition without a permit; 1 Jew who had changed his address without registering this; another Jew found in possession of books hostile to the Reich and 2 Czech workers mobilised for obligatory labour in Germany who had escaped.

The scale of the German searches that night made the Jindra group realise that all the parachute agents in Prague had to be hidden somewhere safe until such time as they could safely be moved out of Prague.

Based on witness statements, an initial description of Gabčík and Kubiš was issued on 28 May, containing the following details:

The first perpetrator: About 30 years of age, 1.65 to 1.70 metres tall with a tanned face, dark full shock of hair, wore a dark suit with small bright stripes. He was bare-headed and [had] broad shoulders. The second perpetrator: 30 to 35 years of age, 1.70 metres tall, heavily built, wore a black untidy suit and black hat. It is very likely that there is in addition a third man who was involved in the attack who cannot be described.

Whilst the search of people's homes had not helped the Germans in their investigation, the crime scene had presented them with a number of important clues: the two briefcases, one bicycle, a Sten gun, a raincoat and a cap. Much attention was focused on the bicycle found at the scene with the briefcase left hanging from the handlebars. Importantly to the Germans, no attempt had been made to remove the serial number, 40363, but attempts to trace the owner of the bicycle proved futile as the manufacturer was unable to provide the sale records for that batch of bicycles.

The bicycle was placed alongside the other recovered items in the window of the Bata shoe shop in Wenceslas Square, while the police also circulated a full description of the bicycle:

Black enamel frame with red and white star, front forks with twelve centimetres of nickel plating and nineteen centimetres long red and white pointed over paint, rear fork black without adornments, black mudguards with one centimetre wide stripe in the middle, rear mudguard showing signs of rust around the fixing holes for the skirt guard and under the rear fork, handlebars pointing slightly upwards, nickel plated, with red paper grips bearing the name of 'J. Krčmář, Velo-Moto, Teplice-Šanov'. Production number 40363. Front wheel: black rim on the right slightly bent after a collision, spokes complete. Rear wheel: one spoke missing, both wheels have black rims with nine millimetres wide red stripes, chain wheel Tordy – made by the Duerrkopp company with a safety lock, the skirt guard in black, red yellow and purple colours is badly damaged. Seat: brown leather, with an embossed logo of a swimming swan on both sides, scale 5055 millimetres, five springs. Tyres: semi pneumatic 28x1in. Accessories: pump, fixed to the left side of the frame, leather tool case with four patent spanners, plain reflective glass at the rear of the fork, pedals with rubber footrests with non-reflective glass.

The initial descriptions of Gabčík and Kubiš had been collated from the first batch of witnesses who had immediately come forward. Other witnesses came forward in the days that followed, especially after the Germans had threatened repercussions for those who purposely withheld information. These descriptions were somewhat varied, both men being described as having black hair or being fair, and either tall and slim or short and stocky. After the war, several of the witnesses said they had given false descriptions to the *Gestapo*.

On the morning of 28 May, Frank flew to Hitler's HQ, where he provided an outline of the evidence, adding that it clearly suggested the perpetrators of the assassination attempt had been parachuted into the Protectorate from England; as a consequence, a tactic of selective terror against the Czechs would be more beneficial than mass reprisals. Frank argued that the arrest of 10,000 Czechs may serve some retribution, but it had the potential to disrupt industrial production, alienate Czechs currently friendly to the regime and suggest on a global scale that the outrage had the full support of the Czech people. Frank proposed it would be better if the Protectorate government mount a determined propaganda campaign against the exiles and their backers in London and Moscow. Frank added that if this did not work, then they could still use what Heydrich had called the whip approach and carry out arrests and executions. Hitler agreed with Frank's plan, but other future events would lead to the use of the whip, which would not go unnoticed around the world.

For now, Hitler and Frank agreed that 1,000 political prisoners would be executed and a reward of 10 million Koruna (1 million Reichsmarks) offered to the person who provided information leading to the arrest of the perpetrators.

It was most likely during this visit that Hitler told Frank that *SS-Oberst-Gruppenführer* and *Generaloberst der Polizei* Kurt Daluege would be appointed Temporary Acting *Reichsprotektor* until such time as Heydrich could resume his duties. Daluege was informed of his appointment on 28 May, and this was confirmed in writing the next day. There was a convenience associated with this appointment, as Daluege was already in Prague having received medical treatment for what has been reported as venereal disease. Daluege's appointment would have dismayed Frank, who found himself overlooked for the position of *Reichsprotektor* for a second time.

Daluege had not been Hitler's immediate choice. The previous day, with his rage still unabated, Hitler had told Himmler that if the Czechs had been unhappy with Heydrich, then he "would send them someone worse! Someone who would be prepared to wade through blood to get the job done.' The man Hitler had in mind was *SS-Obergruppenführer* Erich von dem Bach-Zelewski, a member of the SS who had made a name for himself working alongside the *Einsatzgruppen* SS death squads in the murder of a quarter of a million Jews from Riga and Belarus. In the end, Himmler successfully argued that Bach-Zelewski could not be spared from his role in the East, and Hitler's attention instead fell on Daluege as Heydrich's replacement.

9

Search and Search Again

The Germans reconstructed the assassination attempt several times on the morning of 28 May and took a number of photographs for their investigation, which would be used to support the *Gestapo* report. The items recovered were displayed in the Bata shop window and a huge reward had been offered to those who provided critical information leading to the apprehension of anyone responsible for the attack. The recovery of the items from the scene did lead to anxious moments; the distinctive bicycle had belonged to Marie Moravec, and the hat and raincoat had been borrowed from the flat of the Ogouns. When it was realised that these items might be traced back to them, copies of the cap and coat were made for the Ogouns, but as it turned out the *Gestapo* were not able to trace the owners.

Posters advertising the reward and giving details of the attack were displayed across Prague:

Attempt Upon the Acting Reichsprotektor's Life.

Ten million Koruna reward for all information leading to the arrest of the guilty men. At about 1030 on 27th May 1942, an attempt on the life of the Acting Reichsprotektor SS-Obergruppenführer Heydrich was committed. The Acting Reichsprotektor was travelling from Panenské Břežany by the Kirchmayer Boulevard and his car was turning to the right in V. Holesovickach Street, Prague-Libeň, in order to reach the centre of town. At this point a man stood in the roadway and endeavoured to open fire on the occupants of the car with a sub machine gun. At the same time another man threw a bomb that exploded on contact with the car. After the attack, one of the men ran away along the Kirchmayer Boulevard, Na Kolinske and Na Zapalci; there he entered František Brauner's butchers shop at number 22. He fired several shots from the shop and then continued his flight along Na Zapalci and V Holesovickach, probably towards the centre of town. The other man made off on a bicycle towards Stara Libeň.

The second man is of average height, slim and dressed in a dark brown or black suit and wore a black hat.

The other man, who fled by the way of the Kirchmayer Boulevard and Na Kolinske, answers to the following description: height 5 foot 3 inches to 5 foot

4 inches, broad shoulders, strongly built, round suntanned face, thick lips, dark brushed-back hair, age 30–35. This man was wearing a brown or dark-brown suit with light stripes and brown shoes. He was bareheaded.

One of the criminals left behind a pale beige waterproof silk coat with light buttons. Each man had a dark brown briefcase. These were left at the scene of the outrage. One of the briefcases contained a dirty beige velour beret with the label of the Bila Labut stores. The criminal who fled on foot left a woman's bicycle near the spot; it has the maker's label from Velo-Moto, J. Krčmář, Teplice-Šanov and a manufacturing number of 40363. One of the briefcases found at the scene of the crime was hung on the handlebars of this bicycle.

The criminals must certainly have been waiting for the Reichsprotektor at the scene of the outrage a considerable time, perhaps several hours.

With reference to the promised reward of ten million Koruna for information leading to the arrest of the guilty men, which will be paid in full, it may be pointed out that the following questions arise:

1. Who can give information on the criminals?
2. Who noticed their presence at the scene of the crime?
3. Who are the owners of the objects described, and above all, who has lost the woman's bicycle, the coat, the beret and the briefcases described above?

These items may be seen from 0900 today onwards in the window of the Bata shoe shop at 6 Wenceslas Square, Prague 2.

Anyone who is capable of providing any information and does not come forward voluntarily to the police will be shot together with his family, in accordance with the terms of the ordinance of 27th May 1942, on the proclamation of martial law.

All may be assured that their information will be treated as strictly confidential.

Furthermore, from May 28th 1942 onward, it is the duty of all owners of houses, apartments, hotels etc., to declare to the police the names of persons in the Protektorate whose name has not been registered at the police station. Disobedience of this regulation will be punishable by death.

Information may be given to the Staatspolizeileitstelle at their chief office in Prague at 20 Bredovska, Prague 2, telephone 20041, or at any German or Protektorate police station; and this information may be given verbally or by telephone.

A newsreel which included pictures of the Sten gun was also made and played at every cinema in the Protectorate. Gabčík saw this newsreel when he went to the Flora cinema on Orlická Street in Prague on 30 May, accompanied for cover by Libena and Rela Fafka, to see a film called 'Posvátná Dýka' (Sacred Dagger). This five-minute newsreel was made on the instructions of the Germans by the cameraman of the Czech weekly Aktualita, Ĉeněk Zahradniček, and was compulsorily shown (at least once a day) in all cinemas in the Protectorate.

On 31 May, the Germans issued updated descriptions of the two assassins. Kubiš was now described as: "Height 5 foot 6 inches to 5 foot 8 inches; age 30–35; slim figure. Face round, clean-shaven, full, high cheekbones, dark hair." Extra detail was added concerning the injuries he sustained in the blast: '[He] was bleeding and had a wound on the left cheek and the left ear or temple." The extra information provided on Gabčík confused descriptions, as he was now said to have, "A straight nose, thick lips, high cheek bones, dark brushed back hair."

The Germans also released more information on the briefcases found at the scene, which were described as follows: "One was made of good quality leather, measuring 16⅛ inches by 8¾ inches while the other was brown, worn and made of crocodile skin and measured 12¾ inches by 8½ inches. The side seams have been clumsily repaired with black thread; at the bottom right-hand corner a broad short tear has been sewn together with four even stitches."

Other measures taken made workers absent from their place of employment on the day of the assassination attempt have to account for their movements. The telephone line between Panenské Břežany and Prague was checked, and the Germans found a 'wire tap' had been placed on the line in an amateurish way, but it was not discovered how long it had been in place. The Germans also searched all hospitals in Prague for anyone who had been admitted with facial injuries requiring every doctor in the Protectorate to declare if they had treated anyone with a facial injury.

Indeed, fragments of shrapnel had entered Kubiš' eye, and Doctor Lyčka, who had first attended him, had said removal would require specialist help. Jan Zelenka asked Doctor Sobek – who volunteered at the Masaryk League Against Tuberculosis, which had been a bedrock of the underground in Prague – if he knew a doctor who could help. Sobek, in turn, approached Doctor Milada Franta-Reimová, an ophthalmologist, who removed the fragments of metal from Kubiš' eye. She was later amongst those arrested, and the German report on her claimed, "this doctor did not want to know whom she was treating, but on the other hand she ignored the press and radio announcements that required her to report such injuries. The husband of Doctor Franta-Reimová has been in a concentration camp for a year for being a member of an illegal organisation."

Jindra had given Jan Zelenka the task of finding a safe place for all the parachutists to hide. It was Petr Fafek, another employee at the Masaryk League Against Tuberculosis, who suggested that Zelenka use the crypt at the Church of St Cyril and Methodius. Fafek proposed approaching Jan Sonnevend, an executive at the Masaryk League Against Tuberculosis and Chairman of the Council of Church Elders at St Cyril and Methodius. It helped that all three men were close friends. Sonnevend agreed to ask the curate, Father Vladimir Petřek, if a group of patriots, parachute agents, could hide in the crypt until the Nazi lockdown of Prague had been lifted and the men could be taken to safe houses outside Prague. Father Petřek agreed to meet with Zelenka and outlined the resistance plan of support for the parachutists. Father Petřek said that the parachutists could be brought into the crypt if Bishop Gorazd also agreed. Later, Sonnevend and Father Petřek gave conflicting accounts to the *Gestapo*, Father Petřek saying the approach to hide the parachutists came on 28

May, whilst Sonnevend insisted it was decided to use the crypt on the day before the assassination attempt.

Father Petřek obtained the approval of Bishop Gorazd, and other church officials were sworn to secrecy before the church altar. Warm clothes and food were quickly brought into the church before Zelenka began the process of moving the parachutists into the church crypt, starting immediately on 28 May. The first to be taken in was Jaroslav Švarc (from Tin), then Jan Kubiš on the 29th, Josef Valčik, Jozef Bublik and Jan Hrubý (the latter two from Bioscope) on 30 May, and Adolf Opálka and finally Jozef Gabčík on 1 June.

There was still one parachutist missing: Karel Čurda could not be found. By all accounts Čurda had evaded the German searches and checkpoints and got himself out of Prague after the assassination attempt. He had fled to southern Bohemia and was hiding on his family's farm.

The church crypt ran virtually the entire length of the nave, and originally had two main points of entry/exit and a ventilation slit which opened out on Resslova Street above. One entry point was a staircase in front of the altar, but this had not been in use for some time and was covered by a large concrete slab. The other was at the opposite end of the nave, and was a small rectangular hole covered by a stone slab which could be lifted out to provide a tight entry point into the crypt by ladder. It was a dark, cold and depressing place to stay, but with limited options it offered the agents a secure location to hide.

On the evening of 2 June, the *Protektorate* Government called a public meeting in the Old Town Square to denounce the attempt on the life of the *Reichsprotektor* and proclaim the Czech nation's allegiance to the Third Reich. It is estimated that at least 70,000 Prague residents participated in the demonstration, no doubt the majority attending out of fear for themselves and their families rather than support for the Nazis.

Heydrich was still in the Bulovka under the supervision of *SS-Gruppenführer* Gebhardt and his deputy, Doctor Ludwig Stumpfegger, and the renowned German surgeon, Professor Ferdinand Sauerbruch. Sauerbruch had been Gebhardt's mentor when he was still a student. Gebhardt updated Himmler twice a day on Heydrich's condition.

Following the operation, Heydrich ran a high temperature but there was every expectation that he would make a full recovery. However, Heydrich was still under risk from infection caused by the foreign objects that had been carried into the wounds. Hitler's physician, Doctor Theodor Morell, a close friend of Professor Sauerbach, recommended sulphonamides to treat any infections, but this was rejected by Gebhardt. When Heydrich's temperature increased again on 2 June, together with the discharge of a large amount of fluids, a further operation was considered, but Gebhardt erred on the side of caution and this seemed to be vindicated when, by the morning of 3 June, Heydrich's fever broke and the fluid discharge had noticeably diminished. With satisfaction, Gebhardt informed Himmler that the patient was improving. However, it was a false dawn. Around midday, Heydrich suffered a severe relapse and went into a deep coma from which he would not recover. Heydrich died around 0430 on 4 June. His death was recorded in the hospital records as "348/1942 Reinhard Tristan Heydrich. Cause of death: Gunshot wound/murder attempt/ wound infection."

The post-mortem examination was carried out at 1200 on 4 June at the morgue in the Bulovka Hospital. Present were a number of eminent German medical physicians. The autopsy was conducted by Professor Herwig Hemperl (Department of Pathology) and Professor Günther Weyrich (Department of Forensic Medicine), from the Charles V University, and overseen by Gebhardt and Doctors Dick, Hohlbaum and Sauerbruch, who had been involved in the care of Heydrich.

The main findings of the autopsy were summarised in a short report on 4 June:

1. The surgical sutures were intact and there had been no post-operative bleeding.
2. There were small abscesses in the splenic bed, in the chest wall and diaphragmatic wounds and around the pleural drain, but there were no large collections of pus in the abdominal or thoracic cavities.
3. The pericardial sac contained 100 ml of sero-fibrinous fluid.
4. The coronary arteries and aorta were normal, except for a small atheromatous plaque.
5. The right ventricle, the pulmonary artery and its main branches were filled with fat particles and blood clots. The cardiac valves were intact.
6. The oesophagus contained foul smelling, regurgitated gastric content.
7. The lungs showed the most significant changes:
   a) The bronchi were filled with foamy mucus.
   b) The upper lobes of both lungs revealed severe pulmonary oedema whereas the lower lobes and the left lingual were markedly atalectatic.
   c) There was a right hydrothorax (170ml sero-fibrinous fluid).
   d) The anterior and lateral surfaces of the left lung were fused to the parietal pleura by thick, fibrinious adhesions. A pocket of 50 ml of cloudy, brownish fluid separated the left lung from the mediastinum. Another large pocket (650 ml) lay under the left lung, covering the costo-diaphragmatic recess.

A more comprehensive report was published on 17 June. This included the microscopic and bacteriological findings, and made the following statements:

1. Cloudy swelling of the hepatic, renal and myocardial cells.
2. The diaphragmatic wound, the left pleural cavity and the pericardial sac showed abundance of gram positive bacilli and cocci (mainly streptococci) and especially of proteus bacteriae.

In conclusion, the report stated that death had occurred as a result of septicaemia and shock caused by general infection:

Death occurred after damage to the internal organs (heart, liver and kidneys) as a result of poisoning probably caused by highly virulent micro-organisms. No large amount of pus was found in either the chest or stomach cavities. There were neither signs of pneumothorax nor any encysted secretions in the frontal mediastinal surface of the left lung. The largest secretion above the rear wall of the left lung was drained by using a Petzer catheter. There is no reason to suspect a chemical poisoning caused by the shrapnel.

The delivery of large quantities of morphine to the Bulovka, together with Gebhardt's refusal to use sulphonamides, the only form of antibiotic available to the Germans in 1942, led, certainly post-war, to rumours that Himmler instructed Gebhardt to intervene if Heydrich was likely to survive the operation.

The amounts of morphine delivered to the Bulovka have never been quantified, but it would not be unusual for an active 38-year-old carrying a large frame (Heydrich stood 6ft 3in tall and weighed nearly 15 stone), suffering from painful chest and abdominal wounds, to require large doses of pain relief.

Another theory is that the grenade used in the attack contained a chemical weapon, which caused Heydrich's infection. If this had been the case, then Kubiš, who was wounded by the same grenade splinters, would also have suffered complications from chemical poisoning. However, conspiracy theories are unlikely: Heydrich died due to infection caused by the fragments that entered his body as a result of the grenade explosion.

10

The Funeral and the Hunt for a Young Girl

Shortly after Heydrich breathed his last in Prague on 4 June, the news reached Hitler. He erupted again with furious rage, this time targeting what he saw as Heydrich's stupidity:

> Since it is the opportunity which makes not only the thief but also the assassin, such heroic gestures as driving in an open, unarmoured vehicle or walking about the streets unguarded are just damned stupidity, which serves the country not one whit. That a man as irreplaceable as Heydrich should expose himself to unnecessary danger, I can only condemn as stupid and idiotic. Men of importance like Heydrich should know that they are being eternally stalked like game, and that there are any number of people just waiting for the chance to kill them.

Himmler was also critical: "If, as was the case with Heydrich, you are in the habit of leaving your homes every day, at a particular time and taking a particular route, then you are a sitting target for the lunatic who is lying in wait for you." The Nazi propaganda chief, Josef Goebbels, meanwhile lamented the loss of a committed National Socialist, recording in his diary for 4 June 1942: "The loss of Heydrich is irreplaceable. He was the most radical and successful one in the fight against the enemies of the State."

In public, Heydrich was acclaimed to the German people as the "greatest martyr" since Horst Wessel, the SA leader in Berlin who had been shot by two members of the German Communist Party in 1930. One of Wessel's assassins, Albrecht Höhler, was arrested and charged with his murder. Höhler was initially sentenced to six years in prison, but after the Nazis came to power he was forcibly taken out of jail and killed by the SA. Wessel's funeral was given wide attention in Berlin, with many of the Nazi elite in attendance. After his death, he became a major symbol of Nazi martyrdom and his death was exploited for propaganda purposes. In 1929, Wessel had written the lyrics to a march, which after his murder was renamed the 'Horst Wessel Lied'. It became the official anthem of the Nazi Party, and in 1933 the Nazis raised the status of the song to the co-national anthem of Germany, alongside 'Deutschland über alles'.

Arrangements for Heydrich's laying in state and the return of his body to Berlin started immediately. Heydrich's body remained at the Bulovka until the night of 5 June, when the Germans staged an elaborate midnight procession to move it to Hradčany Castle. It was the most elaborate event seen in the *Protektorate*. The Germans had the streets cleared of the Czechs, and members of the German security services were lined up outside the hospital building as Heydrich's coffin was brought out. The only light came from flaming torches in what was described as the recreation of a "medieval spectacle".

The route from the hospital to Heydrich's laying in state on the forecourt of Hradčany Castle was lined by German troops, and his body was borne on a gun carriage as befitted a military ceremony. It was just after midnight that the procession left the hospital, and it took just over an hour to reach the castle. German cameramen filmed the spectacle so that the Nazis could milk Heydrich's death for their propaganda purposes. They would present the death of Heydrich as heroic, having succumbed to wounds sustained in combat at the hands of cowardly, puppet agents from London.

His body lay in state at Hradčany Castle for two days, with an honour guard present. It was estimated that around 200,000 Czechs filed past his coffin and gave the Nazi statute, fearing what retribution may come their way. On 7 June, in the grounds of the castle and in the presence of Himmler and Hácha's puppet government, the new Acting *Reichsprotektor*, Daluege, delivered a speech in which he said: "We swear to fulfil the political legacy of our dear friend. Nothing is preventing us, faithful to the Führer's order, to finish the work of Reinhard Heydrich in Bohemia and Moravia for the good of the Reich and her great tasks." He added glowing words about Heydrich being a friend of the Czechs and a noble example of the Aryan race, whose name would be carved in their roll of honour. The senior Nazis present would have known the irony in these words, there being a deep, long-standing hatred and contempt between Heydrich and Daluege. Heydrich's coffin was then again placed on a gun carriage and, in another great show of Nazi pomp, escorted to the main railway station in Prague. Here the coffin was taken into the station, overseen by *SS-Brigadeführer* Bruno Streckenbach and *SS-Gruppenführer* Arthur Nebe. The band of the *Waffen-SS Deutschland* regiment played funeral music as the train slowly made its way out of Prague station on its way to Berlin.

When Heydrich's coffin arrived at the Anhalter railway station in Berlin, the cortege was met with similar ceremony, and this continued as it went on its way to lie in state at the *Gestapo* headquarters in Prinz Albert Strasse. The coffin was continuously flanked by an honour guard.

The night Heydrich's body had been moved from the Bulovka to the castle, the criminal investigation continued with further house searches. *Hauptsturmführer* Böhme, head of the security police for the *Protektorate*, sent the following summary report to Daluege and Frank:

The Higher SS and Police Leader of the Reichsprotektor in Bohemia and Moravia Prague, 5th June 1942

B. No. B. d. S. – I – 310/42 g –

Please quote this reference in your reply!

Copy for the Higher SS and Police Leader at the Reich Protector in Bohemia and Moravia SS-Gruppenführer K.H. Frank Prague.

To SS-Oberstergruppenführer Daluege the Higher SS and Police Leader of the Reichsprotektor in Bohemia and Moravia SS-Gruppenführer K.H. Frank Prague.

Morning report.

The search operations on the night of 4th to 5th June 1942 were not carried out at the same extent as previously, due to the fact that a large number of the German police and security people were required for other security tasks in Prague. Nevertheless the following were available and used:

5,213 German police, Wehrmacht, work service, technical emergency aid and other Nazi organisations.

6,403 Protektorate gendarmerie and police.

4,549 forestry personnel, fire department, air raid personnel etc.

They arrested 57 people during last night's searches for reasons of unauthorised possession of firearms, non-registration, anti-state operations, inadequate identity cards, illegal border crossing, escape from prisoner of war camp, vagrancy, etc. Items confiscated were eight firearms, miscellaneous food and beverages, one radio, cigarettes and tobacco.

At midnight, the late SS-Obergruppenführer Heydrich was transferred in solemn procession from the hospital to Prague Castle. President Hácha sent a telegram to the Führer in which he wrote that he and the Government expressed their deepest sadness and unshakable loyalty to the Führer and Reich. The mood of the German population is of increasing bitterness and increasingly strong desire for the sharpest retaliatory measures – the crushing impression on the Czechs continues – compassion is only to be found in the working class.

The enemy radio, which continues to broadcast about the death of the Obergruppenführer accompanied by spiteful descriptions of his person, tries to give the impression that the assassination is the beginning of an uprising by the Czech People and that it is now up to the other oppressed peoples, by starting a second front and breaking the Nazi terror and having the freedom to fight. One of their statements is: 'The European people are the judge and the Czech People the Executioners.' The Gestapo are currently investigating 404 suspects of which 178 come from the Czech population and 62 have already been processed. Although occasionally a connection with the assassination can be found there are no reliable leads yet. Only the escape route of one of the culprits (by bicycle) can be determined for a distance of about 1,700 meters and this has been possible by the use of eye witnesses. Enclosed I attach a copy of a telex to the State Police Headquarters in Prague which possibly contains an important lead. I also enclose a copy of the new evidence regarding the escape route of the one of the culprits.

Signed Böhme

Hauptsturmführer

What this important lead might have been is not known, but the reality was the criminal investigation had made very little progress and now, a week since the attack, the Germans were no closer to identifying or apprehending the assassins. Intense pressure was felt by those involved in the criminal investigation to make some form of progress and, in turn, the Czechs remained fearful of what fury the Germans may inflict upon them.

A German report written the previous day, 4 June, stated: "The basis of the Czech mood was an unpleasant anxiety about pending events which were the subject of numerous rumours. These chiefly dealt with a future wave of executions based on decimation, the execution of Czechs in detention and finally the dissolution of the Protektorate."

In a futile attempt to placate the Nazis, Hácha and his senior ministers travelled in the same train cortege to Berlin as Heydrich's body and attended his state funeral, which was held in Berlin on 9 June. It was a lavish ceremony, held in the Mosaic Hall in the Reich Chancellery, and was arguably the most high-profile funeral held in Germany during the period of the Third Reich. Himmler delivered the eulogy, followed by a short speech by Hitler. In an abject showing of almost paternal responsibility, Heydrich's two young sons were sat either side of Himmler throughout, Lena being unable to attend as she was expecting her fourth child at any moment.

Himmler opened the funeral, addressing the guests thus:

My leader!

Dear Heydrich Family!

Honoured mourning guests!

With the death of SS-Obergruppenführer Reinhard Heydrich, the Deputy Reich Protector of Bohemia and Moravia, Chief of the Sicherheitsdienst and Security Police, the National Socialist Movement has made a tragic sacrifice to the fight for freedom of our people. How incomprehensible to us is the thought that this shining, great human, scarcely 38 years old, is no longer with us and unable to battle along with his comrades. His unique abilities and pure character, his mind, his logic and clarity, are irreplaceable. We would not be abiding by his wishes were we not here with his coffin, heroic thoughts of living and dying investing us, as they once did him.

Our people confronted the death of our dearest. In this spirit we devote our ceremony to honouring him, recounting his life, his deeds, and then returning his mortal remains to the earth. We will fight as he fought during his life and seek to fulfil his role. Reinhard Heydrich was born on 7th March 1904 in Halle on the Saale. He attended elementary school and a Reform School for his secondary level of education. During his school years, in 1918 after the great break up of our people, the 16-year-old student demonstrated his ardent love for Germany by volunteering for the volunteer corps 'Maercker' and 'Freikorps', which were active in the red regions of mid-Germany. In 1922, when soldiering was despised, he enlisted in the navy. He was a Leutnant-zur-See in 1926 and a Oberleutnant-zur-See in 1928. He served as a radio and communications officer and broadened his horizons with foreign duty and travel.

In 1931 he left the navy. Through one of his friends, Eberstein, I met him and inducted him into the Schutzstaffel in July. Heydrich, who had been a lieutenant, became a simple SS man on the small staff of Hamburg together with other noble, mostly unemployed, young men, who found there a true calling. Their duty was with the party and they were involved with propaganda in the predominantly red quarters of the city. Soon after, I brought Heydrich with me to Munich and gave him new duties with the leadership of the SS. During the politically difficult times during the autumn of 1932; he served loyally and steadfastly, despite the many demands upon him. After we came to power, I became Munich police chief on 12th March 1933. I immediately gave Heydrich the so-called political division of the presidium. In no time, he re-organised the division, and in a few weeks transformed it into the Bavarian Political Police.

Soon the division became a model for political police departments in non-Prussian German territory. On 20th April 1934, the Prussian Minister President, our Reichsmarschall Hermann Goering, appointed me to lead the State Police of Prussia and appointed SS-Brigadeführer Heydrich as my deputy. In 1936, the leaders appointed 32-year-old Heydrich, chief of the newly created security police. Besides the secret police, he was responsible for all of the criminal police. The years 1933, 34, 35, 36 were filled with work and innumerable start-up problems. We had to deal with expelling immigrants and traitors. These difficult, painful duties fell to Heydrich's Security Police and the Sicherheitsdienst, which had to earn the respect of the states and the entire empire. By the beginning of 1938, the security police were a strong organisation that could carry out all tasks. Heydrich rendered a great, though unobtrusive, service during the bloodless march into Austria, the Sudetenland and Bohemia-Moravia, as well as the liberation of Slovakia, by arresting opponents and keeping a watchful eye on enemies in various places.

I remind myself to mention here, publicly, the thoughts of this man, who was feared, hated and denounced by sub-humans: such as Jews and miscellaneous criminals. Even many Germans did not understand him. In all measures and actions, he wore the deeds of a National Socialist.

From the depths of his heart and blood he made the world-view of Adolf Hitler a reality. Heydrich solved all problems from a racial point of view. His ultimate goal was the maintenance, protection, and preservation of our blood. To carry out his difficult task, he had to build and lead an organisation, which dealt with evil, criminal, anti-social elements in our society. There was little joy in this work. Heydrich's view was only the best of our people, the racially pure of exceptional character, were viable to battle the elements with negative social sufficient hardness.

He himself was incorruptible. Flat characters and toadies elicited only scorn from him. But truthful, upstanding people, even if guilty, could rely on his knightly nobility and human understanding. Yet he never let anything happen that could damage the whole nation or the future of our blood. One should not forget his truly revolutionary creativity in the criminal police. He approached the question of criminality with a healthy, sober, human understanding. But at the same time, he tried to make the German criminal police a modern and scientific force. As chief of the International Criminal Police Commission he gave to the policemen of the world his wisdom, his experience, and his comradeship. After 1936, when his service began, there was a continuous decrease in crime. Despite three years of war, crime incidence has now reached its lowest level ever. People in Germany can walk down the streets in peace, unmolested, even in the hardest times, in contrast to the 'splendid, humane, democratic countries'. Germans can thank Reinhard Heydrich from the bottom of their hearts for this security.

Both criminal and political miscreants have been severely handled and our security police will continue to do that. Yet after innumerable conversations with Heydrich, I learned that this man, who was externally hard and strict, suffered deeply on account of his duty. When the life of the nation was in question; he was one of the best teachers of National Socialist morals and educated the SS leadership corps of the security service and led it with unimpeachable purity. To the men he commanded, he devoted love and attention, even in the most difficult matters, and showed himself to be a born and bred gentleman. He was a shining example in his willingness to accept responsibility and was a model of modesty. He let his work speak for itself and never boasted his achievements. Many people were surprised he did. He took an interest in all intellectual endeavours of the security service, no matter what their nature. There was not a trace in him of the fusty old policeman. He worked out the scientific basis for everything and applied his findings to everyday questions.

The war arrived with its many tasks in the newly occupied areas, in Poland, Norway, the Netherlands, Belgium, France, Yugoslavia, Greece, and above all, Russia. It was difficult for him, this fighter and doer, not to be right at the front. Besides his tireless devotion to assigned tasks, which he accomplished day and night as one of the most diligent in the kingdom, he spent the early mornings of weeks and months gradually obtaining certification as a pilot and passing his examination as a combat flier. In 1940 he flew combat missions in the Netherlands and Norway. He was awarded the bronze flying medal and the Iron Cross second class. But he was not satisfied. In 1941, at the beginning of the Russian campaign, he flew combat missions, without my knowledge, and I can confirm this fact with joyous pride and certainty. It was the one secret he kept from me in the eleven years we worked together. He was a fighter pilot in a German squadron in southern Russia, and won the Front Flying Clasp in silver and the Iron Cross first class. At this time, destiny reached out to him. Russian flak downed his plane, but luckily he landed between the two lines and dragged himself to the German side, only to go up again the next morning in another plane. I always held to the view that Heydrich did more important work here than as a far off front soldier, even though I understood his need to do what he did.

He was abiding by the law: "do not save your own blood", and proved himself in combat, even though his duty as security police chief was in fact much more dangerous. In September of that year came his greatest task, and, as we now know, his final task. The leader made him Deputy Reichsprotektor of Bohemia and Moravia when Reichsprotektor Neurath became ill. Many Germans and Czechs thought; here comes the fearsome Heydrich, who will rule with blood and terror. But during the following months, he showed the world his positive qualities and applied his creative genius abilities in the fullest measure. He was firm, pursued the guilty, and had enormous respect for German power and law. Yet he gave those who were willing, the opportunity to work with him. There was not a problem in the many-faceted life of Bohemia and Moravia that this young deputy Reich Protector did not solve with aplomb, guided by his understanding of our laws and our Empire.

On 27th May an English bomb hit him from behind. A person paid from the ranks of the most worthless sub-humans had brought him down. Fear and excessive caution were foreign to him, the greatest sportsman of the SS, a bold fencer, rider, pentathlon champion, and swimmer. With courage and energy he defended himself and shot twice at his attackers, though he had been gravely wounded. For days we hoped that his hereditary strength and disciplined, healthy body would overcome his horrible injury. On the seventh day, 4th June 1942, destiny, God the almighty ancient, ended the life of Heydrich, a deep believer but the greatest opponent of the use of religion for political purposes. All of us, including the kingdom's foremost leader, that he served so loyally, are now gathered to honour Heydrich. He was at the time of his death a paragon of happy family life, and his two young sons are here to represent his courageous wife, who is expecting another child. Our leader is awarding Heydrich the gold wound badge, and named, on the day of his death, a Waffen-SS unit on the eastern front, the 6th SS Infantry, 'Reinhard Heydrich'. Heydrich wants to live on in our holy convictions, which were his words. He honoured and advanced the cause of those who shared his blood.

He wants to endure on account of his talents. He was a musical person and a warrior bold, happy and earnest, to unvanquished spirit, a character of unblemished purity, noble, upstanding and unsullied. He has transmitted wonderful virtues to his sons, who honour his blood and heritage. His wife and children deserve our attention and loving care. The SS will look after them well. He wants the SS to live on in our society. His memory will aid us when we have tasks to carry out for the leader and the Reich. He wants to fight along with us, if we remain true to the law until the end. He wants to be our companion in good times and bad. Therefore, he will be present when we are celebrating with our comrades. For the security police and security service he created and founded, he wants to be a model that will never be forgotten, a goal we can aspire to, but never reach. He wants to bear witness for all Germans as a martyr to Bohemia and Moravia, which always will be German lands, as they have been since time immemorial. There, in the world beyond, he will abide among the great battalions of dead SS men. He wants to be with his old comrades: Weitzel, Moder, Herrmann, Mülverstedt, Stahlecker, and many others who in spirit are quietly fighting with us. But it is our holy duty to atone for his death, to take up his tasks, and to pitilessly destroy, without any sign of weakness, the enemies of our people. I have one last thing to say: You, Reinhard Heydrich, SS, were truly a good man. On a more personal level, I thank you for your unwavering loyalty and wonderful friendship, which united us in this life and death cannot obliterate it!

Hitler followed with a short conclusion to this part of the proceedings:

I have only a few words. He was one of the best National Socialists, one of the strongest defenders of the German Reich idea, one of the biggest enemies to all the enemies of the Reich. He is a martyr. He died for the preservation and protection of the Reich. As leader of the party and as a leader of the German Reich, I award you, my dear comrade Heydrich, the highest award that I give you: the Supreme Grade of the German Order.

Heydrich's body was then transported to the *Invalideenfriedhof* in Berlin and lowered into the ground with full military honours.

Some commentators said that Hitler was so overcome with grief that he was unable to say more than a few words at the funeral, but gave full recognition to Heydrich's importance to the Nazi cause by awarding him the highest Nazi award, that of the German Order. This was awarded to an individual for 'duties of the highest order to the state and party'. The first time that it was awarded was in February 1942, when it was bestowed posthumously to Fritz Todt, who had founded the Organisation Todt, which provided the labour force that built the *autobahns* and amongst their many tasks eventually oversaw the building of the concentration camps. Todt had died in an aircraft crash in early 1942 and was replaced in his post by Albert Speer. The German Order was also known as 'the dead hero order', as only two of the 11 individuals to receive it survived the war. Hitler viewed this award as his personal decoration, to be granted to those whose services to the state and party he personally deemed worthy.

If Hitler was overcome with grief, then he had recovered his composure by the time he summoned Hácha and his ministers for the severest of lectures. A humbled Hácha attempted to mollify Hitler by saying that he and all the Czech people condemned the British role in the assassination. This sent Hitler into a further rage, ranting that the assassins must now be receiving shelter from the Czechs. Hitler gave Hácha an ultimation: he would not tolerate any more trouble in the Protectorate, and if the Czechs did not hand over those responsible for Heydrich's death then he would deport the entire population for resettlement.

Hácha then had an opportunity of a meeting with the State Secretary, Otto Meissner, at which Hitler was not present. Hácha wanted to understand if Hitler really wanted to destroy the Protectorate. Meissner gave his opinion that Hitler was clear in what needed to be done, and with regard to the deportation of the Czechs he told Hácha these were Hitler's last words on the subject. It was not a threat Hácha could choose to ignore, but the reality may have been different. For example, the Skoda Works, an important part of the Nazi war machine, needed experienced and enthused workers to continue maximum output.

However, the Germans were determined that the assassination would not go unpunished, and as an initial reprisal a number of Jews from Prague were sent for resettlement to the East. Other more savage reprisals would follow.

11

The Missing Bicycle

One aspect of the criminal investigation where the Germans did obtain information was the escape route of Jan Kubiš from the scene of the assassination towards Libeň. Injured by shrapnel from the grenade explosion, his face was covered in blood, as were his hands from wiping the blood from his eyes. Numerous witnesses came forward who had seen him during his escape, and more importantly, several witnesses reported a man covered in blood leaving his bicycle by the Bata shop in Libeň.

The following is from a *Gestapo* report:

> Prague, 5th June 1942 copy of the telex – FS 1491 from the State Police Headquarters Prague 18 561.
> A) To the RSHA IV A 2-
> B) To the RSHA V Berlin.
> To the Bef. D. Sipo u. d. SD in Prague.
> Urgent.

> During the course of the investigation, new leads were identified for one of the perpetrators who fled the scene by bicycle. His escape route has been determined for a distance of approximately 1,700 metres. In order to obtain further witnesses, a large scale appeal for witnesses by posters was made on the night of the 4th to the 5th of June 1942; efforts were directed exclusively in the district of Libeň.

> One of the assassins fled the scene on a bicycle towards Kirchmayerstrasse-Alt-Libeň. Several witnesses state that he left his bicycle by the Bata shop at the corner of Primatorenstrasse and Slavatastrasse. He then continued on his way on foot. He walked very fast on the left hand side of the Primatorenstrasse in the direction of the railway station at Libeň. The assassin had a bright handkerchief in his left hand during the entire journey on the bicycle and on his walk through the Primatorenstrasse pressed this on his left cheek. A short distance away, he changed the handkerchief to his right hand and hid the right side of his face covering the cheek, eye, nose and mouth. He did this to cover up his facial injuries, which were nevertheless seen by several witnesses. The injury was described that it looked like big drops of bloody sweat on his left cheek. This injury is

either due to rupture of the skin caused by a blast wave or the effect of splinters from the grenade. The following description is given of this man: About 35 years old, about 1.70 to about 1.75 meters tall, slender, round, mediocre face. Dark brown complexion, giving the impression of a southern type. Dark brown suit, which was shabby and worn and a bit too big in the fit. Dark brown soft hat. The behaviour of this man was very striking and unusual, and he was observed by many witnesses. The bicycle he parked at the Bata shop in the Slavatastrasse has a black frame with green stripes. This green stripe was also present in the middle of the wheels (rim). On the mudguard, where the company sign is attached, there are oblique light lines. The handlebars are straight and bent upwards, with bright handles. There was also a handbrake on the wheel.

About 10 minutes after the assassin had left the bicycle at the Bata shop a girl came and collected the bicycle, she came from the direction of the Ludmilastrasse via the Slavatastrasse. The girl rode the bicycle back the same way she had come back through the Slavatastrasse in the direction of Ludmilastrasse. Witnesses gave the following description of the girl; about 14–15 years old. Fresh healthy look and pretty full face. She had dark hair that reached down to her neck. She wore a summer dress. The posters asked: Who has seen these incidents? Who knows the owner of the bicycle? Who knows the girl? Information can be given to any police officer. It should be noted that the reward was increased to 20,000,000 Koruna.

signed Dr. med. Geschke
Standartenführer and Government Director
Gestapo HQ Prague

It is clear that at least four local women either saw the bicycle being left or collected by a young girl. These women were Cecilie Adamová, Žofie Čermáková, Anna Chladová and Františka Sedláková. All of them gave statements to the *Gestapo*. From the information that these women provided, it was clear that the bicycle had been collected shortly after it had been left, therefore, this girl could not live too far away. The Germans thought this may be the important breakthrough that they needed and lead them to the assassins. A major search was decided upon and the area of Libeň was sealed off, with vigorous house-to-house searches undertaken.

Another witness, Václav Třešňák, gave a description of the incident to the *Gestapo*: "On Wednesday 27th May 1942, I drove round from Prague towards Roztok. I was driving along when I saw a girl about 17 years old. She was wheeling a blue men's bicycle and at a great speed. The girl was dressed in a light, wide-cut skirt, and a men's light gray striped jacket. She had short socks. She had curly blond hair."

The following has been extracted from a German report written later in June 1942, when the names of Gabčik and Kubiš were known:

Kubiš parked his men's bicycle in the Slavata-Gasse – corner Primatorenstrasse by the Bata shoe shop and then had walked along the Primatorenstrasse to the apartment of Wenzel Novák in Stranskygasse 3, who had been an active helper in the organisation and had been recruited by Zelenka in January 1942. After he arrived at the apartment and spoke with Mrs Novák and her daughter Jindřiška, he asked Mrs Novák if she could collect the bicycle immediately from the Bata shop, but not to return along Primatorenstrasse as a precautionary measure. Mrs Novák immediately sent her daughter, Jindřiška, there and told her which detour to take. The assassin Kubiš asked the girl what she would say when she spoke to someone, to which she replied that she would say she has come to collect her father's bicycle. The girl came from a side street to where the bicycle was parked, so it appeared that it gave the impression that she came from a different direction than the one in which her apartment was actually located. The appearance of a girl was noticed by witnesses who had already seen a bleeding cyclist and were discussing this on the street corner. One witness, Sedláková, believed that the bicycle was being stolen by the girl and questioned her, whereupon the girl stated that it was her father's bicycle. This woman asked what had happened to her father. She replied; "I do not know yet."

Since the girl appeared barely more than 10 minutes after the bicycle was parked by the assassin at the Bata shop and she said that she had been told of her father's injury and had been sent by him, she could not live too far [away]. This gave an idea of the area to search for this particular girl. The round trip from where the bicycle had been left to the apartment had not been more than 15 minutes, so there were a limited number of blocks of apartments where this girl lived, unless it was an attempt to deceive the investigation. This area was the starting point for a major search which began on 3rd June 1942, and did include the correct apartment. However, this was not successful, because the search concentrated on arresting girls and 250 were arrested which included the girl involved, Jindřiška Novák, but she was not recognised by the witness. The assassin Kubiš, was given a shirt by Mrs Novák, which belonged to her son as the original one had burn marks. The eye injury suffered by Kubiš caused blood to flow from the corner of his right eye and it seemed that damage had been caused to his eyeball or under the eyelid. After the girl had returned with the bicycle and left it in a yard, Kubiš left the apartment and had been given directions to Veitsberg. He went straight to the residence of the family Piskáček, Prague-Vissochan.

As this German report stated, Jindřiška Novák was not recognised by the witnesses. Post-war interviews were carried out with residents of Libeň, who gave statements on this period. František Rotta-Sklenář, director of the girls' school in U zámku in Prague, said:

In the week following the assassination attempt, life in our school was completely normal. But on Wednesday, 3rd June, we could not get into Libeň to get to the school. The Libeň Bridge was closed by the police, and in Palmovka the access to Libeň was closed. Also trying to get to Libeň through Kobylis was not successful. Simply Libeň, or at least the lower part, i.e. the area of our school, was closed by the German Army and no one was allowed to go out either. Occasionally, there was the sound of gunfire. What was going on? We did not get the explanation until the following day. Some woman told the Gestapo that at the time of the attack she saw a cyclist holding a handkerchief to his injured face and she saw him leave a bicycle outside the Bata shop and walked away on foot. About 15 minutes later a girl came; aged about 14 to 15 years old, strong features and she took the bicycle and headed off towards Lidmilině. After this statement, the German Police and Army occupied Lower Libeň on 3rd June and undertook a further rigorous inspection of all apartments. All the girls who were 14 or 15 years old were picked up by the Police and taken to the Petschek Palace. Several hundred girls were taken and a number of pupils from our school were among them. At Petschek Palace, the individual girls were brought to a hall where everyone had to wheel a bicycle. At the same time, the Gestapo watched, probably with the witnesses, through a hidden mirror to see if the girl from a week ago could be identified. The whole search, however, remained unsuccessful. They did not find the girl they were looking for. Then new searches and sweeps began. Men from the Gestapo, once again visited the families of suspected girls, asking where the girl was during the critical time, that is, at 1035–1040 on 27th May, our school was also visited as well. On Friday, 5th June, I had the pleasure to meet the Gestapo for the first time – three came to the school. They specifically asked me if, say, a pupil called Horakova was at school on 27th May. I replied that I did not know, but it could be checked. The class teacher was called and the records checked. We had a scheme where pupils were released for half a day to do work and so we had to check all the records. Questions were asked – when did she leave school and so on.

We kept records of all those who left school early and the Gestapo examined these closely and after about an hour they left but they kept a note of my name and address, but in my mind I felt, "I do not want to see you again." But we soon saw each other again. The next day they came again. The procedure from the previous day was repeated with small changes. They wrote down everything again, listened to everything and left with a friendly "Auf Wiedersehen". I already knew that this is not the last visit.

On 3rd June, the Gestapo arrested Jindřiška amongst hundreds of other girls. They took them all to the Petschek Palace and as you might imagine she was very nervous. It is said she was so nervous she could hardly walk but inside the Palace she hid in an alcove under some stairs, while the other girls were interrogated and made to wheel a bicycle around. As none of the witnesses identified anyone the girls were allowed to go home and Jindřiška joined them and her friends had to support her.

Another witness was Marie Kohoutová, who was 18 years old in 1942:

The Germans who were in our apartment ordered me to wait down the hall. I could not leave the house, the door was guarded. Then they took me to the

Bata shop and there were many girls here, some were even two to three years older than me. Then we were taken by truck to the Petschek Palace – we asked each other where and why they are taking us, but nobody knew anything. We said, "We have not done anything, what can they do to us?" We were not too scared. Upon arrival at the Palace, we were ordered out and they led us through the main entrance. They took us, if I remember correctly, to the first floor into a big hall. I remember there were square apertures in the wall above our faces. There were a row of benches in front of the wall. We had to walk around and we thought we were being spied on from the holes but we could not see them. One of the Germans selected a girl, who then had to walk around in a circle wheeling a bicycle. I cannot remember today whether the girls who were chosen to wheel the bicycle were separated or not after having walked around in a circle. Eventually, the Germans gave us the money for the tram and sent us home.

Eva Miksová, who was almost 13 years old in June 1942, also made a statement:

We could hear much noise outside – shouting and screaming and so we all looked out [of] the window. On the street and on the roofs, the Germans were in uniform, with helmets and rifles. They screamed at us to shut the windows, otherwise they would shoot. The Germans entered the houses and walked from apartment to apartment, banging loudly on all the doors. A German soldier in uniform and a man in civilian [clothing] who spoke Czech came to our apart-ment. I do not know if he was Czech. The German in uniform armed with a rifle went through the apartment. He did not say anything, only the civilian talked to us. When he saw me, he told my mother that I should put on some clothes and I was to go back with them and then come home later. But he did not say where I was going. Mother was not very well and anxious but he calmed her with the words; "Do not be afraid! Nothing will happen to her." But I am not sure she believed this. I dressed and walked down the street leading to the Libeň Bridge (Po Hrázi Street). The soldier still had his rifle outstretched. The streets were empty; no one was in the street. He led me to the Bata shop, where other detained girls had been assembled.

The whole Libeň area had been saturated by the Germans and it seemed like not even a mouse could escape. I think we were waiting for two or three hours before the green military trucks covered with a tarpaulin came in, there were benches inside, the Germans with their rifles and helmets guarding us. They drove us into them and we drove off but they did not tell us where.

Eventually we arrived at the Petschek Palace and the whole street was full of armed Germans and we were led through the main entrance. First they took us to a large room, which looked like a classroom. There were benches and perhaps a blackboard. There was a soldier in uniform here and we were no longer allowed to talk to each other. There we waited a number of hours, maybe two, but it was terribly long. There was only a small group of about 30 to 40 girls. Where the others were put, I do not know. Then a uniformed German came for us and we were led to the cellar. This was scary, dark, without furniture, perhaps just a table behind which was a uniformed German. There was a small window in the wall. They ordered us to walk in a circle around the room, I do not remember how many times we went round and then someone was told to wheel a bicycle. Eventually it was my turn and I think I only did one circuit. The Germans gave the orders as to who was to walk with the bicycle but a Czech person gave us the command in Czech. The behaviour of the Germans was fairly good but even so we were all afraid, we did not know what was going on.

From the cellar room they took us back to the classroom. Everything was done in silence and we had to sit and be quiet. After about an hour of waiting, they gave us money for a tram ticket and sent us home. From the group I was in, all the girls were released. But I have heard that in other groups of girls who were there before or after us, some girls had to go through the process several times. Allegedly, some of the girls were detained. When I came home, it was a warm welcome! My mother did not know where they were going to take me that morning and what they were going to do with me and the other girls. So you can imagine what my mother and the parents of other children had been experiencing. The next day we all got together at school. I did not hear [of] any of my classmates being arrested. However, during the night raid in Prague 8, the Germans arrested many people who did not have their documents in order or were not registered. I cannot imagine, according to what I saw in the Petschek Palace, how the Germans were watching us; that Jindřiška, without any help, avoided walking around. The Germans guarded us well. I do not know how Jindřiška could do it. Perhaps she managed to somehow hide before she went to the cellar. I remember her as a girl of pale skin, black hair and about 13 years old.

The Nováks would have known that Jindřiška, who was of a recognisable stature, may come under enhanced investigation, and so even before the searches commenced, she had her hair, which had been worn long on 27 May, cut short in an attempt to disguise her appearance. It is possible that the female witnesses who were asked to observe the girls in the basement of the Petschek Palace had been having second thoughts and decided not to positively identify Jindřiška. It must be considered unlikely that Jindřiška hid or in some way evaded the process after she had arrived at the Petschek Palace.

The German investigation had been thwarted at a time when they believed they had a definite lead that would take them to the perpetrators of what they saw as a criminal act. They would soon carry out a criminal act of their own in return.

12

Only Corn will be Growing

In 1942 Lidice, situated near Kladno and about 15 miles from Prague, was a relatively sleepy village of around 400 inhabitants, with the majority working in mining or agriculture. This village had come to the attention of the Germans prior to Anthropoid. Corporal Pavelka from Operation Percentage had been captured in October 1941, when he was found to be carrying the addresses of two families who lived in the village. These were the Horák and Stríbrný families, both of whom had sons serving in the RAF in Britain. It is possible that Pavelka had messages from England for these two families, or that the Czech forces in the UK had believed these families would offer help to parachutists given that they had sons serving in the Allied forces. The area around Lidice had also been close to the DZ for members of the Operation Bivouac group, who had landed and then stayed nearby in early May 1942. The village had been searched soon after the assassination attempt, but nothing was found and village life continued unhindered. However, all this was about to change.

Following Heydrich's funeral in Berlin, Karl Hermann Frank reported back to the Prague *Gestapo* that Hitler wanted an act of revenge carried out for the death of Heydrich. Any village found to have harboured Heydrich's killers was to suffer the ultimate fate: the execution of all the adult men, the transportation of the women to a concentration camp and the separation of the children, with those with Aryan racial features to be resettled 'for Germanisation', placed with German families in the Reich and brought up as German. Children who did not meet the racial requirements would be murdered. Finally, the village was to be burnt and levelled.

Then fate, or an act of stupidity, took centre stage. A married man, Vaclav Říha, aged 23, wanted to extricate himself from an affair with his 19-year-old girlfriend, Anna Maruščáková. Říha decided to use the cover of the assassination attempt to write to Anna, saying that he could no longer see her and vaguely suggesting he had been involved in a recent act of resistance. This letter was sent to her workplace, but the day it arrived, Anna was off sick and her employer; Jaroslav Pála, a Nazi sympathiser, opened it. Immediately linking it to the attempt on Heydrich's life, he advised the local constabulary, who in turn informed the Kladno *Gestapo* office. Both Říha and Maruščáková were arrested, after which a strange story emerged. Under questioning, Maruščáková said that Říha had asked her to deliver a message to the Horák family, who lived in Lidice. This message was to tell them that their son was safe and well, and in England. Říha confirmed this when he was interrogated, and he additionally stated that he had met Horák's son in the Protectorate a few days before the assassination attempt on Heydrich. Whom Říha believed he met has never been satisfactorily explained, but after the war Vaněk claimed that this person was not Horák but Valčik.

Whilst neither Říha nor Anna Maruščáková had lived in Lidice, their affair ultimately sealed the village's fate. The *Gestapo* in Kladno and Prague again believed they had discovered a link to the perpetrators, but further investigations and a search of the village failed to link Lidice with any form of resistance. However, by this stage the innocence of Lidice was no longer a consideration for the Germans. Not for the first time, the village had been connected with parachute agents from Britain. The chief of the security police in the Protectorate, Horst Böhme, had spoken to Himmler on the day of Heydrich's funeral and presented the case that the village of Lidice be used for a reprisal. Confirmation was received around 1900 on 9 June, from Himmler, who issued instructions to Frank that Lidice be burnt to the ground and then levelled so that no trace of it remained. Frank informed Böhme of this by telephone, and followed with the words that only corn would grow where Lidice once stood. The name of Lidice would be erased from the map.

Within two hours, German troops had moved in to cordon off the village. The commander on the ground was *SS-Hauptsturmführer* Max Rostock, and his men were accompanied by a propaganda team to record the village's destruction.

The inhabitants were herded into the village square whilst their homes were ransacked. Anything usable and easily portable, such as furniture or prams, was taken away for transport to Germany. The male inhabitants were separated from the women and children and given '*Sonderbehandlung*', a Nazi euphemism for special treatment. They were put into the barn at the Horák farm. Meanwhile, Rostock's troops went round the village with cans of petrol, setting fire to the buildings.

The women and children were driven away to Kladno in trucks. Then the killing of the men started, the executions commencing at about 0700 on 10 June. At first the men were shot in groups of five, lined up outside the Horáks' barn, but Böhme thought the executions were proceeding too slowly so he ordered that 10 men be shot at a time. Mattresses were taken from neighbouring houses and placed up against the wall of the barn to prevent ricochets. The dead were left lying where they fell. By noon, 17 rows of corpses lay on the ground in batches of 10. These were the 173 men of the village, shot in cold blood by a German execution squad. The youngest was just 14 years old, who remained with his father during the separations, and the oldest 84. Another 11 men who were not in the village that evening were arrested and murdered soon afterwards, as were the eight men and seven women of the Horák and Stríbrný families who had previously been arrested. The only adult man from Lidice who survived this tragedy was František Saidl. He had been in prison since 19 December 1938, having accidentally killed his son, Eduard Saidl. He completed his sentence, and claimed not to have heard about the fate of his village until after his release on 23 December 1942.

After the killing had been completed, squads of engineers arrived with explosives to blow up the fire-blackened walls of the buildings. Pioneers with bulldozers then flattened the ruins, uprooted the fruit trees and filled in the lake, diverting the village stream.

The next day, 11 June, trucks arrived carrying 30 Jews from the Terezin camp to dig a common grave for the men executed the previous day.

Ploughs were driven back and forth across the acres of rubble, so that no recognisable outline should remain, and when all was done, they put up a high barbed wire fence around the site with notices in Czech and German which read: "Anyone approaching this fence that does not halt when challenged will be shot."

Some 203 women were arrested and transported from Lidice. They were first taken to Kladno, where, after being held for three days in a school gymnasium, they were separated from their children and sent on to Ravensbrück concentration camp in northern Germany to undertake heavy manual labour. Some women avoided transportation at this time; four, heavily pregnant, were sent to an asylum in Prague to give birth to children they would never see. Seven mothers with children under 12 months old were told they could remain with their babies, although later in the year they too were separated from their children and sent to Terezin and then Ravensbrück. After three brutal years of malnourishment and hard physical work, the surviving 143 women returned home to Lidice.

Eighty-eight children from the village were transported by road to Lovosice and then taken by train to Lodz in Poland, arriving on 13 June. They were held at a former textile factory on Gneisenaustreet. Their arrival was accompanied by a telegram from the *Gestapo* office in Prague which ended as follows: "These children are only bringing what they wear. No special care is required." The children were not sufficiently fed, and were forced to sleep on cold dirty floors without blankets; they covered themselves with their coats if they had brought one with them. Under specific orders of the camp management, no medical care was given to the children.

At Kladno, three children had been selected for Germanisation, although one of these later rejoined the other children at Lodz. Shortly after their arrival in Lodz, another selection process was made by officials from the Central Race and Settlement branch. They chose a further seven children to be Germanised.

It was Adolf Eichmann, one of the main architects of the Holocaust, who gave the order for the murder of the remaining children on 1 July 1942. The next day, the remaining 82 Lidice children were handed over to the Lodz *Gestapo* office, who in turn had them transported to the extermination camp at Chelmno some 70km distant, where they were gassed to death, almost certainly on the same day as their arrival, in Magirus gas trucks.

Three Lidice women at Ravensbrück were later found to be pregnant. Two of them were sent to the asylum at Prague, where they gave birth. The circumstances are not clear, but one of these children was murdered whilst the other survived. The third pregnant woman gave birth at Ravensbrück. Her son was immediately taken away and murdered within minutes of his birth. The seven children who had been aged under 12 months had been sent to a children's hospital in Germany; one died of natural causes but the other six survived. In total, 17 children survived the war from 13 families. Just 11 mothers were reunited with their children at the end of the war.

To try to justify their actions at Lidice, the Nazis issued a statement which read:

> In the course of a search for the murderers of SS-Obergruppenführer Heydrich, it was ascertained that the population of this village supported and assisted the perpetrators. Apart from the help given to them, the population also committed other hostile acts, such as the keeping of an illegal dump of munitions and arms, the maintenance of an illegal transmitter and hoarding of an extraordinarily large quantity of goods which are controlled. The male inhabitants have been shot, the women taken to concentration camps, the children put into suitable educational establishments. The buildings have been razed to the ground; the name of the community has been erased.

Further 'justification' was given to this appalling act when the Germans fabricated a radio-set they said was found in Lidice. It was actually made by Miroslav Wagner, the owner of the Zenit Film Laboratories in Prague.

Harald Weismann, head of the Kladno *Gestapo*, later commented:

> Geschke and Böhme and others showed us the weapons. There was a Colt pistol, several English pistols and a few packs of cartridges. Böhme showed me several sub machine guns, how many I do not remember. Böhme told me; "You see that second report which was checked by our informer proved to be correct because we found these weapons." To my question as to where they were discovered, Böhme said they were found in a mill in Lidice … Today I am – and I must be – of the opinion, that the weapons found in the mill were brought there by agent-provocateurs. Today I understand that the obliteration of Lidice was the biggest outrage in the history of the world. How did Frank manage to get that order from Hitler, I do not know. Geschke and Böhme told me at the time, that there was no evidence against Lidice stating that it was a political necessity and if it was not Lidice, it would have been some other place.

To increase the pressure on the Czech population in the hope of a lead to find the perpetrators, the *Protektorate* Minster of Education, Emanuel Moravec, said in a speech, "Heaven help the Czech nation if the criminals who murdered Acting Reichsprotektor Heydrich are not found. Heaven help them, heaven help them, heaven help them, I repeat three times."

With Lidice erased from the map and the criminal investigation still no closer to a positive lead, *SS-Sturmbannführer* Heinrich Berger came up with the idea of a short-term amnesty for anyone who could provide information on the assassins. Every night, crowds of residents of Prague queued to get a copy of the newspaper with the list of those executed, looking for the names of friends and relatives, now the threat of death for any Czech who had not volunteered information was suspended. However, German rumours suggested that the mass executions would restart, with people selected by using the number on their identity cards. Still the Germans received no real leads; even though they had taken around 300 statements from witnesses, they were still no closer to apprehending the perpetrators. German criminologists expressed the view that fear and anxiety were stopping people from coming forward. Therefore, on 13 June, Karl Hermann Frank issued a proclamation that promised that anyone who supplied information by 18 June would not be harmed. It is also recorded that Hitler had given an order to Himmler for the execution of 30,000 Czechs if this last-chance appeal did not work. What happened in the next few days probably exceeded any expectations that the Germans may have had.

Karel Svoboda. Courtesy MHIP. | Jan Kubiš whilst training in the UK. Courtesy MHIP. | Adolf Opálka pictured at Porchester Gate. Courtesy MHIP.

Josef Bublik. Courtesy MHIP. | Jan Hrubý. Courtesy MHIP. | Jaroslav Švarc. Courtesy MHIP.

Josef Valčik. Courtesy MHIP. | Jozef Gabčik. Courtesy MHIP.

The entrance to Heydrich's villa at Panenské Břežany. Collection NC.

Hácha handing over the keys to the chamber where the crown jewels of Czechoslovakia were kept in a ceremony on 19 November 1941. Courtesy MHIP.

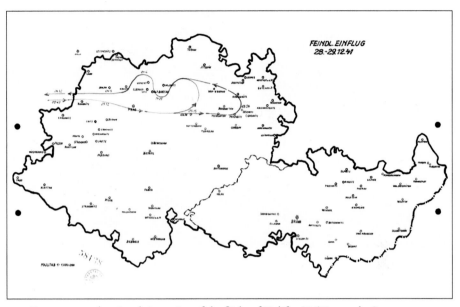

German map showing their version of the flight of Halifax L9618 over the Protectorate.
Courtesy MHIP.

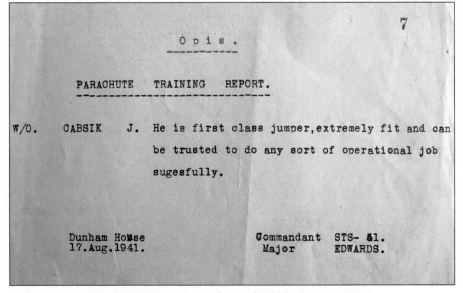

Parachute Training Report for Jozef Gabčik. Courtesy MHIP.

Photograph of Captain A Hesketh-Prichard, from his SOE personal file. Courtesy The National Archives Kew.

Father Vladimir Petřek. Courtesy SP.

Photograph of Major C Clarke, from his SOE personal file. Courtesy The National Archives Kew.

This picture, courtesy of C and T Auctioneers Ltd, is of a striptease suit sold at auction in 2018 which was said to have been found in Czechoslovakia during the Second World War. It sold for £600.

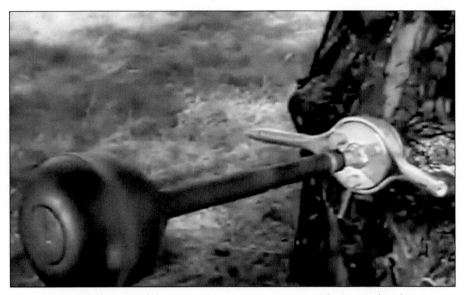

A tree spigot being used during a training exercise. Courtesy The National Archives.

The Heydrich residence. Courtesy Jonathan Saunders.

Karel Čurda pictured in England at Porchester Gate; he was a member of the Out Distance Group. Courtesy MHIP.

Jan Zelenka, another leading figure in the Czech Resistance movement. Collection NC.

Ladislav Vaněk, one of the leading lights in the Czech Resistance movement. Collection NC.

Ata Moravec. Collection NC.

Gerik Vilem, pictured wearing his paratrooper wings. Courtesy MHIP.

The Moravec family, who provided much assistance, are an important part of the story. Here is a pre-war picture with Ata on the left, his mother Marie and Miroslav to the right. Miroslav had escaped to England and was a pilot in 310 (Czechoslovak) Squadron. He sadly died in a flying accident on 7 June 1944. Courtesy MHIP.

Heydrich and Frank in the courtyard of Prague Castle soon after the former's arrival, having taken over as Acting *Reichsprotektor*. Courtesy MHIP.

The grounds of Prague Castle pictured in 2017. Collection NC.

A 1942 image of the Hotel Veselka where Josef Valčik of Silver A worked as a waiter. Courtesy Tony Moseley.

This villa, known as Zámeček, was used by the Germans in Pardubice as a barracks; its grounds were also used as an execution site. Courtesy Tony Moseley.

A parachutist exiting a Halifax aircraft on training exercise. Courtesy MHIP.

Heydrich and Hácha inspecting a hospital train that on 20th April 1942 the Czech people had given to Adolf Hitler as a birthday present. It is said that soon afterwards patriots stated to say that Hitler was so ill he needed a whole train to treat him. Courtesy MHIP.

The corner selected for the assassination attempt – Jan and Jozef decided to wait 'round the corner'. Courtesy SP.

The second modified No 73 grenade which was found in Jozef's briefcase. Courtesy SP.

The assassination scene from the rear; Heydrich's car approached from the right. Courtesy SP.

A general view of the assassination spot. Heydrich's car came downhill and turned right with Jan and Jozef's bicycles left on the right hand side of the photograph. Courtesy SP.

A photograph showing where the bicycles had been positioned across the road from the assassination spot. Courtesy SP.

A view from the other side. Damage to the side of the Mercedes can clearly be seen. Courtesy SP.

This is the road that Jozef ran down pursued by Klein just after the assassination attempt.
Collection NC.

Gestapo photograph looking down on the assassination spot. The locations where the raincoat
(Mantel) and the Sten (M-Pi) were left are also shown. Courtesy SP.

Two Gestapo photographs showing the area around the butcher's shop where Jozef shot Klein.
Courtesy YIVO Institute New York.

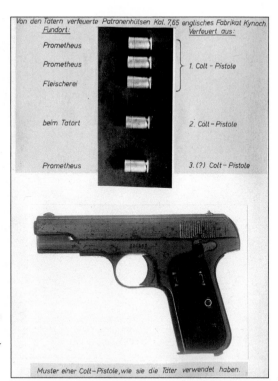

Von den Tätern verfeuerte Patronenhülsen Kal. 7,65 englisches Fabrikat Kynoch.

Fundort:		Verfeuert aus:
Prometheus		
Prometheus		1. Colt - Pistole
Fleischerei		
beim Tatort		2. Colt - Pistole
Prometheus		3. (?) Colt - Pistole

Muster einer Colt-Pistole, wie sie die Täter verwendet haben.

Gestapo photograph of one of the pistols recovered together with some of the cartridge cases fired during the assassination attempt on 27 May 1942. Courtesy YIVO Institute New York.

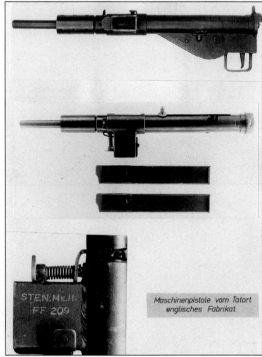

STEN. Mk. II.
FF 209

Maschinenpistole vom Tatort
englisches Fabrikat

Gestapo photograph of Sten FF209 recovered at the assassination scene. Courtesy YIVO Institute New York.

Heydrich being guarded by the SS after his death; this is also the room he stayed in. Collection NC.

The same room pictured in 2018. Collection NC.

The butcher's shop that Jozef ran into close to the assassination spot. Courtesy USM Inc.

Items recovered from the assassination scene – the bicycle, briefcases, hat and coat displayed at the Bata shop in central Prague. Collection NC.

The parachute agents were on the balcony to the right and this Gestapo photograph gives an idea of how difficult it was for the Germans to attack these positions. Courtesy SP.

The catacombs in the crypt with the staircase on the left. Courtesy SP.

Many people filed past Heydrich's coffin at Prague Castle. Collection BG.

Heydrich lying in state in Berlin. Collection BG.

The scene after the Lidice executions had finished. The mattresses were positioned to stop any ricochets from the farm building. Courtesy USM Inc.

Some of the Germans clerks who compiled a list of the property and other items removed from Lidice. Courtesy USM Inc.

The bodies of those executed in the grounds of the Horák farm. Courtesy MHIP.

RAD workers removing rubble from Lidice. Courtesy MHIP.

Front view of the briefcase belonging to Jozef and left hanging from the handlebars of his bicycle. Courtesy SP.

Front view of the briefcase belonging to Jan which he abandoned when escaping from the assassination scene. Courtesy SP.

One of the cells in the basement of the Petschek Palace. Collection NC.

The room inside the Petschek Palace where people waited to be interviewed; it was known as the cinema. Collection NC.

The entry and exit hole for the crypt used by the agents in 1942 viewed from the crypt. Collection NC.

The replacement slab for the one the Germans blew up to gain access to the crypt. Collection NC.

Adolf Opálka after committing suicide on the balcony. He had also suffered a broken right arm during the fighting. Courtesy MHIP.

Post death picture of Jozef Gabčik. Courtesy MHIP.

Post death picture of Josef Bublik. Courtesy MHIP.

Post death picture of Jan Hrubý. Courtesy MHIP.

The trousers worn by Adolf Opálka, showing damage caused by shrapnel and an ankle holster for a pistol. Courtesy MHIP.

A suit belonging to Jan Kubiš recovered from the church. Courtesy MHIP.

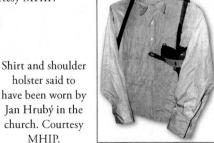

Shirt and shoulder holster said to have been worn by Jan Hrubý in the church. Courtesy MHIP.

Post death picture of Josef Valčik. Courtesy MHIP.

Karel Čurda pictured across the road from the church – third from the right – assisting the Germans in identifying the corpses. Karl Hermann Frank is bending over with his back to the photographer. Courtesy MHIP.

The bodies of the dead parachute agents were laid out on the corner of Resslova Street and what is now known as Václavská. The Germans are assessing their options, perhaps just after they have received the message that Himmler wants the agents taken alive. Collection NC.

The Fire Brigade attempting to put hoses into the crypt. Courtesy SP.

Hoses and battle damage at the ventilation slit. Courtesy SP.

Attentäter Gabčzik, der während des Attentats mit Maschinenpistole ausgerüstet war.

Gestapo photograph of Jozef Gabčik after his death. Courtesy YIVO Institute New York.

Attentäter Kubis, der die Bombe gegen den Wagen von ᛋᛋ Obergruppenführer Heydrich warf.

Gestapo photograph of Jan Kubiš after his death. Courtesy YIVO Institute New York.

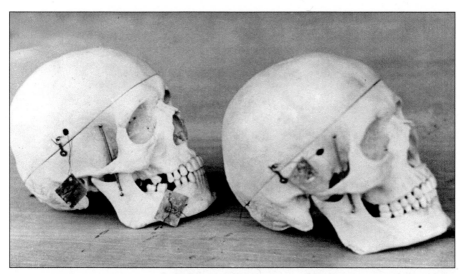

A photograph of the skulls of Jaroslav Švarc on the left and Josef Bublik on the right. Dissection cuts are visible, as are the bullet entry holes. Courtesy USM Inc.

A temporary memorial to Heydrich was erected at the assassination spot on the first anniversary of the attempt. It is said it was only in situ for one day before the Germans took it down. Courtesy USM Inc.

The memorial to the church officials and the parachute agents in Prague. Courtesy Tony Moseley.

A recently installed plaque to Jan and Jozef on the Ellison grave at Ightfield. Collection NC.

The Czech SOE memorial Arisaig. Courtesy Tommy McLeod.

Grenade damage on the floor of the balcony. Courtesy Tony Moseley.

The Kobylisy execution ground pictured in 2017. Collection NC.

The memorial stone at Ležáky. Collection NC.

13

I have some information for you

According to one report, the amnesty was the catalyst for the arrival of another 2,000 statements and pieces of information, including an anonymous letter with a Třeboň postmark that named Gabčík and Kubiš as the two assassins the Germans were searching for.

Meanwhile, in the crypt of St Cyril and Methodius a debate was raging about what to do. News of the atrocity at Lidice had reached the parachute agents. After Lidice, Gabčík and Kubiš discussed the idea with Father Petřek of potentially stopping any further such appalling acts of brutality by the Germans. One suggestion was for them to commit suicide in a park in Prague, with cards round their necks saying they had killed Heydrich. Another more desperate suggestion was to arrange an interview with the hated Emanuel Moravec, the Czech Quisling and Minister of Education, confess what they had done and then shoot him and commit suicide themselves. They were persuaded out of these courses of action by several people, including Father Petřek and Lieutenant Opálka.

It was understood that the parachute agents could not stay indefinitely in the crypt, as in addition to the danger they bought to the church, it was not a healthy place to spend any length of time; it was dark, damp and oppressive and was already beginning to have an effect on the men's health. The only sanitary arrangements for all seven parachutists were a bucket. It was difficult to obtain food and have it brought into the church without arousing suspicion. Bishop Gorazd was fearful of the situation, especially with the German reprisals, and he knew the presence of the agents in the church now endangered all the church members.

Post-war, Vaněk claimed there had been a plan to move the parachutists as soon as the shut-down of Prague had been lifted. They would be smuggled out to the mountain regions, where they would join resistance groups and organise partisan activity. Vaněk even said that Gabčík and Kubiš would be flown back to England by the RAF. However, this is just further evidence that Vaněk's post-war account cannot be relied upon. The RAF did not possess any aircraft that could fly all the way to the Protectorate, land on an improvised strip, collect two agents and then fly back to Britain. Despite this fabrication, it is likely a plan had been formulated to use a police car, coffins and hearses to secretly convey the parachutists out of the city as soon as the opportunity arose.

Vaněk also later claimed that it had been decided that Adolf Opálka would remain in Prague when the other six left. Vaněk said:

> [I said] 'You [Opálka] will stay in Prague: we shall be needing you – you have abilities. The others will go into the country.' Our plan was that four parachutists should go to Kladno in a police car. A Kladno policeman had helped us to find a temporary refuge for them in a warehouse. Kubiš and Gabčík were to go to Oubenice, a village near Benešov; everything was ready for them there, and they would stay with a carpenter. For greater safety we would hide them in some of the coffins that were being taken out of Prague. Kubiš and Gabčík were to stay in Oubenice for a few days. I was to join them there and leave with them for London in a plane sent to fetch us. Opálka had a homing device that would enable him to guide a small plane in to land. While I was away, Opálka was to look after the underground network; and then I was to be flown back from London.
>
> The four parachutists hidden in Kladno were not to remain there long either. We meant to take them to Drahanska Vysocina, the mountains where groups of partisans were hiding. In the forest there lived a reliable Czech, a gamekeeper; and his house had become a kind of headquarters for all the operations carried out by the partisans. The Silver A team, Bartoš and the wireless operator, Potůček, were no longer able to work in the neighbourhood of Pardubice. It was too dangerous for them there, too. For Silver A we had found a hiding place in a quarry near the village of Rousinov, a quarry belonging to the mayor. The mayor was in agreement, and with him keeping watch Bartoš and Potůček would be able to carry on with their work; the transmitter Libuše would continue to send back intelligence for London – if all went well.

There was one parachutist missing from the crypt. Karel Čurda of Operation Out Distance had managed to escape from Prague soon after the assassination and had gone to stay with his family at Nová Hlina, near Třeboň, to the south of Prague. Whilst Čurda may have felt he had the support network of his family around him, they could not offer the resolve of his fellow agents. Both his mother and sister brought pressure to bear on Čurda, and the proclaiming of the amnesty provided him with an opportunity to protect his family. There was also the increased reward of 20 million Koruna. His family's anxiety could not have been helped by several police visits to his mother's home, although these were part of general searches rather than specifically looking for Čurda. Immediately after the amnesty came into force, Čurda took his first step to treachery, albeit a cautious one. He wrote an anonymous letter to the police station at Benesov, south of Prague, naming Jozef Gabčík and Jan Kubiš as the men the Germans were looking for. For the next few days, Čurda sat and waited for something to happen, but there was no public denouncement of Gabčík and Kubiš. His letter had been to no avail. It had been read, but the names were unfamiliar and the Benesov police thought it was one of many similar denouncements, and of no significance.

With the apparent failure of his letter, Čurda decided to travel to Prague and confess everything. He took a train to the capital on 16 June, but he did not know where the other parachutists were hiding. He first visited the Moravec apartment, but nobody was in. At around noon on 16 June, Čurda walked through the doors of the Petschek Palace, the headquarters of the *Gestapo* in Prague. This was not a building any Czech patriot would enter voluntarily, but he did so and told the German manning the front desk that he had some information for them. As first he was treated with scepticism; he was not the first person to walk in claiming that they had information in return for the 20 million Koruna reward. However the Germans soon realised Čurda was the link they had been so desperately waiting for.

It is clear from the translated and captured German documents that Čurda had to prove his credentials. The Germans showed him a number of briefcases, and he was asked to identify which ones had been used by the perpetrators of the attack on Heydrich. As he was able to pick out one of the briefcases found at the scene, the Germans realised that he was worthy of more attention. Čurda stated that this briefcase had been used to conceal a Sten gun, and gave a description of Gabčík. As his description matched that given by witnesses, it became clear that the person sitting in front of the *Gestapo* was a parachute agent, as he claimed. Under questioning, Čurda first gave away the cover names of Zdenek and Ota Navratil. Čurda was searched and his cyanide pill was discovered; further evidence that he was a parachute agent. He offered to help the Germans in return for assurances that his family would be kept safe. Čurda, shown photographs of other parachutists, eventually admitted he recognised them. According to the German report, the photographs were of Pechal, Kolařík, Mikš and Gerik. The *Gestapo* falsely claimed that Gerik was working for them; a standard tactic in trying to turn an agent.

The following is taken from a statement Čurda gave in June 1945:

On 16th June 1942, I travelled to Prague and went to the Gestapo at the Petschek Palace. They began questioning me. To start with they showed me photographs of a few parachutists and asked whether I knew them. I recognised them all; the photographs were of Lieutenant Pechal and of Kolařík, Mikš and Gerik. But I said I did not know them. They beat me, saying they had already captured Gerik and they knew more about it than I thought. Then I admitted I knew the men whose photographs they had shown me. Then they showed me an album with photographs of our Czech soldiers in Poland. I recognised four or five of them and since I was forced to, I told them so.

I also admitted that I was a parachutist, dropped on 27th March 1942 in the neighbourhood of Telc in Moravia with two other men of my team and that we had hidden a bundle in a field; they did not even ask me which of us had hidden it. I also admitted that Gerik was in the plane with me, but that he had not jumped at the same time as I did. I told them my whole history since my landing and betrayed the people who had sheltered and helped me, that is to say my brother-in-law, Antonin Maca at Kolin, the owner of the printing works at Lazne Belohrad, M. Krupka and Alois Moravec, the Svatoses in Michalska Street in Prague, Sergeants Valčik and Kubiš, Madame Baucova and my mother and sister at Nová Hlina.

I know nothing about these people's fate; all I know is that my mother and sister were arrested and then released. Superintendent Jantura and a Gestapo officer called Horny questioned me through interpreters. I did not betray postman Drobil of Jindrichuv Hradec nor Mrvik of Kolin, who gave me clothes. I spoke of the man who had housed us with the Svatoses, but I did not give his name because I did not know it.

They asked me whether I knew someone called Motycka. I did not. They said that was impossible, because Gerik knew him. They also asked me if I was a radio technician and if I knew how to work receivers and transmitters and other instruments. When I said no they were surprised that I did not know how to work them. They questioned me about a man called Navratil, whom I had known in the Czechoslovak battalion in England. I told them he had killed himself cleaning a weapon.

The next day the interrogation went on. This time I betrayed the names of Captain Šustr and Major Blavic, and their duties and where they worked, and the airfields at Velesbourne and near Warwick. I did not admit anything else. As I was forced to do it, I gave away the names of Captain Opálka and Kolařík and the parachutists of two other teams. Since I had seen in the paper that Kolařík's family had been executed I told them where he lived. As for Captain Opálka, I said I did not know where he lived; I told them I had seen him for the last time at the Svatos'. I also told them how he treated me. I admitted that a lady who was a liaison agent had come to see me in Madame Baucova's flat. I betrayed the names of Lieutenant Pechal and Sergeant Mikš, saying that they had come in on the plane with me but that I did not know where they had been dropped.

After the interrogation they took me into the cellar. There I saw Ata Moravec.

However, the one key piece of information the *Gestapo* wanted – the location of the parachute agents' hiding place – Čurda was unable to provide, although under further questioning he did reveal the names and location of safe houses and apartments where he had stayed during his time in the Protectorate. One of the locations he gave up was the apartment of the Moravec family at Biskupcova in Prague. The Moravec home, the hub for the parachutists, was a major lead for the *Gestapo*, who, thanks to Čurda's treachery, were now making real progress. The *Gestapo* had the area around the apartment in Biskupcova discreetly watched whilst a major operation was planned for the next morning. It was the *Gestapo's* SS-Oberscharführer Oskar Fleischer who would lead the operation, which was set for 0400. The area around the apartment block in Biskupcova was surrounded and a squad of men despatched to the Moravec apartment, number 1745/7, on the second floor. Fleischer was a violent man and there was nothing subtle about his approach to the Moravec apartment. Fleischer had hoped, even half-expected to find either one or both of the assassins in the apartment. There was nothing pleasant about his entry into the apartment, and it is believed that the terrified and intimidated Marie Moravec asked permission to use the bathroom to clean herself up. Inside the bathroom she took an L pill given to her just a day or so before by Hana Krupková, who worked as the courier between Anthropoid and Silver A in Pardubice. Fleischer was incandescent with rage when he realised she had killed herself. He had Marie's husband, Alois, dragged off in his nightclothes to the Petschek Palace. There is some confusion over the whereabouts of her son, Ata, at this time. There are two theories – either he was present in the apartment or he was away visiting relatives in Pisek and was summoned back to Prague with a fake telegram saying that his mother was seriously ill and he needed to return immediately. According to Chalupský, the police interpreter who accompanied Fleischer, but an unreliable witness, Ata was in the apartment and joined his father in custody at the Petschek.

The most important question the *Gestapo* wanted answering was where the parachute agents were hiding. At the Petschek Palace the *Gestapo* focussed on 21-year-old Ata; they brutally beat him and then stupefied him with brandy, yet he would not break until finally he was shown his mother's severed head floating in a fish tank. He cried out that all he knew was his mother had told him if ever he was in trouble he should go to the church on Resslova Street in Prague and ask for help. The secret of the crypt was all but out.

The *Gestapo* had not finished with Biskupcova when they arrested the Moravecs. They returned later that morning to arrest Jan Zelenka. Either his name had been given up by Čurda, or there was a rumour was the *Gestapo* found paperwork detailing a suspiciously large amount of meat purchased by Zelenka. A squad of *Gestapo* men was despatched back to Biskupcova to raid the Zelenka apartment. Biskupcova had remained sealed off, so everyone in this street was aware that something dreadful had happened. Zelenka must have been waiting all morning to see if the *Gestapo* would return for him. He was trapped the wrong side of the *Gestapo* cordon. The interpreter, Chalupský, was again on duty and provided an account of what happened when they approached apartment 1837/4, home to Zelenka:

> Fleischer and Herschelmann [from the Gestapo] reached the door and rang the bell. Someone opened the spy hole. "Police! Open up!" Fleischer kicked the door in and at the same time Herschelmann fired at somebody. The shadow of a man ran down the corridor to the bedroom. Another shot was fired but the bullet went through the window and hit the building opposite. We heard a door shut in the bedroom and we found it led to a bathroom where Zelenka tried to lock himself in and take poison. Herschelmann fired at the door furiously. Mrs Zelenka stood in the kitchen. The door opened and out came Zelenka with blood dripping from his injured hand and said; "Here I am." Herschelmann lunged towards him but it was too late; he collapsed foaming at the mouth and died soon afterwards.

Jan Zelenka too had bitten down on his L pill. He was of no use to the *Gestapo* now.

14

We Will Never Surrender!

It was around midnight that Ata told the *Gestapo* about the church on Resslova Street. Pannwitz started gathering information on the church called Saint Karl Borromeo (previously and subsequently the Church of St Cyril and Methodius) and the clergy who ran it. The Germans had summoned every city official they felt could help with regards to information on the church, its layout, the church officials who lived and worked there and how the church was connected to the sewer system. A German policeman called Kurt Friedrich Oberhauser was responsible for religious intelligence, and he had his main informer, a fellow German, Franz Bobe, Prior of the Maltese Order in the *Protektorate*, brought in to the Petschek Palace. It was Bobe who supplied the *Gestapo* with a floor plan and identified the church elders and employees to be arrested.

At this stage the *Gestapo* were unaware whether the parachutists were in the church or a nearby safe house. Karl Hermann Frank, Fleischer and *SS-Hauptsturmführer* Pannwitz wanted the perpetrators taken alive so they could be put on trial and provide a proper conclusion to the criminal investigation. Nevertheless, this also had to be a military operation, and a force of 19 officers and 740 troops from the *Gestapo* and the *Waffen-SS*, under the command of *SS-Brigadeführer* Karl von Treuenfeld, threw a double cordon around the area of the church, had a guard put on every manhole cover connected to the sewer system and set up positions on the roofs of the surrounding buildings. By 0415 on the morning of 18 June, the cordon was established and Pannwitz could proceed.

Between 0420 and 0430, Pannwitz and his group approached the church via the side entrance to the private quarters. The door was opened by the verger, Václav Louda, who was immediately overpowered and arrested. Vladimir Petřek and another priest, Václav Čikl, who had previously been arrested in their homes, were brought into the church via this entrance. This group then cautiously entered the nave of the church. The Germans did not know what they were likely to find. Three of the parachutists had actually spent the night in the balcony alcove above the nave. There were two reasons for doing this; it provided an opportunity to keep watch, and sleeping on the balcony was an improvement to doing so in the crypt. It is virtually impossible that the three men on the balcony – Adolf Opálka, Josef Bublik and Jan Kubiš – did not hear and see the Germans mounting their cordon, and were thus ready when Pannwitz and his group entered the nave of the church. Yet there was no time to warn their comrades in the crypt below, who would soon be awakened by the battle that was about to take place, and the three men took up pre-determined positions ready to fight to the death.

Led by Pannwitz, a search party of 15 *Gestapo* and SS troops moved cautiously into the nave in the half-light of the breaking dawn when suddenly shots rang out from above and a grenade was thrown amongst them. One of the *Gestapo* officers, Kurt Kahlo, was the first to be wounded, shot through the arm. Access to the balcony where the three parachutists had taken up position was by a small spiral staircase. Theoretically, the parachutists held an ideal defensive position, but they had limited ammunition and no means of escape.

Pannwitz's men stumbled back into cover, taking their wounded with them. At the sound of firing from the church, *Waffen-SS* troops positioned on the roof of a school opposite opened fire with their machine guns through the upper windows, and for a short time there was carnage: glass shattered and splintered whilst bullets ricocheted around the church. The thick stonework gave the parachutists some cover, but the Germans in the nave were in danger from their own fire. After a short while the command "Cease fire!" was given and the Germans considered their options. It was decided that the plain-clothed *Gestapo* should step aside and let the *Waffen-SS* handle the attack. Command of the operation now devolved to *SS-Sturmbannführer* Koenig and *SS-Obersturmführer* Sohn. However, there was no easy solution to be found. They wanted the parachutists alive if possible, and the only real access point to the balcony was via the narrow spiral staircase, just wide enough for one person at a time, but now full of furniture thrown down by the three parachutists, which the Germans would need to clear when they made an assault on the staircase. Over a period of approximately two hours, the fighting took on a familiar pattern. Squads of *Waffen-SS* made assaults on the staircase, which was valiantly defended at the top by Opálka as Bublik and Kubiš tried to control the staircase entrance on the ground floor. The three parachutists held off numerous attempts to storm their positions. The interior of the church became a scene of destruction, with wounded Germans surrounded by broken wood, glass and stone fragments. The end finally came at around 0700 when the Germans managed to get a foothold on the balcony, probably due to the defenders running out of ammunition and being rendered barely conscious by grenades. Chalupský, the *Gestapo* interpreter, was present and later described what happened:

> A single shot rang out from the balcony and then there was silence up there, an agonizing silence throughout the church. The SS waited a moment and then proceeded along the balcony. They found three parachutists covered with blood. They came out of the church carrying one body and two dying men. They laid the dead man on a church carpet outside on the pavement. They took the other two off to hospital. The Gestapo took the traitor, Čurda, and Ata Moravec, to the body and asked who he was? Pannwitz did not know who was hidden in the church; perhaps he was thinking only of Kubiš and Gabčík. At first Čurda was silent, then at last he muttered "Opálka".

Opálka's end was likely suicide whilst he still had his wits about him, probably with his last bullet while biting down on his L pill. Kubiš had likely been mortally wounded by grenades and fallen unconscious. Bublik had shot himself through the temple, but reportedly was unconscious but still alive when the Germans reached him.

These two barely alive parachutists were rushed to the SS Hospital in Prague-Podoli, but Bublik died en-route and Kubiš shortly after arrival, neither having regained consciousness. Three brave men with limited ammunition and no heavy weapons had kept many times their number at bay for 2½ hours whilst the Germans were determined to take them alive. This was never an option for the three. Their job had been to hold off the Germans for as long as possible, hopefully giving their friends in the crypt a chance to survive.

Chalupský described the scene at the end of this action:

> I had time to look around as Pannwitz was talking with the SS commander. There were pools of blood on the stairs; that was where they had carried down the bodies of the parachutists. Later I went up into the gallery; the floor and walls were spotted with blood; there were empty cartridge cases everywhere. The gallery was quite large and it overhung the whole of the nave. At the bottom a bricked-up door led to the adjoining house, but the parachutists had not had time to break through it. Indeed, perhaps they had not wished to do so; their companions were in the crypt and they had to gain time for them. They fought to the last bullet.

The Germans were now faced with a question: Čurda had named the perpetrators as Gabčík and Kubiš, but they had only taken one of these two, so where was the other? The Germans had found another set of clothes on the balcony, which they believed meant there was at least one more man hiding in the church in addition to the three who had kept them at bay for so long. Father Petřek was then forced to confess that four more parachute agents were hiding in the crypt.

Chalupský later recalled:

> Meanwhile they were searching the inside of the church for the way into the crypt. The nave was almost destroyed, the windows were broken and the altar overturned. Through loud speakers set up in the street the Germans called upon the besieged men to surrender, promising they would be treated as prisoners of war. The men in the crypt said nothing. I do not know how the Gestapo learnt they were there. Possibly from clues inside the church. No sound had come from the crypt during the battle.

It was realised that there was a small rectangular opening in the floor of the church near the main entrance. This measured about 2ft by 1ft 6in. The entrance stone was moved out of the way, only to reveal a black darkness below. Then a shot rang out from the crypt. Čurda and Ata Moravec were dragged close to the entrance and told to call down for their fellow agents to surrender, Ata refused, but Čurda did not have any scruples about calling down: "Friends, give up! It is pointless. Lay down your arms and nothing will happen to you! Nothing happened to me either. It's me, Karel Čurda." A salvo of bullets greeted these words, now they knew who had betrayed them. Father Petřek was also brought forward and he called out: "They are telling me up here that you should give yourselves up. So I am passing it on. They claim that nothing will happen to you as you will be treated as prisoners of war." The reply came from below: "We are Czechs! We will never surrender, do you hear? Never!"

The only known way into the crypt at that point was this narrow entrance. A plan was devised whereby an SS volunteer was lowered by a rope into the black hole, but as soon as his legs were through he was shot.

The four parachutists in the crypt were Jozef Gabčík, Josef Valčik, Jaroslav Švarc and Jan Hrubý. They had heard the clamour of battle going on above them, but had kept any noise they made down to a minimum. During the battle of the balcony they had known their chances of getting out of the church through the entrance in the floor were non-existent. There was a possibility that they could break into the sewer system, and whilst the battle overhead raged they did make a token effort to dig through the wall, but it was far too thick for the tools they had. Then the noise from above died down; they realised that it was their turn next.

They likely still harboured some faint hope until the stone slab was removed to reveal their final hiding place. By this time Frank had arrived, adding an additional layer of interference to the command structure. Frank reiterated that the parachutists must be taken alive. This order was easier said than done; it was actually the parachutists who could, and would, determine when they died. Plans of the church were reviewed again and another entrance, one large enough to take the coffins down into the crypt, was found by the altar. A squad of SS men cleared away the carpets and other items, exposing a large concrete slab. When tapped it sounded hollow.

Whilst the floor plans were being re-evaluated, a fire brigade crew from the fire station at Sokolská Street had been despatched to the scene. The intention was to incapacitate the parachutists by sabotaging the ventilation shaft, which opened out above head height on Resslova Street. First the Germans had tried throwing tear-gas through the shaft's opening, but the parachutists had a ladder which they could use to get near enough to the opening to throw the tear-gas back into the street. Floodlights were concentrated on the opening in expectation of blinding the parachutists, but they simply shot them out. Finally, someone suggested using the fire brigade to flood the crypt.

The brigade was ordered to put their hoses down the shaft, but this had limited success as by using their ladder and a few shots to keep the firemen back, the parachutists pushed the hoses back out on to the street. A grappling hook was used to snare the ladder and it was dragged out – the defenders had now lost their vantage point. Fireman Karel Hertl hooked the ladder, and with the help of his colleague, Josef Soustružnik, pulled it through the slit. Frank, who was watching from across the road, apparently shouted "Bravo!" and clapped his hands. The hoses were returned and around 3,000 litres of water an hour were sent pouring into the crypt, but a drainage channel meant the level of water rose very slowly and eventually it was decided to turn the hoses off.

Attention was then turned to the second entrance to the crypt and the marble slab discovered in front of the altar. The firemen were instructed to open it up. Chalupský later commented:

> The superintendent sent for the firemen and ordered them to break it. Behind them stood the SS, their weapons in their hands. But the slab held firm and after twenty minutes a fireman tried to explain in pidgin German that it was impossible to deal with it with the tools they had there. The firemen were sent away and the SS engineers came in with explosives. They did something round the slab and then we were told to leave the church. They blasted the slab and the stone broke in two. An eager, inquisitive Gestapo man pulled away part of the wreckage and peered in to see what was inside – bullets whipped past his head. Pannwitz grinned with satisfaction; there were steps leading into the crypt; this was the way down.

It was now only a matter of time for the four remaining parachutists. Chalupský continued his account:

> Once again the SS were called upon. They were to go down the steps, and this time they were sent group by group, in waves of attack. How I admired those men in the crypt; for hours now they must have known that their struggle was hopeless, that sooner or later they would be killed; but they did not give in. They fought like lions. The first SS attack failed. When they had gone a few steps down, a burst of fire stopped them dead and some of them fell; they could not see clearly and the steps being so narrow and steep the wounded men threw the others into disorder. They had to retreat.

Chalupský said the firemen's hoses were again used to pour water into the crypt:

> Now the parachutists' position was becoming critical. Water was flowing into the crypt and they no longer had any way of getting up to the slit to push the hoses out. At the same time the SS launched another attack, throwing grenades and steadily the water flooded into the crypt. Yet the parachutists went on firing. They hit back without a pause, resisting furiously.
>
> Then suddenly, at about noon, four isolated shots rang out below. After that, a great silence. Pannwitz stiffened. He looked at the way into the crypt and beckoned to an SS officer. The SS officer hesitated then ordered two soldiers down into the crypt; they descended cautiously, one step; two steps; three. Still silence. They looked back at the officer who waved them on. They moved further down still, everyone in the church watching them. They vanished into the crypt and then called up; the officer hesitated no longer; with his pistol in his hand

he rushed down. A moment later he reappeared, wet up to the knees and cried "Fertig!" It was the end. It was over.

The four men in the crypt had used their last rounds of ammunition to end their lives. Geschke later wrote to Frank in a report dated 29 June 1942: "The inspection of the four bodies recovered from the crypt confirmed that none of the men died from the fire of the Waffen-SS but they all died because of self-inflicted shots to the head; two of the agents had also taken poison."

Chalupský concluded his account of the end of the siege:

> I went down into the crypt, dimly lit by the little window, the one the water had come through. The place was bigger than I expected. I had to stay on the steps – the floor was quite hidden under the water; a couple of feet or more. I lit a match. There were scraps of paper floating in the water – money and identity cards torn to shreds; they had thought of everything. Bloody marks on the walls; bloody marks on the steps and water everywhere. But the ceiling of the crypt was high and they could have held out a long time, probably for a whole day before it was completely flooded. No, it was not the water that beat the parachutists. There is only one likely explanation – lack of ammunition. Later the crypt was cleaned out; underclothes were found, stoves, tins of food but not a single round of ammunition. A heap of bricks was found near the little window. They had vainly tried to pierce the wall of the church; there was no way out. From that moment on, they had known they were condemned.

The firemen began the process of pumping the water out, and the four bodies were recovered from the crypt and carried on carpets to the corner of Resslova and Václavská Streets. The bodies of Kubiš and Bublik were brought back from the SS hospital around noon; all seven bodies were now lying out on the pavement. The Germans brought a number of people to identify the remaining bodies. The two collaborators, Čurda and Gerik, were asked to identify the bodies, as were Ata Moravec and the courier from Pardubice, Hana Krupková.

Another body was also taken to the street corner; that of Jan Milič Zelenka, the son of Jan Zelenka. Jan Milič Zelenka had committed suicide the previous day, having known that his father had already died and knowing he was a wanted man. He took an L pill in a park in Záběhlice.

After being identified, the bodies were taken away to the Institute of Forensic Medicine and Criminology at the Charles University in Prague for autopsies to be carried out. Meanwhile, back at the church, the Germans were doing their best to turn this episode into a victory. A military band had been summoned and was marching up and down Resslova Street, playing strident Nazi music, in an attempt to conceal what must have been great disappointment that the parachutists had not been taken alive. Whilst the siege had been underway, a message from Himmler had arrived stating that the agents must be taken alive: "Any means should be employed to reassure the assassins in order to capture them alive." But the parachutists were dead and the victory for the Germans was hollow. The subsequent German report would confirm that of the 759 officers and other ranks from the *Gestapo* and *Waffen-SS* who had taken part in the siege at Resslova Street, 14 had been killed and 21 wounded.

15

The Blood-letting Continues

The bodies that had been taken to the Institute of Forensic Medicine and Criminology were subject to post-mortems, which were carried out between 23 and 26 June by Professor Weyrich, assisted by Doctor Steffel. However, before this process was undertaken, numerous people were brought to the Institute to identify the bodies and explain how they had interacted with them.

The following descriptions have been extracted from the German post-mortem reports:

Report number 548 Jan Hrubý carried out on 26th June 1942.
Height 160cm Weight 57kg.
Clothing – dark blue suit with long trousers, two pairs of long johns, underpants, white vest, pale blue striped shirt, dark blue roll necked long sleeved sweater and one right black shoe.
Died from a shot to the head. Anatomical examination shows that the shot was fired to the right temple from a 7.65mm pistol at close range. The bullet exited near the left parietal bone.

Report number 549 Jaroslav Švarc carried out on 24th June 1942.
Height 168cm Weight 64kg.
Fully clothed, dark blue suit, brown woollen pullover, blue sweatshirt, purple woollen vest, striped long johns, blue shorts, grey-brown socks and black shoes.
Cause of death: shot through the head. Anatomical examination shows that the shot was fired to the right temple from a 6.35mm pistol at close range. Smell of almonds in the brain matter and stomach contents suggests that he swallowed poison containing cyanide shortly before death occurred but the poison was not effective.

Report number 550 Josef Gabčík carried out on 23rd June 1942.
Dressed in brown tracksuit, pyjama bottoms, pale blue underpants and two pairs of shorts, two woollen pullovers and blue checked shirt.

Anatomical examination proves that the bullet wound was caused by a high-powered weapon fired close to the right temple. The bullet exited through the left temple.

Report number 551 Josef Valčik carried out on 25th June 1942.
Height 169cm Weight 69kg.
Dressed in dark blue dressing gown, brown striped jacket, grey plus-fours, pink shirt, underpants, dark blue and brown pullover and grey socks.
Originally light brown hair and moustache but dyed black.
Anatomical examination proves that the shot was fired close to the right temple. Suicide by 6.35mm pistol. Penetration wound and exit through the left temple.

Report number 552 Adolf Opálka carried out on 25th June 1942.
Height 178cm Weight 67kg.
Clothing: dark blue tracksuit trousers, pink shirt and a brown woollen sweater.
Died of a shot to the head by a 6.35mm pistol. Anatomical examination shows that the shot was fired close to the right temple. Bullet found lodged in the left temple. He swallowed cyanide before he shot himself. He had also suffered multiple shrapnel wounds from grenade fragments and had a broken right arm.

Report number 553 Jan Kubiš carried out on 23rd June 1942.
Was alive at the church and rushed to hospital but the injuries he had suffered from shrapnel caused massive blood loss and he bled to death.

Report number 554 Josef Bublik carried out on 26th June 1942.
Height 185cm Weight 84kg.
Body dressed in dark blue trousers and pale blue long johns. This individual was of a strong muscular build and well nourished. Anatomical examination showed that he committed suicide with a 6.35mm pistol shot to his right temple. The bullet lodged in his left temple close to his left parietal bone. He had also suffered injuries as follows: multiple shrapnel wounds to both shins, left upper leg and a shrapnel wound on the right side of his neck.

After the post-mortems the heads were removed from each of the seven bodies. The torsos were handed over to be used as training aids by medical students, but some time later were buried in an unmarked grave at Ďáblice cemetery in Prague. The *Gestapo* also ordered that the heads of Gabčík and Kubiš be preserved for posterity, and so were sealed in a preserving solution in glass jars. The skulls of the other five were retained and were put on display in a dissecting room at the Institute of Forensic Medicine and Criminology. The intention was that the preserved heads of Gabčík and Kubiš would later be put on display at the Reich Museum of Criminology, presumably to be established in Berlin after the war.

The deaths of the parachutists was not the end of the criminal investigation. In the days after the shootout at the crypt, the *Gestapo* followed up on further leads given them by Čurda and rounded up more members of the Jindra organisation.

Another parachute agent still at large was Alfred Bartoš, of Operation Silver A. Čurda had informed the Germans that Bartoš led a group that operated in the Pardubice region, transmitting and receiving messages direct with London. On Sunday, 21 June 1942, Bartoš was lured to the Krupka apartment by a message from Hana Krupková, who had herself been betrayed by Čurda and arrested by the *Gestapo*, but offered immunity for her and her husband, Vaclav, if she cooperated. She was escorted to her flat, where she and her guards waited until 1800, but Bartoš did not come. He had in fact been bedridden with rheumatoid arthritis since the beginning of May. Krupková was escorted from the building, but the *Gestapo* left some men behind in the apartment. They were lucky, as a short time later, Bartoš approached the apartment building. He was suspicious; looking up, he thought he saw a man looking down from the Krupkas' window. Realising it was a trap, he turned and ran for his life. Initially he had a good lead over the chasing Germans, but Bartoš was a sick man and soon his pursuers caught up. As the chase continued, shots were exchanged, then Bartoš had the good fortune to pass the Cinema Jas just after a film had ended, briefly obtaining cover amongst the customers who spilled out into the road. However, his luck ran out when, a little further on, at the junction of Smilova and Sladkovského, a group of German *Luftwaffe* personnel were walking towards him. One of the chasing Germans shouted at this group, *"Fallschirmjager!"*, indicating Bartoš was an enemy parachutist. Bartoš, already weakened by his illness, realised his situation was hopeless, put his gun to his head and pulled the trigger. He slumped to the ground, but he was not dead. He was rushed to the Pardubice Hospital and operated on by two senior consultants, Doctors Snopek and Stránský. Their efforts were in vain, and Bartoš died in the early hours of the following day without regaining consciousness. His body was taken to Prague and a post-mortem carried out which reported two bullets found inside his skull. He was buried in an unmarked grave at Ďáblice cemetery.

Either by way of their sophisticated radio detection equipment or from the testimony of one of the many people now arrested, the Germans discovered that the transmitter used by Silver A, codenamed *Libuše*, was hidden in the small village of Ležáky, actually more a hamlet of just nine homes and a mill. *Libuše* had been hidden and used from two local locations – the quarry at Hluboká and later the mill in the village of Ležáky itself.

On 20 June, the *Gestapo* made arrests in the villages of Ležáky, Dachov, Včelákov and Miřetice. Four days later, on Wednesday, 24 June, an operation was carried out against the village of Ležáky, in which members of the *Gestapo*, *Schupos* and SS from Pardubice and Hradec Králové took part. The village was sealed off and its inhabitants were crowded into an abandoned quarry, from where they were later transported to the chateau at Pardubice known as the Zámeček. Meanwhile, all the dwellings in the village were searched and subsequently set on fire. However, *Libuše* had already been moved, so was not found by the Germans. At the Zámeček, the 13 children from the village were separated from their parents and first taken to Prague. They were eventually moved on to Chelmno, where all but two sisters, Jarmila and Marie Šťulík – who had been selected for Germanisation – were murdered. That same evening, 24 June, the 33 adult inhabitants of Ležáky were shot in a makeshift execution spot in the grounds of the Zámeček. As well as the 33 shot that day, another seven people from Ležáky were killed between 25 June and 2 July. A total of 51 villagers from Ležáky were murdered by the Germans in this atrocity.

On 26 June, the Germans announced the destruction of Ležáky as a reprisal for the villagers helping the agents from Britain. The Germans returned to Ležáky in December 1943 and began the process of removing the rubble by using slave labour, but traces of the village remain to this day.

With Valčik and Bartoš now both dead, just one member of Silver A still retained his liberty: the radio-operator, Corporal Jiří Potůček.

Potůček had now been successfully sending messages back to London for many months, but Karel Čurda's treachery meant his luck would soon run out. The final message sent from *Libuše* was on the night of 25/26 June. This message contained the following: "Instead of my radio station, they have levelled Ležáky near Vrb. Kostelec (Skuteč) to the ground. People helping us arrested. Freda's location unknown. People suspicious. Impossible to establish contacts. I am alone." Freda was the code for Bartoš, so Potůček must have been unaware of the events that had taken place at Pardubice a few days earlier.

The job of radio operator was the most dangerous of all undertakings of an SOE agent, and the normal life expectancy when working in enemy-occupied territory was just six weeks. Potůček had managed to survive for six months. After leaving Ležáky, he went to another safe house, a farm owned by Antonin Burdych in the hamlet of Končiny, near Bohdašin, about 100 miles east of Prague and 50 miles north of Ležáky. However, the *Gestapo* eventually traced Potůček to the farm, although when they arrived he was able to open fire and make good his escape into the woods. By 2 July, Potůček had travelled a further 40 miles through the woods, sleeping rough and scrounging whatever food he could. His intention was to reach the apartment of Josef Nováček in Rosice nad Labem, on the outskirts of Pardubice. He was still unaware of the arrests in Pardubice, Nováček having been arrested on 26 June. Finding the apartment empty, in desperation Nováček asked for help from another occupant of the building, Josef Fitzbauer, who not only refused Potůček any form of help but reported his presence to the local police. Recognising that he could not rely on any help, he headed off to the nearby Dubrava woods. Potůček had been walking for many miles; tired and hungry, he decided to rest and soon fell asleep. Potůček was then discovered by a two-man police patrol: Karel Pulpán and František Hoznauer. When interviewed after the war, Pulpán gave a confusing account of what happened. Pulpán on occasions claimed that he called to the figure on the ground to put his hands up and surrender, while the accepted account was that he shot Potůček at close range in the head without a word being said. Pulpán was put on trial and, his testimony not being believed, received five years' imprisonment. His companion on the patrol, Hoznauer, was jailed for two years. Potůček's body was later taken to Prague to undergo a post-mortem before being thrown into an unmarked grave at Ďáblice. Arguably, Pulpán saved Potůček from the rigours of a *Gestapo* interrogation, which would have been his fate if Potůček had been taken alive. He would then have either faced a painful death or, to have any chance of survival, would have to become a turncoat and work for the Germans.

Once all the known parachutists were either dead, incarcerated or in the pay of the Germans, focus for retribution turned on the Czech resistance. Between 28 May and 24 June, a period of less than four weeks, military tribunals in Prague condemned 448 people to death, of whom 381 were men and 67 women. During the same period, the court in Brno condemned another 247 people to death (208 men and 39 women). During the time that the martial law courts were active, 1,585 Czechs (including the 173 men murdered in Lidice) were executed in the Protectorate. These punitive measures were designed deliberately to wipe out the Czech intelligentsia, such as Professor Leopold Šrámek (former Dean at the Czech Technical University), as well as those whom the Germans had directly connected to the assassination attempt on Heydrich. Others were transported to Terezin or sent to work camps in Germany.

Čurda continued to give the *Gestapo* information and divulge the names and addresses of all those who had provided help to him and the other parachutists, so the number of people arrested continued to increase and the resistance was thoroughly broken. Eventually Vaněk was arrested. He immediately offered to help the *Gestapo* in return for his own life, agreeing to set up a radio link with London to send false news. The Germans had been using this tactic successfully in the so-called '*Englandspiel*' from Holland. The *Gestapo* had already started sending messages to London using Potůček's radio and codes, and other materiel captured from Bartoš. Although London responded to the first fake message, they were suspicious; as the Germans did not know the correct security codes to be inserted into every message, the transmissions were soon brought to an end. However, this did not stop the Germans sparing the life of Vaněk, and he also betrayed a number of fellow resistance workers.

By 1 September 1942, the number of Czechs arrested had increased to 3,188, of whom 1,357 were condemned to death by German emergency tribunals. This does not include the 252 individuals in what was known as the parachutist group, the relatives and close helpers of the parachutists; nor the executed villagers from Lidice and Ležáky or those Jews deported to the East for resettlement in the immediate aftermath of the assassination attempt. The *Gestapo* later reported that, "Most of the people who helped the assassins took a pronounced Czech, nationalist, anti-German stance, especially the women. They were often heard to say 'We are proud to die for our country.'"

The so-called parachutist group were shot at Mauthausen concentration camp on 24 October 1942 at two-minute intervals. Included in this killing spree were 12 relatives of Jan Kubiš and 13 of Josef Valčik. Jozef Gabčik's family escaped any sanctions because they were Slovakians and the Nazis found it convenient to maintain the independence of their satellite state.

The Germans immortalised Reinhard Heydrich. The Final Solution, the industrial murder of Jews and 'undesirables', was named '*Aktion Reinhard*'. Trains bearing

'*Aktion Reinhard*' banners moved the Nazi victims direct to the extermination camps at Belzec, Sobibor and Treblinka.

A regiment of the SS, then serving on the Eastern Front as part of the 6th SS Mountain Division, the *SS-Gebirgsjäger Regiment 11*, was renamed the Reinhard Heydrich Regiment. They were granted a cuff title embroidered with the name Reinhard Heydrich. Nineteen streets, squares and parks in the Protectorate were renamed to include the name of Heydrich. A road on the east bank of the Vltava in Prague was one of those renamed (it is now known as the Masarykovo nádraží).

On the first anniversary of the assassination attempt, a memorial bust of Heydrich was unveiled at the location of the attack, with a 24-hour honour guard mounted on it.

The heavily pregnant Lina Heydrich continued to live at the villa at Panenské Břežany. The property and its grounds were technically owned by the state, but Hitler issued a decree on his 54th birthday, 20 April 1943, which ceded the villa to the widow and descendants of Reinhard Heydrich.

However, remaining at Panenské Břežany proved a fateful decision for the family, as further tragedy struck them in 1943. The Heydrich boys, Klaus and Heider, were playing on a bicycle near the villa gates when Klaus cycled through the gates and onto the road, directly in the path of a truck. The driver, Karel Kašparov, who was transporting the village football team back home from a game, was unable to avoid Klaus and the boy was thrown from his bicycle, sustaining fatal injuries. In November 1941, Heydrich had been ceremonially handed the keys to the jewel chamber at St Wenceslas' Chapel in Prague. It is said that Heydrich tried on the crown, in spite of a Czech legend that anyone who was not rightfully entitled to do so would die within a year, along with his eldest son. Heydrich certainly proved the legend, and bad luck remained with the family over the following years.

Operation Anthropoid historian John Martin is one of the very few people that the current Heydrich family have granted an interview to. With John's permission, we repeat here an extract from his interview with Heider Heydrich, who was 8 years old at the time of Anthropoid:

> My brother Klaus and I were very close, almost like twins. Remember, we didn't even go out to school, where we may have met other children. Our teacher, Trude Schilling, came to the house. When Klaus died in 1943, it had a much bigger impact on me than my father's death. Klaus was riding his bicycle and I was hanging on the back of it, when the truck crashed into us, just outside the gates of our home. Klaus was killed but I was uninjured. Klaus was buried in the grounds of Panenské Břežany and I am convinced he still rests there. It was claimed he was disinterred when we left Prague and his body taken with us. Again this isn't true. I can remember the day we left for good. I rode my bicycle around the grounds one last time and his grave was undisturbed.

The trial of those members of the Orthodox Church of Saint Karl Borromeo (St Cyril and Methodius) who had cooperated in the hiding of the parachute agents commenced on Thursday, 3 September 1942, in the Petschek Palace in Prague. Their guilt had already been decided, Himmler having advised Daluege beforehand: "The Führer approved the findings against Bishop Gorazd, Priest Petřek and other priests and members of the church elders who were their accessories. I expect the death sentences to be passed."

Yet the purpose of the trial was supposedly to show the openness and fairness of the Germans. Twenty specially selected journalists were allowed to report on the trial. Geschke, head of the SIPO in Prague, was the Chief Judge. *SS-Hauptsturmführer* Wilhelm Schultze from the Prague *Gestapo* acted as Prosecutor. The trial only lasted a short while; the accused were all found guilty and sentenced to death. As well as the church officials, Anna Malinová, who had been Gabčik's fiancée, was also tried at this court.

Bishop Gorazd was shot at the Kobylisy execution ground the next day, and Father Petřek the following day. A German report about Petřek stated: "The behaviour of the condemned before and during the execution was calm and dignified. He refrained from speaking. His body was taken to the crematorium and burnt there." Others had to wait for their sentence to be carried out. For example, church verger Václav Ornest and members of his family were added to the parachutist group and shot at Mauthausen concentration camp on 24 October 1942.

On 26 September, for what the Nazis declared to be reasons of treasonable activity, the Czech Orthodox Church was disbanded and its property was confiscated. The church on Resslova Street remained closed for the rest of the war. Karl Hermann Frank later concluded: "If the Czech nation is to survive, it cannot be a nation of Petřeks!"

16

Operation Anthropoid – A Summing Up

The actual number of people who died as a result of German retribution to Operation Anthropoid will probably never be accurately known. Whilst the assassination of Heydrich did, in the short term, lead to an outpouring of grief and revenge, it did not stop the implementation of the 'Final Solution to the Jewish Question' which Heydrich had been tasked with. Whether Heydrich had survived or not, his deputy in regard to the 'Final Solution', Adolf Eichmann, remained the major architect of the mass executions that took place over the coming months and years.

The ambitious Sudeten German, Karl Hermann Frank, was passed over for the position of *Reichsprotektor* for Bohemia and Moravia, with Kurt Daluege appointed as Heydrich's replacement. When ill-health forced Daluege to retire in May 1943, Frank was again overlooked when, in August that year, Wilhelm Frick took over in the post. Yet Frank was rewarded for his work: in August 1942, he was made a Minister of State as Reich Minister for Bohemia and Moravia; then in June 1943, he was promoted to *SS-Obergruppenführer* and General of Police in Prague. By the war's end he had attained the rank of General of the *Waffen-SS*.

In 1944, Frank personally conducted anti-partisan operations in Moravia aimed at destroying the Jan Žižka Partisan Brigade. Despite the deployment of 13,000 soldiers and summary executions of civilians suspected of supporting the partisans, the resistance fighters were still able to slip through the cordons set up by the Germans, simply moving their area of operations. Frank falsely claimed that the threat had been eliminated.

Frank was eventually arrested by US Army troops near Rokycany on 9 May 1945. After spending some months in detention, he was extradited to Prague and tried in 1946. Frank was found guilty of war crimes, including the destruction of the villages of Lidice and Ležáky, and was sentenced to death. He was executed at Pankrác Prison on 22 May 1946. He was hung in front of 5,000 onlookers who had suffered by his actions, including the returned women from Lidice. Frank's body was buried in an unmarked grave at Prague's Ďáblice cemetery, not far from where the bodies of the seven parachutists and many of the victims of the German retribution had been thrown into a mass grave.

Heydrich's successor, Daluege, was Acting *Reichsprotektor* until May 1943, when he resigned after suffering a massive heart attack. He spent the rest of the war in western Pomerania, in a house given to him by Hitler. He was detained by British troops in Lübeck in northern Germany and sent to Nuremberg, where he was charged with war crimes. In September 1946, Daluege was extradited to Czechoslovakia, where he stood trial for crimes against humanity committed in the Protectorate during his time as Acting *Reichsprotektor*. Daluege was unrepentant throughout his trial, claiming that he was loved by three million policemen, that his conscience was clear and that he had only followed Hitler's orders. Nevertheless, he was convicted on all charges and sentenced to death on 23 October 1946. He was hung the next day at Pankrác Prison.

Some of the other senior Nazi officials involved in the atrocities were never brought to justice. The commander of the Lidice operation, Max Rostock, ended up working for the communists, and whilst Böhme and Geschke were declared as killed in action, their bodies were never traced.

Of the Czechs who helped the Germans, Vilém Gerik proved a reticent collaborator. Living under 'licence' in Prague, he quickly became disillusioned and tried to escape from the *Gestapo*. He was arrested on 6 April 1943 and placed in solitary confinement in Pankrác prison, before being moved to Terezin and then Dachau concentration camp. At the end of the war the Americans liberated the camp and Gerik returned to Prague, but when it was realised he had collaborated, he was arrested again. In April 1947 he was brought before an extraordinary people's court in Prague on a charge of high treason. He was found guilty and hanged at Pankrác Prison at 1145 on 29 April 1947.

A Czech official who interviewed Gerik in 1947 recorded that Gerik felt the death penalty a disproportionate sentence for the position in which he had found himself in 1942 when he was aged 21. Whilst he did reveal important information to the Germans about SOE training, corroborated information provided by Čurda and was present at the identification of the bodies of the seven parachutists at the church in Resslova Street, for which he was paid a reward, his treachery was nowhere near the same level as Čurda's.

Karel Čurda had been of far more use to the Germans. As well as being rewarded financially, he was given an apartment by the Germans, full German citizenship and a new identity as Karl Jerhot. He married a German, Marie Bauer, with whom he had a son. He was used by the *Gestapo* to trap loyal Czechs and helped in the search for other parachute agents. Čurda was particularly useful in the search for the Antimony group, which had been sent over on the night of 23/24 October 1942 and landed near Roždálovice, north-east of Prague. Their mission was to re-establish links with the resistance and try to find out the fate of the Silver A group. Antimony consisted of three men: Lieutenant František Závorka, Sergeant Stanisav Srazil and Lance Corporal Lubomir Jasinek. Initially they were successful, continuing to evade capture and reporting news of their contacts back to London. But eventually the Germans were able to home in on their radio transmissions and two of the group were corned in Rovensko pod Troskami, about 60 miles north-east of Prague, on 16

January 1943. The *Gestapo* surrounded the house they were sheltering in and called on the pair to surrender, saying if they resisted and opened fire, the village of Rovensko pod Troskami would suffer the same fate as Lidice and Ležáky. Lieutenant Závorka and Lance Corporal Jasinek came out peacefully, but any hopes the *Gestapo* had of taking them alive soon evaporated as both men had swallowed their L pill. This left Stanisav Srazil at large, but he was betrayed by Čurda, who was able to ensnare him in a trap. The *Gestapo* was now in possession of a transmitter and the group's codes and frequencies. *SS-Hauptsturmführer* Willi Leimer convinced Srazil to operate the radio and send fake messages back to London, but Srazil omitted his security code in the few messages he did send, so London did not respond to any of these messages. On 16 April 1944, the Germans decided enough was enough and took Stanislav to Terezin, shooting him four days later on 20 April.

Čurda saw out the rest of the war in the Protectorate. After the war he was quickly tracked down and arrested on 14 May 1945. He was tried for treason, found guilty and hung in Pankrác Prison at 1157 on 29 April 1947, 12 minutes after Gerik. Unrepentant, when asked why he betrayed his comrade's, Čurda answered: "I think you would have done the same for 1 million marks."

Other Czechs who aided the Germans in the immediate aftermath of the assassination attempt were also arrested after the war and put on trial. Marie Navarova, the woman who helped Heydrich at the assassination scene, was arrested for collaboration and committing a crime against the state by helping Heydrich. She was found guilty and sentenced to eight years in prison. Also stripped of her civil rights for 10 years, she died in 1966. Her husband was also found guilty of collaboration and sent to prison in 1948, committing suicide upon his release in 1953.

Franz Brauner, who owned the butcher's shop that Gabčík ran into after the assassination attempt on the morning of 27 May 1942, received payment from the Germans and used the money to buy a new shop, but found himself boycotted by the local people. Later in 1942, presumably as a result of a tip-off from some patriotic Czech, Brauner was investigated by the Czech police and found guilty of selling black market meat since 1940. The *Gestapo* ensured he received a fine rather than a prison sentence. After the war he was arrested and sent to Pankrác. He died in 1977, aged 69.

For the Czech politicians in London, the assassination, as well as the German reaction, put Czechoslovakia back on the political map. A useful comment comes from Jan Masaryk, who said that the Nazi reprisals played straight into the hands of the Czech exiles: "I was in the US at the time of Lidice and making no progress with our propaganda, having exhausted all the possibilities of the situation. Then came Lidice and I had a new lease of life. Czechoslovakia was put on the map again and we had an easy time."

Although the British Government was careful to avoid a direct endorsement of what could be viewed as a political assassination, behind the scenes it certainly supported the efforts of Beneš. A memo was sent from the Foreign Office to the Dominion Prime Ministers on 8 July 1942, which asked them to give as much support to Beneš as possible. Perhaps the biggest political gesture from both the British and Free French was to repudiate the 1938 Munich Agreement, which had carved up Czechoslovakia without giving the people any say in what happened. As a direct result of Operation Anthropoid, the status of the Czech government-in-exile was raised from that of a 'legation' to a full embassy, a step up in terms of recognition and prestige. The British Foreign Secretary, Anthony Eden, made this announcement in the House of Commons in a statement on 5 August 1942:

> I am glad to have this opportunity to inform the House that I have today, exchanged notes with the Czechoslovak Minister for Foreign Affairs in which I stated that the policy of His Majesty's Government in the United Kingdom in regard to Czechoslovakia, was guided by the formal act of recognition of the Czechoslovak Government by His Majesty's Government in July 1941, and by the Prime Minister's statement on 30th September 1940, that the Munich Agreement had been destroyed by the Germans. I added that, as Germany had deliberately destroyed the arrangements concerning Czechoslovakia, reached in 1938, His Majesty's Government regarded themselves as free from any engagements in this respect, and that at the final settlement of the Czechoslovak frontiers to be reached at the end of the war, His Majesty's Government would not be influenced by any changes effected in and since 1938.
>
> In his reply, Monsieur Masaryk, informed me that the Czechoslovak Government accepted my note as a practical solution of the questions and difficulties of vital importance for Czechoslovakia which emerged between our two countries as the consequence of the Munich Agreement, while maintaining their political and juridical position with regard to that Agreement and to the events which followed it. I should not like to let this occasion pass without paying tribute on behalf of His Majesty's Government to the tenacious and courageous stand which the Czechoslovak people are making against their ruthless German oppressors. Acts such as the destruction of Lidice have stirred the conscience of the civilised world and will not be forgotten when the time comes to settle accounts with their perpetrators.

About six weeks later, the Free French followed suit with a similar action. In the presence of General de Gaulle and the Prime Minister of the Czechoslovak government-in-exile, Jan Šrámek, the Czech Foreign Minister, Jan Masaryk, counter-signed a proclamation from the French National Assembly that it now considered the Munich Agreement null and void from the day it had been signed.

On the political front, Operation Anthropoid had almost certainly achieved the aims of the Czech government-in-exile, and indeed brought them fully into the Allied fold. However, the aftermath of the operation cannot have brought much comfort to those in exile. The Czechs were very wary of undertaking any further action in the Protectorate which could bring down on them more savage reprisals. In the spring of 1943, the Russians asked the Czech resistance to carry out sabotage on the Skoda arms factories, but the appeal was rejected. A similar response was given to London when a request for action was asked to be taken against the railways in order to hinder German troop movements to the Eastern Front. It is said that more than 50,000

Czech patriots had been imprisoned or murdered since 1939; a number that Czech circles in London had never thought would be reached.

When the communists seized power in Czechoslovakia in 1948, the significance of Western-led operations was downplayed unless they could be used to the communists' advantage. Czechs who had returned to the homeland having worked for the government-in-exile or SOE were in danger of arrest and imprisonment. Jan Masaryk, the only surviving son of the Father of the Republic, Tomáš Masaryk, was still serving as Foreign Minister after the communist coup. Less than a month later, Jan Masaryk was found dead below the bathroom window in his quarters in Černin Palace. It was announced by the Ministry of Interior as suicide, but the controversy and suspicion surrounding his death continues to this day.

The total number of people who were killed as a result of Operation Anthropoid is generally accepted as being around 5,000. Due to this high cost, Beneš did his best after the war to deny any knowledge of the assassination plan until it was too late to stop it; instead, he pointed the finger of responsibility at Colonel František Moravec. It was not until 1964 that Colonel Moravec spoke out in a public lecture to refute the charge that he alone had masterminded the operation on the orders of the British and without the knowledge of Beneš. Moravec was of the view that Beneš was fully supportive of the operation:

> If Czechoslovakia, instead of yielding to the Munich decision, had fought Germany, as I am convinced it should have done, it would have suffered much greater losses than it did after Heydrich's death, but it would also have earned a worthier place in history. Given the circumstances in which we were placed at the time, it was a good try. It is a good page in the history of Czechoslovakia in the Second World War. The Czech people should be proud of it; I am.

It should not be forgotten that in some of the darkest times in the short history of Czechoslovakia, many of its bravest sons and daughters risked and gave all for the cause of freedom. It is to their eternal memory and heroism that we should remember Operation Anthropoid and ensure that their bravery will never be forgotten:

> We are Czechs! We never surrender!
> *Jsme Češi! Nikdy se nevzdáme!*

Appendices

Appendix A
General timeline for the creation of Czechoslovakia, the road to annexation and Operation Anthropoid and its consequences

31 May 1918	Signing of the Pittsburgh Agreement – a memorandum of intent to declare independence – by the Czechoslovak National Council.
28 October 1918	An independent Czechoslovakia is created. Tomáš Masaryk elected the country's first President.
June 1919	Czechoslovakia signs the Minorities Treaty.
19 May1935	The Sudeten German Party receives over 65 percent of the Sudeten German vote.
14 December 1935	Tomáš Masaryk resigns on grounds of ill-health and is succeeded as President by Edvard Beneš.
14 September1937	Death of Tomáš Masaryk.
12 March 1938	The Anschluss – German annexation of Austria.
15 September 1938	The British Prime Minister, Neville Chamberlain, meets Adolf Hitler in Berchtesgaden to discuss the Sudeten question. Britain and France will guarantee the independence of Czechoslovakia if Czechoslovakia will cede those territories where the German population represents more than 50 per cent of the Sudetenland's total population.
16 September1938	The Czech Government ban the German *Ordnersgruppe*.
22 September1938	Chamberlain meets Hitler at Bad Godesberg for further discussions on the Sudeten question. Hitler demands that Czechoslovakia cede the Sudetenland in its entirety to Germany.
30 September1938	Hitler, Mussolini, Chamberlain and the French premier, Daladier, sign the Munich Agreement, which authorises Germany to occupy the Sudetenland.
5 October 1938	President Beneš forced to resign and goes into exile. He is replaced as President by Emil Hácha.

15 March 1939	President Hácha given an ultimation by Germany; war or a peaceful occupation of Czechoslovakia. Many Czechs flee to Poland or France to volunteer to fight in another nation's army in what they believe will be the coming war with Germany. Colonel František Moravec escapes to London with most of the Staff of the Czechoslovak Intelligence Service. Hitler arrives in Prague at 2000 and stays less than 24 hours.
18 March1939	Baron Konstantin von Neurath appointed as *Reichsprotektor* of Bohemia and Moravia. His position is to protect German interests. (*SS-Brigadeführer* Karl Hermann Frank named as his deputy.)
27 April 1939	A new Protectorate Government is formed with General Alois Elias as Prime Minister. Hacha remains President.
18 July 1939	Edvard Beneš arrives in London. He will form a government-in-exile.
23 August 1939	Germany and Russia sign a Non-Aggression Pact.
31 August 1939	The start of arrests of 3,000 leading Czech figures and intelligentsia by the Gestapo.
1 September 1939	Germany invades Poland.
3 September 1939	Britain and France declare war on Germany.
28 October 1939	Nazi security forces brutally suppress a demonstration marking the anniversary of the establishment of the Czech Republic. Later, the funeral of Jan Opletal concludes in new protests.
17 November 1939	Nine Czech student leaders executed as a result of the anniversary protest; 1,200 students deported to concentration camps.
15 January 1940	Formation of 1st Czechoslovak Division in France. By the end of May this consists of nearly 12,000 men.
10 May 1940	Germany invades France and the Low Countries.
18 June 1940	France asks Germany for an Armistice.
22 June 1940	Evacuation of Czech troops from Port Vendres and Sète by the Royal Navy.
12 August 1940	Formation of 1st Czechoslovak Mixed Brigade at Cholmondeley camp near Chester from the Czech soldiers evacuated to Britain after the fall of France.
28 October 1940	Gabčik and Kubiš amongst those awarded the Czechoslovak War Cross by President Beneš for their valour in the fighting in France.
April 1941	The Czechoslovak government-in-exile considers the viability of sending parachute agents back to the homeland.
18 June 1941	Britain recognises the Czechoslovak government-in-exile in London.
27 September 1941	Reinhard Heydrich appointed Acting *Reichsprotektor* of Bohemia and Moravia. Prime Minister Elias arrested. Elias is subsequently sentenced to death (but held as a hostage and not executed until 19 June 1942).
3 October 1941	In London, in the presence of Colonel Moravec, Lieutenant Colonel Bartík, Major Paleček, Major Krček, Warrant Officer Gabčík and Sergeant Svoboda agree to return to their homeland as an execution team to kill either Heydrich of his deputy, Karl Hermann Frank. Due to a later training injury, Svoboda will be replaced by Warrant Officer Kubiš.
29 December 1941	The Anthropoid, Silver A and Silver B groups return to Czechoslovakia.

Early January 1942	The Anthropoid group's credentials are established with the Jindra Group.
26 April 1942	Operation Canonbury I.
5 May 1942	Operation Canonbury II.
27 May 1942	The attack on Reinhard Heydrich is carried out in Prague.
4 June 1942	Reinhard Heydrich dies at Bulovka Hospital in Prague.
10 June 1942	The town of Lidice is wiped from the map in retribution for the death of Heydrich.
16 June 1942	Karel Čurda walks into the Petschek Palace in Prague.
18 June 1942	German assault on the church in Resslova Street.
24 June 1942	The Ležáky massacre.
5 September 1942	Father Petřek executed in Prague.
29 September 1942	Munich Agreement declared invalid by Britain and Free French.
24 October 1942	The 'parachutist' group of family and close associates are executed at Mauthausen.
9 May 1945	Prague liberated by Russian forces.
22 May 1946	Karl Hermann Frank hanged in Prague.
29 April 1947	Čurda and Gerik hanged in Prague for treason.
27 May 2009	Operation Anthropoid Memorial unveiled at the location of the assassination attempt in Prague.

Appendix B
Parachute groups into Czechoslovakia 1941–42

Benjamin – Otmar Riedl with codes and crystals for the Czech Home Army. Due to a navigation error by the aircrew he was dropped over Austria on the night of 16/17 April 1941 and was arrested soon after landing. He had managed to hide his parachute and equipment, and the authorities did not discover he had landed by air. He was charged with illegal crossing of a border!

Percentage – Corporal František Pavelka dropped near Caslav on the night of 4 October 1941 with a transmitter/receiver and cyphers. He did not remain free for very long as he was arrested in Prague on 25 October 1941. He was executed by the Germans at Plotzensee in Berlin in January 1943.

Anthropoid – Warrant Officers Jozef Gabčik and Jan Kubiš landed near the village of Nehvizdy on the night of 29 December 1941. Their mission was to assassinate the Acting *Reichsprotektor*, Reinhard Heydrich.

Silver A – A three-man group consisting of Lieutenant Alfred Bartoš, Sergeant Josef Valčik and Corporal Jiří Potůček. They were to re-establish contact with Captain Václav Morávek of the Home Army and, through him, a Czech double-agent known as A-54, who worked for German Military Intelligence in the *Abwehr*. Silver A was also to establish intelligence networks and assist with drop zones and arrangements for the arrival of future groups. They were dropped on the same night as the Anthropoid group.

Silver B – This group was also dropped on the same night as the Anthropoid group. It consisted of Sergeants Vladimir Skacha and Jan Zemek. They were dropped with a transmitter/receiver which they intended to pass to the Home Army, and were then to co-ordinate supply drops.

Their equipment was retrieved but later lost and they went into hiding. Both men survived the war.

Zinc – Lieutenant Oldřich Pechal, Sergeant Arnošt Mikš and Corporal Vilém Gerik were sent as a communications team tasked with reinforcing Silver A, establishing an intelligence network in Moravia and also delivering much-needed funds to the Home Army. They left England on 27 March 1942, and were dropped near Gbely in Slovakia in the early hours of the 28th. Pechal shot two German border officials whilst trying to cross into Bohemia and Moravia. He was later arrested. Mikš made it successfully to Prague and was active in the Home Army for a few weeks, but was shot dead by Czech police when attempting to recover buried equipment near Kladno at the end of April 1942. Gerik also made it to Prague, but found all his safe houses had been uncovered by the Germans. He naively decided to hand himself in to the Czech police on 4 April 1942. They immediately handed him over to the *Gestapo*. To begin with, Gerik assisted the *Gestapo* but he then tried to escape into the countryside. He was eventually caught and sent to Dachau concentration camp, but survived the war. In April 1947 he was brought before an extraordinary people's court in Prague on a charge of high treason. He was found guilty and hanged.

Out Distance – A three-man team led by Lieutenant Adolf Opálka, who was supported by Sergeant Karel Čurda and Corporal Ivan Kolařík. They were dropped near Telč in Moravia in the early hours of 28 March 1942. It was an ambitious operation, as they landed with a Rebecca homing beacon which was intended to help guide RAF bombers to the Skoda arms factories in Plzeň. Kolařík was arrested in Brno by the *Gestapo* on 1 April but was able to commit suicide.

Bioscope – Another three-man team, which left England on the night of 27 April 1942. The mission of Sergeants Bohuslav Kouba, Jozef Bublik and Jan Hrubý was to blow up an important railway bridge near Hradnice and a transformer station at Vsetín. They landed northwest of Krivoklat, but within a few days Kouba had been arrested by the Czech police and committed suicide in his cell. Bublik and Hrubý were in hiding in Prague and taken to the church of St Cyril and Methodius.

Tin – Sergeants Ludvik Cupal and Jaroslav Švarc were dropped in the early hours of 30 April 1942 near Třeboň in Bohemia. Their mission was to assassinate the Minister of Education and Propaganda, Emanuel Moravec. It did not get off to a good start, as the men could not find their equipment. Cupal committed suicide in January 1943 to avoid capture by the Germans. Švarc was in hiding in Prague and was one of the parachutists taken to the church of St Cyril and Methodius.

Appendix C
Report on the insertion of parachute agents into the Protectorate

The Wehrmacht representative to the Reichsprotektor in Bohemia and Moravia.

Secret: To the Deputy Reichsprotektor
SS Obergruppenführer General of the Police
Heydrich,
Prag IV.,
Czernin Palace.

As can be seen from this report, it is clear that during the period from August to September 1941 parachute agents have been sent to the Protectorate and to adjacent countries to the east. Agents with a Czech and Slovak background have been sent from the USSR to carry out espionage and sabotage activities in the Protectorate. Sabotage has been carried out in the Protectorate.

The High Command of the Wehrmacht considers it appropriate that the civilian population be given suitable incentives to help combat the enemy parachutists. In the Protectorate this would primarily be in the form of monetary rewards.

I ask for consideration of this proposal.

The Wehrmacht representative to the Reichsprotektor in Bohemia and Moravia

Toussant

Major General

Appendix D
Declaration of the Czechoslovak Government on 29 May 1942

The Czechoslovak Government received the news of the attack upon Hitler's brutal henchman Heydrich in the knowledge that its harassed but undaunted people who are answering with growing resistance the savagery of the German oppressors who, in accordance with Hitler's decision and Heydrich's orders, have been and are striving by means of murder, torture and intimidation to break the resistance of the nation.

With emotion and profoundest sympathy the Government has followed the tremendous sacrifices of the victims who fell during Heydrich's reign of terror from September 28th last year onwards, and it deplores the loss of all those who have thus suffered and to whom future generations for all time will owe a debt of gratitude. With intense admiration it has followed the proud conduct of the nation which even in this murderous tempest did not waver but, on the contrary, strengthened its solidarity and steeled its determination to hold out in the struggle, come what might, until the utter defeat of the enemy.

As the spokesman of the suffering and fighting people the Government of the Republic addresses all the Allied nations and all decent people in the world and calls upon them to hold up to execration the foul wickedness of the Germans led by Hitler and responsible for him. If they are now beginning to murder whole families, this is an act of brutality unique in history and they are thus calling down upon themselves just retribution in accordance with the Commandments of God and Man. There will be no peace and right in the world unless the German crimes are expiated to the full, and unless the Allies secure guarantees that the German nation will never again be able to undertake a new military onslaught against the world.

In the attack on the life of the monster Heydrich the Czechoslovak people is punishing not only the crimes committed against Czechoslovak victims but also against the victims of all the other enslaved nations in Europe. And now in accordance with its old tradition, our nation links up its destiny with the destiny of the peace-loving world. At the moment when in Prague the shots of retribution have sounded forth for all those murdered and enslaved, the Czechoslovak Government in the name of its nation sends to all the fighting and suffering patriots in Belgium, France, Holland, Yugoslavia, Luxembourg, Norway, Poland and Greece, a message of solidarity, admiration and firm faith that beside the four great Allies, the British Empire, the USSR, the United States of America and China, all our lands will share the glorious victory.

The Government is aware that the miserable failure of Heydrich's efforts will now inflame Hitler's henchmen to commit new murders. New Czech victims are already falling in the German execution yards. But this new fury of the Nazis will again be miserably broken by the unyielding resistance of the Czech people and will only strengthen its will and perseverance.

The Government of the Republic calls on all Czechoslovak patriots to stand firmly by one another, to help one another in danger and to scorn everyone who may violate the nation's honour in the hours of trial. The appalling terrorism will only consolidate the unity of all true Czechoslovaks in the Czech lands, in Slovakia and in Carpathian Ruthenia. Whoever defiles himself by collaboration with the murderous enemy will not escape just punishment. We believe, with President Masaryk, that there is no sacrifice dear enough for the conquest and defence of freedom, for there is no true life without freedom.

Appendix E
Message from MX1 (it is believed this was Patrick Howarth) and written to M (the head of operations at SOE) dated 30 May 1942

In the file on Anthropoid at the National Archives at Kew is a document dated 30 May 1942 with the covering note written by 'MX1', which states:

I attach a detailed report on Anthropoid. We hope to have a radio contact tomorrow night, though in the present state of emergency this may not be possible.

From the German broadcasts and newspaper reports it looks as though the operation went mainly according to plan.

I understand that to begin with President Beneš was somewhat apprehensive of the possible repercussions in the Protectorate, but that on second thoughts he has decided that it will stimulate the will to resist at home and gain the Czechs much credit abroad and was well worth it.

Appendix F
Proposed reward payments granted by the Germans to those people who assisted with the criminal investigation

Proposal by the Prague State Police Headquarters of 22nd June 1942, for the people to be potentially rewarded due to their assistance to help capture the attackers on Heydrich.

Proposed list for reward payments.

1. Mrs Marie Navarova, Protektorate citizen, resident of Prague-Pankratz, Prison Administrative Officer.
   Mrs Navarova was the first to try and help the injured Obergruppenführer and to arrange for his transfer to the Bulovka hospital. She also gave a good description of the perpetrator with the sub machine gun and immediately recognised him when shown the seven bodies.
   Proposed Payment   RM 20,000
2. Driver Franz Zitta, Protektorate citizen, resident of Prague-Nusl, Brussgasse 1
   Zitta was the driver of the vehicle which transported the Obergruppenführer to the hospital and assisted with his injuries.
   Proposed Payment   RM 20,000
3. Motorist Theodor Šulc, Protektorate citizen, resident of Prague XIV, Premislufer 485.

Šulc assisted with the transport of the Obergruppenführer to the hospital and also helped with his injuries.

Proposed Payment   RM 20,000

4. Tram driver Josef Klimes, Protektorate citizen, resident of Prague VIII, Steigerwiese 81.
    Klimes helped the injured Obergruppenführer and conducted himself well at the scene.
    Proposed Payment   RM 20,000.

5. Coachman Thomas Grosslicht, Protektorate citizen, resident of Prague-Kobilis, Rumburgerstrasse 3 Wohnaft.
    Grosslicht disregarded his own safety and pursued one of the perpetrators and later helped the injured driver of the Obergruppenführer, Oberscharführer Klein. He even attempted to shoot the offender with the weapon of the wounded Klein; however, he was unable to shoot due to a weapon failure.
    Proposed Payment   RM 20,000.

6. Butcher Franz Brauner, Protektorate citizen, resident of Prague VIII,
    Brauner assisted with the attempt to capture one of the perpetrators and arranged for the transfer of Oberscharführer Klein to a hospital. He gave a detailed description of the offender and later when shown the bodies recovered was able to identify the offender who fled on foot.
    Proposed Payment   RM 20,000

7. Police Officer Michael Lofergyuk, Protektorate citizen, resident of Prague XVIII, Pakomierschitzerstrasse 655.
    Lofergyuk assisted the Obergruppenführer at the scene and escorted him to the Bulovka hospital, from where he made the first report of the attack to the Reichsprotektor's office.
    Proposed Payment   RM 10.000

8. Ivan Loschak, Protektorate citizen, resident of Prague XIX, Fliegerstrasse 17.
    Loschak made an outstanding effort to help the injured Obergruppenführer at the scene and accompanied him to the hospital.
    Proposed Payment   RM 10.000

9. Mrs Helene Pechar, Protektorate citizen, resident, living in Wildenschwert, Pragergasse 236.
    Mrs Pechar behaved well at the scene and gave good descriptions of the perpetrators.
    Proposed Payment   RM 10.000

10. Police Officer Rudolf Schramek, Protektorate citizen, resident of Prague VIII, Rohrgutgasse 15) 1317.
    Schramek distinguished himself by actions and careful handling of evidence at the scene of the crime.
    Proposed Payment   RM 10.000

11. Mrs Berta Zawodnik, Reichsdeutsche, resident of Prague VIII, Schildwachstrasse 16.
    Mrs Zawodnik was present at the scene and provided valuable information in the search for the assassin. When shown the bodies she with absolute certainty identified the one who escaped by bicycle.
    Proposed Payment   RM 20,000

12. Mrs Marie Sprungl, Reichsdeutscher, Prague VIII, Kirchmaierstrasse 1236.
    Mrs Sprungl distinguished herself in the same way as the witness named at 11.
    Proposed Payment   RM 20,000

13. Mrs Agnes Rozek, Protektorate citizen, resident of Prague VIII, Am Libeňer Bräuhaus 1440.
    Mrs Rozek has provided valuable information on what happened at the crime scene. When shown the seven bodies, she recognised the assassin who had escaped by bicycle.
    Proposed Payment   RM 15,000

14. Mrs Frantiska Sedlakova, Protektorate citizen, resident of Prague VIII, Rinbachstrasse 1081.

Mrs Sedlakova made a detailed statement about the assassin who escaped by bicycle and almost certainly recognised him when confronted with the bodies.
Proposed Payment   RM 10.000

15. Mrs Bozona Kalinova, Protektorate citizen, resident of Prague XII, Schwerinstrasse 7.
Mrs Kalinova provided valuable information about the assassin who escaped by bicycle and was able to recognise his body.
Proposed Payment   RM 10.000

16. Security Officer Friedrich Platt, Reichsdeutscher, living at Prague VIII, Kirchmaierstrasse 1236.
Platt provided a detailed statement about the assassin who escaped on foot and positively identified him when confronted with the corpses.
Proposed Payment   RM 10.000

17. Coal merchant Johann Zavazal, Protektorate citizen, resident of Prague VIII, Klein-Holleschowitzerstrasse 88.
Zavazal provided detailed information on the escape route of the assassin who fled on foot and provided very useful information for the subsequent searches.
Proposed Payment   RM 10.000

18. Debt collector Franz Kohout, Protektorate citizen, resident of Prague VIII, Kobilis, Sedlicka 392.
Kohout was a passenger on the tram at the scene and despite several injuries from glass splinters provided a usable description of the offender.
Proposed Payment   RM 3.000

19. Mrs Ruzena Maslova, Protektorate citizen, resident of Prague VIII, Rundbergstrasse 1040.
Mrs Maslova gave a very good description of the assassin who fled the scene by bicycle and recognised him when shown the seven corpses.
Proposed Payment   RM 5.000

20. Fireman Stanislaus Hauf, Protektorate citizen, resident of Prague VIII, Kirchmaierstrasse 1236.
Hauf was able to give a good description of the perpetrators at the scene of the crime and almost certainly recognised the assassin who escaped on foot when viewing the bodies.
Proposed Payment   RM 5,000

21. Mrs Bozena Volvova, Protektorate citizen, resident Kolingarten 15 in Prague VIII.
Mrs Volvova gave a usable description of the assassin who escaped on foot and almost certainly recognised him when confronted with the corpses.
Proposed Payment   RM 3.000

22. Tobacconist Karl Douša, Protektorate citizen, resident of Prague VIII, Rezekgasse 906.
Douša, by his diligence, provided good information about the escape route of the assassin who escaped on foot and a perfectly usable description of the person. He recognised this assassin perfectly among the seven bodies.
Proposed Payment   RM 5.000

23. Tobacconist Wenzel Parzak, Protektorate citizen, resident of Prague VIII, Korsekerstrasse 24.
Parzak gave useful information which was vital in the reconstruction of the crime scene.
Proposed Payment   RM 3.000

24. Tram conductor Wenzel Lastovka, Protektorate citizen, resident of Prague Kobilis, Hornatezerstrasse 649.
Lastovka assisted with information to help reconstruct the events at the scene of the crime.
Proposed Payment   RM 3.000

25. Mrs Hermine Ullmann, Reichdeutscher, living in Prague VIII, Blanikgasse 1050/18.

Mrs Ullmann gave useful information about the assassin who escaped by bicycle.
Proposed Payment   RM 5.000

26. Mrs Karla Vakova, Protektorate citizen, resident of Prague VIII, Sturmfeldgasse 1015.
Mrs Vakova was the only person who was able to give a perfect description of one of the perpetrators whom she saw near the crime scene before it was carried out.
Proposed Payment   RM 5.000

27. Mrs Georgine Kucera, Protektorate citizen, resident living at Prague VIII, Klein-Holleschowitzerstrasse 1156.
Mrs Kucera was able to provide a detailed description of one of the assassins.
Proposed Payment   RM 5.000

28. Mrs Cäcilie Adamova, Protektorate citizen, resident of Prague VIII, Klein-Holleschowitz 1493.
Mrs Adamova was the first to provide information on the bicycle used in the escape. This information was vital in determining the search area in the Libeň district.
Proposed Payment   RM 10.000

29. Mrs Sophie Cermakova, Protektorate citizen, resident of Prague VIII, Rienbachstrasse 1031.
Mrs Cermakova provided valuable information on the bicyclist's escape route.
Proposed Payment   RM 5.000

30. Business Representative Anton Bohac, Protektorate citizen, resident of Prague XI, Brünnerstrasse 116.
Bohac tried to detain one of the assassins at the scene but was unable to do so because he was shot at and so took cover.
Proposed Payment   RM 10.000

31. Metal worker Bohumil Straka, Protektorate citizen, resident of Prague VI, Uraniastrasse 955.
Straka participated in the pursuit of the assassins, gave a valuable description of one of the assassins and also tried to help the injured Obergruppenführer.
Proposed Payment   RM 10.000

32. Innkeeper Anton Marek, Protektorate citizen, resident of Prague-Troja, Steinweg 225.
Proposed Payment   RM 5.000.

33. Motorist Oldrich Vasek, Protektorate citizen, resident, living in Prague VIII, Nadsutko 684.
Proposed Payment   RM 5.000
Nos. 32 and 33 gave assistance to Oberscharführer Klein and took him to hospital in their car.

34. Mrs Katerina Binterova, Protektorate citizen, resident of Prague VIII, Kirchmaierstrasse 1236.
Mrs Binterova provided valuable information about the events at the scene and in particular about the escape route of the perpetrator who escaped by bicycle.
Proposed Payment   RM 3.000

35. Car driver Bohumil Havlicek, Protektorate citizen, resident of Prague XII, Reifstrasse 23.
Havlicek distinguished himself by his conduct at the scene of the crime and provided a particularly valuable description of the assassin who escaped on foot.
Proposed Payment   RM 10.000

36. Messenger Emil Stanek, Protektorate citizen, resident living in Prague X, Kambergerstrasse 46.
Stanek provided useful information on the events at the crime scene.
Proposed Payment   RM 3.000

37. Housemaid Marie Spiclova, Protektorate citizen, resident, living in Prague VIII, Rohrgut 1342 Krcek.

Miss Spiclova voluntarily gave information later at a police station and provided useful information about a perpetrator.
Proposed Payment   RM 3.000

38. Master tailor Vilem Hejl, Protektorate citizen, resident of Prague XII, Silesia 45.
Hejl provided valuable information about previously unknown witnesses.
Proposed Payment   RM 5.000

39. Mrs Helene Havlicek, Protektorate citizen, resident of Prague, Schwanengrund 947.
Mrs Havlicek gave valuable information about the escape route used by the assassin who escaped by bicycle.
Proposed Payment   RM 3.000

40 Tram conductor Franz Zima, Protektorate citizen, resident of Prague VII, Jedlickastrasse 879/52.
Zima gave a good description of events at the scene and also one of the assassins.
Proposed Payment   RM 5.000

41. Guard Stanislaus Dohnal, Protektorate citizen, resident of Prague VIII, Maurerhof 1955.
Dohnal has distinguished himself by his good conduct at the scene and by providing a description of one of the offenders.
Proposed Payment   RM 3.000

42. Tram driver Anton Opletal, Protektorate citizen, resident of Prague XIV, Na Silene Lisce 180.
Opletal gave a detailed description of events at the crime scene and a usable description of one of the assassins.
Proposed Payment   RM 3.000

43. Student Karel Pekanek, Protektorate citizen, resident of Prague VIII, Kirchwassergasse 49.
Pekanek later voluntarily attended a police station to make a statement about the events of the crime and the escape route of the perpetrators.
Proposed Payment   RM 3.000

44. Worker Josef Bilek, Protektorate citizen, resident of Prague XVIII, Ziegelbauerstrasse 3.
Bilek provided a description of the assassin who fled on foot and valuable information on his escape route.
Proposed Payment   RM 5.000

45. Office worker Jaroslaus Pochaska, Reichsdeutscher, living at Prague XIX, Lücherstrasse 20.
Pochaska intercepted an inmate's letter from a Czech prison which yielded information allowing special security measures to be taken. In addition, he personally tried to make contact with illegal organisations in the countryside and was allowed to take his salary for this purpose.
Proposed Payment   RM 5.00046. Doctor Jindrich Pollak, Protektorate citizen, resident of Prague-Dewitz, Dewitzerstrasse 8.

46. Pollak has actively helped to set up anti-resistance groups and information on a large number of capital crimes. Through his active cooperation in the Heydrich assassination case he gave valuable information which helped during the search for the assassins.
Proposed Payment   RM 10.000

47. Police Ensign Johann Anton, Protektorate citizen, resident of Prague-Libeň, Fleischmanngasse 851.
Proposed Payment   RM 5,000

48. Police Officer Karel Hansal, Protektorate citizen, resident of Prague-Libeň, Teufelsfelsengasse 823.
Proposed Payment   RM 5.000

49. Staff Sergeant Josef Kafka, Protektorate citizen, resident of Prague VIII-Libeň, Davidstrasse 1764.
Proposed Payment   RM 5.000
50. Security guard Josef Sotona, Protektorate citizen, resident of Prague-Libeň, Wahlstadt 283.
Proposed Payment   RM 3.000
51. Police watchman Adolf Dycka, Protektorate citizen, resident of Prague X, Theresienstrasse 130.
Proposed Payment   RM 3.000
52. Coachman Jaroslav Kucera, Protektorate citizen, resident of Prague-Kobilis, Striskauerstrasse 730.
Proposed Payment   RM 10,000
Nos. 47 to 52 have assisted in the persecution of two criminals who were arrested in the search for the assassins. Especially commended are No. 47 (Anton), No. 48 (Hansal) and No. 52 (Kucera). Anton also suffered a facial injury during the arrest.
53. Fireman Josef Soustruznik, Protektorate citizen, resident of Prague-Smichov, Brockhoffstrasse 5.
Soustruznik distinguished himself by a particularly brave act at the church in Resselgasse by placing and replacing water hoses in the ventilation window in the church basement.
Proposed Payment   RM 5.000
54. Fireman Karl Novotny, Protektorate citizen, resident of Prague VII, Am Stauweg 42.
Novotny distinguished himself through a decisive action at the church by removing a ladder from the basement used by the assassins and this greatly weakening their ability to defend themselves.
Proposed Payment   RM 5.000
55. Fireman Bohuslav Winter, Protektorate citizen, resident of Prague-Veitsberg, Veitsbergergasse 143.
Proposed Payment   RM 3.000
56. Fireman Karl Hertel, Protektorate citizen, resident of Prague-Branik, Am Hain 35.
Proposed Payment   RM 3.000
57. Fireman Ladislav Klein, Protektorate citizen, resident of Prague-Kobilis, Habernergasse 6.
Proposed Payment   RM 3.000
Those listed from 55–57 have distinguished themselves by their efforts at the church in Resselgasse 82.
58. Pastor Franz Werner Bobe, Reichsdeutscher, resident of Prague III, Karmelitterstrasse 9.
Bobe provided information that the church was being used by the assassins and this helped with the arrest of a main participant.
Proposed Payment   RM 10,000

Appendix G
List of payments from the Prague Gestapo files, 24 December 1942

To the Higher SS and Police Leader SS-Gruppenführer, State Secretary K.H. Frank in Prague
Subject: Reward fund for the investigation into the assassination of SS-Obergruppenführer Reinhard Heydrich.

The reward fund of 2 million Reichsmarks made available by the German and Protektorate Governments has so far paid out 1,539,900 Reichsmarks. The relevant documents concerning these payments can be found in the local files. There is a balance of 460,100 Reichsmarks.

This money is deposited with the German Credit Bank in Prague in account No. 4101.

I have informed the bank that the power to pay out money from the Reward Fund has been transferred from the State Police Headquarters in Prague to the Secretary of State, K.H. Frank, with immediate effect.

The Protektorate Government has not been notified from this office of this decision.

Doctor Gerke

Payments from the Reward Fund

Name	Amount (in Koruna)
Zawodnik, Berta	200.000
Sprungl, Marie	200.000
Platt, Friedrich	100.000
Ullmann, Hermine	50.000
Prochaska, Jaroslaus	50.000
Bobe, Franz Werner	100.000
Müller, Josef	50.000
Navarova, Marie	200.000
Zitta, Franz	200.000
Šulc, Theodor	200.000
Klimes, Josef	200.000
Grosslicht, Thomas	200.000
Brauner, Franz	200.000
Lofergyuk, Michael	100.000
Loschak, Iwan	100.000
Pechar, Helene	100.000
Rozek, Agnes	150.000
Sramek, Rudolf	100.000
Sedlakova, Franziska	100.000
Kalinova, Bozena	100.000
Zavazal, Josef	100.000
Kohout, Franz	30.000
Maslova, Ruzena	50.000
Hauf, Stanislaus	50.000
Volfova, Bozena	30.000
Douša, Karl	50.000
Prazak, Wenzel	30.000
Lastovka, Wenzel	30.000
Vakova, Karla	50.000
Übertrag [transfer]:	3.120.000
Kucera, Georgine	50.000
Adamova, Cäcilie	100.000

Name	Amount (in Koruna)
Cermakova, Sophie	50.000
Bohac, Anton	100.000
Straka, Bohumil	100.000
Marek, Anton	50.000
Vasek, Oldrich	50.000
Binderova, Katarina	30.000
Havlicek, Bohumil	100.000
Stanek, Emil	30.000
Spiclova, Marie	30.000
Nejl, Wilhelm	50.000
Havlicek, Helene	30.000
Zima, Franz	50.000
Dohnal, Stanislaus	30.000
Opletal, Anton	30.000
Pekanek, Karl	30.000
Bilek, Josef	50.000
Pollak, Jindrich, Doctor	100.000
Anton, Johann	50.000
Hansal, Karel	50.000
Kafka, Josef	30.000
Sotona, Josef	30.000
Dycka, Adolf	30.000
Kucera, Josef	100.000
Soustruznik, Josef	50.000
Novotny, Karl	50.000
Winter, Bohuslav	30.000
Hertel, Karl	30.000
Klein, Ladislav	30.000
Knappe, Emil	50.000
Kuba, Rudolf	30.000
Schmidt, Detlef	100.000
Pitermann, Josef	25.000
Raim, Wenzel	25.000
Kopacek, Karl	50.000
Halfar, Anton	30.000
Nemec, Franz	20.000
Hollern, Heinrich	20.000
Kolcava, Ulrich, Doctor	10.000
Dvoracek, Wilhelm	20.000
Gruber, Franziska	100.000
Fritzbauer, Josef	100.000
Koznauer, Franz	30.000

Name	Amount (in Koruna)
Pulpan, Karl	30.000
Überweisungen	
Transfers to offices in Budweis and Königgrätz	23.000
Transfer to office in Iglau	8.000
Transfer to office in Pardubitz	2.000
Panenka, Jaroslaus	10.000
Stepanek, Ladislaus	10.000
Vesely, Wenzel	10.000
Cash withdrawal (reward for 8 Czech Pol.-Agents)	26,000
Cash withdrawal (for Vladimir Moratschewitsch)	10.000
Čurda, Karl	5,000,000
Gerik, Wilhelm	5,000,000
Total	Koruna 15,399,000

In order to take the wind out of the sails of the enemy propaganda, which always blows in a certain direction, I think that two measures are necessary for our policy and for our propaganda:

1. A number of still to be identified people who were arrested in connection with the assassination go unpunished. Our future reputation depends on how we act in the event of further actions of a similar style. (Decree of impunity.)
2. The RM 2 million premium will be paid in whole or in part. The parachute agent Čurda, who, before he gave himself up, made an anonymous report to a Czech Police station and satisfactory evidence of the Czech newspaper used as packing, should also be paid RM 500,000. Another 500,000 RM would be given to assistants in the search or to the Czech firefighters who assisted in the action at the church or distribute it to similar persons. All payments must be published in the press and announced on the radio, stating the names. In addition to providing evidence that we are keeping our promises, this measure has the following additional benefits: Proof is provided that the parachute agents are not a unit struggling to the last breath, but softening and willing to give in. We do not give the Czech people any hope of resistance to the last and of heroism, and moreover London and the émigrés get a shock as their best efforts fail. There is again inconsistency and confusion.

Appendix H
Letter from the Ministry of Foreign Affairs, Czechoslovak Republic, Fursecroft, George Street, London, W1 to His Excellency Mr P. Nichols, The Foreign Office, dated 2 June 1942

Dear Excellency,

I have the honour to inform Your Excellency that the Government of the Czechoslovak Republic has received reports of a new wave of persecution to which the Czechoslovak nation is being exposed.

On May 27th last an attack was made in Prague on the life of Reinhart Heydrich, the Deputy Reich Protector of Bohemia and Moravia. This attack is a manifestation of the opposition and legitimate defence by which the Czechoslovak people are responding to Heydrich's reign of terror dating from his arrival in Prague on September 28th 1941. Reinhart Heydrich, Himmler's right hand, was dispatched to Prague on that date, when it had become clear that all the devices had failed by which Baron von Neurath, appointed Reich Protector of Bohemia and Moravia by Hitler had attempted to break Czechoslovak opposition. It was expected that Heydrich would make use of more stringent methods, and he did so to an inordinate degree. As soon as he entered upon his duties he proclaimed martial law in the most important areas of the country and emergency courts began to carry out their work. It has been ascertained that, by the end of 1941 more than four hundred persons were shot or hanged on charges of subversive activities, agricultural or industrial sabotage, membership of one or other of the former Czechoslovak political parties, often, too, merely for listening to foreign broadcasts and for spreading news obtained in this way. These executions were continued until quite recently, although on a less extensive scale, and the total number of victims of this reign of terror amounts to some five hundred, as far as is known from the official statements of the German courts. These victims comprise both men and women. The actual number cannot be stated even approximately. Under the regime of Heydrich many people were executed without any court procedure, as Heydrich assumed personal responsibility for all the acts perpetrated by the Gestapo.

At the same time thousands of suspects were arrested by the Gestapo, and though many of them were afterwards liberated, the majority were thrust into concentration camps, amongst which the camp at Osvětím has recently become notorious because of the specially barbarous treatment meted out to the Czechs there.

Heydrich swept away the final remnants of any self-government in the Czech territories. General Eliáš, the Prime Minister of the Protektorate Government, was among the first of those who were condemned to death. The Government which had thus been deprived of its leading figure was provided with a Minister of Economics and Social Welfare in the person of Dr Walter Bertsch, a Prussian official completely ignorant of Czech. The actual power is in the hands of Dr Bertsch and the other members of the Government are mere figureheads. Dr Bertsch intensified all the measures concerning the utilisation of output in the Protectorate for the war aims of the Reich. Food rations were drastically reduced, workers were refused the right of free choice of duties, working hours were increased and in every factory of any size a Gestapo cell was installed to detect sabotage. The last measure taken by Heydrich on the day before the attack on his life was a decree introducing conscription for the whole male population of the Protectorate, beginning with those in their sixteenth year. Persons not yet working in war factories were to be sent to labour battalions engaged upon repairing the roads behind the front.

Heydrich at the same time started a ruthless war against Czech education and cultural life in general. Teachers form a particularly high percentage of those who were executed. All Czech institutions of university rank were closed as far back as November 1939, and Heydrich took similar steps in the case of most of the secondary schools, teacher training colleges and higher grade elementary schools. In wireless and the press a campaign was started to gain possession of the 'Czech soul' i.e. to convince the Czech nation once and for all that its function was to be the slave of the Germans, for which purpose it needed only elementary education.

With brutal ruthlessness Heydrich continued and intensified the efforts for the Germanisation of Bohemia and Moravia. German administrative commissars were forced upon purely Czech towns and the last remnants of Czech local government was suppressed. The former mayor of Prague was executed.

Heydrich proceeded in a particularly merciless manner against the Jews. Many persons were executed merely because of their Jewish origin, discrimination against Jews was intensified in the food rationing scheme, several thousand Jews were deported from the Protectorate to Poland under appalling conditions while all the remaining Jewish population in the Protectorate, numbering about seventy thousand persons were incarcerated in the fortress of Terezin, which normally accommodates no more than seven thousand.

By numerous provocative acts Heydrich did all he could, day after day, to wound Czech national susceptibilities. He seized the coronation jewels of the Czech kings, which have also been regarded as sacred national relics, he hounded down the members of the Czechoslovak National Army which during the last war, was established in Russia, France, Serbia and Italy and in articles and speeches he grossly insulted persons whom the Czechoslovak nation has always looked up to as its outstanding representatives.

The steps taken by the German authorities in Bohemia and Moravia as a sequel to the attempt on Heydrich's life vie in their ferocity with any of the German crimes hitherto perpetrated in the occupied countries of Europe. The ferocity of these criminal measures at the same time testifies to the fact that even Heydrich's eight months' rule of terror was not able to wreck the opposition of the Czech people. Under the terms of these measures any person giving any help to the culprits will be shot, and with him his whole family. Here, for the first time, the present German Government publicly proclaim a new and outrageous principle of terrorism, involving the slaughter of women and children if the male members of their family do not comply with the demands of their oppressors. This must never be forgotten.

All persons residing in Bohemia and Moravia who have not yet reported themselves to the authorities were under orders to do so not later than midnight on May 29th. Any persons remaining in Bohemia and Moravia after this time limit without reporting their presence are liable to be shot. The same fate will befall those who harbour after this time limit any persons who have failed to report.

All theatres and other places of amusement and cultural centres have been cleared.

According to the reports which have been received and confirmed, the slaughter of families actually began before the expiry of the time limit for unregistered persons, for as early as May 28th two families including wives and children were shot. In the following few days the same fate befell more than ten families, including a boy of sixteen. According to the reports hitherto available, the number of persons executed between May 28th and June 1st amounted to 107, of whom 22 are women. One of the women was 74 years of age, and she was executed together with her husband, who was 71 years old, her son and her daughter. All these victims belonged to various political parties and they include numerous intellectuals, for example three university professors, one well-known author as well as several high officials, so dreadful was the harvest of German brutality already during the first five days.

In order to justify these executions it is asserted that the victims 1) had harboured persons who had failed to report themselves to the police and who were involved in acts hostile to Germany, or 2) had failed to report themselves to the police in accordance with the regulations issued on May 27th 1942, or, finally 3) had incited the public to shelter the culprits and had expressed approval of the attempt on the life of Heydrich.

The Czechoslovak Government raises the most solemn protest against these barbarous acts which form a blatant negation of all principles of humanity and justice and appeals to the conscience of the whole civilised world. Adopting the fundamental point of view that every nation, in as far as it has not become the victim of direct violence from without, is responsible for the policy of its regime, the Czechoslovak Government declares that responsibility for the crimes committed by the Germans rests not only with the German Government, but with all Germans who were immediately concerned in these crimes, as well as those who assisted them. The Czechoslovak Government will take all necessary steps which it may regard as desirable to secure retribution for these atrocities, and will relax no efforts to bring to account all those who committed these crimes or who were in any way responsible for them, whether they ordered them, carried them out or had any share whatever in them, until the dictates of justice have been fully satisfied, under the terms of the proclamation at the Inter-Allied Conference at St James's Palace on January 13th 1942.

I am instructed to state that the Czechoslovak Government would be grateful if His Majesty's Government would kindly take due note of this resolution. At the same time, I beg to enclose the text of a declaration of the Czechoslovak Government on May 29th 1942.

I have the honour to convey to Your Excellency the assurance of my highest consideration.

Appendix I
Letter from His Excellency Mr P. Nicholls, The Foreign Office, dated 13 June 1942 to the Czech Ministry of Foreign Affairs, Hubert Ripka

Sir,

In Your Excellency's despatch No 79 (2156/5/42) of 3rd June you enclosed a copy of a Note from the Czechoslovak Government regarding the death of Heydrich. In that Note the Czechoslovak Government announce their intention to take all the necessary steps to secure retribution for the acts committed by Heydrich and his subordinates in accordance with the terms of the Resolution signed at the Inter-Allied Conference at St James's Palace on 13th January.

I request that you will acknowledge the receipt of this Note, adding that His Majesty's Government have taken note of its contents. At the same time you should assure the Czechoslovak Government of the deep sympathy of His Majesty's Government with the people of Czechoslovakia in the hard trials to which they are now being subjected by their German oppressors.

I am, with great truth and respect, Sir,

Your Excellency's obedient servant,

For the Secretary of State.

Appendix J
Letter to the Foreign Office from the Czech Ministry of Foreign Affairs, dated 17 June 1942

Your Excellency,

Since the moment when I had the honour to inform Your Excellency in my letter of the 2nd inst., about the new wave of repression which swept over the Czech territories after the attack on Reinhard Heydrich, the German interlopers have subjected our country to fresh acts of terrorism, the barbarity of which, both as regards their character and the methods of their fulfilment, exceed all the other infamies which the Germans have hitherto perpetrated against the populations of the occupied areas.

In my letter I already had the honour to inform you that Himmler, Daluege and their henchmen have replaced their previous system of slaughtering and executing Czechoslovak patriots by another system which involves the cold-blooded murder of whole families, including women and children. In particular, I must emphasise the fact that this method of wiping out whole families has been officially proclaimed by the German authorities as a penalty which will be inflicted upon alleged culprits. In the official proclamation issued at Prague by the German occupation authorities on May 27th last, after the attack on Heydrich, it stated: "Anyone harbouring the culprits or affording them help or having knowledge as to their identity or their whereabouts and failing to report it, will be shot with all his family."

The execution of an alleged culprit, together with all the members of his family has thus been proclaimed as an official penalty, and the German Government, together with its representatives, has accordingly assumed direct responsibility for these acts. The number of persons who between May 27th and June 16th fell victims to this new outburst of German savagery amounts to more than 500. The list of these martyrs provided obvious and unmistakeable evidence that the victims are deliberately selected from all sections of the Czech people. This plainly shows that the Germans are slaughtering innocent people and are perpetrating mass murders, not for the purposes of punishing possible culprits, but solely in order to spread brutal and indiscriminate misery and horror, vainly imagining that in this way they will break the spirit of the Czech nation.

During the days which followed the death of Heydrich the terrorism in our country was intensified in an appalling manner. Not only did the mass executions of whole families of Czech patriots continue to increase, but the Germans committed an atrocity which is without parallel in the history of modern warfare. The Czech village of Lidice near Kladno was razed to the ground, the whole of its male population was shot, the women were thrust into concentration camps while the children, mercilessly dragged away from their mothers, were removed to some unknown destination. A whole Czech village was thus completely wiped out, deliberately, with the full and public knowledge of the German authorities and in accordance with their official public proclamation.

On the subject of the destruction of Lidice, the German authorities issued the following report on June 10th: "In the course of the search for the murderers of SS-Obergruppenführer Heydrich unmistakeable indications were discovered that the population of the commune of Lidice near Kladno had afforded support and help to the set of culprits in question. Proofs were secured without the assistance of the local population, although enquiries were instituted amongst them. Their attitude towards the outrage which thus revealed itself, was aggravated by further acts hostile to the Reich, such, for example, as the discovery of treasonable printed material, stores of arms and munitions, illegal wireless transmitters and extremely large quantities of goods amenable to rationing, as well as the circumstances that the inhabitants of this commune are in the active service of enemies abroad."

By this proclamation, the Germans themselves betray their own arbitrary and inhuman course of action. This outrageous document must be kept on record as a reminder of what the German regarded as adequate justification for sending large numbers of Czech patriots to their deaths and exposing their wives and children to ruin. The Germans do not even attempt to state that they discovered the culprits. They state only that "unmistakable indications" were discovered which tend to inculpate the population of Lidice. And they themselves admit that they secured the accompanying proofs without the assistance of the local population. Uncorroborated allegations of the German subordinate authorities evidently sufficed to let loose this German savagery. It is alleged that the population of Lidice afforded support and assistance "to the set of culprits in question". Yet the Germans have themselves admitted that all attempts to trace those who made the attempt on the life of Heydrich have proved unavailing. Can it be supposed that they would simply have made away with persons whom, by means of torture, they could have forced to provide them with the necessary clues? Only the future will show why the Germans selected precisely the commune of Lidice as their victims. The same thing, however, might have happened to any other Czech commune, because the same dauntless and determined spirit of opposition which pervaded the population of Lidice is alive among the whole of the Czech people.

In the course of this war the Germans have destroyed more than one locality outside the range of hostilities, and have murdered and deported the total population of more than one commune. Never before this, however, I think, have they brought brutality of this kind into the scope of their system of penalties publicly announced and officially approved by the highest authorities even in the actual war zone – outrageous though their system has hitherto been.

The note which I had the honour to communicate to Your Excellency on the 2nd inst. enumerates the measures which the Czechoslovak Government, under the terms of the Allied resolution of January 13th last at St James's Palace, is preparing in order that the culprits may meet with condign punishment. I am enclosing with this note a second resolution of the Czechoslovak Government, passed by the Ministerial Council on the 17th inst. at London, under the chairmanship of Dr E Beneš, the President of the Republic, reaffirming and setting forth in greater detail the former resolution of the Czechoslovak Government and indicating our unswerving determination to proceed to the utmost in order that after the war the demands of justice may be unequivocally satisfied.

I should be grateful if Your Excellency would kindly bring the contents of this letter and resolution to the notice of your Government.

Please accept, Your Excellency, the renewed assurance of my highest consideration.

Ripka.

Appendix K
Letter from the Foreign Office, dated 29 June 1942, to the Czech Ministry for Foreign Affairs

Sir,

In your despatch No 82 of 20th June, Your Excellency enclosed copies of a Note dated 17th June from the Acting Czechoslovak Minister for Foreign Affairs regarding the acts of barbarism committed by the German authorities in the Protectorate, following the attack on Heydrich, and dealing in particular with the German annihilation of the Czech village of Lidice.

In acknowledging the Czechoslovak note of the 17th June, you should inform the Czechoslovak Government that it has been communicated to His Majesty's Government, who wish to assure the Czechoslovak Government and people of their profound sympathy in these further barbarous acts of German oppression and persecution.

I am, with great truth and respect, Sir,

Your Excellency's obedient servant,

For the Secretary of State.

Appendix L
Orders issued to the *Waffen-SS* in Prague for an operation on the night of 17 and 18 June 1942

Distribution:
Commander SS Troops Prague
Commander SS-Wach Batallion Prague
Commander Ersatz Batallion SS-Deutschland Prague

1. Search for parachute agents in the buildings of the area: Karlsplatz west side – Resselgasse – Am Sderas – Sderaser-Lane – Karlsplatz west side. [These are the German names for the streets around St Cyril's church in what we call Resslova Street.]
2. Ersatz Batallion SS-Deutschland cordons off the area mentioned in 1) above.

3. SS-Wach Batallion Prague forms outer cordon: Karlsplatz west side – Trojangasse – Moldauufer a) along the street, b) along the quays – Myslikgasse – Karlsplatz west side.
4. Route of March:
    a) Ersatz Batallion SS-Deutschland: from Nürnbergerstraße via Old Town Square – Wenceslas Square – Water Lane to Karlsplatz;
    b) SS-Wach Batallion Prague: one group via Dientzenhofer bridge and the other via the Smetana bridge.
5. The cordon must start suddenly:
    Start time: 4.10 a.m.
    To be completed by: 4.15 a.m.
6. In the sealed area there are many confusing alleys, passages, tunnels and so on, and it is possible the parachute agents may use these for attacks or escape attempts. Parachute agents are to be apprehended alive.
7. From the issue of these orders strict security is required.
8. Command Posts:
    a) Commander Ersatz Batallion SS-Deutschland Prague corner Karlsplatz and Resselgasse;
    b) Commander SS-Wach Batallion Prague corner Dientzenhoferbrücke – Macha place.
9. I am located corner Resselgasse – Am Sderas.

Signed von Treuenfeld.
SS-Brigadeführer and Major General of the Waffen-SS.

Appendix M
Gestapo report on the assault on the church, dated 29 June 1942

Report from the SIPO Chief Geschke on the Church attack
Secret State Police
State Police Headquarters Prague
Prague II, June 29, 1942.
Bredauer-Gasse 20.
Telephone number 300-41.
B.-Nr. 93/42 – g – II G (SK)
To SS-Gruppenführer and State Secretary K. H. Frank
Subject: Operation of the Waffen-SS on the night of 17th to 18th June 1942.
Report of the BdW-SS of 23rd June 1942.

Attached is the report of the Waffen-SS commander given to me for comments.

The following can be said about the report:
    As far as the BdW-SS speaks of the "SD and SD officials", it must of course be called "officials of the Secret State Police". This confusion is all the more astounding, as the basic discussion for the use of the Waffen-SS took place in the office of the head of the state police headquarters, so the commander of the Waffen-SS had to be aware of the personnel involved in this secret plan.
    In addition, after the SS-Gruppenführer Frank had expressly ordered that the Waffen-SS Commander should provide the Head of the State Police Headquarters in Prague with the necessary resources for this task, he had to use them. The content of the report further compels the following fundamental statement, which has hitherto not been discussed with regard to the success

of the action in agreement with SS-Gruppenführer Frank. Following clear orders, the Waffen-SS cordon was due to begin at 04.10 and finish at 04.15 to assist the secret state police action, although the cordon did not start to deploy till 04.25.

Since it was constantly pointed out during the preliminary discussion, it was possible that there was a second escape route from the church catacombs and an intrusion into the church would only be successful, if an escape of the parachute agents by a possible second exit could be stopped by a cordon of the Waffen-SS. The success of the entire action in the event of a second escape route was dependent on the fact that the Waffen-SS blockade commenced at 04.15 which coincided with the entry of my officers into the church. In fact, the deployment of the Waffen-SS did not start until 04.25, as SS-Gruppenführer Frank could personally ascertain as he was present. If, therefore, a second exit had been available, the murderers of the Obergruppenführer would have been given the opportunity to escape.

1.   We were requested to supply 400 Waffen-SS troops.
2.   The 25 men of the Waffen-SS were not required to "protect" the secret police, the officers of the secret police were issued with close quarter weapons, such as grenades and sub machine guns made available.
3.   As already stated, the cordon of the Waffen-SS did not start until 04.25. The officers of the Secret State Police in the church were immediately fired on after entry, so long before the withdrawal of the Waffen-SS. Of the 25 men of the Waffen-SS, "some did not enter the church", but were still part of the security detail as discussed at the preliminary meeting in my office.
4.   It is completely incorrect that my officers fired from buildings opposite the church through the stained-glass windows and endangered their own men. Secret police officers were not at all in these houses. It was men of the Waffen-SS who were positioned in the school opposite and they opened fire on the church from there. It was not the commander of the Waffen-SS, but me who stopped this senseless shooting because it was endangering my own men.
5.   There was never an order from the Waffen-SS commander to withdraw from the church; the BdW-SS was not entitled to do so either, because until then he was only responsible for the external cordon while I was in charge of the whole action. The officials cleared the church only after they had used their close quarter weapons, especially the hand grenades, and the Waffen-SS Commander refused to provide any further hand grenades. Since without hand grenades any attack was hopeless, the formation of an assault squad from the Waffen-SS was requested as the only way forward by Kriminal Kommissar Pannwitz. This assault troop received all the information that was available, plans of the interior as well as information about the exact location and number of the criminals in the gallery from the Secret State Police.
6.   The comment that two men were taken alive easily leads to confusion because the two agents never regained consciousness.
7.   The comment on the location of the crypt and the presence of other criminals in the crypt were the result of investigation work by the Secret State Police.
8.   The fire brigade was not used by the Secret State Police as an "expert" but as an aid. The head of the fire department declared that the removal of the slab would take 3 to 4 hours if it was not to be destroyed. In contrast, the destruction by detonation took 10 to 15 minutes.
9.   The priest was ordered by the Secret State Police to tell the agents in the crypt to give themselves up and not by the Waffen-SS.
10. According to information from the Fire Brigade, the crypt would have been fully flooded by bringing additional pumps in 1½ hours. If this had been allowed, the Secret State Police would have achieved their goal without further losses. The order of the Waffen-SS Commander to

stop pumping water had been given entirely arbitrarily and without agreement with me as the leader of the entire operation and has led to considerable confusion in the command of the Fire Brigade. The water level also did not rise "very slowly", but had already reached 90 cm in height in the short time the pumps were used.

11. The existence of the stone staircase under the floor in the church was known to the Secret State Police from the beginning, because the priest had admitted it.

12. The autopsy on the four bodies recovered from the crypt revealed that none had been injured by the fire of the Waffen-SS, but that they had all killed themselves by shooting themselves in the head, with two of the agents also taking poison.

13. The fact that a secret transmitter is still to be found in the church is down to the Secret State Police. The church loudspeaker system as far as the BdW-SS is concerned cannot be compared with a transmitter in any way.

In conclusion, it must be stated that all the actions carried out so far with the Waffen-SS have gone smoothly, that only the actions which took place during the night of 17th to 18th June 1942 proved difficult as a result of the frequent personal intervention of the Commander-in-Chief SS which led to difficulties which, however, have not jeopardised the overall result. So far it has not been felt necessary to report on these experiences. However, after the Commander of the Waffen-SS stated in his report of the 23rd of June, that many of them were as a result of suggestions by SS-Gruppenführer Frank, who attended the action, it is regretted therefore that we feel many of their points should be ignored. However, it is still necessary to comment on this report. The experience of this action teaches us that the command relationships must be clearly defined, as has clearly happened in this case by SS-Gruppenführer Frank, and that accordingly interventions of higher ranks in the interest of the success of the entire action must be stopped.

Doctor Geschke
Chief of SIPO in Prague

Appendices L and M are typical of the 'chaos' of Nazi bureaucracy; the *Waffen-SS* getting in a report which blamed the *Gestapo* for the failure to capture the agents alive, and then the *Gestapo* retaliating in kind.

Appendix N
Instructions from Berlin for treatment of captured agents

Telex from the Reichsführer-SS
1. The Chief of the Security Police
2. The Chief of Ordinary Police

Berlin
1. The enemy agents and parachutists have on several occasions previously used the so-called Cyanide tablet to avoid arrest and so ended their lives before they could be interviewed.

2. I hereby mandate that in all arrests in the border area, but also in all arrests by the security police, police officers take the strictest measure to prevent such actions.

3.) The guilty person must always be put in handcuffs and a gag be placed in the mouth.

Signed
H. Himmler
5th June 1942

Appendix O
Preliminary *Gestapo* report on the network of Czech parachutists in Bohemia and Moravia, discovered in connection with the investigation into the perpetrators of the assassination attempt on *SS-Obergruppenführer* Heydrich on 27 May 1942, dated 20 June 1942

I.   On 16th June 1942, at noon, Karel Čurda a Protektorate resident, who was born on 10th October 1911, in Stara-Hlina, Krs. Wittingau, single and a Roman Catholic, whose last residence was Stara-Hlina 1, stated that he wanted to give a statement and asked to be shown the briefcases found at the scene of the assassination, because he thought he knew the owner of one of these briefcases and was also able to provide other relevant information. He said that Jozef Gabčik owned one of these briefcases. He further revealed that Gabčik was also a parachute agent. During interrogation he stated that he was a Czech parachute agent who on 28th March 1942, together with five other agents, had parachuted out of a Halifax transport aircraft into the Protektorate near Worechow, Bez Teltsch.

In the course of further interrogation Čurda stated before being presented with the briefcases that he would definitely be able to recognise the one that was used by the agent Jozef Gabčik. Čurda stated that the briefcase he had seen used by Gabčik before the assassination in the apartment of the Svatoš family in Melantrich No. 15 Prague I, had scratches below the lock. This area had been polished by Gabčik with brown shoe polish. In fact, Čurda immediately recognised this briefcase. The briefcase was found after the assassination attempt at the scene. Further, Čurda stated that Gabčik had a machine pistol a few days before the assassination in this briefcase. In addition, the briefcase contained fresh grass at that time. An investigation into the briefcase by the Forensic Institute of the Security Police in Berlin has shown that the briefcase had been used to transport grass and hay; the opinion was that the last owner of the bag probably had kept rabbit food in the briefcase.

This statement by Čurda gave the impression that he really knew more about the assassination and the group of perpetrators, since the fact that the briefcase had contained grass was only known to a small group of German officials – but not the general public. He named the second assassin as Jan Kubiš, whom he calls a friend of Gabčik. He also confirmed that the personal descriptions of the assassins published by the State Police Headquarters in Prague corresponded to the general descriptions of these two persons. When asked about the motives for his appearance at the State Police Headquarters in Prague, he said that he had heard from the press the news of the shooting of the parents of Czech parachutist Oldřich Pechal, and fearing that his mother, to whom he was very attached, would suffer the same fate, he decided to give himself up. Initially Čurda was unwilling to reveal much information, [and] it appeared he was himself involved in the assassination or at least was very well informed about the perpetrators. Irrespective of this, as a result of his information immediate search measures were implemented.

In support of his statements, he states that on 13th June 1942, he wrote an anonymous letter to the Protektorate General Station in Beneschau, naming the same people as the perpetrators. This anonymous letter was actually handed over by the Protektorate State Police on 18th June 1942. By further cautious interrogation, it was possible to obtain more information from Čurda including contact addresses for parachute agents in Prague, Belohard, Pardubice and Plzeň.

II.   The interrogation of some of the people named by Čurda, in particular Vlastimil Moravec enabled us to gain knowledge of a whole network of Czech parachute agents, including Gabčik and Kubiš, who were described by Čurda as the assassins. It was determined that in Prague the apartments of the following people acted as the main points of contact: Moravec, Svatoš, Bautz, Hošek and Zelenka.

From previous investigations it had been discovered that outside Prague, a close-knit network for helping parachute agents had been set up, which breaks down as follows:

a)   Printer Jan Vojtešek in Belohard,

b)   Electric Board Official Václav Krupka and his wife in Pardubice,

c)   Dressmaker Clucerova in Plzeň, and from the same location contacts by the name of Kral, Bejbl, Hrdelcka.

The arrests of these persons, who are considered to be the main contact points, also resulted in a close-knit network of lesser points of contact, mainly for short-term temporary accommodation so that the total number of people arrested so far in the period from 17th June to 19th June 1942 numbers 51. Further arrests are still to come.

By in-depth interviews of these people, the following information was determined to be the general position:

On the night of 28th to 29th December 1941, a British long-range bomber took off from England and dropped the agents Gabčik and Kubiš in the area of Plzeň and later the agents Valčik, Bartoš and Tolar [Tolar was the alias of Potůček] near Podiebrad. A transmitter was also dropped near Podiebrad. Further interrogations revealed that the parachute agents were all requested to visit the Vojtišek house in Belohard, as they only received further instructions from there. After meeting with the contact, Krupka in Pardubice, they were sent on to other addresses in Prague, Plzeň and Pardubice itself. In Prague, the Moravec apartment became a sort of command post, since several parachute agents were there at the same time, meetings and practical plans were discussed and agreed.

III. From the statements of the parachute agent Čurda, who voluntarily came to the Police, Mrs Krupka and Vlastimil Moravec were identified as helpers of the assassins and were arrested.

Mrs Moravec, the mother of Vlastimil Moravec, was arrested but took poison before she could be questioned properly. She also provided accommodation for the agents on the night of 28th to 29th December 1941. Also other parachute agents and the terrorist group Bartoš, were accommodated in the apartment. At the same time, she served as a courier and helped to find other accommodation addresses as did Mrs Krupka. The Krupkas were mainly the link between Bartoš and all the other parachute agents. The arrested person Vlastimil Moravec acted as special representative of Bartoš at certain times. Moravec provided permanent liaison between the individual parachute agents; while Bartoš worked on the future strategy for his group. He regularly acted as a focal point for communication between the agents and their superiors. He also took on the role of a constant companion to the agents who frequently changed their addresses.

IV. The danger of this group can best be described by the description of two main events, namely the fires near the Skoda Works in Plzeň on the night of 25th to 26th April 1942, and above all the preparation and execution of the attack on 27th May 1942. According to Vlastimil Moravec, the agents Valčik and Kubiš were told around the beginning of April that they had been notified from London that the RAF wanted to bomb the Skoda Works in Plzeň and that they had been instructed to make some sort of preparations, so that the pilots could find the

Skoda Works. Since the parachute agents had no reliable contacts in Plzeň at the time, Mrs Moravec provided them with accommodation. On 16th April 1942, Moravec learned that the preparations for the raid would soon be carried out by the parachute agents.

On 24th April 1942, Moravec escorted, on behalf of Bartoš, Čurda from Pardubice to Plzeň, where Valčik, Kubiš and Adolf Opálka already were present. Then Vlastimil Moravec drove back to Prague taking Gabčik with him. On 25th April 1942 fires were lit, Valčik and Kubiš set fire to one and Čurda and Opálka to the other. The air raid on Plzeň took place that night, but the bombs were dropped 6 km from Plzeň.

V. Vlastimil Moravec further states in his interrogation that he was aware by early May with information provided by Valčik, Kubiš and his mother, that an assassination was being planned against SS-Obergruppenführer Heydrich. He was also aware that Kubiš and Gabčik were ordered to carry out the assassination and that both had already received this order in England. During a discussion at his home, Kubiš showed him a grenade of English origin that it was intended to use in the attack and explained how it worked.

Moravec further stated that he had been informed by Valčik that the assassination attempt on SS-Obergruppenführer Heydrich was originally to be carried out in Panenské Břežany and that Gabčik and Kubiš had repeatedly travelled by bicycle from Prague to Panenské Břežany. According to another statement by Moravec; Gabčik had been using a ladies' bicycle for both the reconnaissance trips and the assassination attempt. The bicycle had been obtained earlier from a Jewish woman called Lydia Bondy, who had been living in Teplitz, but had moved to Prague. Mrs Moravec, who was unable to ride a bicycle, had, therefore, given it to Gabčik, and according to the testimony of her son, all the markings on the bicycle (company name etc) were removed before the assassination attempt. This women's bicycle used by Gabčik was recovered at the scene and taken into safe keeping.

VI. It deserves to be emphasised that until the day of the assassination attempt on SS-Obergruppenführer Heydrich, the parachute agents were housed individually in Prague and surrounding areas. After the assassination, these agents rallied on the instructions of Bartoš in the Karl Borremeus Church, with the permission of the local pastor, Doctor Petřek, who was informed that the persons looking for accommodation were Czech parachutists. Food was supplied by Mrs Moravec. After lengthy interrogations and after overcoming considerable personal anguish Vlastimil Moravec revealed the whereabouts of the parachute agents when he stated that if he was in trouble and on the run he was told by Bartoš to go to the church. A further indication that this was their hiding place was revealed by a statement from Mrs Krupka.

VII. On 18th June 1942 at 04.15 on the basis of information provided by Vladimir Moravec and Mrs Krupka, the Karl Borremeus Church and the surrounding area was cordoned off and kept clear except for authorised personnel. After a gunfight the resistance of the seven parachute agents was ended.

VIII. The identification of the seven dead has so far revealed (in the order of the photographic numbering):
1. Jan Hrubý, born about 1915, is from Moravia (investigations are still ongoing).
2. Jaroslav Švarc, from Moravia, former member of the 4th Infantry Regiment in Hlučin – Moravia (investigations are ongoing).

3.   Jozef Gabčik, born at Poluvsil-Zilina. Gabčik was a member of the former Czechoslovak Railways (CSR), most recently as officer in the 14th Motorised Battalion in Kaschau. Later he was a magazine administrator and on 4th June 1939, illegally joined the Czech Legion in Poland. Gabčik is wanted by the Slovak courts and is listed in the arrest wanted book. Parachute agent Čurda and Vlastimil Moravec have identified him. Gabčik was the sub machine gunner in the assassination of SS Obergruppenführer Heydrich.

4.   Josef Valčik, born 2nd November 1914 in Smolina, Bez. Ungarisch Brod, lately platoon leader in Infantry Regiment 22 in Jitschin.

5.   Adolf Opálka, born 4th January 1915 in Röschitz, former Lieutenant of the Mountain Regiment 2 in Rosenberg.

6.   Jan Kubiš, born 24th June 1913 in Wilimowitz, district Trebič. Known to have served with Infantry Regiment 34 in Moravia-Weisskirchen, [he] was identified by the parachute agent Čurda, Vladimir Moravec and Svatoš. He was also found in the Army service records.

      Note that he has undergone an appendectomy and also a toe of the left foot is displaced to the far left. An expert from the German Forensic Institute – Doctor Steffel – noted on Kubiš both the operation scar and the abnormally placed left toe. In addition, the scars of the wounds caused by the splinters of the bombs on 27th May 1942, which in the opinion of the same expert are about twenty-four days old, can be seen. Kubiš had thrown the bomb at the car of SS Obergruppenführer Heydrich.

7.   Jozef Bublik, born 12th February 1920 in Banov, district Ungarisch Brod, lived until his escape in 1939 at Banov 309.

IX.   The investigations into the head of the Czech parachute agent group, the former Lieutenant in the 8th Dragoon Regiment, Captain Alfred Bartoš, who was in England and now possibly in Pardubice are to be pursued vigorously.

Appendix P
Lidice was not erased from the map

The Germans did their best to remove all traces of the village of Lidice and 'erase it from the map'. However, this did not happen, as once other parts of the world heard what had happened, action was taken. Towns in Brazil, Mexico, Panama, the United States and Venezuela changed their names to incorporate that of Lidice, in remembrance and defiance of the German brutality. Around the world, as far away as San Jerónimo Lidice in Mexico, the massacre is still commemorated every year.

In Britain, strong feelings came to the surface, especially in Stoke-on-Trent, where a resident and local councillor, Doctor Barnett Stross, heard about Hitler's declaration that "Lidice shall die forever" and responded with the opposite: "No. Lidice shall live."

Similar to Lidice, Stoke had a strong mining community, which Dr Stross mobilised. Together with Arthur Baddeley, President of the North Staffordshire Miners' Federation, he launched the 'Lidice Shall Live' campaign on 6 September 1942. Czech President Dr Edvard Beneš attended the launch event. Miners across Stoke-on-Trent and North Staffordshire pledged a day's wage each week to a fund to rebuild Lidice. It was a big sacrifice in an economy already strained by the war, but the miners recognised that it was nothing compared with the suffering of Lidice. By the end of the war, they had raised £32,000 – equivalent to over £1 million today. On 3 June 1945, soldiers from the Red Army erected a monument on the site of the village. In the coming years a new Lidice was built about a mile away from the old village. Today the site of the old village is a national cultural memorial.

A rose garden was also established, created with a donation of 29,000 rose bushes from 32 countries, which has become symbolic of the continuity of life.

Children from Lidice never seen again:

Josef Brehjca
Josef Bulina
Anna Bulinova
Jaroslava Bulinova
Jiří Cermak
Miloslava Cermakova
Bozena Crmakovya
Jiří Fruhaug
Karel Hejma
František Hejma
Jaroslava Hermanova
Marie Hockova
Vara Honzikova
Bozena Honzikova
Zdenek Hronik
Bozena Hronikova
Marta Hronikova
Zdenka Hronikova
Václav Jadlicka
Karel Kacl
Vara Kafkova
Anna Kaimlova
Jaroslav Kobera
Václav Kobera
Milada Koberova
Zdenka Koberova
Hana Kovarovska

Ludmila Kovarovska
Antonin Kozel
Venceslava Krasova
Rudolf Kubela
František Kulhavy
Jaroslav Kulhavy
Miloslav Liscka
Milada Mikova
Jitka Moravcova
Václav Moravec
Karel Mulak
Marie Mulakova
Zdenek Muller
Antonin Nerad
Alena Nova
Milada Novotna
Antonin Pek
Emilie Pelichovska
Václav Pelichovska
Josef Pesek
Anna Peskova
Jiřína Peskova
Miloslav Petrak
Zdenek Petrak
Jiřína Petrakova
Zdenek Petrik
Marie Pitinova
Stepan Podzemaky

Vera Pruchova
Josef Prihodova
Anna Prihodova
Jaroslava Prihodovha
Venceslava Puchmeltrova
Miloslav Radosta
Václav Rames
Jaroslava Ramesova
Bozena Rohlova
Jiřína Ruzenecka
Jiří Seje
Jiřína Souckova
Marie Souckova
Miloslav Souckova
Josef Sroubek
Marie Sroubkova
Jaroslava Storkova
Jarmila Strakova
Ludmila Strakova
Josef Suchy
Wiroslava Syslova
Antonin Urban
Vera Urbanova
Josef Vandrdle
Dagmar Vesela
Karel Vlcek
Jaromir Zelenka
Ivan Zid

Appendix Q
The residents of Ležáky in June 1942

Břetislav Bohač
Marie Bohačova
Antonin Čech
Ludvik Dušek
Marie Duškova
Josef Hrdá
Stanislav Klapka

Josef Bohač
Čeněk Bureš
Marta Čechová
Oldrich Dušek
Aloisie Hrdá
Stanislaw Hrdá
Marie Klapkova

Květoslava Bohačova
Františka Burešova
Vlasta Čechová
Kvéta Duškova
Marie Hrdá
Marie Jamborova
Vlasta Klapkova

Antonin Louvar	Františka Louvarova	Alois Mrkvička
Jaromir Mrkvička	Marie Mrkvička	Antonin Pilař
Miloš Stantejský	Josef Štulik	Václav Štulik
Marie Štulikova	Růzena Štulikova	Jindřich Švanda
Bohumila Švandova	Emilie Švandova	Františka Švandova
Jarmila Štulikova	Marie Štulikova	Helena Skalická
Antonin Skalický	Adolf Sýkora	František Sýkora
Jiří Sýkora	Pavel Sýkora	Emilie Sýkorová
Milada Sýkorová	Milada Sýkorová*	Marie Sýkorová
Břetislav Tomek	Karel Tomek	Karel Tomek*
Růžena Tomková	Růžena Tomková*	

* These three entries were sons and daughters given the same name as their parent.

Appendix R
The *Gestapo* report and footnotes

As stated in the main part of the book, the *Gestapo* was tasked with producing a detailed report on Operation Anthropoid. Only a few copies of this still exist, and to the best of our knowledge the total report has never been included in a book published in England before. We are happy to try to correct this here; although the reader needs to bear in mind that it was painstakingly translated from German and Czech by people with limited knowledge of these languages and we have kept as far as possible to the original text. We are fully aware that there are errors and contradictions in it, and also it was written for the senior leaders of the Nazi regime and tried to paint the German and *Gestapo* actions in the best possible light. Indeed, it is believed that on the day of the assassination attempt Heydrich was in his 'personal' car, registration number SS-4, rather than his official car, SS-3. The *Gestapo* report, probably to try and protect themselves, said that he was in his 'official' car, SS-3.

We have also included as stated the original German names, so, for example, St Cyril and Methodius Church in Prague appears in the report as the Karl Borromeo, Pardubitz is used for Pardubice and Panenské Břežany was called Jungfern Breschan. Also in this report, Czech names were 'Germanised', so, for example, Václav appears as Wenzel. On occasions, to help the reader, the 'Czech' name has been included in brackets.

Additionally, in recent years a document was published in Czech which added information from Czech archives to the original text as footnotes, and a number of these are also included.

Secret State Police Prague, 25th September 1942. State Police Headquarters Prague
Special Commission into the Assassination of the Deputy Reich Protector and Chief of the Security Police and SD SS-Obergruppenführer Reinhard Heydrich.
Final Report.

Introduction.
During the investigation of the Special Commission[1] it became clear that the direct and indirect helpers of the assassins was a large group and that this report does not mention all the people involved and further investigations into these illegal organisations will continue for several months. In addition, Czechs who provide shelter to fugitives who were previously unconnected with the assassination attempt and their circle of helpers will continue to be hunted.

Initial Report and First Acts

The first report of an incident occurred on 27th May 1942, at around 10.50 a.m., when the State Police Headquarters in Prague was informed by the Police Directorate of Prague, Police Commissioner Zenaty, via a telephone message that a bomb attack had been carried out on a senior officer.[2] Further details about the actual location, the extent of the attack and the officer concerned could not be given by the Police Directorate because they themselves only had received a garbled message from the Bulovka hospital, where it was reported this senior officer had been taken.[3]

Immediately, a number of men from the local office went to the Bulovka hospital, where no one could provide clear information either.[4] The situation was eventually cleared up when SS-Obergruppenführer Heydrich was discovered in an operating theatre. The Bulovka hospital was immediately surrounded by a security detail to prevent a repeat of the attack. The crime scene, a few hundred metres away, was then visited, secured and a preliminary scene of crime investigation started. The area was sealed and guarded and on the following morning a detailed analysis of the area was carried out by a team (led by Kriminalrat Kopkow and Kriminalkommissar Doctor Wehner) of the Reich Security Main Office. As an immediate response at around 11.30 a.m., after the arrival of SS-Gruppenführer and Secretary of State K.H. Frank[5], all Prague's arterial roads were closed; as well as stopping all civilian railway traffic leaving Prague.

Appointment of the special commission

The Head of the State Police Headquarters Prague, SS-Standartenführer and Regional Gestapo Director Doctor Geschke immediately set up a special commission headed by Criminal Commissioner Pannwitz to investigate the attack.

Reconstruction of the crime

On Wednesday, 27th May 1942, an attack on SS-Obergruppenführer Reinhard Heydrich was carried out by two unknown perpetrators at 10.36 a.m.,[6] the crime scene was located in the district of Prague VIII at the sharp bend of Kirchmaierstrasse and Klein Holleschowitz. SS-Obergruppenführer Heydrich drove daily from his summer residence Schloss Jungfern Breschan, to Prague Castle. The journey took place on this day as usual in a motor vehicle (registration number SS-3), which was driven by SS-Oberscharführer Johannes Klein. The time of departure from Jungfern Breschan was not known to the public, but it was always between 9.30 a.m. and 11.00 a.m. At the actual time of departure, the Adjutant at the residence contacted Prague Castle by telephone to advise that Heydrich had left.

The journey through the countryside and after crossing the city limits by Prague Kobylisy was quiet and without any disturbance until the bend on the Kirchmaierstrasse – Klein Holleschowitz was reached. At this point, due to the extraordinarily sharp bend, Klein had to slow down and change to a lower gear. As the car came round the bend at a very low speed, a man with a submachine gun pointing towards the Obergruppenführer was standing on the right hand side of the road in the direction of travel of the car. The gunman, who was standing about one and a half metres from the car, followed the movement of the car with the gun, but did not fire a shot. At this moment, when this method of attack had clearly failed,[7] a second man who even the Obergruppenführer's driver had not seen, threw a bomb at the car from a short distance away.

This bomb hit the car on the right rear fender; it then exploded and tore open the right side of the bodywork.[8] The Obergruppenführer was wounded as a result of a piece of bodywork or bomb fragment that went through the right front seat on which the Obergruppenführer was sitting. The splinter penetrated his body and caused internal injuries.[9] At the moment the sub-machine gunner came into sight, Klein shouted to the Obergruppenführer: "Look out, a gunman", or something similar. The Obergruppenführer replied: "Stop, stop now."[10] Shortly after the explosion of the bomb, the car came to a halt; damage from the bomb had caused the car to slow down. The Obergruppenführer and his driver both got out and started to approach the assassins.[11] The gunmen fired from handguns (Colt 7.65mm pistols) at the Obergruppenführer and his driver, but did not hit either of them. The Obergruppenführer had to return to his car after a few steps as a result of his severe injuries and was taken to the nearby Bulovka hospital[12] by a few helpful Czechs who stopped a lorry. At Bulovka an operation was immediately carried out. Meanwhile, Klein chased one of the assassins, along Kirchmaierstrasse in the direction of the city along the Kolin Gardens where the assassin repeatedly fired at Klein but without success. In his attempt to escape, the perpetrator tried to escape through a butcher's shop, but came out again as the shop had no rear exit. In the street outside shots were fired at Klein who was wounded by two shots in his leg and could no longer continue the pursuit. Klein was unable to use his own weapon during this chase because of a stoppage to his weapon.[13] This perpetrator then escaped in the direction of Klein Holleschowitz and [made] subsequent movements towards the Troja Bridge in the city centre of Prague, which are unclear.

The second offender had escaped on a men's bicycle along the Kirchmaierstrasse towards Prague-Libeň and fired his pistol at several pursuers,[14] which aided his escape without interference from them. His escape route was determined by subsequent investigations. He rode the bicycle down the Kirchmaierstrasse and then the Primatorenstrasse to the corner of Slavatagasse,[15] where he parked his men's bicycle in the Slavatagasse outside the Bata shoe shop and then escaped on foot along the Primatorenstrasse in the direction of Libeň. On the basis of witness statements, it was clear that the perpetrator had suffered face or eye injuries, which were bleeding heavily. These injuries caused the offender to cover his face with a handkerchief whilst he was escaping. This action caused him to be noticed by several witnesses and so an accurate description of him was obtained. His bicycle, which he parked at the Bata shop in Slavatagasse, was wheeled away shortly afterwards by an approximately 14-year-old girl. Witnesses who saw this incident had assumed that that the bicycle owner had been injured in a fall and some witnesses spoke to the girl. She explained that she was picking up her father's bicycle. She wheeled the bicycle into Slavatagasse and made, as it turned out after a later investigation, a detour to reach her apartment. This was so as not to betray the direction of this apartment.

At the scene, the assassins had left the following items:

Sub-machine gun (English manufacture)
1 rain coat
1 hat
1 ladies' bike and
2 briefcases

A bomb was found in each case and one spare magazine for the sub-machine gun in one of the briefcases. The briefcase belonging to the assassin who fled by bicycle had been abandoned by the wire fence of a nursery opposite the scene. The other briefcase was hanging from the handlebars of the women's bicycle left behind at the scene, and this contained a bomb and a spare magazine for the sub-machine gun. This bomb was not live, but otherwise ready to use. Presumably, the assassins had made a mistake here by forgetting to insert a detonator. In addition, the perpetrators, as was found by examining the spent bullet cases, used English Kynoch ammunition. From the later investigations by the Forensic Institute of the Security Police in Berlin it was found that this ammunition had been fired from Colt pistols. Also scattered around the damaged car were fragments of metal and pieces of grey insulating tape which clearly showed that the bomb used for the assassination was of the same manufacture as that found in one of the briefcases. The other briefcase, which was left hanging from the handlebars of the bicycle left on the scene (#1 and provided with 2 buckles), was that used by the assassin with the sub-machine gun. The other briefcase thrown away had been used by the bomb thrower.

First reference to English assistance in the act

It was discovered very early on in the investigation based on objects found at the scene that the operation had been carried out by English parachute agents. In late April/early May 1942 parachute agents were dropped in Bohemia together with supply canisters,[16] some of these were later recovered in which a sub-machine gun of the same model as found at the scene, together with similar ammunition, Colt pistols and grey insulating tape were found.[17]

Attitude of the Czech population at the crime scene

The Czech people present at the scene of the assassination were shocked because of the detonation of the bomb and so failed to act quickly. However, some Czechs, including police officers, both on and off duty who were close to the scene did assist but as they were not armed were unable to stop the perpetrators escaping. Some Protektorate citizens did offer assistance to the wounded Obergruppenführer. Amongst those who helped were:

> Marie Navarova, housewife[18]
> Franz Zita, driver
> Theodor Šulc, driver
> and Franz Brauner, butcher, who transported the injured driver, SS-Oberscharführer Klein, to hospital.

These brief accounts of the events at the scene and the escape routes will be ended here, but further investigation added more information and this will be covered later in this report. In essence, the events described here represent the information that was available to the Special Commission in its investigations during the first few days. The larger and more significant measures taken by the Special Commission to obtain information about the assassination and its planning which eventually led to the network of people who had assisted the perpetrators and to the detection and eradication of the murderers is contained later in this report.

Final investigation results on the assassination of SS-Obergruppenführer Reinhard Heydrich

The extraordinary and extensive investigations carried out by the Special Commission have led to the detection and death of the perpetrators of the assassination attempt on SS-Obergruppenführer Heydrich. It is clear and without doubt that after the conclusion of these investigations the identities of those who carried out the assassination and who their helpers were has been ascertained.

The perpetrators are:

Bomb thrower

Czech citizen Jan Kubiš, born 24th June 1913 in Unter-Wilimovic, formerly residing in Wilimowic No. 71, post Libnik, district Trebitsch in Moravia, single, profession unknown.

Army service: Former platoon commander in Infantry Regiment 37 in Moravia-Weisskirchen.

Gunman

Slovak citizen Jozef Gabčik, born 8th August 1912 in Poluvsi, district of Sillein- Slovakia, Roman Catholic, single, blacksmith, last residing in Stranske-Srota No. 135 with his parents.

Army service: Former platoon commander in Infantry Regiment 14 in Kaschau.

Jan Kubiš is the second son of Frantisek Kubiš and Christina, nee Mitiska. This marriage produced four children, three sons and a daughter, of which Jan Kubiš is the second eldest.

Kubiš' father later remarried a divorcee Marie Dusik, nee Cech, she also had four children from this previous marriage and testified that she had four more children with the father of the assassin Kubiš. The eldest daughter brought by Dusik into this marriage produced a child from her stepfather. Frantisek Kubiš was therefore sentenced to one year in prison. The assassin's father, Frantisek Kubiš, was a shoemaker in Unter-Wilimovic and lived in very poor conditions in a small house which had use of a few fields that were badly neglected. The Kubiš family was one of the most mentally unstable in Unter-Wilimovic and enjoyed a very bad reputation in the town because of the circumstances described here. It does not come as a surprise that in such a family relationships are very loose and in some cases nonexistent. He only lived in his parents' house until the age of seven and then was looked after by a relative, his mother's brother, Josef Mitiska. He stayed there until he was 14 years old and so lacked a father figure influence in his life. He has never met some of his siblings.

Josef Mitiska, who was responsible for the upbringing of the young Kubiš is blind and runs a tobacconist in Ptaco. The house is run by his sister, Bernarda Mitiska, and it was in a very poor and modest state. This was the situation that surrounded the assassin from his youth. At the age of 14, Jan Kubiš went to work as a cattle herder and also undertook casual work, without learning a specific profession. At the age of 21, he joined the former Czechoslovak Army, and served with them for a number of years and was eventually promoted to platoon leader. Kubiš then joined the Czech Legion, allegedly via Romania, Turkey and North Africa. He met with Gabčik in France, with whom he stayed together with from then on.

Jozef Gabčik is the fourth child of Franz Gabčik, who was born 13th October 1879 in Skalcko, Sillein. Slovakian born and nationality, Roman Catholic, lives in Skalcko No. 130. He is married to Marie nee Beranek, [who] was born 1st December 1876 in Konska in the district of Sillein, Slovak nationality, Roman Catholic, residing with her husband. The assassin Gabčik has three older siblings, two brothers and a sister, a younger brother died in 1933. The parents are both illiterate, and have paid little attention to the careers of their children, leaving them largely to their own devices as they progress. His father, Franz Gabčik, spent several years in America and returned to his homeland in 1920. He has always shown a conscious Czech-style attitude and is socio-democratically minded.

The assassin Gabčik had lived for two years with his parents after attending elementary school and helped with the house. He then went to Kostelna, where he worked as a trainee blacksmith for four years. After completing his apprenticeship, he joined the former 14th Infantry Regiment in Kaschau, where he remained for several years and became a platoon commander. However, he was dismissed by the military because of conduct prejudicial to good discipline and because he owed 6,000 Koruna. The debts were then covered by his father. After his release from the military, he was employed in Sillein as an ammunition controller and was transferred from there after a short time to Trenčín. Here, however, his criminal tendencies flared up again and he stole army guns and 60 rounds of ammunition. In the course of the investigation about his conduct he asked for and was allowed to take a fourteen-day vacation and he fled abroad to Poland on 4th June 1939. As a holiday reason, he stated that he was going to visit his parents and also to get some documents so he could apply to join the Financial Guard. The Slovak authorities subsequently searched for him without success. His parents and relatives have not heard from him since that time.

The assassin Jozef Gabčik was known as a hermit and of an adventurous nature, who liked to read pulp adventure novels. He had no friends and was considered an outspoken drunkard. It completes the character image of the assassin, that he had no self-discipline, had a low income and was often drunk when he was working. Politically he confessed to be a member of the Agrarian Party and a fanatical Czechoslovak.

After his escape to Poland Gabčik was at Camp Brunowitz near Krakow and from there he travelled via Gdynia to Boulogne in northern France. He then met up with Kubiš in the Legion.

The route for the assassins into the Legion

The escape route of the assassins Kubiš and Gabčik from the Protektorate to the Legion is not confirmed in every detail. There were on the whole two escape routes for potential Legionnaires. One went via Poland – Gdynia and then by ship to Boulogne, the other via the Balkan States, Istanbul, Cairo and thence to Marseilles.

Based on the testimony of escaped Czechs, here is an example of the route into the Legion, from which a clear picture emerges of the individual circumstances, the Legionnaires' movement, and finally their training as parachute agents P

The Protektorate citizen Čurda, who played an important role in the assassination network, had also joined the Legion. On the evening of 17th June 1939 he crossed the border at Moravian-Ostrava into Poland and was taken by a Polish man to Teschen. On the basis of his comments that he "wanted to join up with other Czechs" in Poland; he was taken under guard together with six other Czechs to Krakow. They included as well as Čurda, a former lieutenant from the Army, a senior police officer and a senior administrative official from the civil service. In Krakow, they were taken to the Czech Consulate, and here they were given accommodation and also provided with identity papers in their real names. After three days as a large group of Czechs had arrived in Krakow amongst them four lieutenants and three platoon leaders, they were transferred to the Groß Brunowitz camp near Krakow. There were already 500 to 600 men in this legionary transit camp. The Camp Commandant was a former Czech Army captain. At this camp everyone if they wanted to had to commit to a five-year period with the French Foreign Legion, but with the condition that if war was declared against Germany they would be transferred to a Czech Legion. On 2nd July 1939 this camp was closed and the men moved by rail to Gdansk and from there on the Polish ship *Chrobry* and shipped to Boulogne.

From Boulogne they travelled to Lyon and after thorough medical examinations to Marseilles. In Marseilles, another rigorous medical examination was carried out; those who were not fit for military service with the Legion were rejected and sent to Paris for other duties. A group of those found suitable for service were shipped to Oran in the first days of September 1939, and from there by rail to Sidi-bel-Abbes. The assassins Kubiš and Gabčik were part of this first group transported from Marseilles to Oran. They were then stationed in a camp near La Hadagar Saida for about six weeks and then transported to Oran via Saida. From here a large number of men were transported to Marseille. From Marseille they were taken to a camp at Agde, where they remained until June 1940. After a short period on the German-French front, during which the assassins Kubiš and Gabčik both served in the same unit, they were shipped to Gibraltar and from there in a convoy to Liverpool. They were first accommodated in England in a camp at Cholmondeley Park. After two months, they were moved to Moreton Hall Castle, near Kineton. The Czechs living in these camps, about 150 men, had stayed together for about a year.

Beneš Presents Medals to Kubiš and Gabčik on 28 October 1940

On the National Day of the former Czechoslovak Republic, 28th October in 1940, the Czech Legion held a parade in England before Churchill, Beneš, and senior representatives of the British Army. At this parade, Beneš personally distributed decorations to a number of people including Kubiš and Gabčik.

Training of Czech parachute agents in England

The training of agents in England prior to them being dropped in the Protektorate has been carried out particularly thoroughly. After careful investigation, the parachute agents were selected from members of the Czech Legion, who volunteered to serve in the Protektorate. The agents were almost exclusively former members of the Czech infantry, training and pioneer formations. In isolated cases radio operators of the Czech Air Force were also selected. Several training schools in different parts of England are used, which only have English staff. Basic training was carried out at a school in Manchester, where they were taught weapon training, radio communications, Morse code and parachuting drills. This training was carried out by English instructors in 14 days. Afterwards, the agents were sent back to their parent unit for several months and then called for a six-week special sabotage training course at Camasdarrach near Mallaig in Scotland. This again was run by British Army instructors who taught close combat drills, map reading, Morse code, use of explosives and demolition techniques. Practical exercises were carried out on the demolition of railway tracks and bridges and the theoretical poisoning of drinking water systems. After completing this course, the trainees were taken back to their parent unit. Then they were moved to the Villa Bellasis in Dorking, about 40 km south east of London, and they were transported to their operational airports from here. The radio operators also had to complete a six-week course at the Czech communication station at Woldingham. In many cases the airfield at Tempsford near Bedford was chosen as the departure airfield. The movement of the agents was mostly in groups of three, which were under the command of a former Czech officer.

The communication groups were equipped with a short wave transmitter and receiver, spare parts and also a special short wave transmitter, which bore the code name 'Rebecca'. This is a direction finder apparatus which operates independently for a certain period of time on a particular wave length. British aircrew are therefore trained to pick up the signals within a distance of 150 km [actually around 60km] from the location of the beacon.

The groups selected for sabotage activities were equipped with a large amount of explosive material and special explosive devices for use on railways, bridges, storage tanks and so on. Also included were items which would aid in the production of sabotage devices, such as detonators, time fuses, pressure fuses, acid fuses and other items.

Each parachute agent was also issued with large amounts of German currency, first aid equipment, food for the first few days, sleeping and poison tablets, etc. Their weapons consisted of Colt pistols (7.65 and 9 mm), sub-machine guns and hand grenades. The Colt pistol was in many cases a hallmark of a parachute agent.

Almost without exception, the agents are members of the former Czechoslovak Army. They only received their orders from their respective leader after landing in the Protektorate.

Departure from England and landing in the Protektorate

On 28th December 1941, the assassins took off from England[19] and crossed the Protektorate border shortly before 3.00 a.m. on 29th December 1941. This flight was the first time that parachute groups had been dropped into the Protektorate. The importance of this flight is underlined by the fact that the supervisor of all Czech parachute agents in England, a former captain in the Czechoslovak Army named Šustr, was present in the aircraft. It is even said that on some occasions he controlled this aircraft himself. Šustr only gave the assassins their operational orders during the flight, including where they should go in the Protektorate.

The dropping of the agents took place in two parts. At Nehvizdy located on the road between Prague and Podiebrad; Kubiš and Gabčik landed about 500 metres south of the village [of] Nehvizdy and hid their parachutes and equipment in a hut in a field. This hut was used by the owner as a cattle shed and for storing items. Here they spent the first day and night because the assassin Gabčik had sprained his right foot on landing after his descent. The aircraft then flew north to Kolin, carrying out some circular manoeuvres before turning back towards Pardubice.[20] During this onward flight three other parachute agents were dropped near Pardubitz, the leader of this mixed sabotage and communications group was Captain Bartoš (Motycka), assisted by Valčik and the radio operator was Tolar. This group later re-established contact with the assassins and assisted them in relation to the other tasks that they had been ordered to undertake.

Operations in Plzeň

On 30th December 1941, the assassins Kubiš and Gabčik travelled via Prague to Plzeň and contacted an inspector of the police who lived in Plzeň: Wenzel Kral, Unterberggasse 1.

The details of this contact had been given out by Captain Šustr on the aircraft. They greeted Inspector Kral, using a phrase given to them by Captain Šustr which was "to send greetings from Horak". The assassins had not met him and Kral could not remember at that time who he was, but he accepted the two agents at face value. Kubiš [actually Gabčik] mentioned to Kral that his name was Vyskočil. This and other aliases such as Ota Strnad for Kubiš, were used by the assassins during their stay in the Protektorate.[21]

They advised Kral that conditions in England and the mood in the Czech Legion were not very good. They said the whole organisation was run by Jews and so it was best to come home. An agent who later gave himself up to the Secret State Police confirmed this statement.

Meeting with Beneš

Furthermore, the assassins told Kral that Captain Šustr had travelled in the aircraft from England with them and that they had previously had a meeting with Beneš. This extremely important statement about this meeting with Beneš provides confirmation from the statement of the turned agent. At the end of October or the beginning of November 1941, this agent was in London talking to Lieutenant Hrubec of the former Czech Army from Bernatic near Tabor, when the Lieutenant said that two of the parachute agents had been with the President and they had been dressed in civilian clothes. This phrase in 'civilian clothes' means that they were ready to take off and be parachuted back as agents.

At the time of this conversation, the turned agent knew that only Kubiš and Gabčik had completed their training, and he assumed that they were the two who met with Beneš. Considering that the group to which the assassins belonged was the first closed group of agents dropped in the Protektorate and at the same time, the only group that left between December 1941 and April 1942, it can be concluded with certainty that the agents received by Beneš belonged to this group. They were also far ahead in their training and so other groups can be discounted. The fact that a meeting was held with Beneš and the personal escort of Captain Šustr on the aircraft, speaks clearly for the importance of the orders given to the assassins.

Operations in Prague

On 31st December 1941, Kral took the assassins to the retired police inspector Jan Bejbl, who lives in Plzeň, and then escorted them to Prague. They finally found accommodation in Prague with a postman named Wenzel Ruta, who lived in Prague XI, at Biskupecstrasse 4. They arrived at his residence on 31st December 1941 during the afternoon. When later other Czech women helpers talked about the assassins, they often called them the "New Year's Eve gift". Ruta welcomed the two agents without any hesitation and accommodated them until 5th January 1942, although his apartment only consisted of two rooms. The assassins revealed to people that they had come from England. By chance also living in this building was a teacher: Jan Zelenka. Born in Steinkirchen on 3rd March 1895, now living in Prague XI, Biskupecstrasse 4, new sets of papers were provided by Zelenka and after he had got to know them he invited them to his apartment to discuss details of their operation. This man then became their chief helper and in every way supported the work of the parachute agents.

Involvement of Sokol in the agents' work

The head teacher Zelenka was originally a high ranking official in the Sokol in Dux but moved to Prague as a result of the reorganisation of the Sudetenland. Whilst in Prague he had maintained contacts with others members of the Sokol organisation who had been resettled from the Dux district. After being banned in 1941 many of the leading officials were arrested and those left acted as a support network for the relatives of those who had been arrested. It was stressed again and again by Sokol members arrested in the assassination case that the bond of friendship and patriotism of members led to many close friendships amongst themselves.

The older members some of whom had been part of the movement for decades, emphasize that the arrest of their leading officials, some of whom died in detention (in the concentration camps), was the hardest blow they could have taken. They had felt obliged from previous relationships to help relatives, even if it was illegal. The resulting bitter and embittered attitude of many Sokol officials made working for Zelenka an easy decision. From the beginning of January, 1942, he was probably aware of the order given to the assassins from England. For this attack, directed against the entire Reich, which was so hated by him, Zelenka collected from then on many helpers, whom he found primarily among his Sokol friends. The assassins did not have to worry about their accommodation, food and other care from this point on, because this [was] arranged for them under the leadership of Zelenka.[22] Zelenka when dealing with Protektorate members whom he did not know from his Sokol activities used the name Hajský.

Assistance organised by Zelenka for the assassins from the first days of January 1942 comprised two Sokol officials recruited by him: Wenzel (Václav) Novák, carpenter, born 18th January 1893 in Nebuzel, living in Prague VIII, Stranskystrasse 3 and Jaroslav Piskacek, official with the Bohemian-Moravian Railway, living in Prague IX, Am Ufer 15. These two people assisted with the removal of the equipment and parachutes hidden at Nehvizdy. For this purpose they visited the former Sokol official Frantisek Baumann who lived in Sestajovoc, and was asked to help with transport. Baumann, whose grandparents were Germans from the Sudetenland, agreed to help but allegedly did not actually assist with the request. Baumann, however, was visited by the assassin Kubiš, and Baumann suggested that he hide the equipment in a nearby, abandoned quarry. Novák and Piskáček then spent some time in the countryside near Prague, arranging help from other Sokol officials for the assassins. They found numerous Czechs who provided food, ration cards and money. Even mayors did not shy away from stealing ration cards from their municipal offices for this purpose.

Further contact points and accommodation for the assassins in Prague

Zelenka took care of further accommodation in Prague. The assassins lived for short periods with many Czech families, most of whom were Sokol members. The contact points which were of particular importance for the preparation of the assassination and its execution in Prague are mentioned in detail later. The exact chronological order of the location of the assassins cannot be ascertained in complete clarity, because the two assassins after a few days in Prague formed relationships with women and lived with them several days a week. The women were also unable, as a result of these numerous visits, to identify exactly when they stayed during their five months in the Protektorate.

Relationships of Gabčik and Kubiš

At the beginning of January 1942, the assassin Gabčik first met a young widow on a tram.[23] This widow Anna Malinová nee Komárkova, was born 19th May 1914 in Striberne, but now living in Prague XIV, Linzerstrasse 52, where she owns a small apartment and lives with her young child. They quickly became close friends and an intimate relationship developed between them, which led to Gabčik staying with her for at least a few days and nights a week. Gabčik soon told Malinová, whom she first only knew by his alias, the full story about himself including his real name and background and the general intentions of the agents. She knew that when Gabčik slept with her, he always had a loaded pistol under his pillow. She also saw on several occasions the bombs that Gabčik carried in a briefcase and asked him about the purpose and meaning of these items.

Gabčik told her that they were dangerous and she should never touch these things. She immediately thought that they were bombs but did not want to worry about them. Gabčik had also introduced to Malinová his comrade, the assassin Kubiš. It was suggested that Malinová should find a friend for him also. She did this by introducing one of her work colleagues who was Marie Soukupova nee Kovárniková, born on 4th January 1912 in Ohrazonice, but now living in Prague II, Magdeburgerstrasse 2, and she had a younger single sister who lived with her and so an intimate relationship developed between Kubiš and the sister of Soukupova, she was Marie Kovárniková, an office worker born on 16th February 1914 in Ohrazonice, but now living in Prague II, Magdeburgerstrasse 2.

The assassin Kubiš had also told the truth to his lover about his life and background. Kovárniková eventually became pregnant by him, whereupon one day an alleged Uncle of Kubiš, appeared and told her that she could not have the child, because it was not good to marry during wartime but she should not worry as he would help get her the required treatment. Kovárniková later underwent medical treatment at the hospital in Prague.

These relationships of the two assassins eventually led them to begin to feel comfortable in this bourgeois life (with large amounts of money) and gradually begin to distance themselves from their orders. Zelenka, probably together with the leader of these agents –Bartoš – may have put pressure on them to fulfil their operation, because from the beginning of March 1942 they were living on the run again, in most cases living with a different family for periods of 8 to 14 days. There was no other reason for this measure, because they probably would have lived safer with their lovers. Two locations in Prague where the assassins stayed were of particular importance. In April 1942 they lived with the family of: Alois Moravec, Railway Inspector, born 25th January 1887 in Ratborsch, but now living in Prague XI, Biskupecstrasse 7 and Josef Svatoš, employee, born 8th November 1896 in Prelovice, now living in Prague I, Melantrichgasse 15. In both cases, the major supporters of these illegal activities were the wives, who are fanatical Czechs who have devoted themselves passionately to caring for the assassins. Both families have been fully aware of the identities and origin of the assassins and that they own weapons, explosives and bombs.

Contact point Svatoš

At the Svatoš residence, the assassin Kubiš borrowed a briefcase that had been split at the seams and he immediately repaired in a simple format with black thread. Also at the Svatoš residence in the presence of the family, the assassin Gabčik rubbed his briefcase with shoe polish to try and hide scratches that had been caused by attaching it to a bicycle. Detailed descriptions of both briefcases were later released to the public. The Svatoš family immediately recognised the briefcases, but did not come forward and so withheld information.

Contact point Moravec
Over the years, the Moravec family has become a one-stop-shop for the underground because Vlastimil Moravec, a registered insurance inspector, provided a courier service between Prague, Plzeň and Pardubice. Messages were therefore brought to this apartment and forwarded from there. Mrs Moravec, in addition to the head teacher Zelenka, can be described as the woman who has gone to great lengths to make the assassination attempt a success.[24]

Kubiš shows his bomb at the Moravecs'
Around the middle of April 1942 when the assassins lived with the Moravecs, Kubiš showed his bomb to the son Vlastimil Moravec and explained how they operated. In doing so, Kubiš neatly rewrapped the grey, English insulating tape that had slightly moved on the bomb and explained to him how the detonator worked. This happened on 16th April 1942, the day before the assassins went to Plzeň to prepare for a bombing raid on the Skoda Works.[25] On this day, the other assassin Gabčik , told Vlastimil Moravec that they were planning to assassinate SS-Obergruppenführer Heydrich and that they had already tried in vain once before.

Failed assassination attempt on SS-Obergruppenführer Heydrich
The bomb was to be thrown during a theatre visit by SS-Obergruppenführer Heydrich, however, the operation failed because on the night in question SS-Obergruppenführer Heydrich had visited another theatre. This story seems unlikely, because at that time only one German theatre was in operation in Prague.

Air Raid on the Skoda Works in Plzeň
On 17th April 1942, the assassins drove to Plzeň, to assist with the planning for the bombing of the Skoda Works after Bartoš (Motycka) had received orders from London via the radio. The assassins lived with several agents in Plzeň until 26th April 1942: a tailor, Aloisie Hrdlickova, born 2nd February 1891 in Milovsko, now living in Plzeň, Klattauerstrasse 76 and with a domestic worker, Vera Kucerova, born 15th June 1925 in Plzeň and now living in Plzeň, Resselgasse 4.

The action went completely according to plan. The deployed agents set fire to two barns, one in front of and one behind the Skoda factories. The bombers were also properly briefed, saw the fires, but dropped their bombs 6 kilometres from the target. The petrol for the fires in the barns had been procured by Police Inspector Kral from Plzeň with another assistant.[26] The day before the action, the assassin Gabčik had been ordered back to Prague on the instructions of Bartoš (Motycka) to carry out another task. Presumably, their mission took priority and it was deemed that both assassins could not be lost on this other mission.

Assassination preparations for Jungfern Breschan
On 26th April 1942, Gabčik was handed a ladies' bicycle which the Moravec family had borrowed and it was handed over by Vlastimil Moravec, this is the ladies' bicycle which was subsequently found at the scene of the assassination. The bicycle was handed over to Gabčik at the tram station in Kobilis, the suburb of Prague on the main road to Jungfern Breschan. Gabčik then immediately rode off in the direction of Jungfern Breschan, and so Moravec now suspected that the assassination would take place in Jungfern Breschan. As it turned out by later investigations that was actually true. An assassination attempt in Jungfern Breschan was allegedly not carried out because in the following day's security measures by the SS were strengthened, which also corresponded to the facts.

Meeting of the assassins with SS-Obergruppenführer Heydrich
In the days following the Plzeň operation, Gabčik and Kubiš reconnoitred the road to Jungfern Breschan to familiarise themselves with the movements of the Obergruppenführer and possible locations for the assassnation.[27] They have often sat in shooters huts and when passed by SS-Obergruppenführer Heydrich they greeted him with a deep bow in a subservient Czech way, whereupon the SS-Obergruppenführer gave a friendly greeting in return. Based on testimony from several other people during these trips, the assassins carried their sub-machine gun and bombs with them. They also visited during this period several of their former hosts. They also paid a visit to the family Svatoš around the 10th of May 1942. Gabčik had his sub-machine gun in his briefcase, which was covered by grass.

Contact point Fafek
In the last few weeks before the assassination, the assassins lived at their third important port of call in Prague, the Protektorate citizen Peter Fafek, Accountant, born 30th June 1893 in Dusniky, now living in Prague XII, Gurimerstrasse 11.

Zelenka had asked for their support in February 1942, and the assassins had been living here for around 18 days. They made strong bonds with this family and often visited amusement parks of various kinds with their two adult daughters. The entire family knew that the two men were parachute agents from London. Additionally much support after the assassination was provided by this family. On 24th May 1942, they left the Fafek residence and their location where they stayed on the last few nights before the assassination until 27th May 1942 could not be ascertained, but it can be safely assumed that they lived with their closest supporter, Zelenka.

Efforts to prevent the assassination – Involvement of the illegal Sokol organisation Jindra
One of the leading officials of the Sokol, Ladislaus Vaněk, who was a professor, worked in Brno and lived in Austerlitz, fled because he feared that he would be arrested on the banning of the Sokol organisation in 1941. He was known in Sokol circles under the code name 'Jindra' and began to raise an illegal Sokol organisation, which also called itself 'Jindra'. This organisation existed to help the relatives of arrested members and to look after and provide financial support to members in difficulties. Professor Vaněk (Jindra) has over the course of a year, grown this illegal organisation to a considerable size and it was based in particular on the middle ranks of the leadership. This was not too difficult as many members of the Sokol willingly agreed to help. The Jindra organisation had regional leaders for Bohemia and Moravia and continued to use Gau and Kreisleiter, who joined with many others in providing assistance to the assassins. The head of the illegal Sokol organisation in Bohemia was Franz Pecháček, who lived in Prague-Smichov, Reinergasse 3.

By the end of 1941, Vaněk had already informed the Jindra organisation that a former Sokol official, named Hajský (Zelenka), also ran an illegal organisation providing shelter and food for people living outside the law. Pecháček had already been recruited by Hajský to help with this activity. Since both Jindra and Hajský had a mutual interest, Pecháček arranged a meeting in his apartment, in which Hajský offered to work in the organisation if he were to assume a leading position. At this first meeting, Jindra suspected that Hajský might want to get to know the Jindra organisation and harness it for his own aims and so Jindra rejected the offer. However, three weeks later there was another meeting at the Pecháček residence requested by Hajský and he wanted to have information from Jindra regarding the following three subjects:

1.   Accommodation, travel and habits of the Protektorate's leading figures.
2.   Where the cars used by the senior government members were mostly parked.
3.   How the police protect the leading figures and other security measures they employ.

Information should, if possible, be made available prior to an intended journey of a leading person-ality. If Jindra could not get this information himself, he should call on other people who could. Jindra asked Hajský what this information had to do with the Sokol. Hajský answered that he needed it not as a Sokol official, but as an official of the Czech National Social party (Beneš' party). Finally, he explained that he needed the information for two parachute agents who had an impor-tant job that nobody should know about. Jindra pointed out to Hajský the unknown and serious consequences of an assassination for the Czech Republic. Hajský wanted to fully understand these concerns and finally agreed to a meeting of the parachute agents with Jindra.

Argument between Jindra and Kubiš
This meeting, which was attended by Jindra, Hajský, Pecháček and parachute agent Ota (Kubiš), around the middle of February 1942, was held in the Pecháček apartment. Jindra asked Ota (Kubiš) a question which seemed to catch him by surprise "Who gave you the order to assassinate Heydrich?" Ota is said to have been confused and asked: "How do you know that?" Jindra then with all his persuasive powers made clear to Ota the dangers that such an assassination would bring down on the people of the Czech Republic and would give the Germans a strong political weapon. Jindra added that he felt that people in London had lost their heads completely; otherwise they would not give such orders. Statements by Jindra made an impression on those present and Ota explained that his orders came from the intelligence service, which was in the hands of Colonel Moravec. With that, Jindra explained, he knew that this order came from the mouths of the Czech sham government in London. Colonel Moravec, Jindra said, deserved a court martial for such a reckless order with the repercussions for the Czech people. Ota and Jindra then discussed if it was possible to reverse this order, whereupon Jindra assured Ota that he would do anything he could and would contact London to obtain a cancellation of this order. Ota, on the other hand, agreed that if the order was to be withdrawn then he would in any case postpone the operation as long as possible so that Jindra could obtain a ruling from London. Jindra then actually barred Pecháček from having further contact with Zelenka.

Argument between Jindra and Bartoš
This contact, however, did not break in reality; Zelenka finally arranged a meeting between Jindra and Bartoš, the leader of the parachute agents from Pardubice. Jindra gave Bartoš a detailed account of the consequences of an attack, and Bartoš, who was at first very reserved, finally explained that he did not know of such an operation. He explained, in a very dissatisfied tone, that he was completely astonished at the peace and order that prevailed in the Protektorate and this was not really understood in London. Bartoš finally agreed, though he was only really meant to send back military intelligence, to send a message back from Jindra. However, sometime later Jindra had to obtain further information from the illegal Sokol organisation because London did not recognise this organisation without checking some details.

Argument between Jindra and Kral
In March 1942 Jindra held a meeting with Adolf Opálka (Lieutenant Kral), the leader of a para-chute group, because Zelenka had told him that the assassination was imminent and Jindra wanted to influence Opálka. The two assassins were requested to attend a meeting in Prague as it was known preparations for the attack had already been made. Opálka informed Jindra that he could not really interfere as the two assassins formed a special group on their own. However, since Opálka fully understood the potential repercussions of an attempt and he already had had difficulties with the assassins because of their undisciplined behaviour; he also wanted to try and persuade them to postpone the attempt. Opálka's dissatisfaction with the assassins went so far that he allegedly

threatened to shoot the assassins if they endangered the other agents too much. Jindra learnt at his next meeting with Bartoš that Opálka had actually recalled the assassins from the woods around Jungfern Breschan and a temporary postponement of the act had occurred. At this meeting, the contents of a message which was sent to London was agreed, which contained the following points:

1.   The Sokol does not consider assassination a political weapon.
2.   If anything does happen to the Reichsprotektor another would be appointed immediately.
3.   An assassination will have the worst consequences for the Czech Republic.
4.   Any illegal activity will subsequently become impossible.

This draft was transmitted by the illegal transmitting station Silver A in Pardubice to London in the following format:

Radio message from the Jindra organisation to London:

"At the request of Jindra, whom you recognised on the night of 30th April to1st May 1942, and who has made contact with one of your liaison officers, we send the following despatch, the contents of which have been agreed unanimously:

From the preparations that Ota and Zdenek have made and the places they have been to, despite their continued silence, we conclude that they plan to assassinate H. This assassination would not benefit the Allies and it would have unforeseeable consequences for our people. It would not only endanger our hostages and political prisoners, it would also require thousands of lives being lost, it would throw the nation into unprecedented repression, and at the same time sweep away the last remnants of any resistance organisations. This would make it impossible for anything useful to be done here for the allies. Therefore, we ask that you give Silver (which is the cover name for the Pardubice transmitter [*sic*]) the instruction that the assassination be cancelled.

There is danger in delaying, give the instruction immediately. Should the assassination nevertheless be necessary for political reasons, then it should be carried out on a local Quisling, a likely target being E.M."28 [E.M. was Emanuel Moravec the Propaganda Minister of the Protektorate.]

The next meeting, at which an answer to this message was expected, had been set for the 27th May 1942, at 17.00. The answer was irrelevant as the assassination attempt had been carried out six hours previously. London had therefore given the leader of the illegal Sokol organisation Jindra (Professor Vaněk) the answer to his radio message through their silence. That London must have been very happy with the events, is shown in this radio message, which was sent six days later from London to Pardubice and clearly shows what Beneš thought about the assassination:

Beneš' thanks for the assassination

"3. 6. From the President. I'm glad you're keeping in contact. Thank you very much. I see that you and all your friends are full of determination. It is a proof to me that the attitude of the whole people is rock solid.

I assure you that it will bring success. The actions of the home army are very highly thought of here and calls for great recognition of the resistance of the Czech people.

Your S."

The Assassination

The course of events was exhaustively dealt with at the beginning of the report in the reconstruction of the assassination. After the perpetrators fled the scene in different directions, the bomb thrower Kubiš by bicycle and the gunman Gabčik on foot, they continued their escape routes as follows:

Further escape route of Gabčik

Gabčik arrived shortly after 11.00 a.m. at the Svatoš family residence, one of his former accommodation addresses in Prague I, Melantrichgasse 15. Josef Svatoš described that Zdenek was very excited and nervous and his facial muscles were trembling visibly. He did not have a hat. He was very hot and sweaty and so washed his upper body. Asked by Svatoš why he was so upset, Zdenek replied that he had run very fast and done a horrible job. Mrs Svatoš then returned to the apartment and made Zdenek a citrus drink which he drank greedily. He then put on his damp shirt and asked to leave. He pulled a small pistol out of his pocket and said: "Damn it, you have to take this everywhere with you and it's not much use." He then put his weapon back in his pocket. Zdenek was given a coat and hat by Svatoš. As he was leaving, Svatoš and his wife looked out of the window and saw that he walked calmly to a flower lady, bought a bouquet of lilies of the valley and then disappeared. The Svatoš couple were aware from the condition of Zdenek that he must have done something unpleasant. When they learned in the course of the afternoon through the radio that an attack on the Reichsprotektor had been carried out, they knew immediately that Zdenek and Jaroslav were the two perpetrators. On 29th May 1942 Zelenka (Hajský) confirmed that Zdenek and Jaroslav were the assassins. He also told them that during the search by the police on the night of 27th May/28th May, a parachute agent had been hiding in a light well in his building and had not been discovered.

Further escape route of Kubiš

Kubiš parked his men's bicycle in the Slavatagasse, on the corner with Primatorenstrasse by the Bata shoe shop and then walked down the Primatorenstrasse to the apartment of Václav Novák [and his wife] in Stranskygasse 3, who had been active helpers in the organisation and had been recruited by Zelenka in January 1942. After he arrived at the apartment he spoke with Mrs Novák and her daughter Jindřiška, and asked M if she could collect the bicycle immediately from the Bata shop, but not to return along Primatorenstrasse as a precautionary measure. Mrs Novák immediately sent her daughter, Jindřiška, to the Bata shop and told her which detour to take. The assassin, Kubiš, asked the girl what she would say when she spoke to someone, to which she replied that she would say she has come to collect her father's bicycle. The girl came from a side street to where the bicycle was parked, so it appeared it gave the impression that she came from a different direction than the one in which her apartment was actually located. The appearance of a girl was noticed by witnesses who had already seen a bleeding cyclist and were discussing this on the street corner. One witness Sedlackova believed that the bicycle was being stolen by the girl and questioned her, whereupon the girl stated that it was her father's bicycle. This woman asked what had happened to her father and she replied: "I do not know yet."

Since the girl appeared barely more than 10 minutes after the bicycle was parked by the assassin at the Bata shop, and she had said that she had been told of her father's injury and been sent by him, she could not live too far away. This gave an idea of the area to search for this particular girl. The round trip from where the bicycle had been left to the apartment had not been more than 15 minutes, so there were a limited number of blocks of apartments where this girl lived, unless it was an attempt to deceive the investigation. This area was the starting point for a major search which began on 3rd June 1942, and did include the correct apartment. However, this was not successful, because the search concentrated on arresting girls and 260 were arrested which included the girl involved, Jindřiška Novák, but she was not recognised by the witness. The assassin, Kubiš, was given a shirt by Mrs Novák which belonged to her son as the original one had burn marks. The eye injury suffered by Kubiš caused blood to flow from the corner of his right eye and it seemed that damage had been caused to his eyeball or under the eyelid. After the girl had returned with the bicycle and left it in a yard, Kubiš left the apartment and had been given directions to Veitsberg. He went straight to the residence of the family Piskáček, Prague-Vissochan, who had been helping with the organisation since January 1942 and Kubiš remained here until the following night. He asked them that afternoon for treatment for his eye and Doctor Lyčka was asked to assist.

Medical help for the injured assassin Kubiš
Doctor Lyčka was a district doctor in the capital Prague, former Sokol official and member of the medical group for the illegal Sokol organisation 'Jindra'. Piskáček left to visit him, but met a Sokol official on the way: Antonin Oktabec, mechanic, born on 29th September 1904 in Althütten, but now living at Prague-Karlin, Mühlhauserstrasse 3.

He started a conversation with Oktabec who asked whether he had heard of the assassination and Piskáček replied that he had the assassin at his home. He asked Oktabec if he could arrange for Doctor Lyčka to come to his apartment so that he could treat the eye wound of the assassin. Oktabec went to Doctor Lyčka and advised him of the position but allegedly the Doctor only reluctantly went back with Oktabec. In the late afternoon, Václav Novák and his wife arrived at the Piskáček apartment and Novák asked Piskáček to make sure that the man's bicycle, which was still in his yard, disappeared. Piskáček sent his son to pick up the bicycle and immediately told him that the owner was the Sokol member, Jaroslav Smrž, leatherworker,[29] born 14th September 1904 in Prague and now residing in Prague Wissotschan Kirchenring 660, and asked his son to move the bicycle.

Kubiš, who now had a bandage around his head, remained with Piskáček until the next day, 28th May 1942.

Activities at the Karl Borromeo Church in Prague
Whilst Kubiš arrived the following day at the church of Karl Borromeo, Gabčik lived for another two days until 30th May 1942 with his lover Malinová. In response to the comment that the people that carried out the assassination would make the Czech people suffer which was in a newspaper, Gabčik replied: "The rascal who committed the assassination is now lying in bed with you." On 30th May 1942, Gabčik also went to the Karl Borromeo Church, where five other agents also arrived over the coming days.

Greek Orthodox clergy who were involved with the assassins
Known in Prague as the Church of Karl Borromeo, the church was given by the Czechoslovakian State to the Greek Orthodox Church in 1934. It was named 'St Cyril and Methodius Church' by them, but is not that well known under this name in Prague. The Greek Orthodox Church is better known to the Czech public as the 'Czech Orthodox Church' or 'Orthodox Church'.

The head was Bishop Gorazd, previously known as Matej Pavlik, who was born on 26th May 1879, in Groß-Wrbka, [and] during the 1914 to 1918 World War he was the Catholic priest of the asylum in Kremsier in Moravia. He was a particularly active clergyman, who created a reform movement amongst the Catholic clergy and was in 1919 a leading figure in the 'Jednota', whose slogan was 'going on from Rome'. A delegation of the priests attempted to make Rome agree to these demands such as allowing the clergy to marry and to allow the national language in services. Rome refused. These radical priests then founded a 'Czechoslovak Church' (now the Bohemian-Moravian Church). Gorazd was leader of the movement in Moravia.

This newly formed church had not yet decided completely, whether they should choose a Presbyterian (Protestant) or Episcopal (Catholic) direction. The Episcopal route was out of the question, as Rome was rejected too strongly by the Czech people. The Presbyterian tendency, on the other hand, did not correspond to the religious traditions of the Czech people, which are accustomed to a hierarchical system.

So this newly formed church decided to turn to the Serbian Orthodox Church in Belgrade, to which it felt bound by Slavic sympathy, for help. The Patriarch Demitov in Belgrade finally allowed an Orthodox Church in the Czechoslovak Republic in 1920, to be known as the Czechoslovakian Church and to be headed by Gorazd. In 1921 Gorazd was ordained a bishop in Belgrade. However, in 1923–24 there was a split in the Czechoslovak Church, whereby the Orthodox Church left and became an independent religious community. They received national recognition in 1924 in the Czechoslovak Republic. Their followers are almost exclusively Czechs and to a large extent former Russian legionnaires. This was because many, who had served in Russia during the World War, had been exposed to the Orthodox faith and some had married Russian women.

Their numbers could count upon support from prominent personalities such as General Syrovy and many former officers of the Czech Ministry of Defence.[30] Although the number of their supporters is comparatively low, it has a special significance for Slavism, because it can be regarded as promoting a Pan-Slav movement.

Accommodation, care and security of the assassins in the Karl Borromeo church
The lay committee of the church council of the Karl Borromeo Church was headed by Jan Sonnevend, who was a retired health insurance director who was born on 25th December 1880 in Topolany.

Through his volunteer work in the 'League Against Tuberculosis' (formerly the Masaryk League, which was under the leadership of Alice Masaryk) he continued to work with the accountant of this league, Peter Fafek, who has been mentioned before as a contact. During a conversation about the Karl Borromeo Church, the crypt under the nave was mentioned as it might be possible to use it to store weapons. Later, Fafek told Zelenka about this crypt, who immediately thought this might be a good hiding place for the agents and so negotiated with the pastor of the Karl Borromeo Church to see if this might be possible. The first negotiations then led Sonnevend to speak with the chaplain of the church, Doctor Vladimir Petřek, who was born 19th June 1908 in Olomouc and the pastor Alois Cikl, born 13th January 1900 in Slavietin, who both agreed to accommodate these illegal agents. The time of the first negotiations is different according to the various parties; Chaplain Petřek states the discussions took place only after the assassination, while Sonnevend stubbornly claims to have led the discussion before the assassination attempt. In any case, these negotiations focused on the time around 27th May 1942 and then led to a decision, because on 28th May 1942 the assassin Jan Kubiš was already present in the church. Zelenka personally conducted the recent negotiations with Chaplain Petřek and also discussed in detail the date they could be accommodated there, the care of and provisions for the agents. Certain names were discussed as to help identify the agents and also for them to wear a certain badge. For example, some of them wore a Czech lion on a chain. A woman who has already been mentioned Mrs Moravec also played a crucial role from the start. She met with Chaplain Petřek in the first few days in her apartment, they also met in the church office and she provided food and other daily necessities. After a few days, a total of seven agents, including the assassins, entered the church and were kept hidden in the crypt. Since the crypt was very humid and cold, Chaplain Petřek arranged so that some of the agents could sleep in the choir loft.

The crypt was an ancient burial place for monks and priests and contains about 120 sarcophagi, some of which were still walled up and contained the bones of the dead. Since a large number of people had to be cared for on an ongoing basis, several people were needed to help and these included:

Mrs Moravec
Mrs Fafek and her two daughters
Mr Fafek
Mr Zelenka
Mr Sonnevend
Chaplain Petřek
and an unknown woman.

The eye injury suffered by the assassin Kubiš required further treatment and Chaplain Petřek and Zelenka asked Doctor Sobek who helped the 'League Against Tuberculosis' if he knew anyone who could help and arranged for a friend – an ophthalmologist [–] Doctor Milada Franta-Reimová to help, her date of birth [being] 28th June 1906 in Mittelswalde.

Apparently, this doctor did not want to know whom she was treating, but on the other hand she ignored the press and radio announcements that required her to report such injuries. The husband of Doctor Franta-Reimová has been in a concentration camp for a year for being a member of an illegal organisation. The chaplain, Doctor Petřek, who organised the aforementioned care of the assassins and agents, has gone to great lengths to help them by such things as emptying the bucket used in the crypt as a toilet. He also incorporated every conceivable safeguard to prevent betrayal, by swearing the other two ministers working there to secrecy. Other church officials, who were aware of what was going on, were also sworn to secrecy in front of the altar.

Nevertheless, he was not completely happy with this plan because he also gave one of the church officials called Schweigegeld 500 Koruna. Doctor Petřek soon realised that the assassins were in the church and he discussed the assassination with Kubiš whilst they were there. Kubiš allegedly told him about the preparations of the assassination attempt and their escape routes. With Zelenka Petřek talked about certain subjects in great depth.

Jindra also came to the church and had several conversations with the previously mentioned Lieutenant Adolf Kral and Chaplain Petřek. These conversations revolved around the possible escape of the assassins, which Petřek claims Jindra had attempted to plan. Jindra, on the other hand, claims that he only wanted to lure the assassins out of the church and persuade them to poison themselves in a public park in Prague in order to end the reprisals that the assassination had brought down on the Czech people.

One day, Mrs Moravec came to the church and advised that the assassins had been promoted and awarded a decoration by London. Presumably the news came from the illegal transmitter from Pardubice, because Mrs Moravec had the closest connection with this group.

The Bishop and the Assassins

The Bishop of this church, Gorazd previously known as Pavlik, attended a parish council meeting when the assassins were staying and was advised by Sonnevend and also the Chaplain, Petřek, on the entire recent events in the church. He probably expressed his fear about the dangers that threatened the church, but did not say anything publicly. In the conversation he was even told by Chaplain Petřek that the assassins were in the crypt and the bishop asked, "Are they orthodox believers?" And Petřek replied: "No."

Gorazd then went with this knowledge to Berlin, where he participated in the consecration of a new bishop and the introduction of the Metropolitan Seraphim, and also met with the Church Secretary of the Reich Security Main Office. Although he had hidden the killers of the Chief of the Security Police and the rest of the agents in his church, he quietly negotiated in the office where the assassinated SS-Obergruppenführer was chief.[31] After he returned from Berlin and the agents in the church had been neutralised, he wrote long letters to the Reichsprotektor and various ministers of the Protektorate Government, in which he tries to plead his ignorance of the events at his church. It perfectly paints a picture of this man. If one reads a letter from 1940, which was addressed to the Holy Synod in Belgrade, he wrote that for reasons of expediency he would submit to the Orthodox Church in Berlin and asked the Holy Synod in Belgrade to forgive him.

Moreover, he believed that Germany would soon collapse in starvation and misery with its new rulers. He sent this letter to Belgrade via the then Yugoslav consulate. This hypocrisy and duplicity was maintained by the Bishop until his criminal involvement with the assassins.

A public court hearing regarding the illegal activities of Bishop Gorazd, Chaplain Petřek, Pastor Cikl and Mr Sonnevend was held on 4th September 1942. The four accused were sentenced to death. The verdict was duly carried out. The agents and assassins had been concealed in the crypt of the Karl Borromeo church from 28th May 1942 to 17th June 1942, then in [the] morning of 18th June 1942 the church was stormed and the agents and assassins neutralised. How the Special Commission discovered the trail of the perpetrators will be discussed in detail in this section. This means that a number of the major measures initiated by the Special Commission must be explained, since their consequences ultimately led to the successful location of the assassins and agents.

Examples of Special Measures taken by the Special Commission on the Assassination Day
On the basis of objects found at the scene the special commission was of the conviction that parachute agents had participated in the assassination. The agents' methods of working and accommodation had been previously known and they became known to several families. The Commission considered that the extraordinarily high reward of 2,000,000 Reichsmarks and the death penalty for people found sheltering unregistered people was an essential aid throughout this period.

The major measures taken by the Special Commission were so numerous and varied that it is difficult to give any detail of them in this report; but an overview of the most important criminal and political measures were as follows:

1.   27th May 1942 – 11.30 a.m.
     All routes out of Prague including road and rail were sealed which extended until the early evening. From a criminal point of view, this measure proved to be extraordinarily valuable, because the assassins and their accomplices from that moment on were under the impression that a German security operation of extraordinary size and unusual extent was going to be carried out. As a result of this, witnesses confirmed that the perpetrators felt safer in Prague than in the countryside, leaving Prague was a particular danger and the flat country outside could be combed more thoroughly than a city.
2.   Broadcasting, Press Releases, Billboards and General.
     Bulletins in the press were published in the afternoon of 27th May 1942. Radio messages were transmitted periodically via the broadcasters of Bohemia and Moravia and every half hour via the public address system in the streets of Prague. It had thus been achieved, and with the later articles and cinema coverage, that every inhabitant of the Protektorate was fully informed of the event and the information they needed to provide to the authorities.
3.   Major Search in Prague.
     During the night of 27th/28th May 1942, a search was carried out from 10.00 p.m. to 6.00 a.m., employing more than 8,000 men.
     After the state of emergency was imposed, no person was allowed to be on the streets after 9.00 p.m. The initial plan was to search as many as 35,000 buildings in Prague during this first night, although it was known that not all could be searched in this period. The action only failed because there were too few trained men available and so men untrained in search

procedures had to be brought in. It later turned out that about 70% of the wanted people were affected by this action. These men, mostly parachute agents, hung in the light wells when the apartment blocks were being searched. The light wells were not searched by the untrained forces. This instruction to hide in the light wells has been given to these men by their leadership as it had been noticed in previous searches that the police did not search them. It needs mentioning that it took a considerable physical effort to remain hidden in these narrow shafts for a long period of time.

4. Imposition of a state of emergency in Bohemia and Moravia.

It was stated in Article II from The Decree of a Declaration of a State of Emergency: that whoever harbours, helps or communicates with persons involved in the attack, together with his family, will be executed.

5. Martial Law.

With the imposition of the state of emergency (on the basis of Articles I and II of the decree of the Reichsprotektor in Bohemia and Moravia on the imposition of the civil state of emergency of 27th September 1941) martial law is declared.

6. Obligation to register all persons from the age of fifteen.

Deadline: 29th May 1942 – 00.00. Anyone who remained in Prague who had not registered after the deadline was sentenced to death.

7. Control of the workers' trains, which departed on 27th May 1942, for the Reich.

However, the necessity of this measure proved its worth as one person tried to escape on a workers' train on 27th May 1942, and was arrested. However, this person was later found to be unrelated to the assassination.

8. Immediate Display of Items Found at the Scene.

Items found were displayed in the window of the Bata branch on Wenceslas Square; this is one Prague's largest shops and has one of the largest window displays.

This exhibition was extremely well attended by the residents of Prague but, people who saw the items on display and could have provided information about the items, decided not to come forward.

9. Search of all Hospitals.

For persons with similar injuries to those suffered by the assassin.

10. Interview of all Doctors.

In Prague and the surrounding area for persons who sought treatment for injuries similar to those suffered by the assassin.[32]

11. Burial of Male Corpses.

Burials for males who died aged between 25 and 40 were suspended until 30th June 1942, unless a police permit was obtained. Bodies thought to be suspicious were not to be released for burial unless authorised by the Gestapo.

12. Railway Personnel.

Staff from certain trains and stations, which might have been used as an escape route by the perpetrators were identified and interviewed.

13. Telephone Calls between Jungfern Breschan and Prague.

Telephone records from this and neighbouring villages were examined for the month of May 1942.

14. Telephone Line between Jungfern Breschan and Prague.

The line was examined by specialists from the Reichspost in conjunction with local officials. They found that the line had been tapped in an amateur way but how long it had been in place could not be determined.

15. Identification and Questioning of Residents in the area of the Crime Scene and the Escape Route of the Perpetrators.

     This measure has led to the identification of witnesses who, in spite of all the appeals and publications, did not come forward, mainly because they considered their information so insignificant that they thought it would not be of any use to the police.

16. Identification and Interview with the tram crews and passengers who passed the scene on the morning of 27th May 1942.

     Other measures that were gradually implemented in the course of the investigation:

17. Use of Special Search Squads in the Area of the Crime Scene.

     For this action the best investigators were used. The teams were given a free hand and used the information gained from new evidence. They mingled with and studied the habits of the people in the area of the assassination. Whilst the information gained from this work was not always decisive for the investigation, at least in psychological terms the attitude of the Czechs and the resulting conclusion for further action by the Special Commission was of considerable value.

18. Two cinema newsreels.

     Two short films (with and without sound) about the items recovered at the scene.

19. Bill Posting in the Local Districts.

     These posters were put up in such large numbers that each house received several copies.

20. Property Identification by the Criminal Police.

     To try and identify the owners of the objects found at the scene of the crime, all persons resident in the Protektorate (Germans, Protektorate citizens and foreigners) were asked if they knew any of the items found. They had to either confirm or deny this and sign a list. Up till the time that the perpetrators were neutralised, more than 7 million people had not been asked this question and it was thus discontinued.

21. The Ladies' Bicycle.

     This was left behind at the crime scene and after it had been traced as originating from the Teplitz-Schönau area, a special team was deployed there.

22. Dust and Dirt on the Ladies' Bicycle.

     To determine the origin of the dust and road dirt under the mudguards of the ladies' bicycle, a geologist was consulted, and he advised several areas in which the bicycle had been used. This report proved to be correct.

23. Investigation into the displaced persons from the Sudetenland.

     The possibility that a displaced person had brought the ladies' bicycle to Prague in the autumn of 1938 existed, and therefore these Protektorate members (about 40,000) were checked against the repatriation lists.

24. Briefcase with Glass Bead Contents.

     A forensic investigation had found in one of the briefcases tiny glass beads often used on women's evening dresses. On the basis of this information extensive investigations were made in the glass bead manufacturing and processing industry.

25. Permanent Checkpoints.
    a)   Railway stations
    b)   Railway trains
    c)   Vehicles
    d)   Hotels
    e)   Port facilities

26. Random Checkpoints.
    a)   Restaurants, cafes, bars etc.

b)   In allotments and orchards
c)   Shops
d)   Residential buildings
e)   Random searches of districts, hostels etc.
f)   Cinemas
g)   Roads and parks
h)   Swimming baths
i)   Trams and tram stations

27.   District Wide searches in the Entire Protektorate by the German Ordinary Police.
This measure served less for criminal reasons but more to install a climate of fear in the population, which made them fear reprisals for illegal acts and prevented them from accommodating strangers. Each night a random district in the Protektorate was searched.

28.   Review of all new registrations throughout the Protektorate.
This measure was extremely difficult to carry out because of the prevailing circumstances in the Protektorate, because it was customary not to match a new submission with a de-registration.

29.   Introduction of Compulsory De-registration in the case of a New Police Registration.

30.   Freight trains were searched at the border crossing.

31.   Search on 3rd June 1942.
This was carried out by 650 men in a specific sector of the district of Prague Libeň. This search was to try and find a girl who had picked up the men's bicycle used by one of the assassins from the Bata branch in the Primatorenstrasse corner Slavatagasse in Libeň. The search did not identify the girl; who nevertheless was amongst the 260 girls arrested because of their age and appearance. The witnesses who were asked to identify the girl, were very scared because of possible revenge action by the assassins, and so they did not identify this girl out of those arrested 260.[33]

32.   Review of all Girls' Schools in Libeň.
All students who were absent on the day of the assassination were apprehended and their reason for being absent from school checked.

33.   Declaration by Protektorate Physicians.
After the attack all the doctors in the Protektorate had to sign a pre-printed, written statement that they had not treated people with certain injuries. In addition, they had to commit to report anyone who did ask for treatment for the described injuries. If there was any doubt, they were required to advise the police the details of those seeking treatment. The doctors who actually treated the assassins have signed false statements.

34.   All Workers of Prague.
Workers who were not at their workplace on the day of the assassination attempt were to be identified and checked.

35.   Czech workers in the Reich.
Workers who were not at their workplace on the day of the assassination attempt were to be identified and checked.

36.   Czech prisoners.
Prisoners who had been released from prison at the time of the assassination or who had recently been released have been identified and checked.

37.   Male relatives of those who had been sentenced by the Special Court in 1941.
Those people who had a relative who had either been shot or died in a concentration camp were identified and checked.

38.   Search for all Identity Papers issued in Brno.

It turned out that most of the illegal residents possessed papers issued from Brno and that several parachute agents from London were provided with such papers. The Protektorate authorities had to check that all people with papers issued from Brno had indeed been issued [with them] by the Protektorate and whether the person matches their stored personal data. Once the papers had been verified a further pass was issued. This measure made the assassins and their helpers very anxious and so dare not use public transport.

39. Involvement of Collaborators.

As a result of information received from this source much essential information has been provided and led to search opportunities in Prague and against certain groups of people.

40. Cooperation with Other Authorities and Services.

In order to implement all of the above measures, each of which required a particularly large amount of work and support, it was necessary to make extensive use of other authorities and services. With very few exceptions, this cooperation has been smooth and worked extremely satisfactorily. The Czech authorities and the Czech Police have been severely affected by the events and have in fact spared no effort in using their officers until they are utterly exhausted.

41. Impact of the German measures on the Czech Population and the Conclusions drawn from it.

For 15 days the Czech population was in constant turmoil due to the published daily lists of court judgments and by the rapid consequences of the measures outlined here which were continually addressed, checked and amended, so that a strong German security presence was noticeable. Since some rumours circulated that the Germans were indiscriminately picking out innocent people for revenge, or if they speak to the Secret State Police, some people no longer dared to reveal their knowledge to the authorities.

In the first few days after the assassination, the Czech people had realised the horrific consequences and fear grew amongst the population and a sense of paralysis crept in. After a few more days this fear was replaced by a sense of being punished by the German authorities. The feeling that it was now 'too late' to report as a witness was a feeling that was so common that no one dared to speak to the authorities. In order to gain knowledge of this situation, the special search teams sent out have done valuable work. Since only a very small number of reports and statements from the Czech people were received in the first fourteen days as a result of this climate of fear; it was decided to announce a 48-hour immunity period. Anyone who filed a report in this period went unpunished, even if he himself was charged with sheltering unregistered persons. (Supplementary Decree of Article II dated 27th May 1942 amending the Decree of 16th March 1942). This immunity was issued as a decree of the Reichsprotektor and was later extended to four days at the instigation of the Reichsprotektor. It came into force on 14th June 1942 and was to be in place until 18th June 1942.

41. The Reaction of Foreign Countries and the Czech Population to this Decree.

This idea was from the outset regarded as an attempt to make the Czechs cooperate by other means, on the basis of the knowledge of the psychological attitude of the Czech Republic. From enemy propaganda, this sincerely meant and carried out measure, has been presented as a German ultimatum that the Secret State Police have announced to the Czech people that if they do not respond there will be reprisals. The Czech Exiles claim that one in every ten Czechs will be shot if this decree does not lead to the perpetrators of the attack. Since this decree was particularly strongly commented on in the Protektorate press and on various occasions with the headline 'The Last Deadline' this view has become strongly accepted by foreign countries' propaganda. The consequence of this was that due to the immunity period and fearing the ultimatum, parts of the population that could give even the slightest clue to help the investigation, rushed in a panic to the offices of the German police. There were so many people wanting to give information that the State Police Headquarters in Prague was unable to cope with them on the first day. In the first 48 hours more than 650 people volunteered information, of which more than half made no usable statements. In contrast, there [were] only 309 responses from the Czech population during the previous 19 days.

42. Valuable Information that came in and steered the Investigation in New Directions.

On Tuesday 16th June 1942, at noon, among the people who reported to the State Police Headquarters in Prague, was a young Czech who claimed to have information about one of the briefcases that had been displayed at the Bata shop. This Czech was particularly notice-able by his uncertain and hesitant demeanour. He was subjected to a very thorough exami-nation asking questions which went beyond this general statement and he revealed that he had seen this briefcase in the possession of a young man whom he did not know, but who happened to have been staying with a Czech family in Prague at the same time as him. Appeals about the briefcase had been very numerous in the press but had never had any success, because they were mostly answered by people trying their luck, possibly to try and claim some of the large reward money on offer. This Czech [was] Karel Čurda, who described the first time he saw the briefcase and that freshly cut grass was in the briefcase at that time. By saying this Čurda instantly became of note because the Forensic Institute of the Security Police in Berlin after an investigation had determined that in one briefcase traces of leaves and dry stem, a piece of coal leaf and two leaves of mug wort, etc. had been found. When several briefcases were presented to Čurda, he instantly and without hesitation picked out briefcase (No. 1), which was actually the briefcase of one of the perpetrators and in which the plant traces had been found by the forensic investigation. The interview with Čurda was then carried out vigorously, as well as him being body searched [and this] led to his confession that he was a parachute agent. He was still extremely anxious and disturbed and could allegedly give details of the entire agent network in the Protektorate. It actually turned out through later investigations that he knew only parts of the activities of the agents and their network of helpers. This was due to many members of the organisation never using their real names.

Karel Čurda [was] born 10th October 1911, in Stara-Hlina near Wittingau, [and is a] Protektorate citizen, single, Roman Catholic religion, one illegitimate child aged 2½ years, son of a forestry worker, Franz Čurda, and mother Rosa nee Novakova, living in Nova-Hlina. He left school in 1933 and then worked in agriculture in Nova-Hlina. On 1st November 1933, he joined the 29th Infantry Regiment in Neuhaus for his national service and afterwards stayed in the Army until 10th June 1938 and left as a platoon leader. From 11th June 1938 to 17th June 1939, he worked in the Czech Financial Guard at Had in Huldschinerländchen. On 17th June 1939, he fled to Poland in his uniform to join the Czech Legion. According to his own statements, the reason for his escape was not the new political situation in the Protektorate, but allegedly with dissatisfaction in his new position and a desire for adventure.

The escape route to the Legion was the usual one; from Poland to France to North Africa and back to France and then finally after the collapse of the French Army, to England. He served in England with Kubiš and Gabčik and knew them from the camps and attendance on the same courses. But he already knew them from France. He also attended the secret agent school in England and undertook the normal training programme. On 25th March 1942, he was flown to the Protektorate, but could not be dropped because of fog. The attempt was repeated on 29th March 1942, and this time he was dropped near Telsch in the district of Jihlava. The leader of this group was Lieutenant Kral, who has been mentioned earlier. He was not given a specific task but followed the orders of the leader of his group Adolf Kral.

The decision by Čurda to turn himself in was due to the harsh measures that had been taken by the Germans since the assassination. The parents of a parachute agent known to

Čurda had been shot dead. This fact deeply troubled Čurda, and he feared for the life of his aged mother, with whom he had hidden for some weeks in a hayloft. He therefore surrendered, trusting in the promised immunity from punishment. Although in his heart, Čurda never really believed this promise and that the German authorities would spare his mother and relatives. During the period of his six-week detention, Čurda was treated with the utmost courtesy and given many privileges but always felt that he would still be shot and this made interrogations with him extremely difficult. For example, after having been interrogated for several hours during which he seemed anxious, he was searched thoroughly and a well concealed lethal pill commonly used by parachute agents was found on him.

43.   Searches of the first safe houses on 17th June 1942.

Because of his extensive interrogation, a total of eight safe houses used by the parachutists were identified, four in Prague, one in Plzeň, one in Bad Belohrad, one in Pardubice and one in a village near Tabor, each were subjected to a surprise search on the same night. Čurda was not sufficiently knowledgeable about the importance of the individual houses in terms of their importance in the overall organisation. In fact, there were three addresses in Prague which were of particular importance to the parachutists and assassin network, which were not yet known at the time of the initial interrogation. The contact points in Prague [were]:

Jan Zelenka, (Hajský), Head Teacher

Prague XI, Biskupecstrasse 4

Josef Svatoš, Employee

Prague I, Melantrichgasse 15

Alois Moravec, Inspector (BMB)

Prague XI, Biskupecstrasse 7

Heinrich Bauc, Haulage Contractor

Prague XIV, Lumirgasse 601

The importance of Zelenka and Mrs Moravec has previously been emphasised in this report. Both were fanatically determined Czechs who had assisted with the assassination and knew every detail of its execution. They were both prepared from the outset that one day the police would be able to identify them. They were also, like most other senior helpers, equipped with lethal pills given to them by some of the parachute agents. In the early hours of 17th June 1942, when officers entered the Zelenka apartment using the usual security measures, Zelenka confronted them with the words: "Gentlemen, I am at your disposal." Two minutes later he was dead.[34] Exactly the same event took place at the apartment of Mrs Moravec, who also collapsed a few minutes after the appearance of the officials. They had both killed themselves using the lethal pills they had been given. Among those arrested was the Svatoš family, from Prague I, Melantrichgasse 15, where Čurda had a conversation with a parachute agent, and saw one of the briefcases found at the scene. This Czech person, whose real name was Gabčik, had a briefcase with him at the Svatoš family residence which contained grass,[35] under which Čurda claims to have recognised the parts of a sub-machine gun. The model of the sub-machine gun was known to Čurda because he had trained with this model in England. This point of contact [which] appeared after his first statement was to be a most important clue and worthy of further investigation. It could allow the origin of the two briefcases, which were found at the scene, to be identified. Furthermore, further names of offenders and a large number of other contact addresses were obtained; all of which were searched on 17th June 1942.

As a result of these interrogations, it was possible to identify more people who had assisted the perpetrators, so that by the evening of 17th June 1942, over eighty people had been arrested who had supported the assassins. However, some people who had helped;

disappeared immediately after the assassination or had no contact points except Zelenka and Mrs Moravec. These two had taken poison at the time of their arrest. So the focus of the interrogations was on the family members of these two people. Mrs Zelenka, suffered from severe heart disease and was extremely nervous and so could give no information. Zelenka's son had disappeared without a trace and was a few days later found dead in a forest near Prague. He had also poisoned himself. Meanwhile, the son of Mrs Moravec, who had at first denied any knowledge of the assassins and agents, confessed after seeing the corpse of his mother. He held out until late in the evening of the 17th June 1942, when he revealed an essential fact that his mother had told him that if he was ever in serious trouble he should go to the crypt of the Karl Borromeo Church for assistance. It turned out that he had known of this shelter since 2nd June 1942.

44. Hiding the assassins and preparing for their capture.
It was believed that this statement was true as it had been confirmed by information gained from other interrogations, especially from Mrs Krupka (the most important point of contact in Pardubice). Since the Karl Borromeo church in the Resselgasse is located near Charles Square, right in the centre of Prague and it was thought that for some length of time between five and eight people had been hidden here, there was no doubt that the clergy knew of this fact. But with the arrest of so many of their points of contact and helpers it was likely that the perpetrators would be soon warned that their hiding place was becoming dangerous.

This was proved to be a fact as only a small number of the helpers were aware of this contact point. It also turned out that an unknown person (but most likely the chaplain) telephoned the Moravec apartment on the afternoon of 17th June 1942, stating he was from the Karl Borromeo church and asked why Mrs Moravec had not come to the church. It was also suggested that one of the agents (Adolf Kral) that same afternoon was to have brought coffee and cake to the church. Through the skilful work of the Gestapo officers located in the apartment of Mrs Moravec, they convinced the pastor that all was well and seemingly no suspicions were raised. On the following day, on the 18th June, 1942, when the chaplain repeated his call, and Mrs Moravec was again not available it is likely some doubt would have crept into the mind of the caller. Given the overall caution exercised by the assassins and agents and clergy in the church, the church may well have been empty when entered.

45. Operation at the Karl Borromeo Church.
It was just before midnight on the 17th June, when the suspicion that the assassins were in the crypt of the Borromeo Church emerged and it was agreed there was no time to lose, because a wait of about 24 hours or even 12 hours could prevent a success. There was no doubt that according to previous experience, the assassins would not be taken alive and would prefer to fight and kill Germans in preference to surrender.

The special commission was faced with the situation that the assassins would be found dead and, under slightly better circumstances, badly injured. At least it seemed better to have the assassins dead rather than having to find them again. If they did not have an underground exit from the crypt it was expected they had a good defensive position and would fight.

During the night of 17th/18th June 1942, an exhaustive investigation into the exact layout of the crypt and church was carried out and any possible escape routes. Experts in the fields of buildings and professors and so on were consulted and were then detained for the duration of the action at the Gestapo HQ. Any interrogation of the clergy, inspection of the church itself or the church officials, was deliberately avoided, so as not to endanger the operation in the least. Previous experience with the Czech State Police meant that it was certain that no Czech could be trusted with the details of this investigation. Additionally, approaching the City Planning Department, Post Office and other authorities, which could actually have helped greatly, were omitted, so that the Czechs employed there could not communicate details of this operation to illegal organisations.

46. Operation to arrest the assassins.

After this preliminary work had been carried out the decision was made that night to immediately inform SS-Gruppenführer, Secretary of State Karl Hermann Frank, who then took part personally in the meetings and ordered the mobilisation of a Waffen-SS battalion for securing the area. The Waffen-SS were given 5 minutes notice to move. At 0415 on 18th June 1942, a cordon around the church was imposed and the operation of the Gestapo then began. The outer cordon had to be some distance from the church, because underground in Prague is a system of old passages and sewers and the possibility of an escape was quite high. Amongst other things, the River Vltava is only about 300–400 metres away, and it might have been possible to escape using sewers. The area in which the church was located was searched by a party of 65 men under the leadership of SS-Hauptsturmführer Leimer and the search then pushed forward concentrically on the church. The team in the church, which later also entered the crypt was under the leadership of SS-Hauptsturmführer Pannwitz and consisted of 15 men. Shortly before the operation began, the pastor and chaplain of the church were arrested in their homes and made to show the officials the entrances to the crypt. The chancery clerk who was arrested when trying to enter the church, who lived in the rooms adjacent to the nave, said he did not know anything about the crypt. The Gestapo team entered the nave through two doors leading directly from his residence.

The church is a classic late Baroque building designed by the German architect, Dietzenhofer, and is one of the best monuments of Prague. It has a nave and a flat gallery without railings on the street side of the Resselgasse and a choir loft on the Sderaz-Gasse, both of which can be reached via a spiral staircase, which begins in the nave and ends in the choir loft.

After entering the nave, machine guns were positioned at the two entrance doors to secure the area and prevent escape. The search of the nave was completed in less than five minutes and in two places signs were found that a crypt must be present. But before moving the heavy flagstones that led to the crypt, the choir loft and gallery needed to be searched. Access to the spiral staircase was closed by a locked iron door. At the same moment that officers had opened the door and were about to ascend the spiral staircase shots were fired towards the officers on the spiral staircase and nave. The enemy agents were well hidden behind metre-thick columns, but could be held down by machine gun fire. One of the officers was lightly wounded during this first engagement. In this situation, taking the enemy alive was completely impossible. The enemy put up stiff resistance and would not surrender and so had to be killed although some of them committed suicide by shooting themselves or taking poison. After a thorough examination of all available options (using the roof, adjacent houses etc., to gain access), an attempt was made to disable the enemy with hand grenades. This did not succeed, and the enemy continued to fire and also threw grenades from the gallery, probably three. After thorough preparation the enemy was then destroyed after an assault by troops from the Waffen-SS using machine guns and hand grenades. From the gallery and choir three agents were recovered either dead or badly wounded:

1. Kubiš (Navratil, assassin, bomb thrower – body No. 6),
2. Kral (Adolf (Opálka), body No. 5),
3. Bublik (body No. 7).

Kral was already dead. Kubiš and Bublik displayed signs of life. They were immediately taken to the SS military hospital to try and keep them alive, but both died.[36]

Clothing was found in the choir loft which suggested that at least three more people still had to be in the church. The chaplain of the church, Doctor Petřek, who had taken cover when the first firing began, knew the situation in the church. He finally admitted that there were four men in the crypt under the nave. This crypt was accessible from the nave through a rectangular hole in the floor and then using a ladder to descend several metres. Another entrance, where a larger staircase leads into the crypt, was covered by a large stone slab. Everything was tried to get these four men to come out alive. The chaplain and the pastor, both of whom the agents had known and cared for in the crypt, spoke to them through the rectangular hole. They told the agents that resistance was futile and that it would be better to surrender. Three times they were asked to come out. They answered on the first occasion: "Never", on the second time "Never" and on the third occasion: "Czechs never surrender."[37]

These answers and the length of time that the enemy had remained in the crypt led us to believe that no escape route had been found. Since entry into the crypt would have caused heavy casualties, because at first the only entry was through the rectangular hole and allowed the enemy to shoot each person who entered individually, other efforts had to be made.[38] Firstly, tear gas was used; however, it was not effective as not enough gas was available to form an effective concentration. Another attempt was made with the assistance of the Prague Fire Department. Through a ventilation slit located in the church wall, which was the only link between the crypt and the street (Resselgasse), four hose lines were placed through the slit and with the help of two pumps water was pumped into the crypt. The aim was to try and force the enemy out of the crypt due to a rising water level. If some more pumps had been used it is possible within two hours the enemy would have been forced out. The enemy, who had not reacted to the tear gas, responded violently to the water attack as a ladder was used from the inside to force the hoses back out, they also fired through the ventilation slit and threw petrol bombs. Fire was returned by the Waffen-SS who formed the cordon and they also used hand grenades. A particularly brave fire fighter was able to reinsert the hoses under enemy fire.[39] After 40 minutes, the water level had risen by only about 1 metre using the two engines. The Waffen-SS suggested that volunteers should be lowered down through the rectangular hole; this was not approved by me because of the danger to human life. Three volunteers were lowered into the crypt but immediately came under fire from the enemy and had to be withdrawn, all three were wounded. After this the Waffen-SS fired down into the crypt from the nave and also threw hand grenades. After evacuating the wounded, a second wave of Waffen-SS stormed the crypt but found the enemy already dead. Four men, one assassin and three agents, were in the crypt and had all committed suicide by shooting themselves in the head. These four men were:

Gabčik,

Valčik,

Švarc and

Hrubý.

The crypt was, as it turned out, extraordinarily large. It occupied ¾ of the area under the nave and had a wide corridor in the middle and a total of 120 catacombs on both sides. Some of these still contained bones from pastors and monks buried there. Empty catacombs had been used by the agents as storage spaces and also for sleeping. The following items were later recovered from the crypt:

Sleeping bags

Mattresses

Clothes, cooking pots and a stove

Oil lamps

Toiletries and other items necessary for daily use

Food

10 pistols and 1 revolver with ammunition

Among them were Colt pistols, calibre 7.65mm, No. 540 416 and No. 539 370, which the two assassins had fired during their escape after the attack. Later examination by the Forensic Institute of the Security Police confirmed this.

With the neutralisation of the assassins and the five other agents, the direct perpetrators of the assassination attempt on SS-Obergruppenführer Heydrich were identified, located and killed.

47. Verification of the Identities of the Perpetrators Kubiš and Gabčik.

The special commission's role before the action in the Karl Borromeo church was very clear and it was to identify and trace the assassins. However, after the action was concluded in the Borromeo Church, further measures were carried out which without doubt clearly proved the identity of the assassins. Since they had both died, it was expected, that enemy propaganda would state that the German findings were false. All seven bodies were photographed in the Department of Medicine at the Charles University in Prague after thorough autopsies and witnesses who had seen the two assassins at the scene were shown the bodies. In addition, two parachute agents who knew the assassins from the Legion time in France and also during training in England were shown the bodies.[40]

48. Evidence.

1. Pistols from which the cases found on the scene were fired.

    The 10 pistols, which were recovered from the Karl Borromeo church and used by the agents and assassins, were sent immediately to the institute of Forensic Science of the Security Police in Berlin for comparison purposes. The Institute of Forensic Science, in its report of 19th June 1942, reference No. 1860/42 CTI determined that the Colt pistol, calibre 7.65 mm No. 539 370 is the pistol, from which the three bullets recovered from the walls of the printing house, Prometheus in the Kirchmaierstrasse and in the area of the shop owned by the butcher Franz Brauner, were fired. The cases found there had been fired, during the escape of the machine pistol gunner (Jozef Gabčik), at the driver of the Obergruppenführer, SS-Oberscharführer Johannes Klein, who chased him. It is thus clear that the weapon used by the machine gunner was in the Borromeo church. In the same report it is stated that the Colt pistol, calibre 7.65 mm No. 540 416, had fired the fifth cartridge case which was found at the crime scene at the intersection of Kirchmaierstrasse and Klein Holleschowitzerstrasse. It was here that a shot was fired by the bomb thrower (Jan Kubiš). Thus, it is clear that the weapon used by the bomb thrower was also in the Karl Borromeo church.

2. Sub-Machine Gun.

    The parachute agent Čurda, who had given himself up, had seen Gabčik, who was known to him from England, at the Svatoš house in Prague carrying a briefcase containing a sub-machine gun filled with grass. When shown all seven dead bodies Čurda recognised the make of the sub-machine gun and identified body No. 3, Jozef Gabčik, as the person who had the briefcase with the sub-machine gun at the Svatoš house. Mrs Svatoš also identified that corpse No. 3 was that of Zdenek (code name of Gabčik), who had the briefcase containing the sub-machine gun at her house.

3. Briefcase belonging to the bomber.

    Mrs Svatoš stated when confronted with the bodies that body No. 6, Jan Kubiš, was the person who had borrowed a briefcase from her husband. When the recovered items were displayed at the Bata store she immediately recognised the briefcase, but for understandable reasons did not come forward.

3a. Briefcase of the machine gunner.

She also identified body No. 3, Gabčik, as the person who had owned the other briefcase that had been on display at the Bata store. Both briefcases have been shown to her and she has recognised both of them due to various features. One had been repaired in her apartment while she was present and on the other, Gabčik had covered a scuffed area with brown shoe polish. All of these features were immediately recognised by Mrs Svatoš.

4. Bombs.

Vlastimil Moravec when confronted with the seven bodies identified body No. 6, Jan Kubiš (bomb thrower), as the agent who had shown him and explained the workings of the bomb. Additionally in his presence, Kubiš had unwrapped the grey tape from the bomb and wrapped it up again neatly.

5. Self-confession by Jan Kubiš to his lover Marie Kovárniková.

Kubiš, who was known to his lover as Jaroslav Navratil or Ota, testified that he had visited her the day after the assassination and stated to her that he had committed the assassination with one of his comrades. At that time Ota had a badly inflamed right eye. Kovárniková had recognised her lover Ota, Josef Navratil, from the publication of pictures of the assassins in the newspapers. She identified the body of Jan Kubiš when shown his corpse.

6. Confession of Gabčik to his lover Anna Malinová nee Kovárniková.

Gabčik told his lover, to whom he also revealed his real name, but whom she had originally known as Vyskočil, when he was in bed with her that his comrade Ota had committed the assassination. His lover had used the words to him that it would be the reds that had carried out the assassination, because now the Czech people must pay for it. Gabčik replied to her literally: "The red that did the assassination is now lying in your bed." In addition, Malinová said that Gabčik once had in his briefcase three egg-sized items. When she questioned him about these, he explained that she did not need to know that but should not touch these items as they could easily explode. She assumed they were bombs.

7. Ladies' bicycle left behind at the crime scene.

By reconstructing the course of events of the crime, the ladies' bicycle left behind at the scene must have belonged to the machine gunner, because hanging from the handlebar was a briefcase and inside it was a filled magazine for a sub-machine gun. In addition, later investigation showed that this briefcase was seen in the possession of the machine gunner Gabčik, by Čurda, at the Svatoš residence and the same briefcase was identified by Mrs Svatoš. (The briefcase was filled with grass, under which a sub-machine gun was hidden. The briefcase was buffed with shoe polish in various places.) The origin of the women's bicycle confirms the investigative work. The ladies' bicycle was the property of a Jew, Lydia Bondy nee Holzner, born 3rd September 1921 in Teplitz-Schönau. Her father, the Jew Holzner, bought the bicycle that was recovered at the scene for her in 1935 in Teplitz-Schönau from a bicycle dealer called Kretschmer. Franz Holzner died in 1937. In September 1938, the Holzner family moved from Teplitz-Schönau to Prague. The women's bicycle was taken and constantly used in Prague. Because of the heavy traffic in Prague, Mrs Bondy stopped cycling in September 1941. At that time she passed it on to a colleague, a nurse called Marie Sebesta, who was residing in Prague-Radlitz. Then Mrs Bondy gave the bicycle to the sister of Mrs Sebesta, Mrs Kouthan, who lived in Prague XVI, Radlitzerstrasse, when she stayed for six weeks in this apartment. Later it was returned to Mrs Sebesta, where it was stored in the basement until shortly before Christmas 1941. The Bondy family had a close friendship with the Moravec family (helpers to the parachute agents in Prague). In particular, the son, Vlastimil Moravec, who was friendly with the Bondy daughter and was able to borrow the ladies' bicycle just before Christmas. The Moravec family were already looking after securities and a large sum of money on behalf of the Jewish family. Bondy to stop this falling into the hands of the German authorities. The ladies' bicycle was stored in the Mercury Garage in Prague. On 26th April 1942, Vlastimil Moravec personally handed over the women's bicycle to the assassin Zdenek (Josef Gabčik) in Prague-Kobilis. From this point on, the women's bicycle was freely available to the assassins and then it was left behind at the scene. The women's bicycle was recognised by all the persons mentioned in this section.

Vlastimil Moravec, when confronted with the bodies, stated that body No. 3 (Josef Gabčik) was the person to whom he had passed the ladies' bicycle on 26th April 1942. Moravec had already learned before the assassination from his mother and the parachute agent Valčik that this ladies' bicycle would be used as part of the assassination attempt. After the publication of the picture of the bicycle, Moravec and his mother recognised the ladies' bicycle as the one that had been in their possession with them and they talked about what to do next.

Witnesses who recognised the assassins when confronted with the seven bodies.

8. SS-Oberscharführer Johannes Klein – driver of the SS-Obergruppenführer
9. Douša, Karl
10. Brauner, Franz
11. Großlicht, Thomas
12. Navarova nee Strasnicka, Marie
13. Platt, Friedrich
14. Huff, Stanislav
15. Wolf, Bozena

The persons mentioned from 8 to 13 clearly recognised body No. 3 as the machine gunner (Gabčik) and those named from 14 to 15 as the person who fled after the attempt on foot. This was the machine gunner Jozef Gabčik.

16. Maslova nee. Zaruber, Bozena
17. Müller, Josef, police officer
18. Zavodnik, Marie
19. Sprungl, Marie
20. Rozek, Agnes
21. Sedlackova, Frantiska

The persons mentioned from 16 to 20 recognised body No. 6 when shown the seven bodies as the bomb thrower (Kubiš).

Moreover, the person named at 21 again recognised the cyclist who had escaped from the scene of the attack and was wounded in the face. In addition, another 10 persons who were at the scene or on the escape route when confronted with the bodies had not clearly seen the faces of the perpetrators, so they were unable to provide any additional information.

Names of helpers of the assassins who recognised them from the preserved heads of the assassins Kubiš and Gabčik.[41]

22. Kovárniková, Marie, lover of the assassin Kubiš, whom she knew as Jaroslav Navratil

23. Soukupova nee Kovárniková, Ludmilla, lived with her sister Marie K. and was a friend of Kubiš

24. Malinová, Anna, lover of the assassin Josef Gabčik

The persons mentioned from 22 to 24 immediately identified and with no doubt the head of body No. 6 as Jaroslav Navratil (Kubiš), who they knew had carried out the assassination and had been wounded in the eye.

25. Piskáček, Antonia

26. Piskáček, Jaroslav

The assassin Kubiš went to the Piskáček residence immediately after the assassination attempt and the injury to his eye was noted. The Piskáček couple recognised the head of body No. 6 again without doubt as the assassin, who was known to them as Ota.

27. Ruta, Václav,? quartermaster for Strnad and Vyskočil from 31st December 1941 to 5th January 1942, when confronted with the two preserved heads of bodies No. 3 and 6 [identified them] as those who stayed with him during that period.

28. Kovárniková, Marie

29. Soukupova nee Kovárniková, Ludmilla

30. Malinová, Anna

31. Piskacek, Jaroslav

32. Kral, Wenceslas

The people mentioned from 27 to 32 correctly identified the preserved head of No. 3 as Zdenek. Malinová, who was his lover, also knew him by his real name of Jozef Gabčik.

33. Novák, Václav, senior

34. Baumann, Bretislav

These two people almost certainly recognised the head of body No. 6 as Strnad. Baumann stated he was the man who came to him and asked him to help hide the parachutes.

35. Linking of Ota and Jaroslav Navratil with Kubiš.

Body No. 6 has been recognised by numerous witnesses as either being known to them as Ota or Navratil. Parachute agent Čurda, identified body No. 6 as Jan Kubiš and emphasised that this was his real name.

36. Linking of Zdenek, Broucek and Vyskočil with Josef Gabčik.

As already mentioned, a number of witnesses recognised body No 3 as that of Zdenek. The parachute agent Čurda, recognised Josef Gabčik and stated that this was his real name.

However, the lover of Gabčik, Malinová, who knew that Zdenek was really Jozef Gabčik, recognised him in photographs and as a corpse.

37. Statement of Krupková, Johanna.

In the evening of 27th May 1942, in the apartment of the Moravec family, Mrs Moravec told Krupková that the assassination attempt on SS-Obergruppenführer Heydrich had been carried out by the two parachute agents Ota and Zdenek.

38. Statement by Vlastimil Moravec.

On 28th May 1942, Valčik told Moravec that Ota and Zdenek had committed the attack. His mother added that Ota had been seriously injured in one of his eyes. This conversation took place at breakfast at the kitchen table in their apartment.

39. Men's Bicycle.

About four weeks before the assassination, Václav Khodl got this bicycle from his uncle, Jaroslaus Smrž. Khodl's mother, Mrs Emanuele Khodl, told her son that he should not return the bicycle to his uncle for the time being. She lent it to the assassin, Jan Kubiš, whom she knew was a parachutist. Kubiš brought the bicycle back to them. Two days before the assassination, Kubiš wanted to borrow from Mrs Piskáček her son's bicycle but they refused. Therefore the day before the assassination, Kubiš visited Mrs Khodl and borrowed from her again the men's bicycle belonging to Mr Smrž. After the assassination, Kubiš rode to the Bata shop in Libeň and left the bicycle and walked to the house of the Novák family. Mrs Novák asked her 14-year-old daughter, Jindřiška, to pick up the bicycle from outside the Bata shop, and doing her best to avoid attention she placed it in the yard of her house. The husband, Václav Novák, went with his wife to Piskáček in the evening of 27th May 1942, to request that the bicycle that was in their yard be moved. The son of the Piskáčeks picked up the bike and was supposed to take it to the Khodls' and if there was nobody there, take it to the apartment of the Šmrzs. Piskáček took the bicycle directly to Smrž and it was left in this apartment. The Novák and Piskáček families were fully aware that this men's bicycle had been used by the assassin.

Further Investigation into the Circle of Helpers of the Assassins.

After the extermination and annihilation of the assassins and their direct helpers in the Karl Borromeo church, whilst it was clear that the assassins had been identified; the investigation work of the special commission was by no means finished. Only now, in unprecedented detail, were their widely spread circle of helpers rounded up, although some of the most important heads and officials were still able to flee. Extensive manhunts were mounted to find Doctor Lyčka, who treated the bomb thrower on the assassination day, and Professor Vaněk (Jindra), the head of the Sokol organisation.

It became clear during this phase of the great resistance shown by the Czechs that in spite of the law, coercion and the threat of death, many Czechs preferred to die than cooperate with the German authorities. For example, during the hunt for Doctor Lyčka, it became known that he was still in Prague and staying with some friends. Two friends, who had been arrested and could be subject themselves to punishment by death for failing to reveal information, refused to reveal any information. One friend, called Caloun, who is an official of a German company and has a monthly income of RM 1,000, and whose wife works in the film industry and also earns a lot of money, declared that Lyčka would probably take his own life rather than surrender. It was made clear to Caloun, and he fully understood, that every night of freedom for Doctor Lyčka costs a new blood sacrifice for the Czech people, because by Doctor Lyčka approaching other Czechs and asking for accommodation, it threatens them with the death penalty. He himself stated that he has no false illusions regarding non-cooperation with the state police and was not prepared, like so many others, to assist the state authorities. Caloun had the demeanour of a normal citizen and was a good businessman, but was convicted within 24 hours. Caloun is only a harmless example of the harshness with which the Czechs pursued their illicit aims by sacrificing their own lives.

Zelenka and his son, Mrs Moravec and others took poison and the two assassins shot themselves. The detainees are constantly trying to use poison or firearms to avoid arrest, or to take their own lives in other ways. This situation made it necessary for the officials of the State Police Headquarters in Prague to have to disguise themselves in ever more ingenious ways so as to be inconspicuous to the people they wanted to arrest. They disguised themselves as employees of the gas board, street cleaners, workmen, chauffeurs, patients, postmen, etc., to try and take people alive. In many cases, not only the use of firearms, but other weapons have been used, which often led to success only with the use, by the authorities, of heavier weapons, such as sub-machine guns and hand grenades. During the arrest of the Czech, Oldrich Frolik, whose residence was used as a safe house until 15th September 1942, he still had hidden weapons, ammunition and grenades at his home. Frolik was immediately well prepared to defend himself with a firearm and shot and injured two officers from the State Police Headquarters in Prague. The arrest of this determined fugitive Frolik was only achieved by a large scale undercover operation. Frolik was offered by one of his associates an escape from Prague in a truck. However, this plan originated from this office and the truck was provided by the Secret State Police; he was overpowered with four other criminals after a heavy fight. All these measures meant that the investigation process was extremely protracted. The head of the illegal Sokol organization, 'Jindra', Professor Ladislaus Vaněk, was also identified but only arrested in another undercover operation after eight weeks of preliminary work. Jindra was guarded by heavily armed men but still managed to take poison. For a year he had adopted the name of a friend of his who was now serving in the Czech Legion and was a former staff captain. Jindra also lived partly with this man's wife as her husband and continued to draw his monthly pension. His organisation was so large that it cannot be detailed here and several months' investigative work needs to be carried out to reveal the entire network. The leader of the terrorist group and agent who is often mentioned in this report is called Bartoš, and his radio operator was Tolar, who escaped after the assassination of the men at the church; both were also identified but shot in a fire fight.

Despite the difficult circumstances described here in the identification of the network of helpers and despite the tough doggedness and reckless determination of the Czechs involved, the work of the Special Commission was carried out with such little loss on both sides, that this success is only due to the incalculable and outstanding commitment of the officials of the State Police Headquarters in Prague.

Motive.

The motives that led the Czechs to their actions are partly contradictions in themselves. Although Jindra tried to prevent the assassination attempt he was powerless to stop it. Vaněk finally offered to assist us to prevent further grave consequences for the Czech people and because he had come to the conclusion that he was able to work with the State Police and so help the Czech cause rather than illegally for Beneš' devastating policy. Whether this was the result of propaganda broadcasts or he changed his view about his organisation, is not known. This willingness of Jindra to help us made a very serious impression.

Another example is the chaplain Doctor Petřek, who is considered to be the typical representative of the Czech intelligentsia. Doctor Petřek was born in Belgrade and since his time at the University of Belgrade has been aware of influences of German scientific material, institutions and achievements. Petřek has been influenced exclusively in his studies by German intellectuals. He says that he had never been anti-German and had not shown any pronounced Pan-Slavic stance, even though he was a Greek Orthodox pastor. Out of historical philosophical considerations and objective observation of the political conditions of the last few decades, he has come to the conclusion that the historical task, which was set by the providence of the German people, is at present being solved. Orders given by France and England were a thing of the past. He was convinced that the German people will fulfil their historic task and that it will not hinder anyone, let alone the handful of Czechs who exist in the world. In the area of Bohemia and Moravia in 20 years, they may still speak Czech, but only think German; this was his firm belief. Although he saw the situation objectively, he has not been able to avoid the question posed to him by the parachute agents from London in any other way than in a Czech-chauvinist sense. He states that after all he is still a Czech and cannot refuse the help of a member of his nation. In addition, the men were indeed sent from London and it was felt they had a better overview of the world situation from there rather than those in Prague; and if the time has come for such actions, then you cannot set aside the fact they you are a Czech. Doctor Petřek has had no inhibitions in this regard from his point of view as a pastor. His attitude has only been determined by his loyalty to Czech folklore.

Another motive in support of the assassins and their accomplices was found in the group of people who were members of Sokol, those who had bitterness towards the Germans for dissolving the organisation and those who had known people who had been arrested and placed in concentration camps.

The women who worked with particular fanatical zeal in the entire organisation either have a son in the Legion, like Mrs Moravec, or are guided by maternal instincts, such as Mrs Fafek, who wanted to be a motherly figure to the parachutists. In some cases, however, the motives of some of the female helpers were found to be sexual.

Among the women and Sokol leaders, a particularly prominent chauvinist attitude has been noted, which did not conceal their anti-German sentiments, even in interrogations with the secret police, and many said that the Czech bloodshed as a result of martial law in the autumn of 1941 fuelled their desire for revenge. These outspoken anti-German Czechs consider themselves innocent of any wrong doing and are treated as martyrs.

In conclusion for the motives given, many state that the assassination attempt was a military task ordered from London. More than three hundred people have been identified as helpers in the assassination operation or knew about the perpetrators and a list of these follows later. These Czechs were driven in their actions by the motives already cited.

Conclusion.

The picture of the origins and execution of the attack can be clearly drawn after the investigation work carried out. It was not the Protektorate who sent men to the execution chamber. It was Beneš himself who met the assassins before their departure, who heard the warnings from the Czechs who remained at home and who feared the cruel consequences of this murder, but who, after the act, expressed his gratitude to the murderers. Beneš found two of his countrymen, degenerate characters when in their homeland, loafers and drunkards, worthy of handing over a bloody calling card for their so-called Government-in-Exile. He has himself and with his supporters turned racially inferior human beings into murderers. He has the full support of his host country, England, and through its aid, by supplying training, weapons and the carrying out of the actual assassination of SS-Obergruppenführer Heydrich, we come to the conclusion that it was: 'Made in England'.

Pannwitz.

Kriminalrat.

I.   Contact Points

    A.   In Prague:

        1.   Bauc, car contractor, National Community

        2.   Bockova, wife

        3.   Bradac, master tailor

        4.   Brychova, wife (divorced)

        5.   Dubova, wife, Red Cross

6.   Fafek, accountant, Sokol
7.   Hosek, official of the Prague High Court, Sokol
8.   Jesenska, dentist
9.   Khodl, inspector at the Avia Prague
10. Kovárniková, factory worker
11. Löbl, wife
12. Malinová, factory worker
13. Moravec, retired chief inspector of the Bohemian-Moravian Railway
14. Novák, carpenter, Sokol
15. Piskáček, technical officer at the Bohemian-Moravian Railway
16. Pouznar
17. Ruta, post-assistant
18. Sedlak, commercial clerk
19. Soukupova, worker
20. Svatos, Registry resident
21. Vicherkova, wife
22. Zajickova, widow
23. Prochazka, former captain of the CSR, currently out of service
24. Hrncirik, coffeehouse owner, Sokol
25. Karban, official
26. Frolik, mechanic
27. Bradac, master tailor

B.   In Plzeň:
1.   Hrdlickova, wife (widow)
2.   Kral, Rayon inspector
3.   Kucerova, merchant
4.   Bejbl, retired police inspector

C.   Other contact points:
1.   Vojtisek, printer, Sokol Bad Belohrad
2.   Vojtisek, owner of a printers
3.   Vykouk, debt collector, Sokol Radotin
4.   Krupka, official of the Bohemian Electricity Association, Pardubice
5.   Burdych, farmer, Upper Kosteletz

D.   Support to the parachute agents was given by:
1.   Bejbl, Plzeň, retired police inspector
2.   Kaliberova, Prague housewife
3.   Smrž, Prague Sattler (Sokol)
4.   Sramkova, Prague housewife
5.   Zelenka, Prague head teacher (Sokol)

E.   Before the assassination, the following people were aware of the attack:
1.   Kovárniková, factory worker
2.   Moravec, Alois, Retired Chief Inspector of the Bohemian-Moravian Railway
3.   Moravec, Vlastimil, organisation official
4.   Svatoš, Josef, Sokol
5.   Svatoš, Frantisek, Aide, Sokol
6.   Krupka, Wenzel, official of the Bohemian Electricity Association, Sokol
7.   Krupka, housewife
8.   Zelenka, headteacher

9.   Vaněk (Jindra) Ladislav, Professor, Sokol

F.   The following people knew who had carried out the assassination:
1.   Fafek, accountant, Sokol
2.   Franta, ophthalmologist
3.   Gorazd, bishop
4.   Hansl, store man
5.   Hejl, private servant, Sokol
6.   Hruskova, dairy worker
7.   Jesensky, dentist
8.   Khodl, inspector at the Avia Prague
9.   Kovárniková, factory worker
10.   Kuthan, locksmith
11.   Louda, church official
12.   Lyčka, Doctor
13.   Malinová, factory worker
14.   Miniv, director of district health insurance
15.   Moravec, Alois, retired chief inspector of the Bohemian-Moravian Railway
16.   Novák, carpenter, Sokol
17.   Oktabec, mechanic, Sokol
18.   Rysavy, treasurer, Sokol
19.   Smrž, saddler Sokol
20.   Sobek, Doctor at the Central Insurance Institution, Social Democrat, Freemason
21.   Sonnevend, church elder
22.   Soukupova, worker
23.   Spinarova, dentist
24.   Svatoš, Aide, Sokol
25.   Svatoš, Aide, Sokol
26.   Sverak, Doctor
27.   Zajickova, widow
28.   Zelenka, head teacher, Sokol
29.   Hruskova, dairy worker
30.   Stanovsky, canon

G.   The following people were aware that the assassins were in the Karl Borromeo church:
1.   Fafek, accountant, Sokol
2.   Fafkova, housewife
3.   Fafkova, a member of the league to fight tuberculosis
4.   Fafkova, a member of the league to fight tuberculosis
5.   Gorazd, bishop
6.   Gruzinova, secretary of Bishop Gorazd
7.   Jesensky, dentist
8.   Moravec, retired chief inspector of the Bohemian-Moravian Railway
9.   Moravec, wife
10.   Moravec, Vlastimil, organisation official
11.   Mühlmann, housewife
12.   Ort, official
13.   Petřek, chaplain of the Greek Orthodox Church
14.   Rysavy, taxman
15.   Sobek, Doctor

16. Sonnevend, church elder
17. Sverak, Doctor
18. Zelenka, head teacher, Sokol
19. Vaněk, professor, Sokol member (technical director)
20. Cikl, pastor of the Borromeo church

H. The following people were probably aware that the assassins were hiding in the Karl Borromeo church:
1. Louda, church official
2. Ornest, master tailor, part-time church official

I. Perpetrators of Illegal Activity:
1. Baumann, farmer
2. Bockova, housewife
3. Brych, merchant
4. Brychova, housewife
5. Bubnik
6. Caloun, notary, Sokol
7. Cernicky, book binder, Sokol
8. Falta, commercial employee
9. Geisler
10. Hampel, railway worker
11. Hejcmann, official, Sokol
12. Hofmann
13. Hosek, official of the Prague High Court, Sokol
14. Janickova, housewife
15. Rezek
16. Kabrt, farmer
17. Kaliberova, housewife
18. Karban, official at the Ministry of Economy and Labour
19. Klikar
20. Klouda
21. Kral, engineer
22. Krovak
23. Kubica, teacher, Sokol
24. Marecek, loading supervisor, Sokol
25. Merta
26. Moravec, merchant, Sokol
27. Münzberger, tram conductor, Sokol
28. Nitka, merchant
29. Panes
30. Pelcak
31. Pleskot, director
32. Polak, widow
33. Pouznar
34. Rebec, cutler
35. Riha, iron worker
36. Slavicek, official
37. Shejbal
38. Schulz

39. Šustr
40. Stary, gardener
41. Strnad, court official
42. Vanik, master carpenter
43. Vejvoda
44. Zemanek, architect
45. Trojan, managing director
46. Opicka, city secretary
47. Jedlan, carpenter
48. Carabel, carpenter, National Conciliation
49. Vyhnis, senior teacher, National Conciliation
50. Hes, watchman, Sokol official
51. Koudela, official of the Bohemian-Moravian Railway

J. The following people provided food for the assassins in the Karl Borromeo church:
1. Fafek, housewife
2. Fafek, civil servant
3. Fafek, civil servant
4. Petřek, chaplain
5. Zelenka, head teacher, Sokol
6. Moravec, housewife

Footnotes

1   After the attack on Heydrich, a special investigative commission was established at the Prague State Police Headquarters to look into the details of the assassination. From a document dated 29th September 1946 which includes post-war German language testimony by former *Gestapo* criminal commissioner Heinz Jantur, headed 'Assassination of the *Reichsprotektor, SS-Obergruppenführer* Reinhard Heydrich':

Fervent activity broke out. Under the leadership of the criminal commissioner Pannwitz, the head of the IIG, a special commission was set up. It consisted of the most capable officers. At the direction of the Main Office of Imperial Security, the heads of the [Prague] service and also the state police in Berlin, Dresden, Cheb, Liberec and Karlovy Vary had to second about 20 officials. Together with the necessary steno typists, the special committees numbered around 120 people. I belonged to the commission as a deputy head of the IIG. The main office of the Criminal Police Prague was also called to co-operate by supplying clerical support.

It was decided to split the investigation as follows:

1.1) Criminal Commissioner Schultze investigated all traces of the parachute agents and the people around them,

1.2) Criminal Commissioner Pannwitz was responsible for all contacts gained in the city of Prague,

1.3) Criminal Commissioner Morbeck investigated activities outside Prague, but within the jurisdiction of the Prague State Police, i.e. in Bohemia,

1.4) Criminal Commissioner Leimer was in charge of all leads that led outside the jurisdiction of the Prague State Police,

1.5) Yantur has taken over the duties of the Criminal Investigation Service.

The Evaluation Committee was later subordinated to Criminal Commissioner Lüss from the Criminal Police in Prague.

Pannwitz's memoirs from 1959: "Immediately after the assassination, the commission was sent reinforcements of officials from many cities in the Reich, including Dresden, Leipzig,

Berlin, Hanover, Munich and Nuremberg. Additionally, police reinforcements arrived to cope with certain aspects of the investigation.

"Police officers carried out certain tasks without the aid of a forensic special commission, probably on the orders of their political masters. This was not good for practical work. Employees from the Reich did not know the Czech language, nor the conditions under which they needed to work in the Protektorate, so they could only act as auxiliary forces or help local officials. The Commission, which was tasked with investigating the assassination, was given a clear structure under these conditions. There were, however, about 1,200 officials who were working for the Commission and had to be managed in their work. The leadership of the Commission was subordinated to all heads of the secret state police and their officials. Each report or individual search was written down and transferred to the headquarters of the Commission where they handled the matter. Here it was decided whether it would be eliminated or further investigated. Everything that did not involve the assassination was returned to the reporting office. The Commission worked very quickly, concentrically and without a break. Within this framework, much use was made of the best officials, carrying out all the urgent investigations. For example, a suspect cyclist was identified within half an hour after being reported and 30 officers put on the case. A special search squadron found every imaginable situation and carried out documentary checks in hotels, trams, market places and bus and railway stations. We know that the actions of this search led the parachutists' leader, Lieutenant Bartoš, to order all seven agents in Prague to hide in the crypt of the Karl Borromeo church."

2   Heinz Jantur's statement from 1946: "If I remember correctly, the first report on the assassination was received by the state police from Doctor Ženatý from the *Protektorate* Police. The report stated that an assassination attempt on a senior German officer had been committed in Prague-Libeň. At this time I was the Air Raid Defence Officer and was in the Old Market with my then commander, the criminal commissioner, Pannwitz. We were notified by phone and hurried to the crime scene. At the hospital, Criminal Commissioner Pannwitz discovered that the victim of the assassination was *SS-Obergruppenführer* Heydrich. Doctor Ženatý arrived with a larger number of officials, taking care of the police closure of the hospital."

3   Pannwitz's memoirs of 1959: "A few minutes after the assassination attempt, a liaison officer for the Czech and German police forces, Commissioner Ženatý, told me that the police had reported that a senior officer of the *Wehrmacht* had been injured in a bombing. The Czech police were probably afraid, so he acted as if he did not know anything, and that he just heard something very vague. Such reports, which reported attacks on the *Wehrmacht*, were very common, and often they were false, so there was a tendency in the state secret police not to respond to them and wait for details from the Czech police. In this case, however, Ženatý decided to visit the crime scene, although he had only vague information. There were two more officers present from the police station where the report came from. There he was told that the injured general was in Bulovka and that he was thought to be the *Reichsprotektor*."

4   Pannwitz's memoirs from 1959: "There was no information at the hospital; nobody seemed to know anything, so it was decided to enquire in every room in the surgical department. At the entrance to one of the operating theatres, Heydrich was discovered; he was sitting in the middle of a trolley. Two nurses were putting ice on his forehead and his cheeks; he had two injuries in his back. Heydrich turned around, recognised the police official and asked him where his briefcase was. He was told that everything was present, although we did not know for certain. Heydrich was due to fly to the *Führer*'s Headquarters in the morning, and he had some secret papers in his briefcase. The briefcase remained lying in the car and a Bohemian

woman helped arrange transport for him to the hospital. The Professor said he should immediately be operated on, which commenced within 10 minutes."

5   Pannwitz's memoirs of 1959: "The first measure was the order to close the city of Prague in
order to prevent the escape of offenders to the countryside; at the same time, power should be
demonstrated. The *Wehrmacht* closed the entire area of the city; it was extremely difficult, if
not impossible, to get out of the city. The 24-hour train service was stopped, every single one
of them. Eventually this was rescinded but strict street controls were carried out. These measures made the perpetrators stay in the city. At the same time, 35,000 buildings were searched
in the evening and night after the assassination. These searches required the deployment of
about 12,000 men from various organisations, even the Czech police. From the beginning,
no direct success was expected; only the population should be given to understand what
the danger was to keep the perpetrators hidden. The first afternoon a state of emergency,
including a curfew for the night, a ban on public events, and so on, was introduced. Later, it
was discovered that an apartment in which one of the perpetrators was hiding was searched.
Military troops had little criminal training or knowledge, and their job was to look for illegal
residents. When the search squad appeared, the fugitive went into a ventilation shaft near the
bathroom or toilet and was hanging on a window ledge for almost ten minutes. About 650
people were arrested this night, whose papers were found not to be in order. Some of them
were arrested and questioned by the Czech police; others were of no use to the investigating
commission and were released again."

6   Heinz Jantur's testimony from 1946: "On 27 May 1942 at 10.35 a.m. a bomb attack on
SS-Obergruppenführer Heydrich was committed in Prague-Libeň, where he was badly injured.
Heydrich was on his way from his summer residence in Panenské Břežany to the Prague Castle
and was sitting in the right front seat of his car beside the driver. In the so-called hairpin bend
on the junction of Kirchmaierovy and Primátorské in Prague-Libeň, two unknown men
suddenly emerged, the first of whom attempted to shoot *SS-Obergruppenführer* Heydrich
with a sub-machine gun. But the weapon did not work. When Heydrich saw this, he ordered
the driver to stop. At this point, the other man threw a grenade at the car from a distance of
about two metres. It hit the right rear door, exploded and a large splinter penetrated through
the seat's back and metal fragments and padding from the car and seat entered Heydrich's
back.

   "The perpetrators immediately fled. Badly wounded, Heydrich stepped out of the
stationary car and tried to fire his gun, but for some reason the weapon failed. Shortly after,
he had felt very unsteady and had to lean on the car."

7   Pannwitz's memoirs of 1959: "Both bombers took positions on the edge of the road, one
and a half metres from the passing car; Gabčík stood there, hiding the Sten sub-machine
gun under his raincoat, which he had placed over his arm. When the car became level with
him, he raised the sub-machine gun in the direction of Heydrich – he was no more than
one metre away. He pulled the trigger once, more than once, but the weapon did not work.
Potentially Heydrich could have been hit 32 times. Gabčík dropped the weapon and ran
away. Heydrich's driver was watching everything."

8   Pannwitz's memoirs of 1959: "The car was still moving slowly when the second assassin,
Kubiš, threw a bomb which hit the car in the rear right fender. This assassin was concealed
behind a streetlight at a distance of five metres from the first assassin and acted after the failed
machine gun attempt. The assassin had to handle the bomb very carefully. It had a highly
sensitive detonator."

9   Pannwitz's memoirs of 1959: "The bomb exploded on the rear fender – the car was hit in a
relatively unfavourable place. The rear of the car was torn and the splinters tore through the

back of the seat on which Heydrich was sitting. Two fragments penetrated his back. One was a small splinter, but entered the spleen. The car had horsehair cushions and some of these also entered Heydrich. As a result, blood poisoning led to the death of Heydrich's nine days [*sic*] after the attempt. Also, in spite of orders being issued that steel sheets should be installed in the seat backs this had not been done."

10   Pannwitz's memoirs of 1959: "According to the regulations governing drivers of leading officials, it was their duty to speed up and drive away from the scene if such an event occurred but Heydrich commanded: 'Stop!' The driver complied with this order, when he should have ignored it and driven away."

11   Pannwitz's memoirs of 1959: "Heydrich jumped immediately out of the car and tried to shoot at Kubiš, who was only a few yards ahead of him. From the side pocket of the car, he pulled a lightweight 7.65 calibre pistol to fire at Kubiš. But the weapon did not work as he had forgotten to load it."

12   The undated post-war testimonies of the Bulovka hospital staff, which were recorded by an official of the Ministry of National Defence. It is not a verbatim record of testimony in the form of a witness statement or a consistently recorded narrative in a third person. Both possible ways of recording are mixed up. Witness names are also missing. However, the factual testimony is authentic:

From the statement of Doctor Pěnkavy: "Heydrich got out of the car and went to the entrance. He was placed in a wheelchair and taken to the elevator with a guard. Heydrich said, '*Rufen sie den Burg.*' (Call the Castle) They went into an examination room and then with Doctor Jarolímka he went to the operating room where they stripped him. Nothing but a small wound in his back. Heydrich said, '*Die Mappe geben sie mir her?*' (Where is the folder they gave me?)

"Heydrich was pale, but he was standing. Heydrich called Jíravský at the Castle, where they did not believe him at the beginning. Later, the chauffeur Klein was brought in."

Further testimony was given by Doctor Jarolímka: "My nursing sister said, 'They say they brought the *Reichsprotektor* here.' We had all heard the blast some time before. He appeared and Pěnkava ran towards him. Jarolímka together with his nursing sister from Brno whose name I cannot recall, and Pěnkava stripped him in the hall, dragged off his shoes, etc. They asked him, 'Are you hurt? Are you in pain?' He was pale. Doctor Jarolímka discovered a lump in the lumbar region, close to his spine, which was accompanied by a little bleeding. There was a German in the porter's office, who phoned the *Gestapo*. In a few moments, Frank and the others were here. The German, Doctor Dick, who also ran out of his surgery, was examining Heydrich and found that the kidney was not bleeding. An X-Ray was taken and it showed a piece of shrapnel, a piece of sheet metal, horsehair, etc. from the seat. After the examination Heydrich moved alone to the trolley and said: 'I will go alone.'

"His briefcase was placed on the floor next to his leather coat. Then he was taken to the second operating room, where a brief operation (investigative) was carried out. Although Doctor Dick assured him he was a German professor, Heydrich wanted another German surgeon present. In the first operation an incision was made in his back and splinters, fragments of steel plate and bristles were removed. During the second surgery when his abdomen was opened up his spleen was removed which was then put into formalin and stored. At first Heydrich was feeling ok, but on the fourth day peritonitis occurred and on the sixth day sepsis set in. He received a transfusion, even on his last morning – the eighth day, when he died."

Statement of Nurse Ena Kolarova: "Heydrich was getting worse in the corridor. Doctor Dick told him that it was a serious wound and he would call Professor Hohlbaum; a German who worked at the Jirásk Clinic. During the operation, the Czech Müller was also present. They called her [Kolarova] that night before Heydrich's death to bring Doctor Dick to his room with the items needed for a transfusion. She glanced through Heydrich's door and he was very yellow, almost deathly."

13   Pannwitz's memoirs from 1959: "His driver also jumped out of the car and pursued Gabčik, the assassin with the sub-machine gun. It was impossible for him to get to his bicycle, and he therefore ran in the opposite direction. The SS driver was about 15 metres behind him and almost managed to catch him up when Gabčik started shooting wildly from his Colt pistol. The driver also pulled out his pistol and wanted to fire, but the gun did not work, as he accidentally released the magazine from his Walther pistol. If the magazine is only a millimetre out, the weapon will not work. The driver did not have enough intelligence to stop for a moment and check his pistol. In that case, the defect could have been rectified and the offender would not escape. So he carried on chasing the man virtually unarmed. The perpetrator ran into a shop to try and escape through a rear exit. However, there was no rear way out, so he had to come out the front and ran into the driver who had reached the area. Gabčik fired; the driver suffered a wound in his knee and was unable to follow him. So this offender also escaped."

Heinz Jantor's statement from 1946: "*SS-Oberscharführer* Klein also left the car and started pursuing the offender – the gunman with the sub-machine gun. He ran a bit up the Kirchmaier, that is, in the direction that *SS-Obergruppenführer* Heydrich had come, and then turned left into the narrow street where he entered a butcher's shop owned by someone called Brauner. Klein chased him there and tried to fire at him several times. However, the gun did not work out (as we later discovered his pistol, a Walther-PPK, 'did not have a sufficiently loaded magazine'). Klein hid behind the flower box in front of Brauner's shop. The assailant fired at him several times from the shop, and when he knew that Klein could not shoot back, he left his position and fired at him in the legs, so Klein collapsed. The owner of the butcher's shop, Brauner and a carrier, I cannot remember the name anymore, but Brauner or the carrier took Klein's pistol and pursued the fleeing man.

"But possibly for the reasons already described, they could not use the weapon. At the intersection of the street where Brauner lives, Kirchmaierstrasse [in fact Holešovičky] both gave up the chase, because the assassin had a big lead and apparently disappeared from sight. He probably jumped onto a passing tram. Then the carrier and Brauner took Klein, who was unable to walk, to Bulovka Hospital."

14   Post-war testimony from a tram conductor, František Carda, given on 15 September, 1945:
1)   Were you present at the scene of the crime of the assassination of Heydrich and what did you initially see?
       "On the day of the assassination I was working in a No. 3 electric tram as a front-driver. I had just left the depot when a blast occurred, and then the electricity immediately stopped. I immediately jumped out of the tram and went to see what was going on. Meanwhile, I heard shooting. The car was not far from us, about six to ten feet away. I saw a German follow the perpetrator who was on a bicycle and fired at him. I think it was Heydrich. After chasing him for about twenty metres Heydrich returned to the car. He examined the discarded sub-machine gun and then examined the briefcase and the coat that was thrown away by the attacker. The second officer pursued the other assailant who ran in the direction of Kobliyska and then turned away into Kolinske. The pursuer was still running behind this attacker and I did not see him anymore. I do not remember, however, if the attackers fired back at their pursuers."
2)   What did you notice about Heydrich's car?

"When the attackers disappeared, I went to the car and I saw it was damaged. Heydrich stood at the car, with one hand holding his back and I saw that when he unbuttoned his tunic he was bleeding. Also standing by the car was a lady, who was about 40 years old, and allegedly German, who also spoke Czech and urged us to call for help. A van belonging to a small delivery company called Holan was stopped and, with the help of several people, Heydrich was put in the back of the van."

3)   Who was still present at the assassination?

"A driver Lašťovka Václav, the second driver of the car Zima František and another electrician Klimeš. Other people I do not know."

4) Were you questioned by the *Gestapo*, how often and for how long?

"I was interrogated twice by the *Gestapo*. For the first time on the day of the attempt, they took us by car to Petschek Palace and interrogated us individually. My interrogation lasted about one hour. The second time I was interviewed again in Petschek Palace on the second or third day and again for about one hour."

5)   How much did you receive as a reward and in what form?

"I did not get any reward."

6)   Do you have anything else to mention?

"I note that I did not volunteer to help the Germans but they came to us. Also as a Bohemian I knew that the assassination had been carried out by committed patriots and I did not want my testimony to hurt anyone. I would point out that, in my opinion, no one had to report to the detriment of the attackers if he did not want to. I was offered a high reward when describing the perpetrators but I said that after the blast I was taking care of the wounded electricians, which was my duty to do, and after I did that, everything was over."

15   Heinz Jantur's testimony of 1946: "The second offender, the bomb thrower, ran across the Kirchmaierstrasse to the telegraph pole where he had left his bicycle. He tried to ride towards the city centre. He was also chased by pedestrians and he fired several times as he was riding his bicycle and also at a policeman from around Libeň, who was waiting at the tram stop. As was later found out from eye witness testimony, he was holding a handkerchief to his face as small pieces of shrapnel from the grenade caused him injuries to his face."

16   Pannwitz's memoirs of 1959: "The intact bombs found at the scene contained a well-known English manufactured plastic explosive. Other items found were English insulating tapes, English detonators and English flares known to us since the campaign in North Africa. Also because an English sub-machine gun was used, very quickly we did not have any doubts about where the assassination had been planned from."

17   Heinz Jantur's testimony from 1946: "*SS-Obergruppenführer* Heydrich was first helped by the wife of the then prison doctor at Pankrác Navary, who happened to be at the crime scene. She helped him so he could sit back in his car and then stopped a passing van. With her help and with the help of the driver, Sulce; Heydrich was transferred to Bulovka Hospital."

18   The departure was originally scheduled for October 1941, and a meeting was held on 3 October and Colonel Moravec gave a speech to the members of Anthropoid. At this time the group consisted of Jozef Gabčik and Karel Svoboda. However, Svoboda was injured and replaced by Jan Kubiš:

Moravec said to Gabčik and Svoboda: "You are informed by the radio and newspapers about the senseless killing at home. The Germans murder the best of the best. The Germans continue waging war against our people, who only have the means for weak retaliation. We can do so and we must hit back strongly. At home our forces have been working and are now in a situation where their possibilities are limited. There is a lot of help we can give from outside. One of these tasks will be entrusted to you. The month of October is the month of our national holiday, our liberation. It is necessary in this situation, when our people will celebrate the saddest holiday of their liberation, to make this holiday significant. It was decided that you would do something that will be recorded in history. There are two main people in Prague who represent this evil regime, K. H. Frank and Heydrich, the newcomer. In our opinion, as well as our leaders, one must try to pay for it to show that we are exchanging blow for blow. It would, in principle, also be the task you will be entrusted with. Tomorrow you are going to do some night parachute jumps and you will then go home to carry out an action. This will also need to be done alone, for reasons that will be clear to you and potentially without cooperation from our home forces.

"You will get from our Home Army full protection and synergy. But you must create the method and time of the task yourself. You will be dropped in an area that ensures you your best chances. You will be equipped with everything that we can provide you with. As we know the situation in our country, there will be good people who will help you. However, you should act carefully and with balance. I do not have to repeat that the task is historically momentous, but it is a great risk. It depends on what assumptions you make, your cleverness, and so on. We'll talk about things again when you come back from supplementary training. As I said, the task is serious. Your heart must be in this. If doubts arise after what I have said, say so. The departure of both will take place around the 10th October."

19   Pannwitz's memoirs from 1959: "After the detection of enemy parachute aircraft, the Germans developed a particularly successful defence, which led to the rapid arrest of the agents and the capture of the majority of their material. A brief outline of the method: The German air defence had an airborne warning service spread over the entire territory which identified enemy aircraft and then notified the appropriate authorities. Time, flight direction, and eventually its height were recorded on a large map.

"During the flight, I immediately raised an alarm and calculated the speed of the enemy aircraft between the reported points. If it remained the same, for example, 400km/h, everything was ok but if the speed between two reported points dropped rapidly, for example to 100–150km/h, it meant that the enemy aircraft had most likely descended to about 250m, circled over the ground and dropped agents or material. The authorities in this area were immediately alerted and all available military and police units were sent out to search for agents or material. In this way, we usually started a search two hours or so after the drop, almost every time finding material and sometimes agents. They often were able to get away from their landing point but without their valuable equipment. The enemy – whether from England or Moscow – did not know anything about our tactics and continued to use the same ones for the whole war."

20   The men of Anthropoid received fake *Protektorate* documentation in England before their departure. At some point details of their false identities were recorded and these are the details:

Personal Documents. Gabčik: Civil *Protektorate* number 3501, issued by the District Office in Prostějov on 27 February 1940, signed, v. z. Kropáč, and issued in the name of Zdeněk Vyskočil, locksmith, single, born 8 April 1912 in Prostějov. Described as having an average figure, chestnut hair, brown eyes, nose obtuse, normal mouth, healthy teeth.

Personal Documents. Kubiš: Civil *Protektorate* issue 5481/39, issued by the police headquarters in Brno on 27 October 1939, and issued in the name of Otto Strnad, worker, single, born 24 June 1913 in Rosice, in the district of Brno. Described as having an average figure, chestnut hair, blue eyes, nose pointed, normal mouth, healthy teeth.

Václav Kral provided documents to the parachute agents from local sympathisers which confirmed that they were unfit for work. He even supplied personal worksheets dated 30

December 1941 (Jan Kubiš filled his out under the name of Otto Strnad, and Jozef Gabčik under the name of Zdeněk Vyskočil).

The aforementioned forms from late1941/early1942 were accompanied by a post-war opinion of the Ministry of Defence, to which photocopies of these forms were sent to assess their authenticity. The Ministry's opinion was: "The handwritten copy of this photocopy was compared on 25th March 1947 with the manuscript of Jan Kubiš, who together with Jozef Gabčik carried out the assassination of Heydrich, and it was with all certainty that the application was filled in by Kubiš."

This supported by the testimony of Ladislav Krale, dated 27 May 1946:

"Václav Kral was my cousin and I knew he was involved in the underground organisation and that he was working with parachute agents who had been dropped in our country. In late 1941 or early 1942 he visited me in my office accompanied by an unknown man and asked me to provide papers for this stranger as well as another man who could not attend because he had an injured leg. He told me that both of these men had been parachuted in from England and they needed new papers and asked if I could help him. He told me about two people who needed new papers; one of them was called Otto Strnad, while the other one was Zdeněk, but I do not remember the surname. I supplied new documents with the appropriate stamps as well as photographs.

"After the death of Heydrich photographs of the assassins were published in the newspapers and I recognised Gabčik and Kubiš as the two men who I had produced documents for and who I later found out had lived with Václav Král."

Further testimony comes from Doctor Stanislav Hrubý; this was published in the *People's Law*, No. 83, 19 August 1945, under the title 'Thus, the assassination of Heydrich':

"Sometime in January 1942, an existing patient Jarka Piskáček, brought to me a man with a leg problem and he was a new patient to me. I treated him without asking anything. At the beginning of February, Piskáček reported that he was looking after two parachutists from England who had a great mission to undertake in the *Protektorate*. To make sure they were legal I suggested they needed sick notes and suggested they contact some friends of mine at the Prague Health Insurance Company in Prague II, Švehlovo nábř. Now we know that it was comrades Fafek and Miniv, who willingly provided workbooks for the parachute agents. At the end of February, Jarka Piskáček brought them to my surgery where I gave them both false sick notes as if they were unable to work. I first signed off Josef Strnad with a duodenal ulcer. His papers were saying that he lived with the Khodlovy family in Vysočany, Waldecká Street. The second note was in the name of František Procházka with a diagnosis of an inflamed gall bladder. He also lived in Vysocany, with the Piskáčkovy family on Na břehu. After this another friend Doctor Lyčka from Karlin wrote a review report every week and confirmed their inability to work."

21 Post-war testimony by Jana Zákoucká dated 21 September 1945, which outlined how she supported the parachutists:

    I.   Have you worked with Mr Zelenka-Hajský?

    "Through Antonín Oktábec I was also involved with my husband in the group of Mr Zelenka-Hajský. Over the course of time, I definitely knew about the involvement of other families, namely the families of Brychta, Pecháčkova, Hejlova, Nováková, Piskáčkova, Strnadova and Doctor Lyčka.

    II. Did you know that this support for was for the parachute agents?

    "Mr Oktábec told us: 'Parachute agents have been dropped in the *Protektorate* and it is our duty to help them.'"

    III. What help did you provide?

"Initially, we provided food coupons, cigarettes, and later we supplied food. After the assassination we provided waterproof clothing, coffee, tea, oil, alcohol, magazines and books. We have been told that these items were needed because they were going somewhere where it was cold and damp. As was later discovered, it was in the church at Resslova Street. My husband had stored a large number of biscuits as emergency rations."

IV.   Did you ever come into direct contact with the parachute agents?

"I never came into direct contact with the parachute agents, but once as Mr Oktábec and I were walking along a street he pointed someone out to me and said, 'That is one of them.' Later I found out it was Valčik."

V.   Did you know anything about the planned assassination?

"I knew with my husband that the parachute agents had an important task, it was even said that an assassination of historical significance would be undertaken, but no one knew whether an assassination of Heydrich or Frank would be committed. We even knew about potentially three places where the assassination was to take place, namely: Vysočany nad Bulovkou, Klárově on a sharp bend below Chotkový but the third location was not known to us. It was even said to us that a parachute agent would use an animal to make an assassination attempt. Later, a trained dog was spoken about. Furthermore, Mr Oktábec told me that they had reported to London that the time was not yet right, but London said, 'Carry out your mission.'"

VI.   How did you and your group act after the assassination?

"That same evening we had a meeting with Mr Oktábec, where we had already learned the details of the fitters that worked for Frigera who assembled ice and coolers for Heydrich. Montéři said that he heard in the hospital that Heydrich had stated in a very angry tone that every tenth resident from the street where the assassination occurred was to be shot. I also know that Mr Oktábec and Mr Hejl had an order on the day of the assassination to be in the vicinity of the assassination spot to help if needed. Doctor Lyčka was later that day invited by Mr Oktábec to visit him and he came dressed as an electrician. They went to Rustonky where he treated an injured parachute agent. Doctor Lyčka said after he had treated the agent that he was leaving for Vysočan.

"I am sure that Mr Zelenka-Hajský knew in advance where the parachute agents would hide after the assassination. Mr Oktábec told me that Mr Zelenka was a frequent visitor to the church and one night, despite the fact that there was a curfew, he was stopped by a patrol when he was on his way to the church.

"Mr Zelenka also worked with Mr Vosmik, the son of a butcher from Libeň, who was supposed to be executed with his whole family. According to others, his wife told the police that she had contact with the parachute agents."

VII. Do you have anything else to say?

"The second day after the assassination, I was sent to see Mrs Anne Zákoucká in Libeň where I was to meet with Mrs Novák. Here I had to tell her to change the appearance of her daughter, Jindřiška, a little and to say that she was ill and could not attend school. After the attack one of the perpetrators arrived on a bicycle near the house of Mrs Novák and left the bicycle outside a nearby shop. There was blood on the bicycle and he went to their house where he washed himself. The girl, Jindřiška, who had just come back from church, was sent to collect the bicycle. She was told to take an indirect route home and to try and not to speak to anyone. She brought the bicycle home but was questioned by two women. That same day, an unknown young man came to the house and took the bicycle. The perpetrator was provided with new clothes and the original clothes were immediately burned. On the 9th of July, the family of Novák and other families were arrested in the evening and they were all executed.

22   The *Gestapo* officials were likely to be fooled into believing Anna Malinová had met Gabčik accidentally in a tram. This possibility cannot be excluded, but Jaroslav Čvančara's hypothesis is that Anna's girlfriend Ludmila Soukupová and her sister Marie Kovárníková knew Kubiš before the war because they all came from the same village of Ohrazenice near Dolni Vilémovice. After her arrest, Marie Kovárníková and Anna Malinová tried to make out that they were just 'mistresses of the bombers' and tried to persuade the *Gestapo* that Kubiš and Gabčik did not take part in the action against Heydrich. The women also concealed the existence and activity of František Šafařík. He was a former pupil of Jan Zelenka-Hajský and at the same time an employee at the Prague Castle. He provided information to the women on Heydrich's activities in Prague and details of how Heydrich travelled between Prague Castle and Panenské Břežany. Fortunately Šafařík remained unknown to the *Gestapo* and so survived the war; she died in 1970.

This is the account which František Šafařík gave in Prague on 24 April 1946: "I came into contact with some parachute agents through my teacher, Jan Zelenka, whose code name was Hajský, who had taught me at school. In the spring of 1942, Zelenka often visited me and asked about my work at Prague Castle, where I worked in the maintenance department. We also discussed the situation around Heydrich and then in the early months of 1942 he introduced me to two men. I found out they were Jozef Gabčik and Jan Kubiš, who told me they had parachuted from an aircraft near Plzeň and were selected to carry out an assassination of a high-ranking German official. Zelenka asked me to give them as much information as I could about Heydrich's movements especially by car. To this end I met with both of them several times. Kubiš also came to the Castle several times to look at his car. I left messages with two women, whose names I never asked, at a dead drop at a house near the Castle. I gave them the necessary reports of planned departure and expected arrival times of Heydrich together with other details, such as whether or not he was accompanied by an escort.

"I would also point out that my teacher, Jan Zelenka (Hajský), with whom I made a deep friendship, was the leader of a group of assassins and also the main organiser. At one of the meetings with Zelenka, he mentioned to me that a couple of boys from England had come to him and asked me to find some shelter for them. He suggested that the catacombs under the Castle might be an appropriate place, but I regretfully had to tell him that this hiding place would not be too good because many people would have known about it and, as a result, we dropped the idea."

23.   One of those who provided food for the parachute agents and escaped detection was Eduard Kučera, and on 1 October 1945 he gave an account of how he got involved and the help he provided:
What did you know about the parachute agents?
"In March 1942, through Mrs Marie Moravec, I met the parachute agents Valčik, Gabčik and Kubiš. I would like to point out that since 1922, I have known Mrs Moravec and she was a very good friend and I knew the whole family well."
What did you do to support them?
"Mrs Moravec came to me in Brno and asked me if I could obtain large quantities of food without it being well known. She later confessed to having a large number of young men from England and had to look after them. I was able to obtain four pigs for her. She also asked for cigarettes, clothes and other foodstuffs apart from meat. When I heard what she needed them for I did everything I could do to help.

"At various times numerous parachute agents stayed with me. They told me their names but they did not talk about the tasks assigned to them nor did I ask them anything. Probably in the middle of April, Valčik was with Mrs Moravec when the posters of Valčik appeared with a reward for information about him.

"One time he and I looked at a poster; [we] read the description of Valčik and he said, 'So they cannot know me.' About three days later he went to Prague. After this I only saw members of the Moravec family and supplied them with food. After the assassination, Mrs Moravec again asked me to help with food, especially tinned food as they are all hiding in a shelter somewhere in Prague."

Do you have anything else to mention?

"The link between me and Mrs Moravec was Mr Krecbach in Prague. After the parachute agents were shot in the church and with Mrs Moravec arrested, my son came to me and drew attention to what had happened to the Moravecs. I was afraid but somehow I was not identified. Mrs Moravec was a very intelligent woman, a patriot and carried on fighting against the Nazis till the end."

24. Testimony from Vladimír Tichot, who was one of the people who let parachute agents stay in his home:

What did you know about the parachute agents from Prague?

"About 14 days before Easter 1942, Mrs Moravec came to tell me that she had brought a parachute agent whose name I did not know (later I discovered it was Valčik) and he stayed in my apartment for about 14 days. On Whit Saturday, he left but during his stay with me, he brought friends to stay on about six occasions and later when their pictures were in the newspapers I found out one of them was Gabčik."

What did you know about these parachutists?

"After he had been with me about five days, Valčik asked me to go to Plzeň with him. When we got to Plzeň we split up but on the way I had talked about the geography and other things we would see. He did not tell me why he was going there. It became clear very soon that he had gone to Plzeň to help with the British bombing raid.

"Another time, Valčik asked me if I knew anyone else he could stay with for a few days and I was able to help. But he never told me anything about what he had done or what he was planning to do and I never asked him either."

Do you know if he met other people?

"I know he was in touch with Mrs Moravec, the Sulková family and once he told me that he had been staying with a teacher in Strašnice but he did not say the name."

How did Valčik live during his stay?

"We were provided with some food and although we were offered money by Valčik for his time with us we did not take anything."

Did you contact Valčik after the assassination?

"On the third day after the assassination, Valčik came to us and we let him stay but he moved on again the next day. Later, I was asked by Mrs Moravec to lend her a kerosene stove and fuel for the boys. I gave this to Mr Sulková."

Do you have anything else to say?

"Valčik was a very intelligent man and he told me once that when he was in confession in Moravia, he confided to the priest why he was here. I would also like to point out that Valčik never mentioned his tasks to me and he even denied that he was a Moravian, although you could see it at first sight."

25. Pannwitz's memoirs from 1959: "How difficult the situation of the parachute agents was in the *Protektorate* can be shown by the preparations for the bombing of the Skoda works in

Plzeň, which took place on the night of 25th/26th April 1942. Lieutenant Bartoš did not want to ask for help from the local Czech population or the Czech resistance movement, therefore he ordered several of the parachutists to assist in the preparations. The raid did eventually take place and before the raid, barns were set on fire to direct the bombers, and a Rebecca homing beacon was used, but the raid was a total failure. The bombers arrived but the agents had to do everything by themselves, without the help of others, and they were not able to light the fires in the two barns at the same time. Such was the lack of willingness of local Czechs to participate in sabotage."

26. Pannwitz's memoirs from 1959: "Heydrich was personally instructed to follow Hitler's orders concerning the travel of senior officers. He agreed with the general measures, but he clearly refused a travelling escort as he said it would damage German prestige in the *Protektorate*. Although prior to his arrival von Neurath travelled with an armed escort. He always had an arrogant attitude and he believed none of the Czechs would do anything to him. But we had his opinion recorded and referred to it in Berlin – after the assassination had happened we were covered for this absence of an escort by this note."

27. Pannwitz's memoirs from 1959: "In the complex processing of the information regarding the background of the assassination, we also had copies of radio messages which the parachute agents had sent to London. Among the decrypted messages was the following:

The President received a question from the agents asking if a person with the code name Jindra might send him a message about the agents in the *Protektorate*. This message contained the following: 'As we can deduce from the actions of our two friends, the assassination of H. is now planned. This assassination will not help the Allies, and would have far reaching consequences for our nation. It would endanger not only our hostages and political prisoners but it could result in the loss of thousands of other lives, and plunge the nation into unprecedented oppression, while at the same time it would sweep away the last remnants of any surviving organisation and therefore prevent anything more being done for Allies.'

"The next section of text is not exactly known, but it literally said: 'I urge that the assassination be stopped and that an order saying the same should be sent to our friends. However, if the assassination is necessary for foreign policy reasons, they should target a local Quisling, first of all to E. M. Jindra.'

"Who was the sender of this telegram? Lieutenant Bartoš, the leader of the radio operators, was dead. So no one could give us any information. Finally, we found out that the person code named Jindra might be a Czech professor called Vaněk of Brno, who had been the leader for more than two years. He was being actively sought by the Brno *Gestapo*. The search for him continued yet it was not until mid-August that we were able to trace him, yet he managed to avoid the police several times and was finally arrested in September 1942. When we spoke to him after his arrest we told him his cover name was Jindra and his real name, he replied: 'Oh, then you are Mr Müller from the German police who has been looking for me for 8 weeks.' It surprised us how well informed about us he was, including the workings of the department, colleagues and many other details.

"After the first shock of arrest Vaněk was willing to talk sensibly, especially when we presented him with his message sent to Beneš. The mobilisation of the Czech nation to partisan action to the Germans' rear would eventually require much higher human sacrifices than the deployment of soldiers in the field. Because the Czechs were exempt from military service there was nothing for them at this time other than to wait. In addition, the weapons supplied to Germany from factories in the Czech territory were so significant that the Germans would certainly not retreat in the event of riots and would act in any way to maintain that territory. Hitler was of the opinion that Europe is dominated by the one who has the Czech space – the centre of Europe. Considering this, Vaněk came to realise that riots or rebellion against the Germans would be a suicide of the Czech nation. Vaněk also spoke about his interviews with the bombers and other parachutists who repeatedly stated that they were deliberately fed false information about the situation in the *Protektorate* and he said more often than he himself believed that the Czech nation should wait. But the agents had taken a military oath, they cannot get out of it and their tasks have to be fulfilled.

"Urgently, Jindra demanded that Bartoš issue orders to the two agents to stop the attempt [but] all approaches were refused [by Gabčik and Kubiš]. Jindra was a highly educated man who above all had the best interests of his people as his aim. He was deeply convinced that the Czech nation was not at all in a situation where it could influence the results of the war, and therefore wanted to prevent absurd sacrifices. Finally, he said he was willing to come to an agreement that he and his Sokol organisation could take part in organising internal policies in the *Protektorate*. He would remain in contact with us as well as the Czechs, so we could have contact with England. We could then feed misinformation to London. Agents, who, on the basis of these false messages, would be sent to the territory of the *Protektorate*, would be interned under German-Czech supervision when they were Czechs and Slovaks. In any case, they should not be prosecuted. London was to be misled by reports of successful agents' actions. The leadership of the special commission had confidence in Jindra and understood the benefits of such a development. Nobody believed he would be against such a proposal.

"But suddenly things changed. The *Gestapo* leader was informed of this conversation, having the Commission's head summoned and ordering the immediate surrender of Jindra to the State Police. Thus, Jindra was moved to the insignificant position of an arrested Sokol leader. For two years, he was subjected to petty, humiliating interrogations. His fate is not known to me.

"In this situation – just as in the case of Lidice – the representatives of power, the head of the *Gestapo*, the commander of the security police and Böhme, showed how dangerous and stupid the leadership was."

Heinz Jantur's statement of 1946: "It must be emphasised that the leaders of the resistance organisation, 'Jindra', Professor Vaněk, who was arrested on 4th September 1942, knew of the planned assassination of Heydrich. Today, I cannot say whether Vaněk was connected with the agents or whether he received the information because of his ongoing radio link with the Czech government in London. Through radio messages the resistance organisation warned the government in London against this act; as such an act would require unheard of bloody sacrifices by the Czech nation."

28. Post-war testimony by Antonie Bejckova (sister of Jaroslav Smrž and Ema Khodlová):

When did you meet and under what circumstances did you have dealings with the parachute agents Gabčik and Kubiš?

"When I visited my sister Mrs Emanuela Khodlová, probably in January (shortly after their arrival) I was introduced by her and I recall one was called Stejskal and I have forgotten the name of the other."

What did you talk about and what did the gentlemen say about you?

"During this visit there was also another parachute agent, Opálka, whom I was introduced to. Opálka said, 'You probably do not know what we are. One day you will read the newspapers and you will know what we are about.' Gabčik and Kubiš only talked about general things. I visited my sister during the morning and my visit lasted for about an hour."

What did you think about them?

"They were trusted, for my sister was my sister."

How many times did you see them and where?

"Every time I visited my sister, I met the two of them, Gabčik and Kubiš, both day and evening. Some evenings Gabčik, Kubiš, my sister, my brother-in-law, my sister's son and me played cards."

How many times when you visited your sister did you see the agent Opálka?

"Only once."

Were Gabčik and Kubiš accommodated with, and fed by your sister?

"Gabčik and Kubiš were staying with my sister in one room all the time until the assassination of Heydrich. They were there for about three months. They ate with my sister and with Mr Piskáček."

Who brought parachutists to your sister and asked for their accommodation?

"The two parachute agents were brought by my brother Jaroslav Smrž, who lived in Prague."

Why did your brother suggest the two agents stay with your sister?

"Because he had a small apartment and two small children, while his sister spent a lot of time living alone and had a bigger flat."

Where did your brother meet your other parachute agents?

"He met with the above-mentioned parachute agents probably through Mr Piskáček. I do not know who was staying with Mr Piskáček and who he met. He turned to my brother perhaps because Mr Piskáček was the chief of Sokol and my brother was his deputy."

When did the above-named parachute agents leave and return to your sister?

"The above-named parachute agents left at various times of day and night. Frequently they came in the early morning, but they never mentioned where they had been and what they were doing."

How were they armed?

"They were armed with Sten guns and pistols. They also had grenades. They always carried pistols with them, and when they went to sleep they put them under their pillows. They were always telling my sister about the danger that she and her family could be in and said they would shoot it out with the *Gestapo* if they came to the apartment."

Who gave the parachute agents transport?

"About six weeks before the assassination, my sister borrowed my brother's bicycle and gave it to one of the agents. According to my sister's statement, the second bicycle was borrowed from someone in Žižkov. My brother-in-law, Khodl, removed the number plate from the bicycle about 14 days before the Heydrich assassination."

Where did the parachute agents sleep the night before the assassination of Heydrich?

"Gabčik and Kubiš slept the night before the assassination with my sister, i.e. from 14th to 15th June 1942 [*sic*]. I did not visit my sister this day."

Why did your sister tell you to visit the next day?

"She asked me if I heard what had happened. I said 'Yes' and then she said, 'That's what my boys did.' When they left, they did not say where they were going to. On the day of the assassination, they borrowed a coat from my sister which had been borrowed from Václav Hofman, a carpenter in Vysočany."

When and under what circumstances did you see or meet the agents after the assassination of Heydrich?

"The next day after Heydrich's assassination, when my sister returned from shopping, she had a newspaper in the mailbox (a special edition of Heydrich's assassination), on which was written: 'Mama, tell Big Dulich [Jan Kubiš] to wait for me on Flora. Dulisek [Jozef Gabčik].'"

What did your sister do with this message and how did she arrange a meeting?

"Big Dulich did not visit my sister, so my sister could not pass the message on."

What happened to the bicycles which the parachute agents used on the day of the assassination?

"I knew that when the Germans were asking for information about a missing bicycle they had also recovered a man's hat, briefcase and overcoat, but the bicycle they were looking for had been hidden.

"The son of Mr Piskáček brought this bicycle to my brother and then brought it to me. I hid it in the bathroom. On the same day, the police came to us but I showed them a ladies' bicycle – they were looking for a man's bicycle. Fortunately, the police did not really search the apartment and so did not find the bicycle. The next day my brother took the bicycle away."

Did the parachute agents visit your sister after the assassination?

"The agents visited my sister a day before the final shoot out in the church and suggested that they spend the night in her apartment. They said they had orders to stay in the church at night so could not disobey this order."

How did you find out that the assassination was carried out by the parachute agents that your sister sheltered?

"The day after the shoot out in the church, my brother-in-law, Václav Khodl, showed me the newspaper with photos of Gabčik and Kubiš, where it said they were the murderers of Heydrich. My brother-in-law said to me on the bus, 'Do you recognise them?' There were a lot of people on the bus and I did not know if anyone was watching us so I did not say anything. In the evening when I returned home, my daughter showed me a photograph of the agents in the newspaper. She said to me, 'Mother, these two gentlemen were with my aunt.' I replied, 'Emo, please do not even think of it.'"

How and from whom did you find out that the parachute agents were killed in the church?

"According to photographs and some names given in the newspaper, I knew that they were the agents who had stayed with us. The photograph used of Gabčik was good, but the one of Kubiš was bad, probably taken after his death, with a noticeable wound on his throat."

Who told you the names of the parachute agents?

"In June, they issued a brochure about the participants in the assassination of Heydrich. I learned about the church, where Gabčik and Kubiš were killed. This told us that the agents had shot themselves."

Where was the operational material and weapons of the agents stored?

"The weapons of the parachute agents were buried in the garden of the house where my sister lived in Horní Počernice. The coveralls of Gabčik and Kubiš and one parachute were placed in a children's coffin and buried in the cemetery in Ďáblice. The funeral was arranged by my brother, Václav Smrž, on the basis of a fake death certificate and who issued this certificate I do not know. The second parachute was left with my sister Ema Khodlová. About 14 days after my sister's arrest, I went with my husband to her apartment for the purpose of destroying any traces of the parachute. The parachute was cut in half and one half taken away and handed over to a man called Dejvic. The other half I burned in the bathroom. I handed the parachute rigging lines to Mr Šimandl."

What happened to the bodies of the parachute agents?

"A parish office official at the church in Resslova Street told me that the heads of Gabčik and Kubiš were stored in alcohol in the Pathological Institute until the time of the revolution. During the revolution, the *Gestapo* collected the heads and drove off in the direction of Barandov. An official of the Institute followed them on a bicycle until he lost them in Barandov because the *Gestapo* were in a car."

29. Pannwitz's memoirs from 1959: "The church community in Prague was not great. A church arose from the necessity of providing religious support for the Russian Orthodox wives of

Czech Legionnaires who had returned from Russia after the First World War. Because many of the Legionnaires were the leaders of the first Czech Republic, a significant part of the prominent members of that time belonged to this religious community."

30   Pannwitz's memoirs from 1959: "Other clergymen who had been working in prisons and psychiatric hospitals admitted during the trial that since 1939 Bishop Gorazd had been spying against Germany in favour of Russia through his Episcopal letters.

"When Chaplain Petřek informed him [Bishop Gorazd] of the presence of the assassins in the church, he asked only if they were Orthodox and left it at that. During the time when the bombers were already in the crypt of his church, he sent a telegram to the German authorities and left for Berlin to express his condolences on the death of the *Reichsprotektor* and discuss religious affairs in the Reichs Main Security Office. Everyone was of the opinion that the Orthodox Church should always provide a refuge for political refugees. Chaplain Petřek, a highly educated man, swore two church officials to secrecy about the agents in front of the altar and then gave each of them 50 Reichsmarks.

Heinz Jantur's statement from 1946: "As well as Petřek it was found out that two church officials knew there were people hiding in the church. In addition, the Patriarch of the Greek Orthodox Church in Prague knew as well. It is known to me that Petřek gave a very comprehensive testimony, because whilst they were hiding in the church he spent a lot of time with them and discussed many things. Petřek also personally took charge of all the food delivered by the supporters and handed them over to the agents."

31.   Pannwitz's memoirs from 1959: "All 7,000 doctors in the *Protektorate* had to declare in writing that they did not treat any man with similar facial and eye injuries that Kubiš had suffered."

32.   Pannwitz's memoirs from 1959: "When the assassin, Kubiš, fled from the crime scene, he was able to use his bicycle. The escape route was precisely reconstructed because Kubiš covered his wounded eye with a handkerchief and so was recognised by many people. At a street corner he left his bicycle propped against the kerb and walked away. Two women who were present at this time noticed it. Then they saw that about 10 to 12 minutes later, a 14-year-old girl came and walked away with the bicycle. Since the initial search for this girl did not yield any results, the search area from where the bicycle was left was extended in all directions. It was set by the distance someone could walk in eight minutes. This search area was sealed off in the early hours by the *Waffen-SS* and all girls who were around 14 years old were detained. All the girls had to walk past the two women and then 12 were selected to walk with a bicycle and five were considered to be of special interest. The girls were released with an apology but their homes and families were put under surveillance."

Heinz Jantur's testimony from 1946: "Only on about 1st June 1942, several women from the area of Libeň came forward as a result of a special appeal asking for information on the escape route of one of the assassins by bicycle. Some witnesses commented that they saw a man on a bicycle holding a handkerchief in front of his face, while others confirmed that the cyclist was bleeding from his face. It was clear he had left this bicycle outside a Bata shop but I do not remember the name of the street now. Other witnesses also reported that they soon saw a girl aged between 14 and 16 taking the bicycle from outside the Bata shop. One of them even spoke to the girl and asked why she was leaving with the bicycle. The girl replied to her that the bicycle belonged to her father and she was collecting it. On the basis of this evidence, we were very confident that at least the girl must live close by. Therefore, on the next morning, 3rd June, a large search was organised and all girls aged 12 to 16 were detained for questioning. The girls detained were first assembled at the Bata shop and they were initially screened there.

"Also if anyone was found during this search with facial injuries they were also detained. If I remember correctly, 42 girls were selected for further questioning and they were made to walk in front of three or four of the witnesses. For this purpose each of the girls had to walk a bicycle around a room and the witnesses had to say whether they recognised the girl or not. This resulted in the number being reduced to eight or 10 girls. I have to add here that the witnesses wanted to avoid [being seen by] the girls and so watched through a small hole in the wall so the girls did not know who the witnesses were. None of the witnesses recognised anyone. We knew later the actual girl was detained but managed to escape detection. But we arrested the family later after the attack on the church. For completeness, I add that the *SS-Gruppenführer* Nebe, Head of Unit V at the Reichs Main Security Office, personally supervised the preparation of the above described action in Libeň on 3rd June 1942.

"Criminal Commissioner Leimer also received a promising lead from the Warsaw police headquarters in the very first few days. There was a man in custody who said he had something to do with the assassination of Heydrich. If I remember correctly, this was a spy that had been working for both sides – the USSR and Germany. But it turned out he had nothing to do with the assassination of Heydrich."

33. *Gestapo* officer Josef Chalupský's testimony dated 25th September 1945, regarding the death of Jan Zelenka-Hajský, whose arrest he attended: "It was about 5 o'clock in the morning when I joined the arrest team as an interpreter. In total there were about six or seven *Gestapo* officials in the arrest team as Fleischer had assumed that parachute agents would be in [Mrs Moravec's] apartment. He [Fleischer] had been to some extent warned by what had happened when Mrs Moravec had been arrested a short time before. She was given permission to go to the toilet and when she came back, she dropped to the ground and was foaming at the mouth. Her husband said that it was a heart attack. However, she was found to have taken poison. Mr Moravec and his son were taken to the *Gestapo* HQ and interrogated. At about noon, Fleischer called me with Herschelmann and said we must immediately go to the same street to carry out further arrests. It was the apartment of Zelenka. The apartment was on the first floor on the left. Fleischer went with Herschelmann to the front door and rang the bell. Heller and I stayed on the stairs and watched as Fleischer kicked down the door and almost immediately Herschelmann shot someone. A few seconds later we entered the apartment and Herschelmann reported that he had seen Zelenka running into the bathroom. Then Zelenka said 'I'm coming out' and as he appeared from the bathroom he dropped down dead – he had also taken poison. It was found to be the same poison as used by Mrs Moravec. Zelenka was transported to the Pathology Institute and his wife was arrested. I think that it was the same day that the Czech police reported that Zelenka's son had been found dead in a park – he had also taken poison. I was convinced that the apartments of Moravec and Zelenka were revealed by Čurda. However, it is possible that Zelenka's apartment was revealed by the younger Moravec, who also revealed that the agents were hiding in the church in Resslova Street. Zelenka was slightly injured by a shot from Herschelmann and I think also Fleischer fired several times.

34. Grass carried as food for a rabbit in a briefcase was not unusual for that time in Prague. In 1942, rabbits were kept in almost half of Prague's buildings as the food situation increasingly became worse. Most people lived in apartments without gardens, so collecting grass as rabbit food was not uncommon.

35. Pannwitz's memoirs from 1959: "Information came in from various sources about the crypt in the church but it was decided to start the search the next morning. But we did not know where the assassins were and it was around midnight on 17th June 1942 when we took the decision. During this time we took all conceivable steps to find out the layout of the crypt

and church. We knew the agents were likely to be well-armed, would put up a stern resistance and we also had to consider possible escape routes they might use. During the night various people were called upon to provide information: the head of the city building office, the staff of the church buildings, the sewage network and so on. They were kept in custody until the action was over for fear of information getting out to the agents. With the help of the *Waffen-SS*, three cordons at varying distances from the church were set up. All sewer outlets were guarded and teams were placed in buildings, cellars and on roof tops.

"The cordon started to be put in place [at] 4.15 a.m. on 18th June. The clergy were questioned and at first denied any knowledge of agents hidden in the church. When the first group of civilian officers went into the church, they found a church official sleeping in a room. He also claimed he did not know anything. In that room the windows were protected by heavy iron grilles, but on one of them the grille was obviously recently broken and removed. The official could not explain why this was so. Approximately two minutes after entering the main part of the church, a concentrated fire from the choir loft was directed at the officers. One officer was wounded in the hand. Soldiers with machine guns, positioned at the entrance to the church, immediately opened fire. Agents then threw a bomb into the area of the altar that did not hurt anyone, but just set the tapestries on fire. Access to the choir loft was up a narrow staircase and it was easy for the agents to keep the officers at bay. The only possible method of attack seemed to be by using hand grenades. It was decided to let the *Waffen-SS* take over the attack as they were better equipped but it was a difficult task to overcome the assassins. When eventually the *Waffen-SS* reached the choir loft they found three agents – two who had taken poison and were already dead and the third was Kubiš, who had been the bomber at the assassination attempt and he was still alive. He had suffered concussion from the blast of a grenade and tried to take poison but fell into unconsciousness and died. His immediate transfer to the hospital was arranged but all the physicians' efforts to keep him alive were in vain. He died about 20 minutes after arrival at the hospital. It was a heavy loss for the criminals."

Heinz Jantur's testimony from 1946: "In the morning of 18th June a massive effort was undertaken to capture the bombers. K. H. Frank also appeared in the office. The *Waffen-SS* had been instructed by Frank to create two cordons around the church – one inner and one outer. A larger number of military units were used as buildings near the church had to be included in the cordon so that any possible escape routes for the agents could be cut off. The Criminal Commissioner entered the church with about 15 men. The Chaplain Petřek was brought in by Schumm and ordered to show us where the agents were hiding. He refused to say anything. Then soon afterwards firing began and one of the officers was shot in one of his thumbs. Hand grenades were thrown by both sides. The agents' resistance was gradually broken. One was hit by two grenades, another was also severely wounded and the third was hit by gunfire. Three agents were found in the choir loft. Two of them, despite heavy injuries, had shot themselves in their heads and died. If I am not mistaken, the third man was transferred to the SS hospital in Podoli, where he also died after a short while."

36. Pannwitz's memoirs from 1959: "We knew that Gabčik, who had been the gunman at the assassination, was still missing. Chaplain Petřek watched the battle going on in the church and revealed that there were seven men in the church. So there were still four men to find and they were in the crypt. The first three men killed were forced to sleep on the balcony as they found it too cold in the crypt and did not have time to hide before we entered the church. The Chaplain described the situation in the crypt and to our astonishment he told us that there was no escape route from there. The agents were like rats in a trap. In the crypt there were recesses where coffins had been kept but many were empty and so the agents used them for storage and to sleep in. The entrance, which had previously been used to take the coffins

down into the crypt, had been sealed and so there was only a small entrance we could use. As a professional policeman I wanted to close the investigation and obtain a complete story of the assassination and so we wanted to take the agents alive. So we sent the Chaplain to negotiate with them. Agents from the crypt answered that they were Czechs and would not surrender. They were well armed and anyone who entered the opening was shot. We made many offers, but they refused everything."

Heinz Jantur's testimony from 1946: "We knew that there were more than three agents. According to information from Čurda and others none of the three dead corresponded to the description of one of the two perpetrators of the assassination. Petřek was very energetically questioned as to where the others were. After some initial hesitation, he finally admitted that four men were hiding in the crypt beneath the church. Then he showed us the entrance. To prevent unnecessary bloodshed, these four agents were repeatedly encouraged to surrender. But they said they would not even think of it and fired a few shots to reinforce this. We had a great interest in taking the assassins alive and we took measures to try and get them to leave the crypt voluntarily. The Fire Brigade was called in and pumped water into the cellar with two hoses. During this time the agents repeatedly succeeded in pushing the hoses out of the opening leading to the crypt. The Fire Brigade continued to put hoses into the opening and eventually one fireman managed to hook the ladder they were using to reach the slit and pulled it out. However, after a certain period of time we realised that the water level was only rising very slowly in the crypt and that it might be that the water was leaking away somewhere. The pumping was therefore ordered to be stopped.

"The *Waffen-SS* were told to attack but any efforts resulted in them being wounded, two seriously and one lost an eye. Hand grenades were also used but it had no effect. Shortly afterwards four shots rang out and it all went quiet. Someone entered the crypt and found that all four agents had killed themselves with a shot to the head. The bodies were identified by a number of people and K. H. Frank took a great interest in what was going on. Among the agents were the two bombers [*sic*] Gabčik and Kubiš. Gabčik [*sic*: Kubiš] had a great number of facial scars that were a result of a bomb explosion."

37. Pannwitz's memoirs from 1959: "We were trying to make them uncomfortable in the crypt. The Fire Brigade were called; they tried to flood the cellar using a number of hoses. It was an unpleasant job for them as the agents were using a ladder to reach the level of the ventilation slit and pushed the hoses out and also fired out into the street. The SS fired back but without success. When the water level in the crypt reached a level of about a metre, tear gas grenades was thrown in. But it did not have much success as the gas escaped through holes in the church floor and affected officials who were in the church. However, we believe that both tactics weakened the resolve of those in the crypt to resist; even so the siege had been going on for about 6 hours. The senior commanders were becoming restless either from misunderstanding the position or stupidity.

"Then it was decided to contact a German hospital and see if a quick-acting narcotic could be used that would render the agents unconscious. After about 20 minutes' discussion it was found that nothing suitable was available. It was then decided by the *Waffen-SS* commander, Treuenfeld, that his men would enter the crypt in what I would call an arrogant move as any protests were waved aside.

"The head of the Commission immediately explained to Frank the pointlessness of this order and made it clear that it was important to get the agents alive. If we wanted them dead we could have thrown many hand grenades or bombs into the crypt many hours ago.

"It turned out that Treuenfeld had said to Frank: 'Herr *Gruppenführer*, I'm asking for permission to send a squad into the crypt and we are being blamed here!' Frank had already agreed to this and I feel would be ashamed to take back his order. Three men from the squad were lowered into the crypt and were consequently shot. After these failures we found the main entrance to the crypt and broke open the slab.

"All four agents shot themselves soon after this and before we entered the crypt. Among these four was Gabčik. Half an hour later, Himmler, who had been kept informed of what was happening, sent a message that the assailants should be captured alive."

38. Post-war testimony from fireman Ladislav Klein dated 10 July 1945: "On the day of the attack on the church I was on duty at the Central Station when two appliances from the station were ordered to the area of the church. The first appliance went to Wenceslas Street; the other was in Resslova Street below the church. The firemen in Resslova Street were under the command of Binder and Commander Klouček was in Wenceslas Street. We were in Wenceslas Street and told not to leave the appliance and to ignore any military actions that took place in Resslova Street. We stood there for about half an hour.

"During this period Binder came to the car and asked if anyone knew what the inside of the Karl Borromeo church in Resslova Street was like. In particular, Binder was wondering if the church had escape passages which the killers of Heydrich could use. But no one knew the church, so Binder went away very annoyed.

"The first order was issued by Binder or Klouček, I cannot remember exactly which of them it was, but I think that it was Klouček, who was our immediate commander. It was an order to put the pumps on standby and to move round to the church. Hoses were connected to nearby fire hydrants and I was ordered to put a hose into the ventilation slit. It was a difficult task for me as a new fireman and was possibly why I was chosen. Water was pumped into the crypt for about half an hour. We could also see that there was a ladder inside the crypt and an order was issued to pull it out. I hooked the ladder and others such as Hertl, Novotny and Soustružníka helped pull it out. When the ladder was out Karl Hermann Frank came forward and it seemed he was pleased that the ladder had been removed.

"Then the crypt was attacked by the Germans with tear gas bombs. After this we got involved with various actions including putting up lights inside the church and also some outside which shone directly at the ventilation slit and then pumping water out of the crypt when the action was over. I cannot remember today the sequence of events that took place in Resslova Street because of the fact that all the actions were carried out in a hurry, so I could not follow them. In my defence, I would point out that I was just doing my job at Resslova Street, and I was a very inexperienced fireman. For what reason I was awarded the 30,000 Koruna reward I do not know. But it was definitely not for one particular action. The reward was given to us at the *Gestapo* HQ in a gathering of about 80 people, some in uniform and some not. I was not too happy with getting the reward and wanted to give it to a charity, share it amongst other members of the crew; but we were forbidden to do so by Binder and Klouček. We were warned that such an act would be treated as an insult to the donor – The German Reich. However, I did have to donate 2,000 Koruna from my reward as my contribution towards a celebratory party organised by Klouček. This party was mainly attended by *Gestapo* members and members of the German police."

Testimony from fireman Josef Soustružníka: "I was on the night shift on 16th to 17th June 1942 at the fire station in Sokolská. In the morning of 17th June at about 6.45 a.m. we were given the order to go to Resslova Street. I was in the appliance commanded by Binder the Reich Controller. When we arrived at the church on Resslova Street, we saw that the area was full of *Gestapo* and SS men.

"At first we were ordered to stay in the appliance and only after some time we were given orders by the SS to pump smoke and water into the crypt. My job was to collect items from the appliance to assist with this. After various attempts to get into the crypt we were ordered to break the slab which was in front of the altar to gain access to the crypt but we did not have good enough tools to do this. After the action was over we were ordered by the SS to bring the corpses out. I declare that all the work we did was under coercion and overseen by armed SS men. Later as a reward for our actions at the church both Novotny and I were given a reward of 50,000 Koruna. This was the highest paid to a fireman and that's because we were both involved in removing the ladder from the crypt that the agents had been using. It was the most dangerous task but we could not refuse to do it because armed SS were close behind us. Other firemen received 30,000 Koruna. This reward was paid in instalments and I had to give 2,000 Koruna to Binder to help pay for the party that he organised for the people that took part. I note that Binder received the Iron Cross II for his actions on this day. I wanted to give my reward to the Red Cross but Binder would not let me. I did not spend any more of the money and still had 48,000 Koruna at the end of the war. Even though I am under investigation I declare that I have had no benefit from this reward. I did not want the reward. Why did I get a reward? I do not know but I had a job to do and was threatened with death if I did not carry it out."

Post-war testimony of fireman Karel Novotny dated 13 November 1946: "I was a fireman in Prague in 1942. On that critical day in June in 1942, an alarm was sounded. We got into the appliance and found we were going to Resslova Street. On the way, German patrols stopped and checked us and we were made to wait in Wenceslas Street for further orders. At about 10 o'clock orders came but we already knew what was going on. Controller Binder (a German) had asked us who knew about the church on Resslova Street and whether it had any secret passages. We said we did not know and then the order came to prepare the pump. We had to pump water into the crypt. We had to do this under fire from the agents in the crypt but no one was hurt but the hoses were damaged. Then we had to fix spotlights shining onto the ventilation slit but they were fired on and hit and also some petrol bombs were thrown. Then we managed to hook out a ladder the agents were using and we were able to get hoses into the crypt. Then we were told to stop pumping water and later Binder told me to ring HQ and ask for a diving unit. When I came back after doing this and reported to Binder, we were trying to break open the slab in the church which led to the crypt but were unable to do so. Then the Germans took over and later I heard several shots ring out which I think was the agents killing themselves. Later after the bodies had been removed we were ordered to pump out the water from the crypt which was about 30cm high. We later received a reward at the Petschek Palace in a sealed envelope in which I found a bank book for the *Creditanstalt der Deutschen*. This was for the amount of 50,000 Koruna. The highest rewards were in this amount. I did nothing special, just what I was ordered to do. Failure to obey them meant death for us. Why I received the highest reward is not known to me. I used the reward to support my mother, who was a widow. Then I later got married and used the money to set up home with my wife."

39.   Post-war testimony of Josef Pánka, a university lecturer at the Institute for Forensic Medicine in Prague, dated 19 October 1945.

1.   What do you know about the dissection of the bodies from the autopsy?

"After the closing of the Czech University in Prague I was moved in November 1940 to the German Institute for Forensic Medicine. The professor was Günther Weyrich. I was employed as an assistant and during autopsies I took notes. On 18th June 1942, seven corpses from the church on Resslova Street were brought in. All the corpses had gunshot wounds apparently after committing suicide and only one was showing wounds from a grenade. According to the photographs I was presented with I certainly recognised Kubiš and Valčik. I cannot remember the other photographs I was shown. Four unknown men escorted by *Gestapo* officers and one of them in a straitjacket were brought in to identify the corpses. After having been recently shown a number of photographs I think one of these men was called Ĉoupka [*sic*]. One man was in a straitjacket. He was a taller figure, had blond hair which was cut short, his face was swollen but I cannot give a more detailed description. It was obvious that he suffered a great deal. When asked if he could identify any of the corpses, he said he did not know any of them. Another man [these two men were Hrubý and Bublik] said he recognised two of the bodies and claimed to have jumped with them somewhere near Teplice. According to the photographs I have been shown I believe this was Gerik."

2.   How were the corpses treated?
"About the third day after the corpses were brought to us, the heads of the corpses were removed and two were kept in alcohol. These preserved heads were those of Gabčik and Kubiš. The bodies were given to the Anatomical Institute as specimens for German students to use for training. The heads were kept by us until 20th April 1945, when a German called Steffel put them in a sack and carried them away."

3.   What else do you remember?
"I remember that an SS man and Vyhnal brought the corpses to us. The dead were mostly wearing sweaters and trousers if I recall correctly. The clothes were mostly removed by Vyhnal. When I searched the clothing belonging to Kubiš, I found a wallet in which there was a picture of St. Anthony but otherwise it was empty."

Post-war testimony dated 5 September 1945, from František Vyhnal: "At the time of the assassination of the former *Reichsprotektor* Heydrich I worked at the Institute of Forensic Medicine. After the action at the church seven corpses including the two who carried out the assassination were brought to the Institute. The autopsy on these parachute agents was carried out by Professor Weyrich and Doctor Steffel and I assisted them together with another Czech named Králík. It is true that I cut off the heads of the parachute agents and two of the heads – those who assassinated Heydrich were preserved and placed in glass jars. The heads were then put on display and Professor Weyrich was placed in control of them. At the end of the war the heads disappeared but I do not know where they went as I was then serving in the German Army. As far as the bodies of the agents are concerned I know for certain that they were handed over for teaching purposes at the medical school. Also, the bodies of other people executed were handed over to us and then buried either in a common grave at the Olšany Cemetery or transferred to the medical school."

Further testimony from František Vyhnal from his statement dated 30 October 1946: "I moved in 1937 to Prague where I was employed for a couple of years as a bricklayer and then in early 1940 I moved to the Pathology Institute at the German University where I was employed as an assistant. In 1943 I enlisted into the German Army but I do remember the autopsies of the parachute agents. After the Heydrich affair, corpses of various agents were brought to the Pathology Institute to have autopsies carried out on them. It is true that I scalped one of the corpses but his head was cut off by Doctor Steffel. I also remember that the *Gestapo* brought in a Czech – a parachute agent who had a battered and bruised face and they showed him the bodies of several agents who had been in the refrigerator for about three weeks and they asked him if he knew any of them. He denied having known any of them. I declare they did not listen to him. I was present at this interrogation because I held the keys to the refrigerators and I was ordered by the *Gestapo* to open the one where the parachute agents were stored. It is also known to me that the heads of the seven agents shot in the church in Prague were examined in the Institute. Details are known by Pánek who also worked with me in the Institute."

Undated testimony from Josef Pánek: "In 1942, when the assassination of Heydrich was carried out, the parachute agents were taken to the Institute for Forensic Medicine and an autopsy performed by Professor Weyrich and Doctor Steffel. I remember that other parachute agents were brought in by the *Gestapo* to identify the corpses. The heads of Kubiš and Gabčik were cut off and preserved in alcohol-filled jars. These heads remained in the Institute until about 14 days before the end of the war when an unknown official from the Prague *Gestapo* collected the heads and as I later found out, the heads were burnt at the crematorium in Prague."

40. Testimony from Heinz Jantur in 1946: "The dead were taken to the Institute of Forensic Medicine and Criminology at Charles University. During the following days various witnesses from the assassination spot and other places were brought to the Institute to try and identify the perpetrators. About 20 witnesses identified two of the bodies as the assassins who fled on foot and by bicycle. This backed up the identification from Čurda. The heads of the two assassins were then kept in the Institute of Forensic Medicine and later were also shown to some of the helpers whose houses they had stayed in and they also identified Gabčik and Kubiš."

41. Pannwitz's memoirs from 1959: "When the chapter of the final report was drawn up, which discussed the motives that drove Czechs to assist the perpetrators before or after the assassination, it had to be noted that most of them were members of Sokol. The number of assistants who knew exactly what the agents were in the country for was very small. The number of people arrested as direct helpers was around 50. How did it happen that the Sokol members were represented in such a large number? After all, there [were] other much more forceful and vocal opponents of the Germans. The Sokol, once founded by the Sudeten Germans, a union with civic and sporting aims, was dissolved by the 'Czech Government', without German participation. After the *Gestapo* arrived they arbitrarily confiscated the assets of Sokol and took into protective custody as political hostages many senior members of Sokol. The reaction to this was much indignation and led to the start of organised illegal activity with naturally a much larger anti-German stance than before."

Appendix S
Memorials concerning those involved in Operation Anthropoid, the Czech Forces and SOE.

This short appendix is not intended to be an exhaustive one but lists some of the memorials known to the authors at the time of publication:

In the United Kingdom:
The Czech Memorial at Cholmondeley Castle.
The Czech Parachutist Memorial to Operation Anthropoid in Leamington Spa.
The headstone to the Ellison family that commemorates Jan and Jozef in St John the Baptist Churchyard, Ightfield, Shropshire.
The Czech SOE Memorial at Arisaig, Scotland.
The Czech Memorial and graves (military and military veterans) at Brookwood Military Cemetery, Surrey.

In the Czech Republic:

An Operation Anthropoid Memorial on the drop zone at Nehvizdy.

The Czech Resistance Memorial to Operation Anthropoid on Zenklova in Prague – this is at the assassination spot.

The National Memorial to the Heroes of the Heydrich Terror at St Cyril and Methodius Church in Resslova Street, Prague.

A memorial plaque to Jan Kubiš on the town hall in Dolni Vilemovice, where he was born and also an exhibition to him in the Town Hall.

A memorial to those executed at the Kobylisy firing range in Prague.

Memorial plaques at two of the most important locations where support for Operation Anthropoid was found in Prague: 1745 and 1837 Biskupcova Street – these were the residences of the Zelenka and Moravec families.

In Slovakia:

A memorial plaque to Jozef Gabčik on the house where he lived in Poluvsie.

A statue to Jozef Gabčik located in his home village of Poluvsie.

A statue of Jozef Gabčik in Zilina on the Závodská cesta.

In Germany:

A memorial to all those executed at Mauthausen concentration camp.

Appendix T
A few words about Operations Silver A and B and their consequences.

As previously described, Silver A consisted of their commander Lieutenant Alfred Bartoš, Sergeant Major Josef Valčik and Lance Corporal Jiří Potůček, who eventually arrived in Pardubice in early 1942. They received help from many people in this area but in particular the Krupkas. This couple were also involved in helping to arrange a meeting between Alfred Bartoš and an initially suspicious Captain Morávek of the 'Three Kings' group. Later, Hana delivered messages to Josef Valčik after his arrival in Prague and helped Alfred Bartoš decode messages.

The Krupka flat in Pernerova was only yards away from Josef Valčik at the Hotel Veselka run by Arnošt Košťal. Several other important families with resistance connections lived in the same street. Amongst them were Alfred Bartoš' mother Antonie and her sister Františka Jirásková, who was married to Čeněk Jirásek, who repaired radios. There was also Bedřich Schejbal, Františka's son from her first marriage (to a cousin of Alfred Bartoš), and Alvín Palouš, a local businessman who owned an electrical factory. Alfred Bartoš knew this area well. He came from Sezemice u Pardubic, previously attending the cavalry school in Pardubice opposite the Hotel Veselka. Václav Krupka had also studied at the same military establishment and the two men had met each other before the war. Alfred's decision to return to a place where he was well known, now using the alias of a dead man 'Motyčka', was perhaps tempting fate more than a little. The chance of recognition was always a possibility and he was spotted on at least one occasion. The Krupkas had first become involved in the operation at the suggestion of two of their good friends, Czech patriot and former motorcycle speedway rider František Hladěna and his young wife Taťána, who recruited them to help the parachutists. Franta Hladěna was a well-known figure around Pardubice as one of the founders and competitors of the '*Zlatá přilba Československo*' motorcycle race in 1929. Before moving to the Krupka flat, Alfred Bartoš had stayed with the Hladěnas, arriving at their flat with Jiří Potůček on 3 January 1942. Taťána Hladenová and Hana Krupková were of similar age and best friends. They were both to work together as resistance couriers during the crucial first six months of 1942. The Hladěna couple eventually both paid the ultimate price for their involvement with the Silver A operation. František Hladěna died mysteriously, while held in custody by the *Gestapo* at the '*Oberlandrat*' building in Pardubice. No one alive today knows the exact circumstances of events. František Hladěna, having been arrested, was taken for interrogation early on the morning of 20 June 1942 along with his wife. During this fateful day he was either thrown or jumped through one of the upper stairwell windows on the third floor of the building, falling to his death on the cobblestones of the rear courtyard below. His wife Taťána, almost 20 years junior to her husband, is listed amongst those executed at the '*Zámeček*', Larishova vila, on 2 July 1942. One single gunshot wound to her body and no other sign of injury suggests that she was not executed by firing squad with most of the other prisoners, some of whom had signs of rough treatment and multiple injuries. She had been brought back to Pardubice from interrogation in Prague, having been taken there the previous day for questioning, where she refused inducements to cooperate with the *Gestapo*.

In contrast to the Hladěnas, the Krupka couple were able to survive the war, while many of their resistance compatriots did not. Václav Krupka spent the remainder of the war in Flossenbürg concentration camp, while his wife remained free, under the protection of Wilhelm Schultz, the *Gestapo* officer who had carried out her interrogation. Hana was one of the people brought to the corner of Resslova Street in Prague to help identify the bodies of the parachutists taken from the church. Later, her situation would become controversial and cause problems for Hana Krupková for many years after the end of the war. Even today, there is still no plaque on the building where the Krupkas lived, to record their brave work for the resistance movement. Hana eventually had to divorce Václav and, after many years of trying, was finally given permission to leave Czechoslovakia.

The Hladěnas and Krupkas were only arrested because they were betrayed by the testimony of parachutist Karel Čurda, who incriminated them and the whole resistance movement all over the Protectorate, from Plzeň to Prague and beyond to Pardubice, in the days after 17 June 1942. Čurda had previously visited the Krupka flat in Pardubice and passed on this information, plus the details of almost everywhere else he had been and everyone he had met, to the *Gestapo* in Prague. This information helped to start a chain of events which would have serious consequences for many. On 21 June, a trap was set in place to catch the illusive Alfred Bartoš when he called at the Krupka address. Two *Gestapo* officers, Hubert Hanauske and Josef Krebs, were waiting at the flat for Bartoš to arrive. Bartoš, as expected, called at 7 p.m. that evening and rang the bell at the main entrance on the ground floor. Looking up to the flat window on the fourth floor, he saw two men staring back down at him. At this point, Bartoš decided to make his escape through the streets of town. Some witnesses say he ran off in the direction of the stadium (the Letni *stadion*, built in 1931 close to Pardubice Castle), but this seems unlikely, as he found himself pursued by the *Gestapo* agents, so he ran in the opposite direction. It was well known that *Gestapo* officers had accommodation at a house in the street '*u Stadionu*'. Bartoš would have known this and kept away from the area of the stadium at all costs. As the chase progressed, shots were exchanged several times by both sides as Bartoš tried to shake off his pursuers in the crowds outside the Gloria cinema, near to Smilova ulice. Turning left into Smilova, Bartoš desperately looked for a safe place to hide. On the left side of Smilova was the surgery of specialist Doctor Bartoň. The doctor had previously assisted the parachutists and Bartoš tried to break into the locked building without success. Further along Smilova, there is a crossroads where Smilova and Sladkovskeho meet. Today, as in 1942, there is a chemist shop on this corner. It was here, finding his path blocked by *Luftwaffe* personnel and with the *Gestapo* men pursuing close behind, that Alfred Bartoš put his own pistol to his head so that he would not be taken alive. Fatally wounded, he died in hospital during the early hours of the following morning at 2.10 a.m. An autopsy carried out in Prague on 27 June found that two bullets had been the cause of death.

Ležáky was a small stone-working community made up of nine buildings and 53 inhabitants, 20 miles or so south-east of Pardubice and between the larger villages of Miřetice and Vrbatův Kostelec a few miles to the east. From the early days of the German occupation, resistance had been active in Ležáky. Bohumil Laušman, the leader of the Social Democratic Party, had fled Czechoslovakia to Britain in 1939. He was the man responsible for the arrival of the parachutists at Ležáky, having passed on the names and addresses of citizens who could be trusted to the Czechoslovak Ministry of National Defence in Exile, in London. As early as October 1941, František Pavelka (Operation Percentage – the first parachutist to successfully land in the Protectorate) had used a hideout at Nasavrky to the west of Ležáky, based on information provided by Laušman. During a six-month period between October 1941 and April 1942, four groups of parachutists were dropped into this region of East Bohemia (Percentage, Silver A, Silver B and Intransitive). The resistance group Čenda (named after local man Čeněk Bureš) had been active in Ležáky and the surrounding villages. Eight men formed the prominent members of Čenda: Josef Šťulík, Jindřich Švanda, Čeněk Bureš, Miloš Stantejský, Karel Svoboda, Karel Kněz and the Vaško brothers, Jindřich and František. Karel Kněz, an important member who was Head Constable at Vrbatův Kostelec, in 1939 had helped supply weapons to the resistance from the police storage depot. The Čenda group grew in size to over 20 members and were in regular contact with larger national resistance groups, ÚVOD and PVVZ. It was nearby in the Hluboká quarry owned by František Vaško at Dachov that radio operator Jiří Potůček had set up the transmitter Libuše, successfully making contact with London from his hiding place in the roof of the machine plant. Finding a suitable safe place from where to transmit messages was always a problem for Jiří Potůček. The transmitter Libuše was often moved around to different locations in the wider area, including Lázně Bohdaneč to the north-west of Pardubice (where Potůček's radio aerial was recently discovered in the roof of a house – exactly as he had left it in 1942), before being concealed at the Ležáky mill of Jindřich Švanda towards the end of May, with Jiří Potůček hiding close by. Following the Čurda betrayal, a bicycle messenger, Luda Matura from Pardubice Svitkov, arrived to warn Jiří Potůček and the members of Čenda about the arrest of the associates of Silver A in Pardubice. The *Gestapo* began checking identity papers in Ležáky and looking closely at the quarry of Hluboká and the Ležáky mill. Arrests were made, including the miller, Švanda, but the Libuše radio set had already been removed on 18 June, along with radio operator Jiří Potůček, who was one step ahead. The messages from Libuše to England began on 15 January 1942, with the last message being sent on 26 June 1942.

Time ran out for Ležáky on the morning of Wednesday, 24 June 1942, with the arrival of some 500 SS men and Protectorate gendarmes sent by Gerhard Clages, commander of the Pardubice *Gestapo*. Clages ironically had a '*chata*' (weekend cottage) at Dachov, the place where Jiří Potůček had set up his radio. Clages' men arrived shortly after midday. The village was surrounded and closed off to the outside world. Villagers were brought together, including children, and identity papers checked. Altogether, 47 men, women and children were taken from Ležáky before the afternoon was over; most adults to be imprisoned and later executed at Pardubice Zámeček, the 'Larischova vila'. Anything of value was taken and the village, which had existed since at least 1651, was set alight and burned down.

Pardubice Zámeček, Larischova vila should not be confused with the much larger white Zámeček in the oldest part of Pardubice, but it is a mistake that is regularly made. The Zámeček, Larischova vila where the Ležáky people were taken is in the district of Pardubičky, to the east of Pardubice, in the direction of Černá za Bory. A mysterious building with many names, it is often described as a manor house rather than a castle, even though it has a recently rebuilt imposing gothic tower. When the Larischova vila was built over 130 years ago, as a residence for industrialist

Jiří Larisch-Monnich, the area was very different, with open fields for horse jumping and hunting. The building changed hands several times before 1939, and a riding school operated here from 1937. By the time of the Protectorate, the Zámeček had new residents and became a barracks complex for the German reserve police battalion '*Böhmen*'. The battalion had a strength of some 200 men, who were put in place to control the activities of the citizens of Pardubice and protect armament production. By 1944, the police battalion had been moved elsewhere and the buildings were used by Fire Brigade Police troops who had previously been garrisoned in Plzeň.

The cellars of the Zámeček became a temporary prison for the residents of Ležáky, alongside many of the patriotic helpers of Silver A from Pardubice, Hradec Králové and other places in the surrounding area. People such as Věra Junková, the girlfriend of Alfred Bartoš, and Doctor Bartoň, whose wife Emilie Bartoňova later died at Auschwitz on 23 December 1942, found themselves held in the cells here amongst many others. More than 40 people, including the villagers from Ležáky, were shot in one day at the execution site, in the sand pits near Zámeček. Between 25 June and 2 July 1942, more than 190 Czech resistance members who had helped the parachutists of Silver A were executed here. The firing squad was made up of soldiers from the German Police Regiment at Kolin. Afterwards, the bodies of those executed were cremated in Pardubice and their ashes dropped into the Labe from the river bridge. An impressive memorial stands at the execution grounds, and the Larischova vila Zámeček building is currently (2018) undergoing a major reconstruction. The building is open to the public on certain dates, when it is possible to visit the site. Larischova vila has had a chequered history since 1945, finally belonging to the Foxconn company and falling into disrepair, before the building was donated to the Czech Legionnaires in 2014 for restoration. Many local people in Pardubice remain unaware that the building still exists. We have been told several times that it does not, but this is not so. The Larischova vila still stands, hidden amongst trees and the tall blue office buildings of Foxconn. The rebuilding project continues to gather pace and more major improvements are planned in the future.

The story of Ležáky does not end with the executions in Pardubice, as not everyone died there. Thirteen Ležáky children had been held prisoner in the coal cellars at Larischova vila. They were moved by train to Prague, probably very late in the evening on 24 June. Witnesses at the railway station in Pardubice mention seeing children looking "very dirty" (from the cellar coal dust) waiting for the train. From Prague they were sent to Łodz in occupied Poland. Eleven of the Ležáky children and one girl from Lidice died in the mobile gas vans at the death camp at Chelmno. Two Ležáky sisters, Jarmila and Marie Šťulík, were considered suitable for 'Germanisation' and placed with German families. They were traced by Police Inspector Josef Ondráček and brought back to Czechoslovakia after the end of the war. Unlike Lidice, Ležáky was never rebuilt. Ever since 1945, the site has become a memorial, with stone monuments marking the place where the foundations of each house or building once stood. There is also an excellent museum here.

By the end of June 1942, radio operator Jiří Potůček was the 'last man standing' in the Pardubice region from the original three parachutists of the Silver A mission. Josef Valčik had left town, joining Anthropoid and meeting his fate in the crypt at the Church of St Cyril and Methodius in Resslova Street, Prague. Alfred Bartoš had lost his life following the gun chase through the streets of Pardubice on the evening of 21 June. Most of the Pardubice resistance members had either been killed or arrested, while perhaps a few remained free in hiding. This left Jiří Potůček in a very isolated position, with few people to turn to for help. The resistance movement around Pardubice had been dealt a hammer blow and people were reluctant to help a wanted man on the run.

On 30 June, Jiří Potůček found himself far away from Pardubice in the small village of Končiny near Bohdašín, in the northern hills below the Krkonoše Mountains. He was hiding at the farmhouse of the Burdych family. The *Gestapo* appeared, looking to ambush and arrest him, but Potůček was able to get away, firing with both pistols as he made his escape. For almost 48 hours and over many miles, he was on the move through the countryside heading south back towards Pardubice, avoiding patrols searching the woods to find him. Towards the end of the third day, Potůček had walked over 50 miles and was now back at Rošice and Labem, a village on the outskirts of Pardubice. He was trying to reach the flat of Josef Nováček, but luck was against him. Josef Nováček had been arrested on 26 June. Potůček then asked another resident, Josef Fitzbauer, for help, but he did not want to become involved and turned him away.

By now exhausted and hungry, Jiří Potůček walked through the woods towards the Trnová forest, north-west of the river Labe close to Pardubice, where, unable to carry on any further without rest, he decided to sleep for a while, concealed in a ditch. Some short time later, he was discovered by a Protectorate gendarme, Karel Půlpán from Pardubice-Doubravice. Půlpán shot the sleeping Jiří Potůček without warning, using his CZ 24 pistol. After the war in 1948, Půlpán was put on trial, although he claimed he fired accidently. Whether or not this is true is debatable, and only Půlpán knew his true intentions. By killing Potůček while he slept, Půlpán had spared him a difficult interrogation at the hands of the *Gestapo*; a dead man cannot be forced to give up information. Půlpán received a sentence of five years' hard labour, and his colleague František Hoznauer, a local councillor, two years' hard labour for his participation in the killing of the parachute agent. Ironically, messages were still being transmitted from London for Jiří Potůček as late as August 1942, by which time he had been dead for several weeks. The Pardubice *Gestapo* sent the body of Jiří Potůček to Prague for a post mortem to be carried out. Afterwards, the remains of the last member of Silver A were buried at Prague Ďáblice cemetery, in a communal unmarked grave, in the same area where the other fallen parachutists came to rest. The four members of Burdych family from Končiny who had tried to help Potůček were all executed. A memorial to Potůček was erected soon after the war, at Trnová, the place where he died, but removed following the rise of communism. The original memorial was replaced after 1968, using granite from the destroyed village of Ležáky. In recent years, new memorial stones to the other parachute groups have been added to the site, and a memorial park, opened in 2010, now stands at this spot. Nearby streets of new housing in Trnová were named after the parachutists. A large number of rectangular cast metal plaques were commissioned at the end of the war to the victims of the '*Heydrichiada*' and placed on the buildings where the deceased resistance members had lived around Pardubice. Not all of these now remain, as many of the older buildings were replaced over the years and the plaques lost. One of these plaques commemorates Alfred Bartoš at the place where he died.

Meanwhile, the two men of Silver B – Staff Sergeant Jan Zemek and Sergeant Vladimír Škacha – were dropped near Kasaličky and their task was to deliver a radio to a resistance group known as Introduction. Introduction had links with Jan Zelenka and later the Anthropoid group in Prague. The mission started badly, as the radio they were carrying for use by the resistance was damaged on landing and some equipment lost. This was only the first of numerous problems for Silver B. Although both parachute agents had been trained in the use of explosives and demolition techniques, neither were able to repair the damaged set, much to the frustration of Vladimír Škacha, as he stated in an interview after the war:

"Why did the people who prepared the operation not think that the addresses we had been given to contact would be unwilling or unable to help us? London expected that these people would help but were absolutely unsure why one of us [Škacha] had not been trained as radio operator? Why was our equipment so primitive? I was thoroughly trained in demolitions and had been proven as a good shot on the ranges. But I did not have a decagram of explosives … I had a radio transmitter I could hardly work and I was unable to repair it."

The addresses of resistance contacts supplied to Silver B proved to be of no practical use. They now found themselves in a difficult situation, miles from where they should be, unable to ask for help by radio or on the ground. In these circumstances, the two men did the only thing possible. They contacted relatives of Jan Zemek near Brno, where they stayed while unsuccessfully trying to contact members of the local resistance. Both parachute agents remained free, moving around from different hiding places. Vladimir Škacha narrowly avoided capture by the *Gestapo* in December 1942 and escaped. It was not until January 1945 that he was finally caught in Moravská Ostrava, following a shootout, and sent to Flossenbürg concentration camp. He survived Flossenbürg and was liberated when units of the US Army reached the camp near the pre-war borders of Germany and Czechoslovakia on 23 April 1945. Jan Zemek stayed in hiding near Kyjov in southern Moravia, joining partisan units at Osvětimany near Buchlov in March 1945. He was involved in several operations against the Germans.

Ultimately, the mission of Silver B failed due to a series of events beyond the control of the parachutists. These could with hindsight possibly have been predicted beforehand, but were not sufficiently addressed in advance. The Silver B mission is unusual, as both members of the operation survived the hostilities. Vladimir Škacha emigrated to Canada in 1968 and died in Toronto in 1987, while Jan Zemek lived in Moravia until 1994, when he died in Brno.

Bibliography

Břečka, J., *Moravian, Slovakian and Czechoslovak Parachute Operations from the West during the Second World War* (Brno: Moravské zemské muzeum, 2015).

Burian, M., Knížek, A., Rajlich, J. and Stehlík, E., *Assassination: Operation Anthropoid 1941–1942* (Prague: Military History Institute Prague, 2007).

Čvančara, J., *Anthropoid* (Prague: Centrum české historie, 2017).

Hanzliková, R., *In the Ležak Stream Valley* (VEGA-L, 2009).

Ivanov, M., *Target Heydrich* (New York: Macmillan Publishing, 1974).

MacDonald, C., *The Killing of Reinhard Heydrich* (New York: Da Capo Press, 1998).

Ivanov, M., 'The Assassination of Reinhard Heydrich', *After the Battle*, issue 24.

Martin, J., *The Mirror Caught the Sun, Operation Anthropoid 1942* (John Martin Ltd, 2009).

Moravec, General F., *Master of Spies* (London: Sphere, 1981).

Šmejkal, P. and Padevět, J., *Anthropoid* (Prague: Academia Praha, 2016).

Šustek, V., *Atentát na Reinharda Heydricha* (Prague: Scriptorium, 2013).

Weisz. G., MD FRACS MA and W. Albury BA PhD, 'The attempt on the life of Reinhard Heydrich, architect of the final solution: a review of his treatment and autopsy', *Israel Medical Association Journal*, 2014.

Files from the National Archives Kew:

FO817/7 Foreign Office Czech Embassy file: Political: attack on Heydrich and German reprisals

HS4/30 SOE Czech Legion

HS4/35 SOE Canonbury 1 and 2: bombing and sabotage of Skoda factory

HS4/39 SOE Anthropoid, Silver A and Silver B

HS9/321/8 SOE personal file C. Clarke

HS9/1211/7 SOE personal file A. Hesketh-Prichard

HS9/1421/8 SOE personal file J. Strankmüller

KV2/2942 Security Service file on Edvard Beneš

WO178/21 War Diary 22 Military Mission

WO208/4472 Intelligence file on Reinhard Heydrich

The authors wish to thanks the following for their help:
John Martin
Martin Bull
George Scott
Anita Moravec-Gard
Zdeněk Špitálnik
Marta Majerčik
Richard Jopson
'Stan' B. Štěpánek
Colonel Frantisek Bobek. CsOL Chrudim (Pardubice Zamecek)
Jiri Hofman CsOL Chrudim (Pardubice Zamecek)
Marek Melša
Pavel Šmejkal

Index

Index of People

Index of Places

Index of General & Miscellaneous Terms